THE FORAGING SPECTRUM

《《《《《《《《《《《《《《《《《《《《

THE FORAGING SPECTRUM

DIVERSITY IN HUNTER-GATHERER LIFEWAYS

ROBERT L. KELLY

SMITHSONIAN INSTITUTION PRESS

Washington and London

Figure 7-4 is adapted from *The Mardudjara Aborigines* by Robert Tonkinson, copyright © 1978 by Holt, Rinehart and Winston, Inc., reproduced by permission of the publisher

Copy Editor: Peter Donovan
Supervisory Editor: Duke Johns
Designer: Janice Wheeler

Library of Congress Cataloging-in-Publication Data
Kelly, Robert L.
    The foraging spectrum : Diversity in hunter-gatherer lifeways / Robert L. Kelly.
        p.   cm.
    Includes bibliographical references and index.
    ISBN 1-56098-465-1 (cloth : alk. paper). — ISBN 1-56098-466-X (paper : alk. paper)
    1. Hunting and gathering societies. I. Title.
GN388.K44   1995
306.3'49—dc20   94–21100

British Library Cataloguing-in-Publication Data is available

Manufactured in the United States of America
02 01 00 99 98 97 96   5 4 3 2

∞ The paper used in this publication meets the minimum requirements of the American National Standard for Permanence of Paper for Printed Library Materials Z39.48-1984.

For my parents, who showed me the paths in the forest

CONTENTS

LIST OF TABLES

PREFACE

I remember that I was amazed. Amazed at the faces of Tasaday men and women looking back at me from the pages of *National Geographic* in 1972. To a young high school student who yearned to travel to exotic places and to study prehistoric peoples, those photos of the Tasaday afforded the opportunity to do both vicariously. Here was the Stone Age! Hunters and gatherers, unsullied by civilization, who lived "much as our ancestors did thousands of years ago" (MacLeish and Launois 1972:219).

Anthropology, the Tasaday, and, I like to think, I myself have come a long way since 1972. It is still not clear who the Tasaday really are—conscious players in a hoax perpetuated by the Philippine government or unwitting pawns in a larger geopolitical game—although it is clear that they are not and never were isolated Pleistocene relics (see Headland 1992). But their legacy continues in both the anthropological and, especially, the public perception of hunter-gatherers. Alleged relics of an earlier epoch, people that time forgot, hunter-gatherers are seen as humanity stripped of its technological trappings. Thus they are described in the popular media by what they lack. The Tasaday, for example, had "no agricultural implements . . . no woven cloth . . . no pipes . . . no pottery . . . no weapons . . . no word for war"

(MacLeish and Launois 1972:242). Hunter-gatherers seem to be "man in the raw state of nature" (Holmberg 1950:261).

Opinions have long differed on whether humanity in its alleged raw state was a good thing or not. Some people come down on the side of Jean-Jacques Rousseau's Noble Savage, while others see humanity's darker side in "primitive" society, where people's lives are, in the memorable words of Thomas Hobbes, "nasty, brutish and short." Hunter-gatherers today are used by the popular media as a foil to our own industrialized society, to demonstrate its failures or successes. Some see in hunter-gatherers evidence of an evolutionarily ingrained propensity for savage hunting and bloodshed, a biological imperative for carnage (see Cartmill 1993), while others see in these same societies an inherently kinder and gentler form of human organization that could even provide a model for corporate culture (Bernhard and Glantz 1992). In popular books such as *Clan of the Cave Bear* and movies such as *Quest for Fire* and *The Gods Must Be Crazy,* hunter-gatherers are schizophrenically portrayed as what we think we used to be: the original hippies or the ultimate road warriors. They represent either a simpler, more egalitarian past to which we should return, or they are evidence that we have yet to overcome our club-wielding troglodyte heritage. Though diametrically opposed, I think it can be argued that both these images of hunter-gatherers are based on unilineal evolutionism (see chapter 1), the idea that all human societies progress through the same evolutionary stages, although at different rates, by improving their moral and mental capacities.

Anthropologists have spent a considerable amount of time trying to teach the public that this method of accounting for human diversity is wrong. Stated bluntly, living hunter-gatherers are not the alter ego of Western civilization; they are not "simple" societies; they are not humanity in a state of nature; they are not Pleistocene relics; they do not preserve an ancient way of life; we cannot reconstruct ancient human society by extrapolating backward from living hunter-gatherers.

Yet we social scientists ourselves are guilty of some of the same tendencies towards simplification. Portrayals of foraging societies in many theoretical formulations, especially in textbooks, ignore or downplay the importance of modern social and economic contexts and of variability among those who hunt and gather to obtain their food. I can appreciate that some simplification is necessary in teaching or building theory. But too much unwittingly lends itself to facile constructions of other people's lives and to erroneous understandings of both evolution and the factors that affect the lives of living foragers (nearly all of whom are adversely impacted by the intrusion of Western society into their lives).

This book is a contribution to combating both of these problems, the tendency for anthropologists to simplify hunting and gathering societies and the tendency for students to misunderstand the factors that condition human differences. To achieve this goal, this book focuses on variability in the foraging lifeway, and examines the factors that may account for this variability within the perspective of behavioral ecology. It is not a thumbnail sketch of the foraging lifeway. Although some may find this frustrating, one more description of a fundamental hunter-gatherer lifeway could only propagate a new stereotype.

I have written this book for two audiences. First, I hope to provide those who teach introductory anthropology with some knowledge of the range of lifeways encompassed within the category *hunter-gatherer,* and direct attention to the causal variables that lie behind this variability. I want students to understand that if a behavioral or cultural characteristic—sharing, for example—is common among hunter-gatherers it is not just because they are hunter-gatherers, or because they preserve some core trait of humanity, but because of a set of conditions that may be prevalent among living hunter-gatherers. This is achieved here by focusing on how foragers differ in terms of subsistence, mobility, demography, sharing, territoriality, and social and political organization. Rather than leave students with a yearning for another time or another place, an approach that focuses on the relationships between behavior and environment, though less romantic, can provide students with the tools to see how structural elements of their own society encourage (or discourage) certain behaviors.

Second, this book is also for advanced undergraduates and graduate students. It assumes some knowledge of anthropology, but does not assume familiarity with the hunter-gatherer literature or behavioral ecology. My goal is to provide an overview, and, consequently, some fascinating topics have been shortchanged. I will leave them to the student to investigate further. I must admit that in writing this book I had my own undergraduate archaeology students in mind. I hope this book helps them, and students like them, to avoid falling prey to the temptation to use a modern hunter-gatherer people, or some amalgam of foraging societies, as an analogy for reconstructing the past. However, data from ethnographically known foragers are still useful to archaeologists in constructing models to be tested with archaeological data. We cannot allow ethnographic data to "tyrannize" our reconstructions of the past (Wobst 1978), but at the same time we cannot forgo a rich source of ideas and hypotheses. We cannot look to living foragers for analogues of prehistoric ones, but we can use data from them to test some ideas about human behavior. Simply put, I hope this book will encourage students to think more theoretically.

Finally, a word about words and a caution about data. In recent years the term *hunter-gatherer* has been discarded by some in favor of the more generic term *forager.* This term avoids privileging the hunting side of hunter-gatherer. However, I will use both terms interchangeably simply to avoid monotony. Also, the appellations given to different groups of hunter-gatherers change as anthropology educates itself, as the subjects of anthropology are given a greater voice in ethnography, and as societies change and redefine themselves. I try to strike a balance between terms that will assist the student in exploring ethnographic literature and terms that will not insult members of foraging or formerly foraging societies who might read this book. Also, in some places I use the ethnographic present tense, but the reader should not assume that the particular group has not changed between the time of ethnographic study and today. Likewise, where the past tense is used, the reader should not assume that the group discussed no longer exists. Finally, the student should be cautious in using the data presented in tables here uncritically. These data were collected under diverse conditions and in different ways. I have provided them to indicate some of the variability present among foragers, and as a guide to potential sources of data. But the student is advised to consult the original sources before using any data reproduced here for his or her own further analyses.

It has been more than twenty years since I first looked in wonder at those pictures of the Tasaday. I no longer see them as the faces of ancient relatives. In the daily activities of foragers, for the most part I now see costs and benefits of resources, caloric returns, differences in time allocation, opportunity costs, utility curves, and fitness benefits. But occasionally I can also see beyond these, to the human side of the evolutionary processes that shaped and continue to shape the remarkable diversity of humanity. And I am no less amazed.

ACKNOWLEDGMENTS

This book has been written over many years and I will undoubtedly leave out many deserving individuals from this list. To them I say that your input has nonetheless been greatly appreciated. I would be remiss if I did not first acknowledge a large debt to David Hurst Thomas, who, through the archaeology of the Great Basin, introduced me to hunter-gatherers, and to Lewis Binford, who has shaped much of the way I approach anthropology. Without their guidance and patience over the years I would not be in a position to indulge in the pleasure of thanking them.

This book began to take shape while I was a Weatherhead Fellow at the School of American Research in 1988–89. I am grateful to the School for that opportunity and for providing me with a stimulating group of scholars to talk anthropology and to play pool with: Michael Brown, Winifred Creamer, Ron Grimes, Jonathan Haas, Grant Jones, Jerry Levy, and the late Bobby Wright, Jr. Other writing time was made possible by Victor Olorunsola, the late Dean of the College of Arts and Sciences, University of Louisville. Lin Poyer made it possible for me to sit on an island in Micronesia and complete the first draft.

Many people have read and commented on portions of the manuscript or complete drafts. These include Ken Ames, Robert Bettinger, Jane Collier, Eric Ingbar, Robert Hard, Robert Hitchcock, Julie Peteet, Lin Poyer, Russell Reid, Steve Simms, Eric Alden Smith, John Speth, and Robert Tonkinson. I would especially like to thank Eric Alden Smith, the Smithsonian Institution Press reviewer, who gave the manuscript more attention than it deserved, and improved the final version enormously. I cannot say that I took all of the advice given to me, and I alone am responsible for errors and shortcomings. Robert Hitchcock, Peter Brosius, Barry Hewlett, and P. Bion Griffin graciously made photographs available to me. Peter Donovan diligently and skillfully copyedited the manuscript, while Duke Johns guided it through the production process.

This book has taken me away frequently from those close to me, and forced them to put up with my foul moods, ravings on evolutionary theory, and bouts of forgetfulness. So, to Lin and to Matthew I say, it's finished! but most of all, I say thank you.

HUNTER-GATHERERS AND ANTHROPOLOGY

1

... where every man is Enemy to every man ... wherein men live without other security, than what their own strength, and their own invention
shall furnish them withall. In such condition, there is no place for Indus-
try; because the fruit thereof is uncertain: and consequently no Culture of
the Earth; No navigation, nor use of the commodities that may be im-
ported by Sea; no commodious Building; no Instruments of moving, and
removing such things as require much force; no Knowledge of the face of
the Earth; no account of Time; no Arts; no Letters; no Society; and which
is worst of all, continuall feare, and danger of violent death; And the life
of man, solitary, poor, nasty, brutish and short.
political philosopher (Hobbes [1651] 1968:186)

To date, the hunting way of life has been the most successful and persistent
adaptation man has ever achieved.
anthropologists (Lee and DeVore 1968:3)

Hunter-gatherers have always played a pivotal role in anthropological theory.
Nineteenth-century evolutionists looked upon them as living fossils of early
human society. Émile Durkheim's theories of religion and society relied
heavily on Australian Aboriginal cultures. A. R. Radcliffe-Brown's studies
of the Andaman Islanders and Australian Aborigines were the ethnographic
foundation of structural-functionalism. Cultural ecology was grounded in
Julian Steward's intimate knowledge of the lifeways of western North America's Shoshone and Paiute. Australian Aboriginal ethnography figured prominently in Claude Lévi-Strauss's search for the elementary structures of
kinship. Indeed, Aram Yengoyan once observed that virtually the entire
history of anthropological theory could be written in terms of Australian
Aboriginal—hunter-gatherer—ethnology (1979). Hunter-gatherers figured
prominently in anthropological theory because they were thought to preserve or be an avenue to the reconstruction of an ancient condition of humanity, the hunter-gatherer evolutionary "stage." This stage, so the story
goes, accounts for 99 percent of human history and was the context in which
humanity evolved its fundamental attributes (Lee and DeVore 1968:ix). In
fact, the idea of a primitive society—wherein lay the origins of religion, the

I

division of labor, and kinship—was the very foundation of anthropology as a discipline (Kuper 1988). An understanding of the hunter-gatherer lifeway, then, is essential to any critique of anthropological theory (Bettinger 1991).

But who are hunter-gatherers? Their image has changed dramatically over the last century as particular ethnographic cases waxed and waned in popularity. In the first part of the twentieth century the Australian Aranda served as the primary anthropological model of hunter-gatherers; later it was the Shoshone of western North America, and, after the "Man the Hunter" conference, the !Kung, or Ju/'hoansi[1] of Botswana; today, the Paraguayan Ache are gaining prominence in the professional literature. Sometimes hunter-gatherers are defined economically, as people without domesticated plants and animals (except dogs), although this definition subsumes a variety of social forms. Or they are defined socially, as *band* societies, people who live in small groups, with flexible membership and egalitarian sociopolitical relations, a definition that subsumes a variety of economic forms (Lee 1992). Through the years, as the ethnographic cases representing the archetypal hunter-gatherer society changed, so did its characteristics: from Radcliffe-Brown's patrilineal horde to bilateral bands with fluid membership; from Man the Hunter to Woman the Gatherer; from egalitarian bands to rural proletariat; from isolated Paleolithic relics to marginalized but full-fledged members of the contemporary world system.

Yet even a cursory perusal of ethnographic literature shows that there is considerable diversity among ethnographically known hunter-gatherers, even within a delimited region such as the Kalahari Desert (e.g., Kent 1992; Barnard 1992). Hunter-gatherers everywhere manifest a variety of kinship systems, for example. Hunting is important in some societies; in others, gathering is critical. Some have been more substantially affected by colonial governments than others. Some are very territorial, others are not. Some are egalitarian while others are ranked societies. The list goes on, and includes variability in work effort, fertility, health, mobility—in all areas of life.

Anthropologists are aware of this variation.[2] But for many years the objective of hunter-gatherer research has been to seek out the essential core of the hunter-gatherer lifeway and consequently to ignore or explain away variability as the product of extraordinary natural environments or particular historical circumstances. Elman Service, for example, in his classic synthesis *The Hunters,* explicitly excluded Northwest Coast peoples from consideration because they were adapted to a rare environment where food resources were said to be abundant. Although shifts in models or archetypes reflect genuine advances in knowledge and understanding, they also reflect shifts

in emphasis—the highlighting of particular points along a continuum of behavior. For each model proposed, variation is recognized, but eventually
winnowed out, leaving behind a unitary description of the essential hunter-
gatherer. At most we are given two categories, such as "simple" and "complex" hunter-gatherers (see chapter 8), with one of these normally privileged
as capturing the essence of the hunter-gatherer lifeway.

There are indeed behaviors and cultural concepts common to many ethnographically known hunter-gatherers. But even where a behavior is common to modern hunter-gatherers, it may only be so because of the current
prevalence of a causal variable—for example, circumscription due to European colonization, trade, habitation of marginal environments, or low population density, and not because that behavior is inherently associated with
"the" hunter-gatherer lifeway (Ember 1975; Schrire 1984a). Whatever is
commonly associated with ethnographically known hunter-gatherer economies cannot be causally linked with hunting and gathering because *hunter-
gatherer* is a category we impose on human diversity—it is not itself a causal
variable. The reasons for the existence of features that lead us to categorize
societies must be empirically established rather than assumed at the outset.
To an extent, the issue is whether one finds what is common or what is
different among living foragers most intriguing. My position is that we cannot truly understand what is common without also understanding what is
different.

My goal in this book is to review some of what anthropology has learned
about the variability among ethnographically known hunter-gatherers
(figure 1-1). As the term is used here, hunter-gatherers refers to those groups
of people who have traditionally been recognized by anthropology as
hunter-gatherers. That is, the history of the field, rather than some other
criterion, defines the subject. These people are indeed those who do or did
procure most or all of their food from hunting, gathering, and fishing. But
the reader should know that many people who traditionally have been labeled hunter-gatherers do grow some of their own food, trade with agriculturalists for produce, or participate in cash economies, though ethnographies
often downplay the significance of these activities.

This book has been written with archaeologists in mind, although it contains no prehistory and is by no means limited to archaeological interests. As
an archaeologist I know that there is seldom enough time to read even a
limited range of the ethnographic literature and, consequently, that this
tempts archaeologists to see the entire prehistoric world of hunter-gatherers
through the lens of Ju/'hoansi, or Shoshone, or Nunamiut ethnography. My

Figure 1-1. World map showing locations of some of the foraging societies discussed in the text. Drawn by Dan Delaney.

goal is to give fellow archaeologists, and ethnologists who are not specialists in hunter-gatherer studies, a sense of the variation that exists among hunter-gatherers and some idea of what might account for it. I do this by examining several areas of behavior: subsistence, mobility, trade, sharing, territoriality, demography, and sociopolitical organization. I have had to leave aside many other important areas, such as cosmology and religion.[3] An ecological perspective of one form or another has guided much research undertaken since midcentury, and this book reflects that perspective. In the final chapter I discuss how anthropological analysis has attempted to reduce the variation among living hunter-gatherers in order to reconstruct an "original" human society. I argue for the alternative goal of understanding variability among ethnographically known hunter-gatherers within a body of theory in order to make effective use of ethnological (and ethnoarchaeological) observations in studying the past.

To situate this book in the context of hunter-gatherer studies, I will briefly review the history of hunter-gatherer research in terms of three models: the patrilineal/patrilocal model, the generalized foraging model, and the interdependent model. First, however, I turn to an earlier era, and consider the place of hunter-gatherers in nineteenth-century thought. Although later models are often responses to the shortcomings of nineteenth-century evolutionism, we have nonetheless inherited some characteristics of that century's intellectual stance.

HUNTER-GATHERERS IN PRE-TWENTIETH-CENTURY THOUGHT

As the study of human diversity, anthropology began as soon as the first hominids wondered why the people in the next valley were different. But more conservatively, anthropology appeared as a formal discipline in the late nineteenth century. Like much of Western thought, it was intellectually rooted in Enlightenment philosophy, in which ideas about so-called primitive societies, including hunter-gatherers, played a key role.

Enlightenment philosophy revolved around the notion of progress. In a world thought to be created by a perfect God, diversity in humanity was related to differences in the degree of perfection. Progress was movement toward moral perfection. Just as God could be ranked above the whole of humanity, so could cultures and ethnic groups be ranked in their respective degrees of perfection. The history of humanity was seen as operating according to universal, natural laws that led to the moral development of people, and that was evidenced by the increasing subjugation of nature by people. Progress in this view was affected by environmental and technological factors, but it arose primarily from increasingly rational thought. Allegedly unable to think rationally, members of less advanced societies were controlled by nature; thinking rationally, members of advanced societies controlled nature.[4]

During the nineteenth century, the pageant of technological advancements uncovered by archaeologists and enshrined in the Stone, Bronze, and Iron Ages made clear to intellectuals of the time that Europeans had passed through earlier stages in their progress to modernity. Anthropology developed as part of late-nineteenth-century efforts to reconstruct these past stages. These efforts included Lewis Henry Morgan's *Ancient Society* (1877), Henry Maine's *Ancient Law* (1861), John Lubbock's *Prehistoric Times* (1865), and Edward Tylor's *Primitive Culture* (1871).[5] These early evolutionists, however, faced a problem. Reconstructing prehistory requires archaeological evidence, the physical record of the human past. Although sufficient archaeological research had been conducted in the late nineteenth century to discern a past, this past was difficult to interpret. It revealed technological advances and a cumulative domination of nature, but had nothing to say about kinship, or politics, or social organization. To reconstruct prehistory where archaeological data were lacking or insufficient, the evolutionists fell back on ethnography and the *comparative method*.

The comparative method was formally developed by Auguste Comte, although its intellectual pedigree can be traced back at least to the Greek philosophers (for a history and critique see Bock 1956). In linguistics, it was a method of reconstructing dead languages; in biology, a way to reconstruct extinct species; and in anthropology, it was a way to reconstruct the European past. Stated simply, the comparative method took existing cultural (and biological) diversity in the world and turned it into an evolutionary sequence. Different peoples represented different stages in humanity's march to perfection.

The theoretical paradigm of the evolutionists provided the justification for this methodology. Couched within Enlightenment notions of progress, early evolutionist thinking also included themes of a "struggle for existence" and "survival of the fittest," themes that students of anthropology know best from the writings of Charles Darwin and Herbert Spencer. But Darwin's notion of natural selection played no role in the work of early evolutionists. Instead of a selective process, evolutionists saw change as transformative along a more or less single scale of progress. Evolution resulted from the accumulation of ideas over time that improved peoples' minds and morals. The struggle was humanity's upward movement toward the perfection of God. Evolutionists such as Morgan saw that some societies moved along different pathways due to the effects of diffusion and their environments. Nonetheless, they were primarily intrigued by the general tempo of this process. Thus, Morgan could describe world history in terms of seven periods, the lower, middle, and upper status of Savagery, the lower, middle, and upper status of Barbarism, and the status of civilization, each with its critical discovery or invention that improved humanity's condition and insured its progress.

This of course raised the question of why everyone was not the same. The Enlightenment paradigm provided the answer: variability among the world's peoples was attributed to variability in the tempo of mental improvement; some peoples moved ("progressed") up the evolutionary ladder more quickly than others.[6] Handily enough for the evolutionists, less advanced societies could therefore be seen as relics of an earlier age, "monuments of the past" (Morgan [1877] 1963:41). By putting the world's peoples into a ranked sequence, human prehistory could be reconstructed.

The criteria for constructing evolutionary sequences were various, and included technological, social, political, intellectual, and moral factors. The ethnocentrism of the comparative method was shown in these criteria, for invariably European society was the standard against which all other societies were judged. Monogamy was superior to polygamy, patrilineal descent was better than matrilineal descent, monotheism was morally superior to ancestor worship, science was the successor to religion. Rankings often had a strongly racialist basis, with people of color at the bottom and Europeans (and especially northwestern Europeans) at the top of the sequence. "Few would dispute," Tylor asserted, "that the following races are arranged rightly in order of culture:—Australian [Aborigines], Tahitian, Aztec, Chinese, Italian" (Tylor 1871:27). To be fair, some authors, such as Morgan, attributed some differences to environment or technology, but ultimately cultural progression was linked to biological affinity (see Harris 1968:137–41 on the racial determinism of Morgan and Tylor).

Some scholars used this racist underpinning of the comparative method to justify the placement of hunter-gatherers at the lower rungs of the evolutionary ladder. Modern hunters were represented as descendants of prehistoric ones and could, Sir John Lubbock claimed, shed light on the past for the same reasons that modern pachyderms could tell us about prehistoric ones (1865). William Sollas compared the reconstructed physical features of Neandertals (which we now know to be incorrect) and Australian Aborigines to assert that the latter were lineal, unevolved descendants of the former. To Sollas, Bushmen were Aurignacians, and Eskimos were descendants of the Magdalenians, genetic relics of Upper Paleolithic peoples. (Sollas recognized that this was a tenuous approach, but with few archaeological data at his disposal he saw no more secure alternative "in a subject where fantasy is only too likely to play a leading part" [1911:70].)

Two other related factors helped place hunter-gatherers near the bottom of the evolutionary scale in these nineteenth-century schemes. First, they had few belongings. Of course, it is obvious that material goods could only be a hindrance to nomadic peoples, but in the minds of nineteenth-century European scholars the causal arrow was reversed. Hunter-gatherers were nomadic because they were intellectually incapable of developing the technology needed to permit a sedentary existence—agricultural implements, storage facilities, houses, ceramics, and the like. Were their moral and intellectual character to be raised, hunter-gatherers could settle down and reap the material rewards of progress.

Second, because many were nomadic, hunter-gatherer peoples had concepts of private property quite different from those of Europeans. While we shall see in chapter 5 that it is incorrect to say that there are no territorial boundaries among hunter-gatherers, the subtlety of the ways in which hunter-gatherers relate people to geography was lost on European explorers and colonizers. To them, hunter-gatherers had no concept of private property, a sure sign of arrested moral and intellectual development.[7]

In addition to its racist implications, we can see that the comparative method yielded "a philosophy of history that was identical with the set of assumptions used to arrange social or cultural differences in a presumed temporal and developmental series" (Bock 1956:17). If Australian Aborigines, for example, matched Neandertal "culture" so well, it was because Europeans had already presumed what Neandertal culture was like. This was hardly a demonstration that the Aborigines were a relic population. The comparative method seemed to work so well because it conveniently began by assuming the past it claimed to discover. Primitive or "primal" society was a chimera, a figment of the collective imagination of early evolutionists (see Kuper 1988).

While the comparative method was not without its contemporary detractors (most notably Franz Boas), it continued to influence anthropological research well into the twentieth century. The hunter-gatherer lifeway came to be represented as something undesirable, something humanity had to leave behind. Early twentieth-century descriptions of hunter-gatherers left students wondering "not only how hunters managed to make a living, but whether, after all, this was living" (Sahlins 1968:85). Allan Holmberg described the Bolivian Sirionos' adaptation to the tropical rain forest as ineffectual, their lives as dominated by a continual concern for food, their personalities as ungenerous and quarrelsome (1950; see commentary by Isaac 1977). Jules Henry asserted that the Kaingang (Botocudo) of Brazil "resented" their former nomadic way of life (1941:3). Viewed as too lazy, improvident, or stupid to grow their own food, hunter-gatherers were seen as people who had failed to move to a higher level of development. Alternatively, they were people who had been forced by agriculturalists into marginal areas where life was precarious, and were thus prevented from evolving further.

Anthropology eventually left this sad image behind (see below). But there was another legacy of progressive evolutionism that anthropology found harder to shake. Victorian scholars could see that human societies were incredibly diverse. They assumed that this diversity came from a single original social form, a prehistoric hunter-gatherer (rather than arboricultural) Adam and Eve. Why? The comparative method sought regularities, not patterns. Evolutionists looked for what was common among societies that they had already decided belonged in the same stage. Some differences arose from diffusion and environment, but if the major cause of change was the accumulation of ideas over time, then in the early stages of development not enough time would have passed for much variation to arise from any of these factors. There should, therefore, be less diversity in the early reaches of human evolution, when people were hunter-gatherers, than in later stages.

Although anthropologists have dismissed unilineal evolutionism and the particular notion of progress behind it, this part of the nineteenth-century paradigm continues. In the models developed in the twentieth century to describe hunter-gatherers, variation was something to be explained away in searching for the essential hunter-gatherer. We can see this in formulations of the patrilineal/patrilocal band, the generalized foraging, and the interdependent models.

THE PATRILINEAL/PATRILOCAL BAND

Beginnings are always hard to pinpoint, but the formal concept of a patrilineal, patrilocal band can perhaps be attributed to A. R. Radcliffe-Brown and his description of Australian Aboriginal social organization, especially that of the Kariera and Aranda (1930–31). Radcliffe-Brown argued that all Aborigines prior to contact lived in patrilineal/patrilocal *hordes*. Sometimes the hordes were described as small patrilineal groups, sometimes as clans, and sometimes only as something like clans. Whatever it was, the horde owned a specific tract of land containing its totemic sites, to which it had exclusive use rights. Radcliffe-Brown described the horde as politically autonomous, with no provision whereby a man could leave his own to join another. The horde was also the basic war-making unit.

While the term *band* had been in use for many years, it was not until 1936 that Julian Steward formalized the concept. Looking beyond Radcliffe-Brown's Australia, Steward saw variability in band composition, and he described three major types: *patrilineal, matrilineal,* and *composite* bands. Patrilineal bands had local exogamy, group sizes of fifty to a hundred, political autonomy, patrilineal descent and land inheritance, patrilocal residence, and communal land ownership. Theoretically, they consisted of a single lineage. Patrilineal bands were said to be the most common social form,[8] and, for Steward, this meant they were the earliest. Matrilineal bands mirrored patrilineal bands, but with matrilineal descent and matrilocal residence. Steward attributed matrilineal bands to factors such as a shortage of men in the wife's family, more favorable conditions in the territory of the wife's family, the desire to secure assistance of the wife's mother in child rearing, the lack of women for exchange with the wife's band, or to diffusion of practices from a neighboring area. Steward gave matrilineal bands little consideration and, in later years, he all but omitted discussion of them (e.g., Steward 1955).

Composite bands consisted of several independent families, were endogamous with bilateral descent, and had no rules of residence. Composite bands were frequently larger than patrilineal ones due to more abundant food resources, especially herds of migratory game. Steward saw composite bands as resulting from a variety of factors, especially their size and the prior subdivision of land into family tracts for special economic purposes (e.g., Algonquian and Athapaskan fur-trapping territories, Speck 1915), although the band might still be the political unit. Interband adoption and the legitimacy of cross- and parallel-cousin marriage, Steward argued, also encouraged the formation of composite bands.

Steward saw that some groups, such as the Western Shoshone and Eskimo,[9] did not fit into his classification. For these people, Steward claimed, there was no political unit beyond the family. He described this as the *family level of integration,* and attributed it to harsh environments that prevented the formation of bands.

Although Steward clearly recognized that not all hunter-gatherers fit the patrilineal-band model, the exceptions were given only slight attention. One reason is that Steward first thought the origin of patrilineal bands was to be found in natural male dominance (1936:333, although he later dropped this idea; 1955), and in the need for males (brothers) to bond together in order to hunt communally. Steward also argued that a hunter needed to remain in the area of his childhood, since he assumed that local knowledge was a prerequisite for successful hunting. Though Steward claimed he had ascertained "the causes of primitive bands through analysis of the inner functional or organic connection of the components of the culture and their environmental basis" (1936:344), he gave nearly equal weight to a priori land-use precepts, adoption practices, kinship, and ideas of human nature (male dominance and territorial ownership).

Service later critiqued Steward's typology, and in the process discounted variation even more (1962). Whereas Steward saw the composite band as the result of ecological factors preventing the formation of patrilineal bands, Service claimed that composite bands as well as family-level cases were the result of depopulation and the fragmenting effect of European contact. Service emphasized postmarital-residence rules more than Steward had, since he felt many cases of unilineal descent were de facto descent groups resulting from a postmarital-residence rule (1962:30–33, 60). Therefore, Service always referred to *patrilocal* bands. Because these bands appeared to be common among hunter-gatherers, and because they appeared in many environments, Service concluded that the patrilocal band was the earliest form of human organization above the level of the family. And, in contrast to Steward, Service took the position that "ecological adaptation has nothing whatsoever to do with preventing or 'frustrating' the formation of the patrilocal band," since the patrilocal band was not an adaptation but an "inevitable" form of social organization (1962:108). Thus, it could be extended to our earliest ancestors.

Within a few years, *patrilocal band* became nearly synonymous with *hunter-gatherer* (Service 1966; Williams 1974). Yet, from the beginning, it was clear that the patrilocal-band model could not accommodate all known hunter-gatherer societies. In Australia, the mismatch between the model and ethnographic reality was argued in terms of whether the data were derived from hunter-gatherer behavior or from ideology. Since Radcliffe-Brown recorded "memory culture," he recorded the ideology of land-use and descent rather than the actual behavior, but he assumed the two were the same (Peterson and Long 1986:18). Melvin Meggitt and especially Les Hiatt criticized

Radcliffe-Brown's reconstruction of the patrilineal horde as far too simple, static, and ignorant of variability in the ethnographic record (Meggitt 1962; Hiatt 1962, 1965, 1966, 1968; see review in Keen 1988).[10] Hiatt further pointed out that matrilineages existed, although they were not corporate land-owning or food-gathering units, and, most important, that economic relationships to land had to be differentiated from ritual ties.

Arguing that Hiatt had oversimplified Radcliffe-Brown's analysis, W. E. H. Stanner tried to resolve some of the ambiguity in the concept of horde in Australia with the concepts of *estate* and *range* (1965). An estate is an area that is traditionally recognized as the territory ("country" or "dreaming place") that "belongs" to a patrilineal-descent group, whereas range is the actual land over which a foraging group may roam. Sometimes estate and range are identical, but often the range is much larger (see Barker 1976). Patrilineal groups could cut across what were recognized as boundaries on other social levels, and members from many totemic-descent groups could make up a food-gathering unit. Also, many patrilineal groups did not have distinct territorial boundaries encompassing their totemic sites, and food-gathering units could move through areas containing the totemic sites of others.

Clearly, ethnographers recognized variability in Australian Aboriginal social organization. Radcliffe-Brown himself had recognized this variability and that is perhaps one reason why his definition of horde was so hard to pin down. Ethnographers argued over whether this variation should be attributed to environment or to European contact, over whether data collected years after contact was valid, and over the ecological basis of patrilineal hordes (Stanner 1965; Birdsell 1970). But they also argued about whether the variation was significant. Was it that there were other forms of local group organization no longer fully recognizable (L. Hiatt 1968:100), or were these organizations only variations on a theme, not important enough in themselves to call for explanation? The critical point is seen in Stanner's observation that "in remarks of wide application, [Radcliffe-Brown] tended to refer to hordes; in matters of detail or in analysis, to clans" (1965:8). Consequently, in the minds of many anthropologists, especially those outside of Australia, the clan and horde became synonymous. Any hints Radcliffe-Brown gave of variability—permeable boundaries, for example—were largely ignored by his readers (see Stanner 1965:15–16) and, in more general discussions, by Radcliffe-Brown himself. Anthropology was looking for a single *descriptive* model of hunter-gatherer social organization.

By the 1960s, however, many anthropologists recognized that there was much variation among hunter-gatherer social organizations that could not be subsumed under the patrilineal/patrilocal-band model. A new synthesis was in order and it was provided by the "Man the Hunter" conference.

THE GENERALIZED FORAGING MODEL

In 1966, seventy-five scholars from around the world met in Chicago to discuss the state of knowledge about hunter-gatherer peoples. Organized by Richard Lee and Irven DeVore at the urging of Sol Tax, the "Man the Hunter" conference proved to be the century's watershed for knowledge about hunter-gatherers.

The conference covered the topics of marriage, demography, territoriality, social and political organization, and evolution; it employed data from Africa, Australia, the subarctic, Arctic, South America, and North America, from ethnographic as well as archaeological cases. It provided new perspectives on marriage practices, filiation, descent, and residence. Despite its title, the conference introduced anthropology to the importance of plant food and women's labor in hunter-gatherer diet, both of which eventually led to new interpretations of human evolution (see Slocum 1975; papers in Dahlberg 1981).

Environment and subsistence took on increased importance at "Man the Hunter." Marriage practices, for example, were presented as ways of creating social ties to distant areas to facilitate migration in times of local resource failure. Group movement, size, and membership were seen as responses to local food density and variability. Lee characterized the Ju/'hoansi adaptation as "long term," adapted to environmental conditions as they are manifested over decades. In contrast to earlier descriptions of them as evolution's failures, in the late 1960s hunter-gatherers gained a reputation as savvy lay ecologists. They were *t'xudi kaus,* as the Ju/'hoansi might say, masters of cleverness and bush lore.

"Man the Hunter" created a new model of hunter-gatherer society, the *generalized foraging model* (Isaac 1990). In this model plant food, rather than meat, is the focus of subsistence. Defense and territoriality are unimportant and population is kept in balance with food resources through intentional cultural controls. "Man the Hunter" codified the importance of sharing, bilateral kinship, and bilocal postmarital residence in the hunter-gatherer adaptation.[11] Part of the new model was explicitly set forth in Lee and DeVore's conception of "nomadic style." It consisted of five characteristics:

(1) *Egalitarianism.* Lee and DeVore argued that mobility constrains the amount of property that can be owned, and thus serves to maintain material equality.

(2) *Low population density.* The food supply indirectly keeps population growth rate and density low so hunter-gatherers live in small groups, coming together seasonally in large aggregations for social purposes. Population is kept below carrying capacity through intentional, conscious controls such as abstention, abortion, and infanticide.

(3) *Lack of territoriality.* Long-term adaptation to resource variability requires that hunter-gatherers be able to move from one region to another, making defended territories maladaptive.

(4) *A minimum of food storage.* Since the group is nomadic, and food plentiful relative to population density, Lee and DeVore assumed that long-term storage would be unnecessary.

(5) *Flux in band composition.* Maintaining social ties requires frequent movement and visiting, which also discourages violence since disputes can be solved through group fissioning rather than fighting.

Notwithstanding the many exceptions, hunting and gathering as an economy became equated with the band as a social form. When Leacock and Lee, for example, discuss hunter-gatherers, they only (and explicitly) discuss band societies, excluding such groups as those of North America's Northwest Coast (1982a). Foragers of the Kalahari Desert, and especially the Ju/'hoansi, came to be regarded as the quintessential hunter-gatherers (figure 1-2).

The most critical part of the generalized foraging model, and the most enduring legacy of the conference, was Marshall Sahlins' eloquent formulation of the "original affluent society" (1968, 1972). In the 1960s and 1970s many people, anthropologists included, were dismayed with the state of the world. A grinding war of attrition in Vietnam and widespread environmental degradation led many to reject the materialism of Western society. Nineteenth-century notions of progress collapsed, and instead of an inexorable climb upwards, evolution now seemed a downward spiral from an initial state of grace, a fall from Eden. Increasingly dissatisfied, Westerners searched for an alternative way of life, where material possessions meant little, where people lived in harmony, where there were no national boundaries to contest.

It was in this social context that Sahlins proposed the concept of the original affluent society. Prior to "Man the Hunter" the hunter-gatherer lifeway

Figure 1-2. A Southern Kua woman prepares to cook the head of a donkey for two female-headed households in the Western Sandveld of the Kalahari Desert. The woman to her right pounds maize received in exchange for work in the fields of a nearby cattle post. While Bushmen were regarded as the quintessential hunter-gatherers in the 1960s and 1970s, they lived interdependently with agropastoralists. Photograph taken in August 1975. Courtesy of Robert Hitchcock.

had been viewed as one of continual fear and starvation, a perpetual and barely adequate search for food. Inspired by economist John Kenneth Galbraith's *The Affluent Society,* Sahlins argued that ethnographic data actually painted quite a different picture: hunter-gatherers spent relatively little time working, had all the food they needed, and spent leisure hours sleeping or socializing. The devil-may-care attitude toward the future, which many early explorers and ethnographers interpreted as stupidity or foolishness, Sahlins claimed was an expression of self-confidence and assurance that the environment would meet one's needs. The carelessness with which many hunter-gatherers treat material goods, previously interpreted as the inability to recognize personal property, was, Sahlins argued, a response to a mobile lifestyle in which permanent material goods are a hindrance. In Sahlins' memorable phrase, the foraging economy was a Zen economy: wanting little, hunter-gatherers had all they wanted. In the 1960s and 1970s, it was a very attractive image.

But Sahlins' primary purpose in proposing the original affluent-society model was to counter the prevailing argument in anthropology that hunter-gatherers did not have "elaborate" culture because they did not have the time to develop it. Paleolithic hunters, the argument went, adopted agriculture and animal domestication to relieve themselves of the time-consuming burden of hunting and gathering. They were evolution's success stories. Living hunter-gatherers, on the other hand, were the misfits or the unfortunates who had been pushed into environments hostile to agriculture. Spending all of their waking hours in the food search, hunter-gatherers could not develop elaborate culture because they did not have the spare time to build temples, carve stelae, or erect pyramids. To overturn this deeply held misconception, Sahlins felt it necessary to use the "most shocking terms possible"—thus the overstatement of the original affluent society (1968:85). In his 1968 paper, Sahlins dramatized the fact that Australian Aborigines and the Ju/'hoansi work only a few hours a day, yet, even with this abundance of free time, they did not develop civilization. Thus, the development of writing, arts, architecture, and the like required something more than free time. In particular, they required material investment. Among nomadic peoples, material belongings are a burden. No matter how efficient or attractive an implement may be, if it can be manufactured at the next campsite, why bother carrying it? An implement that cannot be readily manufactured must be extremely useful to be worth carrying. This is largely why hunter-gatherers, in the eyes of many explorers, had cavalier attitudes toward personal property. If hunter-gatherers have all they want because they want very little, perhaps it is because they cannot afford to want very much.

Given the social context in which the idea was proposed, it is easy to understand how the image of hunter-gatherers as "affluent" captured wide attention.[12] Left unelaborated, however, was the relationship between the economic constraints of foraging, social relations, material goods, and culture (see Bird-David 1992a,b). By centering attention on Sahlins' claim that hunter-gatherers do not work a lot, anthropology replaced one facile stereotype with another.

In the years since 1968, anthropologists have used the concept of affluence in different ways. For Sahlins, and many other anthropologists as well, affluence was inherent in the economy of hunting and gathering; therefore all hunter-gatherers were, by definition, affluent. But in reality, when these anthropologists thought about hunter-gatherers they were only thinking of groups such as the Ju/'hoansi (and sometimes only the Ju/'hoansi)—groups that fit the image conveyed by the generalized foraging model (Bird-David 1992b). As with Service's model, matrilineal, avunculocal, sedentary, territorial, warring, ranked societies (e.g., those of North America's Northwest Coast) were excluded from the generalized foraging model. Anthropology's view of foraging societies became quite myopic. In archaeology, the concept of affluence had a particularly dramatic effect on theories explaining the origins of agriculture. Long seen as a great improvement in human life, agriculture came to be represented as a lifeway adopted only under dire circumstances.[13] Theories explaining the origin of agriculture focused on how population growth and migration to environmentally marginal areas forced hunter-gatherers to leave their life of leisure behind, become agriculturalists, and work for a living (e.g., Binford 1968; Cohen 1977).

Other archaeologists, however, reversed the affluent-forager image, labeling groups with high population densities, many material belongings, and food storage as the most affluent—people who, in contrast to Sahlins' original formulation, apparently wanted a lot and got a lot—and desert hunter-gatherers as the least affluent (e.g., see papers in Koyama and Thomas 1981). In fact, some argue that Northwest Coast society, with its elaborate mortuary feasts and material culture, is a product of an environment that contains abundant food resources (see chapter 8), that is, a product of the free time that resource abundance permits. This is precisely the relationship that Sahlins had tried to counter!

Different uses of *affluence* were partly generated by a misunderstanding of the original concept, but they were primarily generated by efforts to account for variability within a single descriptive model of hunter-gatherer society. At "Man the Hunter" there was disagreement over most generalizations about hunting and gathering, and discomfort over the fact that generalizations could be made only if certain groups were set aside. George Murdock, for example, was struck by the uniformity in hunter-gatherer social organization and division of labor—if the Australian Aborigines were left out. Based on statistical tests that utilized data from Murdock's ethnographic atlas, John Whiting showed that hunter-gatherers were significantly different from agriculturalists in a number of categories—but again only if the Australian Aborigines were ignored (Lee and DeVore 1968:336–37). Teeming with sodalities, Australian Aborigines did not fit into Service's evolutionary paradigm. The Australian Aborigines were a particular bugbear at the conference, defying easy inclusion with other hunter-gatherers. They were often treated as a special case, as were Northwest Coast and equestrian Plains

Indian societies. Conference participants admitted to considerable variability among foragers, but were unwilling to give up the general category of hunter-gatherers. (And, reading between the lines, there seemed to be some disagreement among participants as to whether they should define hunter-gatherers in social or economic terms.) There was tension between those who sought universal characteristics of a modal form of hunter-gatherer society (e.g., Williams 1968:126), and those who felt it necessary to account for variability. DeVore cautioned participants that "we might well be suspicious of any generalization that was intended to apply to all men who have ever hunted in any place or at any time" (Lee and DeVore 1968:339). While participants recognized variability, then, there was still a nagging sense that there ought to be something socially and culturally unique and common to all people who hunt and gather for a living.

Even leaving aside exceptions such as Northwest Coast societies, a typology or definition of band societies continued to be elusive. Though a proponent of typologies in 1955 (Steward 1955:180), late in his life Steward claimed that the year-to-year fluctuations in group composition made it difficult to define bands "either as a generic category, as a series of subcategories, or as some kind of subdivision of larger social units" (1969b:290). He questioned whether "we have any cross-cultural types that are truly identical structurally" (1968:322) and suggested that "minimal importance should be ascribed to a search for criteria of bands and to a construction of a typology of bands" (1969a:187). Instead, he recommended that "it may be far more profitable to search for those processes which have brought about the distinguishing characteristics of societies under this very broad category" (1969a:187). Steward was not waffling when he saw a typology of bands as being directed by and toward a study of the processes that brought bands into being. He was instead expressing the frustration everyone at the time felt over the desire to study hunter-gatherers as a social or economic type without being able to define what that type was. This is the dilemma of categorical thinking, a problem that is neither new nor unique to anthropology.

But, if the "Man the Hunter" conference tore down one theoretical model to replace it with another, the new model was itself soon to be dismantled, for the very research it inspired was rapidly producing information for which it could not account.

A key question raised by several researchers goes to the heart of the generalized foraging model by challenging the concept of original affluence: how much do hunter-gatherers work, and why? Reexaminations of Ju/'hoansi and Australian work effort do not support Sahlins' claim. Kristen Hawkes and James O'Connell found a major discrepancy between the Paraguayan Ache's nearly seventy-hour work week and the Ju/'hoansi's reportedly twelve-to-nineteen-hour week (1981). The discrepancy, they discovered, lay in Lee's original definition of work.[14] Lee counted as work only the time spent in the bush searching for and procuring food, not the labor needed to process food resources in camp. Add in the time it takes to manufacture and maintain tools, carry water, care for children, process nuts and game, gather firewood, and clean habitations, and the Ju/'hoansi work well over a forty-hour week (Lee 1984; Isaac 1990). One of the sets of Australian data that Sahlins used came from what was literally a foraging experiment of only a few days' duration, performed with nine adults and no dependents. There was little incentive for these adults to forage much (and they apparently were none too keen on participating—see Bird-David 1992b) and the results are undoubtedly nonrepresentative (Altman 1984, 1987).

More accurate estimates of the time hunter-gatherers spend foraging and processing the resources they bring back demonstrates that some hunter-gatherers work at subsistence pursuits for seven, eight, or more hours a day (table 1-1; see also Hill et al. 1985).[15] But many hunter-gatherers do not spend much time out foraging, and some only forage every other day or so. Why don't they forage more? Do they intend to have an affluent life of leisure?

At the "Man the Hunter" conference, Lorna Marshall pointed out that Ju/'hoansi women may not work as hard as they could because in gathering more than needed a woman would soon be confronted by demands to share the fruits of her extra efforts, and face accusations of stinginess if she refuses. Knowing that extra labor does not benefit her family, Marshall argued, a woman intentionally restricts how much she gathers (Lee and DeVore 1968:94).

Such intentional restrictions on productivity may be common, and with good reason. Through an insightful computer simulation, Bruce Winterhalder showed that even if a few members of a foraging band should elect to increase their productivity, they could cause disaster for everyone in the group. By working long hours and taking in more food than is necessary, hard-working foragers could deplete local resources quickly, causing large fluctuations in population growth rates that could eventually result in group extinction (Winterhalder et al. 1988; Winterhalder 1993). Winterhalder found that the effect of increased foraging effort is abrupt, and even small

Table 1-1. Foraging and Work

Group	Foraging hrs/day female	Foraging hrs/day male	Foraging hrs/day both (mean)	Working hrs/day both (mean)	Reference
South America					
Ache	1.3	6.9		6	Hill et al. 1985; Hurtado et al. 1985
Hiwi (late wet)[a]	2.6	1.3			Hurtado and Hill 1987, 1990
Hiwi (early dry)	2.2	1.7			Hurtado and Hill 1987, 1990
Hiwi (late dry)	1.6	2.0			Hurtado and Hill 1987, 1990
Hiwi (early wet)	1.5	2.2			Hurtado and Hill 1987, 1990
Africa					
Ju/'hoansi	1.8	3.1		7	Lee 1979, 1982
BaMbuti (nets)				8.5	Harako 1981
BaMbuti (archers)		5.0			Harako 1981
BaMbuti (nets)			10		Terashima 1983
BaMbuti (archers)			8.1		Terashima 1983
Efe Pygmy (men)		4.6		6.3	Bailey 1991
≠Kade	2.4	6.3		9.5	Tanaka 1980
G/wi			5.2		Silberbauer 1981a,b
Hadza			2		Woodburn 1968
Hadza (dry season)	2–6				Hawkes, O'Connell, and Blurton Jones 1989
Hadza (wet season)	4–8				Hawkes, O'Connell, and Blurton Jones 1989
Kutse (Bushmen)[b]		2.6			Kent 1993
Australia					
Australia Coast				3.8	McCarthy and McArthur 1960
Australia Coast				5.1	McCarthy and McArthur 1960
Australia Interior			3		Curr 1886–87
Australia Interior			2–3		Grey 1841
Australia Interior			2–4		Eyre 1845
Ngadadjara	4.5			7	Gould 1980
Western Desert	4–6				Tindale 1972
Southeast Asia					
Paliyan			3–4		Gardner 1972
Agta (male)		7.5			Estioko-Griffin and Griffin 1985
Agta (female)	6.2[b]				Goodman et al. 1985
Ihaya Agta (female)				4.2	Rai 1990
Ihaya Agta (male)				7.7	Rai 1990
Batak	2.9	4.1			Endicott and Endicott 1986
North America					
Tlingit				6.5	Oberg 1973

Note: Work includes both foraging and food processing/preparation.

[a]Female work effort given is for nonnursing or postreproductive women; nursing or pregnant women work less.

[b]Includes hunting only, dry season; 1987–91.

increases in work effort can change an environment that is replete with food into one that is barren. Hurtado and Hill provide tentative support for this argument in their analysis of the Venezuelan Hiwi's foraging activities (1990). The Hiwi do not forage for more than an average of two to three hours a day because their net caloric intake might actually *decrease* due partially to the difficulty of working during the hottest part of the day. This would probably dramatically decrease women's fertility, a fact that Hiwi women seem to recognize.

So do foragers have all they want because they want very little? Winterhalder argues that Sahlins' "Zen economy has an ecological master" (Winterhalder et al. 1988:323) and that we can expect variability in how much effort foragers put into foraging depending on a number of environmental factors. The concept of original affluence cannot account for variability in forager work effort and reproduction or for conditions that lead to increased work effort and population growth (Blurton Jones, Hawkes, and Draper 1994; Winterhalder and Goland 1993; see chapter 6).

It also now appears that many hunter-gatherers are also chronically undernourished and undergo dramatic seasonal fluctuations in weight and nutritional status that, for women, affects fecundity and the welfare of nursing offspring.[16] Members of that quintessential affluent society, the Ju/'hoansi, "are very thin and complain often of hunger, at all times of the year. It is likely that hunger is a contributing cause to many deaths which are immediately caused by infectious and parasitic diseases, even though it is rare for anyone simply to starve to death" (Howell 1986b:173–74; see Isaac 1990). And the Ju/'hoansi, like all hunter-gatherers, are also susceptible to periodic and seasonal famines (Hitchcock and Ebert 1984). This is not just a product of contact. A growing body of archaeological data also demonstrates that prehistoric hunter-gatherer peoples in a variety of environments lived physically demanding lives, and frequently witnessed severe seasonal food shortages (e.g., Yesner 1994).

Life among some hunter-gatherers may also be more violent than previously thought. Per capita homicide rates among some hunter-gatherers, including the Ju/'hoansi, are quite high, rivaling those of large North American cities (Lee 1979:398–99; Headland 1988). Lee counters this observation by arguing that were it not for medical facilities, violence in North American cities would lead to many more deaths, and greatly increase the homicide rate over that of the Ju/'hoansi. It is also apparent that some violence is due to the sedentization process that requires people to aggregate into large groups, and to the unrestrained use of alcohol (Kent 1990). Nonetheless, the Ju/'hoansi do experience violence, and many other hunter-gatherers fought and raided one another for revenge, food, and slaves.[17] Other hunter-gatherers are also far more territorial than the Ju/'hoansi, including some in the Kalahari Desert itself (Heinz 1972), and vigorously defend their territorial boundaries, sometimes through violence.

The emphasis on plant food in the generalized foraging model also does not apply to all hunter-gatherers. It is obviously not true of Arctic foragers, but it is also untrue for many who live in lower latitudes. Using the ethnographic atlas, Carol Ember showed that as a simple statistical percentage, meat was more important than plant food, and, not surprisingly, that men contributed more to subsistence than women in the majority of societies (1978).[18] Brian Hayden also found that whereas hunted food provides a mean of only 35 percent by weight in a sample of forager diets, it provides at least half of many groups' total caloric needs (1981b). Hunting is important to foragers, but we should not return to a pre-"Man the Hunter" stereotype. Instead, we need to understand how foragers make decisions about what and how much to hunt.

Others have found that the alleged egalitarian relations of hunter-gatherers are pervaded by inequality, most notably but not only between the young and the old, and men and women (Woodburn 1980; Hayden et al. 1986; Leacock 1978; see chapters 7 and 8). Food is not shared equally, and men and women in a hunter-gatherer camp may eat very different diets, with women often eating less meat than men (Walker and Hewlett 1990; Speth 1990). Archaeologists have found increasing evidence of prehistoric nonegalitarian hunter-gatherers in a variety of different environments (Price and Brown 1985b), most of whom lived under high population densities and stored food on a large scale. None of this contradicts the traditional definition of egalitarianism, but it does point out that the social relationships of hunter-gatherers are more complex and diverse than once assumed. It is certainly erroneous to equate a hunter-gatherer economy with band society.

In the twenty years after the generalized foraging model was formulated, anthropologists encountered serious discrepancies between it and ethnographic reality, some of which we have noted above. However, the most serious criticism of post-"Man the Hunter" research was the recognition that living foragers are not isolated from the world system. This has resulted in a new approach to modern foragers, the interdependent model.

PROFESSIONAL PRIMITIVES AND THE INTERDEPENDENT MODEL

One purpose of "Man the Hunter" was to help resolve what many saw as difficulties with the patrilocal-band model. But also, in the early 1960s, astonishing discoveries made at Olduvai Gorge and elsewhere demonstrated the antiquity of the human species and renewed the desire to use living hunter-gatherers as a source of insight for reconstructing the lives of early hominids. Lee and DeVore explained that "Man the Hunter" was organized

> to follow logically from an earlier symposium on the Origin of Man. . . . Current ethnographic studies have contributed substantial amounts of new data on hunter-gatherers and are rapidly changing our concept of Man the Hunter. Social anthropologists generally have been reappraising the basic concepts of descent, filiation, residence, and group structure. In archaeology the recent excavation of early living floors has led to a renewed interest in and reliance on hunter-gatherer data for reconstruction, and current theories of society and social evolution must inevitably take into account these new data on the hunter-gatherer groups. (Lee and DeVore 1968:vii)

While no anthropologist at "Man the Hunter" would have said that living foragers were *exactly* like Pleistocene ones—not even Victorian scholars made this claim—it was not clear how theories of social evolution were supposed to take into account the new data on hunter-gatherer groups. The issue is critical for archaeology because modern foragers do not, in Sahlins' phrase, live in a prehistoric world of hunters, but in a world of IBM, Coca-Cola, World Bank-sponsored cattle ranches, international lumber markets, and guerrilla movements. All live physically and socially on the outskirts of societies different from their own. They interact with these societies through trade, marriage, and employment, and have done so for some time (Spielmann and Eder 1994). The Penan of Borneo gather rattan today for the world market and probably traded with Chinese merchants at least as long ago as 900 A.D. (Hoffman 1984). In Africa, many Bushmen[19] were impressed into modern military forces because of their knowledge of bushlore; some may have oscillated among pastoralism, agriculture, and foraging for centuries (Gordon 1992; Wilmsen 1989a; Denbow 1984; Wilmsen and Denbow 1990). African Pygmies were involved in the ivory trade long before Europeans penetrated the Ituri Forest (Bahuchet 1988). In North America, Algonquians trapped beaver almost to extinction beginning in the early sixteenth century for the manufacture of hats and other goods in Europe. The

Shoshone preyed on the livestock of mid-nineteenth-century California-bound immigrants, and California hunter-gatherers were devastated by disease and acts of genocide beginning in the eighteenth century. Down under, Australian Aborigines traded with Macassans from the Celebes well before British colonization (Meehan 1982:16). After contact, immigrants hunted Aborigines for sport on the mainland and in Tasmania. Virtually no hunter-gatherer in the tropical forest today lives without trading heavily with horticulturalists for carbohydrates, or eating government or missionary rations.[20] Some authors have even suggested that it is impossible to live in the tropical rain forest as a hunter-gatherer without the carbohydrates and iron tools provided by horticulturalists (e.g., Bailey et al. 1989; Headland and Reid 1989).[21] Terry Rambo predicts that Southeast Asian foragers would cease to exist if trade with villagers were cut off (1985:31).[22]

In brief, long before anthropologists arrived on the scene, hunter-gatherers had already been contacted, given diseases, shot at, traded with, employed and exploited by colonial powers, agriculturalists, and/or pastoralists. The result has been dramatic alterations in hunter-gatherers' livelihoods. Family trapping territories among the Naskapi and Montagnais were probably adaptations to the fur trade, rather than precontact forms of land ownership (Cooper 1946; Leacock 1954, 1969). Amazonian and Canadian groups responded to European colonization by separating into family groups and marketing forest produce—rubber in one case, furs in the other (Murphy and Steward 1955). Other hunter-gatherers sold their labor to colonists and colonial enterprises, often with disastrous consequences (e.g., Gould, Fowler, and Fowler 1972; Krech 1983). Those people labeled hunter-gatherers today rarely obtain all their food from hunting and gathering—some do a bit of agriculture, some receive government welfare, and some do wage labor (figure 1-3). Others are also deeply involved in cash economies, making crafts and gathering forest products to sell on the world market (see Peterson and Matsuyama 1991). They often live on cultural "frontiers," shifting between foraging and wage labor or commercial foraging (Gardner 1993). Some retreat into forests or deserts to avoid conscription, taxes, and the administrative arms of colonial powers (Feit 1982; Gardner 1993; Nurse and Jenkins 1977; Woodburn 1979). For others, foraging is a political message, a way to reaffirm their cultural worth (Povinelli 1992; Bird-David 1992a,b). Reanalyzing the concept of original affluence, Nurit Bird-David suggests that modern hunter-gatherers have a "cosmic economy of sharing," with social systems designed so as to incorporate non-hunter-gatherers' resources and yet maintain a foraging way of life (1988, 1990, 1992a,b). There

Figure 1-3. A family of Mikea, seasonal foragers in southwestern Madagascar. In the dry season this family gathers roots in the forest to eat and to sell; in the wet season they will move into a semipermanent hamlet and grow maize through slash-and-burn horticulture. They participate in a nearby village's market and frequently work for wages. Photograph by the author, July 1993.

can be little doubt that all ethnographically known hunter-gatherers are tied into the world economic system in one way or another; in some cases they have been so connected for hundreds of years.[23] They are in no way evolutionary relics, and using these people to interpret the living floors of Olduvai Gorge is no straightforward exercise.

In the mid-twentieth century, anthropologists saw the effects of contact between hunter-gatherers and "outside" societies as something that could be eliminated or neutralized, like noise in a radio signal, allowing reconstruction of the precontact lifeway. In the 1980s, however, some anthropologists argued that the effects of interaction cannot be subtracted from hunter-gatherer lifeways. Efforts to do so, the argument goes, encourage a view of hunter-gatherers as "primitive and isolated—incomplete, not yet fully evolved, and outside the mainstream" (Headland and Reid 1989:43). In fact, some argue that the structure of hunter-gatherer systems is *only* to be understood in terms of how hunter-gatherers interact with non-hunter-gatherer societies. Hunter-gatherers of today, Tom Headland and Lawrence Reid claim, remain as hunter-gatherers "because it is economically their most via-ble option in their very restricted circumstances. . . . [they carry] on a life-style not in spite of but because of their particular economic role in the global world in which they live" (1989:51).

This observation encouraged some to move away from the ecological par-adigm of the 1960s and 1970s, and the generalized foraging model has now been replaced, in some quarters, by what we will call the *interdependent* or to use the Seligmanns' term, the *professional primitives* model.[24] Unlike previous models, it has nothing to do with reconstructing an earlier stage of human evolution but it does make some serious claims about the role of ethnogra-phy in reconstructing the past.

Given the important place of the Ju/'hoansi in hunter-gatherer anthropol-ogy in the 1960s and 1970s, it is understandable that much of this new per-spective centers on reinterpretations of Lee's ethnography of that group. Briefly, Edwin Wilmsen, James Denbow, and others argue that the Ju/'hoansi and other Bushmen have not been "pure" hunter-gatherers for at least sev-eral hundred years, perhaps more than a millennium. Instead, the revisionists argue that the Bushmen have been in close contact with African and Euro-pean traders, and have shifted among foraging, agriculture, and pastoralism in response to changes in the regional social and political reality of southern Africa (Wilmsen 1983, 1989a, 1992; Wilmsen and Denbow 1990; Denbow 1984; Gordon 1984, 1992). Bushmen society and culture are formed not only by ecology, but by south African political economy as well. For ex-ample, Bushmen egalitarianism is seen by some not as an adaptation to the exigencies of nomadic life in the desert, but as a response to domination by hierarchical outsiders (see discussion by Woodburn 1988), a product of the Bushmen being the lowest stratum in a class society (Wilmsen 1983; 1989a; Gordon 1984).

Carmel Schrire and Wilmsen criticize Lee for characterizing the Ju/'ho-ansi lifeway as "an elementary form of economic life" (Lee 1969:73) and as "the basic human adaptation stripped of the accretions and complications brought about by agriculture, urbanization, advanced technology, and na-tional and class conflict" (Lee 1974:169; Schrire 1980, 1984b). In his major monograph on the Ju/'hoansi, Lee argued that "the first order of business is carefully to account for the effects of contact on their way of life. Only after the most meticulous assessment of the impact of commercial, governments, and other outside interests can we justify making statements about the hunter-gatherers' evolutionary significance" (1979:2). Schrire and Wilmsen argue that such an approach is impossible, for once the effects of contact are subtracted, there is nothing left. Wilmsen, in fact, argues that his own work with the Bushmen has nothing to say about hunter-gatherers: "in the Kalahari, we are some thousand years too late for that" (Wilmsen 1989a:57). Ignoring the political and historical context of the Bushmen or any foragers, Wilmsen and Schrire argue, treats them as being outside history, and ignores the exploitation and inequality that characterize their lives.[25] Thus, many adherents of the interdependent model are concerned with understanding the modern political reality of hunter-gatherers' lives and with assisting their claims to land and political autonomy (see papers in Leacock and Lee 1982b; Wilmsen 1989c).

The specifics of Bushmen history are best argued by experts on the Kalahari.[26] However, two issues raised by this debate are central to current anthropological perspectives on hunter-gatherers.

Who are hunter-gatherers?

The first issue is whether the sociocultural trends observed among modern hunter-gatherers are associated with hunting and gathering itself, or are a product of hunter-gatherers interacting with non-hunter-gatherers:

There can be no doubt that, one way or another, all [ethnographies] describe societies coping with the impact of incursions by foreign forces into their territories. Anthropologists have used these studies to postulate commonalities among groups in their search for those features that are residual or intrinsic to the hunter-gatherer mode. The big question that arises is, are the common features of hunter-gatherer groups, be they structural elements such as bilateral kinship systems or behavioral ones such as a tendency to share food, a product of interaction with us? Are the features we single out and study held in common, not so much because humanity shared the hunter-gatherer life-style for 99% of its time on earth, but because the hunters and gatherers of today, in searching for the compromises that would allow them to go on doing mainly that, have reached some subliminal consensus in finding similar solutions to similar problems? (Schrire 1984b:18)

By identifying this issue, Schrire raises important questions, although her focus remains on commonalities among hunter-gatherers, not on variability. Like its predecessors, the interdependent model runs the risk of constructing a new stereotype—one that considers the particular historical circumstances of different peoples, but still reduces variability by arguing that allegedly common characteristics are a product not of social evolution or ecology, but of interaction with non-hunter-gatherers.

But not all relations of contact are the same (Schrire and Gordon 1985:2; Lee 1988; Spielmann and Eder 1994). Peter Gardner points out that encapsulation can result in sociopolitical domination, disruptions in economies due to diseases, displacement, exchange, cash foraging, and/or the development of dependence upon neighbors (1993). Perhaps the Bushmen are egalitarian because of contact with colonists and traders. But, whereas Northwest Coast hunter-gatherers eventually became a conquered people, contact with colonists and traders initially made them more warlike and more socially stratified (Ferguson 1984). David Stuart also shows that Tierra del Fuego's Ona and Yahgan responded differently to European encroachment due to their different social organizations and environmental conditions (1980). Not all aspects of modern hunter-gatherer organization are products of encapsulation (Woodburn 1988). We should "consider the possibility that foragers can be autonomous without being isolated and engaged without being incorporated" (Solway and Lee 1990:110).

The concern with contact-induced change threatens to reduce analysis of variability among hunter-gatherers to a new stereotype, one that focuses on issues of power and control, that treats modern hunter-gatherers only as disenfranchised rural proletariat, and that ultimately denies the usefulness of the study of modern hunter-gatherers for understanding prehistory. This is as much of an oversimplification as was the generalized foraging model. And it is as much an overstatement to claim that modern ethnography is useless to prehistory as it is naive to suppose that the effects of contact can be subtracted from living foragers.

Marxist approaches

The second issue raised by the interdependent model concerns the ecological paradigm of post-"Man the Hunter" research. With increasing interest in how foragers are encapsulated within the world system has come an increased concern with political economy. As a result, Marxist approaches have made inroads into hunter-gatherer studies. We can only give a simple description of these approaches here.

Marxist approaches rest in one way or another on Karl Marx's concept of the *mode of production*. Briefly, the mode of production is made up of the means of production (land, raw materials, and labor) and the social relations of production (the way in which products are distributed and the labor process is reproduced). Although other factors were important, Marx saw the means of production as strongly conditioning the relations of production.

Marx divided capitalist societies in their simplest form into two classes: those who owned the means of production and those who owned only their labor, which they sold to the class of owners. The owners sold goods on the market for profit—whatever remained after paying taxes, capital investments, and laborers. Classical economics saw profit as capital to be invested in the economy for the good of all. Marx, however, saw profit as exploitation. Since the owners of the means of production control profit and pay themselves from it, maximizing profit maximizes their return. And, since labor is the most expensive element of production, owners maximize profit by reducing the cost of labor—by replacing workers with machinery, by paying workers as little as possible or by moving where labor is cheaper.[27] Thus, capitalism entails social relations that initially facilitate production but which eventually come to exploit workers.

Why do workers put up with this? Marx argued that the owners of the means of production also control a society's ideology—the explicit ideas of the social relations between the classes. Marx argued that the actual relations of exploitation were masked or mystified by an ideology in which owners claimed to work for the good of society, and in which workers were doing their part by remaining workers. Driven by the ever-developing forces of production and the increasingly constraining relations of production, the contradiction between the actual and professed social relations in a society eventually produces class conflict when the working class recognizes the discrepancy between the two. Attempts to resolve the contradiction produce class struggle, resulting in the formation of new classes, which renews the cycle.

Initially, it was the apparent absence of these elements from the lives of hunter-gatherers that inspired some analysts to discover in them a truly classless society, or "primitive communism." (Lee [1988] attributes recognition of this not to Marx, but to Lewis Henry Morgan, whose work later inspired Engels [1884].) Hunter-gatherers are, the argument goes, evidence of a precapitalist mode of production, the *foraging mode of production*. Lee describes this mode of production as one in which social relations enforce equal access to resources (1988). It includes:

(1) collective ownership of the means of production (land and its resources),

(2) the right of reciprocal access to the resources of others through marriage or other social ties,
(3) little emphasis on accumulation (and, in fact, opposition to hoarding),
(4) total sharing throughout the camp,
(5) equal access to the tools necessary to acquire food, and
(6) individual ownership of these tools (Leacock and Lee 1982a:8–9).

Some theorists see the foraging mode of production as grounded in the lack
of control over food production and the inevitable diminishing returns of
foraging that produce movement and the consequent lack of interest in material goods and land ownership (Meillassoux 1973). Tim Ingold, on the
other hand, places greater emphasis on social relations, arguing that hunter-
gatherers hunt and gather not just to eat, but to maintain a specific order of
social relations, those emphasizing egalitarianism and the collective appropriation of resources (1987, 1988).

Leacock and Lee claim that the foraging mode of production (and consequently primitive communism) is only applicable to band-living peoples,
that is, hunter-gatherers who have egalitarian social systems (1982a:1). But
many hunter-gatherers do not fit this model. Along with Marxist approaches
has come a growing concern with describing and accounting for people who
are economically speaking hunter-gatherers, but who do not fit the definition of the foraging mode of production.

When defined in terms of social relations, hunter-gatherers are often divided into two types, egalitarian and nonegalitarian (Keeley 1988; see chapter
8), or what Woodburn labels *immediate-* and *delayed-return* hunter-gatherers
(1980). In immediate-return systems no surplus is created, and resources, especially food, are consumed on a daily basis. These are egalitarian hunter-gatherers, in Woodburn's formulation, and include groups such as the Hadza, Mbuti,
and Ju/'hoansi. Woodburn's description of immediate-return hunter-gatherers is close to Leacock and Lee's description of band societies. Delayed-return hunter-gatherers, on the other hand, are those who reap the benefits
of their labor some time after investing it. This category includes primarily
hunter-gatherers who store food for later consumption. But it also includes,
in Woodburn's conception, Australian Aborigines, because adult men give
kinswomen away as brides in the expectation that their patrilineage will receive a bride in return in the future; thus, men store obligations in the form
of women (see also Testart 1987, 1989). Extensive food storage does appear
to be associated with nonegalitarian sociopolitical organizations among foragers, although it is not clear how (or even if) storage itself necessarily results

in exploitation of those who cannot control access to the stored resources by those who can (Keeley 1988; Testart 1982; see chapter 8).

Delayed-return or storing hunter-gatherers do not fit the model of primitive communism, a fact elaborated upon by theorists representing structural Marxism. Blending Marxism with French structuralism, structural Marxists argue that hunter-gatherer society is to be understood largely in the same terms as class or capitalist society. Therefore, structural Marxists assume that hunter-gatherer society is also driven by inherent relations of exploitation and by contradictions between social relations and ideology. Just as the generalized foraging model focused on immediate-return systems to the exclusion of others, structural Marxists appear to focus on delayed-return systems. Structural Marxists place much greater emphasis on the social relations of production than do dialectical materialists such as Leacock and Lee. Though they do not go so far as to argue that the social relations of production are determinant, structural Marxists do see them as dominant:

social relations can themselves establish the context for change and generate a dynamic which fuels further changes. While social relations are influenced by other variables (such as environment, demography) they have their own internal dynamics and because it is here that decisions are made they may be viewed to a large degree as primary. (Lourandos 1988:150; see also Godelier 1977; Bender 1985; Meillassoux 1973)

Structural Marxists focus on social relations that generate surplus food or resources that are used in competitive activities between local groups. Through such activities certain individuals profit by gaining prestige from the labor of others. Though it would seem that structural Marxism is suited to the study of delayed-return systems, in fact, structural Marxists assume there are exploitative relations in all societies, relations that are masked by ideology. For these theoreticians, social change arises from individuals negotiating the contradictions within their social order. Social change, they argue, is largely produced by the operation of social relations of production.

There are a number of difficulties with structural Marxism as it is applied to hunter-gatherers (see discussion in Bettinger 1991). Since Marx's social analysis was designed with class societies in mind, one can question its applicability to the band societies of many hunter-gatherers. Many Marxists, however, argue that classes are not necessary for a Marxist analysis to proceed, since all societies contain contradictions and exploitation at some level between groups that theoretically approach classes in nature, for example, gender and age groups (Bern 1979; Woodburn 1982). Among some Australian Aborigines, for example, old men control the distribution of women as wives; young men acquire wives largely by obeying older men, hunting for them, and allowing them to distribute the product of the hunt. Likewise, men who have received wives are in debt to the older men who gave them wives until they are able to return a woman as a wife. Woodburn sees this as establishing inequality and exploitation between older and younger men (1982)—although unlike true classes, where there is limited social mobility, all surviving young men in the group eventually become older men.

But, even if exploitative relations exist between groups approximating classes in all hunter-gatherer societies, it is clear that these are not all the same. The competitive feasts of the Kwakiutl, for example, are not found among the Ju/'hoansi, and, even if we accept Woodburn's analysis, the nature of Australian Aboriginal gerontocracy is certainly different from Northwest Coast society (which in places included a slave class). Left unclear is what generates different levels and forms of inequality (see chapter 8). It is probably true that all hunter-gatherer societies contain contradictions that mask and propagate exploitative relations, and all modern (and many prehistoric) foragers constitute a class relative to their nonforaging neighbors. Marxism can be a powerful explanatory framework for understanding the operation of a group's internal dynamics, the relationship between foragers and their neighbors, and the manipulation of the symbols of ideology. But Marxism loses its power as an explanatory framework when it views all hunter-gatherer societies as essentially similar (whether they are "primitive communists" or incipient capitalists). This generalizing is not unique to Marxism. And though Marxism is an explanatory framework rather than a descriptive model like the patrilineal-band and generalized-foraging models, it shares with those models a tendency to offer stereotypical images rather than an understanding of variability.

HUNTER-GATHERERS AS A CULTURAL TYPE

Throughout the history of anthropological thought, the stereotypes of hunter-gatherers have changed from one extreme to another: from a vision of lives that were nasty, brutish, and short, to lives of affluence; from a diet of meat to a diet of plant food; from egalitarianism to inequality; from isolated relic to rural proletariat. Anthropology sought to explain "the" hunter-gatherer lifeway by seeking generalizations, usually drawn from a very small sample of societies, sometimes from only one. There is nothing wrong with seeking generalizations; indeed, this is part of the obligation of a scientist. But generalizations should not mask the underlying variability; rather they should be steps toward understanding it.

At this point my reader is probably wondering how I justify writing a book about hunter-gatherers if I see so little utility in that category. In a number of ways, hunter-gatherers as a group differ statistically from those other categories of humanity so dear to anthropology: horticulturalists, agriculturalists, pastoralists. Likewise, hunter-gatherer bands differ from tribes, chiefdoms, and states. In the past, anthropologists have felt the need to search for what is common among hunter-gatherers in contrast to these other categories, that is, to seek what is essential to the hunter-gatherer lifeway. This search has played an important role in understanding cultural evolution by pointing to correlations that give us clues to the causal variables involved in creating cultural diversity, by identifying differences between those we call hunter-gatherers and those we give other names. Yet, "it is not whether phenomena are empirically common that is critical in science . . . but whether they can be made to reveal the enduring natural processes that underlie them. . . . In short, we need to look for systematic relationships among diverse phenomena, not for substantive identities among similar ones" (Geertz 1973:44). To search for relationships between monolithic categories such as *technology* and *social organization,* or *economy* and *society,* or *hunter-gatherers* and *agriculturalists* only obscures the mechanisms and processes that result in human cultural diversity (see E. Smith's response to Testart [1988]).

Many researchers today do recognize variability among hunter-gatherers but treat it typologically, dividing them into dichotomous types: simple/complex, storing/nonstoring, delayed-return/immediate-return, mobile/sedentary, foragers/collectors. But we also hear today in anthropology, and in hunter-gatherer studies in particular, a call to move away from the typological approach of cultural evolutionism and toward theoretical frameworks that explicitly account for variability: "strategies that cannot cope with the similarities and differences found among hunter-gatherer societies suffer greatly by comparison with strategies that can cope with them" (Harris 1979:79).[28] We are moving out of one fascinating period of exploration and into another equally fascinating period of explanation.

By critiquing the category of *hunter-gatherer* I do not mean to suggest that *all* categorization in anthropology is useless. Anthropology is a continual process of constructing and deconstructing analytical categories. Indeed, typological thinking may be an inescapable part of being human. But a category is useful only if it helps point to the processes at work that create the human diversity that is temporarily pigeonholed (and ultimately only modestly described) by that category. The angst expressed over the category of hunter-gatherers in many forums today signals that the category has reached the end of its useful life in anthropology. Used self-consciously, however, there is nothing wrong with the term *hunter-gatherer*—as long as we recognize that it carries no explanatory weight, that it is only a heuristic and pedagogical device.

Therefore, I use the traditional anthropological category of hunter-gatherer as a subject for this book in order to demonstrate the variability within that category—to deconstruct it, if you will. In focusing on variability I hope to discourage descriptive, typological approaches that proceed in a dictatorial fashion, where one model is toppled only to be replaced by another that is different, perhaps more politically fashionable, but just as restricted in scope. I hope in this book to give readers some of the background and means to developing theories aimed at explaining variation.

Consequently, despite the title of this book, I am not so much interested in hunter-gatherers as I am in the factors conditioning human behavior and culture—for example, constraints on foraging, factors affecting trade and territoriality, and the ecology of reproduction. From current literature, it often seems that what is taken to be relevant to understanding hunter-gatherers is not assumed to be likewise relevant to other traditional social categories. The environment, for example, often figures prominently in analyses of hunter-gatherer societies, but less so in studies of agricultural societies. Yet, in fact, much of what is written here should be applicable to other traditional cultural types in anthropology. Agriculturalists, for example, continue to hunt and gather (see papers in Kent 1989c), and the same approaches used to analyze foraging can also be used to analyze gardening (e.g., Cashdan 1990; Keegan 1986). Likewise, approaches to understanding variability in hunter-gatherer demography, land tenure, or kinship should be applicable to nonforaging societies. In other words, general theory should account for diversity across the conventional categories anthropology imposes on humanity, not just within them.

HUNTER-GATHERERS AND ECOLOGY

I assume that adaptation to the environment plays a major (but by no means singular) role in conditioning the variability seen in hunter-gatherer societies. Thus, this book emphasizes ecological approaches focusing on behavior and decision making that revolve around time, energy, and reproduction (Smith and Winterhalder 1992b). I follow Pianka's broad definition of ecology as "the study of the relations between organisms and the totality of the physical and biological factors affecting them or influenced by them" (1978:2) but add to it a concern with human social relations, perception, and enculturation.

Many proponents of Marxist approaches or the interdependent model downplay or even denigrate the material constraints of life. This is odd, for while these analyses frequently rail against the reduction of social relations to economics, they are often grounded in economic and environmental explanations. Marvin Harris, for example, argues that Godelier's analyses of Australian Aboriginal section systems and the BaMbuti mode of production are ultimately grounded in ecology (1979:231–32; see chapter 7). While we should remember that modern hunter-gatherers are not isolated, and that the pure hunter-gatherer cannot be distilled from the enclaved hunter-gatherer, at the same time we should not assume that interaction and trade is all there is to modern hunter-gatherers (as some suggest—see Hoffman 1984). Though subsistence studies should not be taken out of context, recent studies of hunter-gatherers receiving at least half of their diet from government rations or store-bought goods have nonetheless advanced our understanding of factors conditioning hunter-gatherers' subsistence.[29] While coping with the political environment, hunter-gatherers still must eat and deal with their physical environment. Discounting ecology, especially subsistence-related issues, discounts what must have been important to prehistoric hunter-gatherers and what is equally important to modern ones. We can examine how people make decisions and adapt to their physical and social environment, regardless of whether they are "pure" hunter-gatherers or not.

Human interaction with the environment is not the foundation of human society, nor is it a theoretical panacea. Although human decisions are made within an ecological framework, they are also made within historical and cultural constraints. There is no perfect match between culture and environment, and ecological perspectives cannot explain the particulars of Australian Dreamtime theology, Bushmen kinship, or Kwakiutl mythology. We cannot sort behaviors into those that are "ecological" and those that are "social" or "cultural," as Ingold has repeatedly pointed out (1987, 1988). But we have to start someplace, as long as we recognize that beginning with the environment does not make an ontological statement about culture. While an understanding of human interaction with the environment will not come easily, it is in my opinion the most straightforward task before anthropology at present. In the next chapter, we will briefly trace the development of ecological thought in anthropology, concluding with a discussion of behavioral ecology, which is rapidly developing as a useful context in which to understand variation among hunter-gatherers.

ENVIRONMENT, EVOLUTION, AND ANTHROPOLOGICAL THEORY | 2

While it is true that cultures are rooted in nature . . . they are no more
produced by that nature than a plant.
anthropologist (Kroeber 1939:1)

We hate the lions, leopards, and spotted hyenas because they will hurt us.
The antelope hate us because they see our fires at night and N!adima
[God] has told them that these fires are to cook them.
G/wi man (Silberbauer 1981a:63)

There seems little room for argument with Kroeber's assertion that a society is not a direct product of its environment. Yet we cannot deny that we are part of nature; we live with the same ecological realities that the G/wi acknowledge. Social scientists have long been interested in the relationship between human culture and the environment, although its importance in American anthropology has waxed and waned over the last hundred years.

The use of *environment* as an analytical concept has improved dramatically in recent years, but anthropology still faces the daunting task of relating cultural diversity to environment in a consistent theoretical fashion. In recent years, gains have been made by uniting an ecological with an evolutionary perspective in a field known as behavioral ecology. We will consider this theoretical paradigm in this chapter, but we must first briefly consider two earlier paradigms, the culture-area concept and cultural ecology, since much of the research and data discussed in this book was undertaken within them (see Ellen 1982 for a thorough treatment of ecological thought in anthropology).

THE CULTURE-AREA CONCEPT

The theater in which the play of American anthropology would be performed was built by Franz Boas. As a response to the ethnocentrism of late-nineteenth-century evolutionism, Boas emphasized the holistic study of cultural traits and downplayed the importance of evolutionary classifications. For Boas, culture traits such as drums, shamanism, masks, or myths could originate in different cultures for different reasons. They could, therefore, only be understood within their own cultural and historical context and could not be taken as evidence of a society's position on an evolutionary scale. For Boas, the source of culture was culture itself, that is, independent invention, history, or diffusion. The environment could establish possibilities or limits, especially in terms of food supply, but it had no control beyond this.

However, whereas Boas argued that culture traits did not necessarily evolve as aggregates, when his students constructed distribution maps of culture traits among North American Indians it became evident that traits were geographically concentrated. Otis Mason was the first to call such regions *culture areas* (1894), but it was two students of Boas, Clark Wissler and Alfred Kroeber, who tackled their implications.[1]

Wissler could see that culture areas, defined by a constellation of culture traits, coincided with the geographic range of a major food, such as bison, salmon, wild seeds, maize, or caribou. Culture areas were in fact named after the primary source of subsistence, the Bison Area, for example, or the Eastern Maize Area. Wissler explained the connections between culture and environment as being mediated by a subsistence technology that was linked to the particular food being consumed. He argued that a culture became best adjusted to the subsistence of a region at what would become the center of a culture area where "ideal conditions" prevailed (although the center could be defined by historical or ethnic as well as environmental conditions—Wissler 1926:372). From here, culture traits spread outward at a constant rate of diffusion, eventually forming the culture area when they reached the geographic limits of the primary food resource.

The culture-area concept was fraught with a number of practical and theoretical difficulties. Defining a culture area was often difficult since some aspects of culture (e.g., religious practices or kinship terminology) cut across what otherwise appeared to be cultural or geographic boundaries. And the larger a culture area, the greater the environmental and cultural diversity encompassed within it, the greater the number of possible connections between environment and society, and the greater the difficulty in sorting them out, or in discovering cross-cultural correlations between culture and environment. There was no explicit method to identify the "typical" traits of a region, or what the "ideal conditions" were that gave rise to these traits, except that both should be at the center of a culture area. It is easy to see that preconceived notions about the adaptation of, for example, a bison-hunting region, probably played a large role in defining "typical traits."

For our purposes, what is most important is that the culture-area concept left vague the actual causal links between culture and environment. This was in part a result of Kroeber's and Wissler's theoretical stance. Although Kroeber admitted that "every culture is conditioned by its subsistence basis" and that there are "relations between nature and culture," he only begrudgingly gave the environment any significant role in producing cultural diversity (1939:3). In the final analysis, Kroeber could say only that environment limited the possibilities of culture, and that methodological difficulties precluded any further theorizing: "the interactions of culture and environment become exceedingly complex when followed out. And this complexity makes generalization unprofitable, on the whole. In each situation or area different natural factors are likely to be impinging on culture with different intensity" (1939:205).

My feeling is that Wissler was not as willing to throw in the towel as Kroeber. I think he suspected the existence of a mechanism to account for the similarities of different tribes living in the same ecological region, but he never found it. Instead, his reasoning became circular: once bison hunters, for example, adapted to bison hunting, they tended to consort with bison hunters and to stay within bison-hunting territory; thus, they shut themselves off to diffusion and remained bison hunters. Once adjusted to their environments, cultures changed slowly, and could move beyond the boundaries of their environment only with great difficulty. When natural and cultural areas coincided, all cultures on the continent were at their "climax"— a vague concept that culture-area theoreticians never adequately defined (Harris 1968:376–77). In the end, there was no choice but to turn to migration, diffusion, and historical factors to explain change.[2]

CULTURAL ECOLOGY

At about the same time that Kroeber was publishing culture-area maps, one of his students, Julian Steward, was already attempting to resolve the deficiencies of the culture-area concept. Steward rejected the "fruitless assumption that culture comes from culture" and focused on the relationships between society, technology, and environment, an approach he labeled *cultural ecology* (1955:36).

Originally, cultural ecology was not a nomothetic approach because it sought "to explain the origin of particular cultural features and patterns which characterize different areas rather than to derive general principles applicable to any cultural-environmental situation" (Steward 1955:36). Nonetheless, cultural ecology had to make some assumptions about "general principles." Central to the methodology of cultural ecology was the concept of the *culture core*, which was defined as those behaviors most closely related to the extraction of energy from the environment. Other aspects of society, such as social organization and ideology, were built upon the core but were also easily affected by historical and cultural factors, such as innovation and diffusion (Steward 1955:37–41). These factors were primary for Kroeber but secondary for Steward. Echoing his nineteenth-century predecessors, Steward said this would be true especially in the case of hunter-gatherers:

among the simpler hunting and gathering peoples, the nature of the social unit was determined to a very large extent by the processes of cultural ecological adaptation, that is, by the nature of social interaction required for subsistence in a given environment by means of a given technology. The social environment, as contrasted with the natural environment, is also a factor in shaping the nature of any society but its role is minimal in most of these cases. (1969a:188)

Steward saw the culture core as the foundation of any society, but he did not use a well-defined method to determine the core elements in specific ethnographic cases. He impressionistically noted which cultural behaviors seemed to be closely tied to "significant" features of the environment—such as distributions of water, plants, or game—although these features were also not selected by an explicit method (1955:93). And, although Steward noted that the environment was culturally perceived, he did not examine the implications of this observation. Steward was adamant that core elements and important environmental features were to be determined by the empirical evidence of each ethnographic case. However, since there was no explicit method of identifying the culture core, it could be whatever an anthropologist wanted it to be (Harris 1968:661). For Steward, it was subsistence technology.

In focusing on the culture core, Steward tried to define how technology and environment shaped society and set the stage for different lines of social development ("multilinear evolution"). In defining bands, for example,

Steward noted how the ecological similarities of different environments exploited by a simple technology could limit production and population size and thus produce similar social organizations (1936). While Steward allowed that culture-historical factors played a large role in conditioning the form of secondary, or noncore features, he focused attention on how the culture core shaped them. (Toward the end of his career, however, Steward viewed the culture core in a less deterministic fashion.)

There is a parallel to the culture core in the notion of *base* in Marxist approaches to hunter-gatherer societies where the "mode of exploitation of the land [is] the determining factor in a society of hunters . . . since we have deduced logically from there the economic, social and political organization, as well as their religious representations" (Meillassoux 1973:199). It is this deterministic hierarchy that has caused some to label cultural ecology as vulgar Marxism, for in it "an apparent hierarchy of institutions [implies] a determinate hierarchy of functions" (Ellen 1982:60; see also Geertz 1973:44). Steward indeed sought deterministic, not probabilistic relations between environment, technology, and society. Harris sees this as a major flaw in cultural ecology (1968:668).

Steward's approach had a dramatic impact on American anthropology in the 1950s and 1960s (Vayda 1969; Cox 1973), especially in hunter-gatherer studies. Since hunter-gatherers at this time were viewed as relics of, or analogues to, early human societies, and since evolution was seen as an additive process, many anthropologists agreed that "at the foraging level of cultural complexity, the cultural core constitutes most of the total behavioral pattern" (Bicchieri 1969a:chart). There was nothing for the core to determine, since hunter-gatherer society was nothing but culture core!

Cultural ecology encouraged a number of detailed studies of the subsistence practices of hunter-gatherer societies (e.g., Bicchieri 1972; Lee and DeVore 1968; Damas 1969d). It affected the specific content of these studies variously, but for the most part, cultural ecological studies tried to account for cultural behaviors by showing how they were necessary to the act of getting food, or how they improved foraging efficiency, reduced risk, or netted the highest returns. Moore, for example, explained scapulamancy (the use of burnt caribou scapulae by the Montagnais-Naskapi to divine the direction of a hunt) as a way to randomize hunting excursions and avoid repeated hunts to one area (1965). Moore argued that this made the most efficient use of time in an area where prey are widely scattered and mobile. Damas argued that the size of Inuit winter camps—about 50 to 150 people—increased the number of hunters in a group and maximized the probability that a kill would be made each day since "the lone hunter or even several hunters have little chance of success" (1969b:51). Damas concluded that Inuit settlement size was an adaptation to the environment because it probably maximized hunting efficiency, although no quantitative data were available to test this proposition. Bicchieri compared the subsistence practices, social organizations, and religions of the Bushmen, Hadza, and the net-hunting and bow-hunting BaMbuti, concluding that those hunter-gatherers who lived in "restrictive" environments had fewer options and that, therefore, the core had a greater influence on the secondary features of the sociocultural patterns (1969a,b). Sociopolitical organizations of those living in "permissive" environments, Bicchieri argued, could be affected by other cultural processes, such as diffusion. Yengoyan suggested that Australian marriage practices, which insured that men acquired wives from (and thus constructed affinal ties with) distant groups, was an adaptation to the Australian desert, where people had to move in with others in times of drought (1968). Both Suttles (1968) and Piddocke (1965) saw Northwest Coast potlatches—large feasts at which a chief gave away blankets, coppers, canoes, or even slaves to a guest village to acquire prestige—as adaptations to population pressure and potential resource failures. The feasts were said to insure the redistribution of goods, and to construct debts and alliances to cope with times of food shortages.

The infusion of systems theory and the ecosystem concept into anthropology in the late 1960s produced an invigorated cultural ecology that encouraged measurement of the complex relationships between people and their environment; it therefore related cultural behaviors in a more rigorous and empirical fashion to the environment (Winterhalder 1984). The application of the ecosystem approach is best known through non-hunter-gatherer studies, especially Roy Rappaport's study of New Guinea Tsembaga Maring horticulturalists (1968) and R. Brooke Thomas's study of Andean horticulturalists/pastoralists (1973). These researchers focused on reconstructing the flow of energy through the cultural system and on modeling how elements of the system were interrelated. Rappaport, for example, demonstrated the intricate connections between pig and human population sizes, warfare, gardening, and rituals. He saw the ritual system not just as a reflection or validation of subsistence behaviors, but as an integral part of the entire system. In Rappaport's words, the Tsembaga lived in a ritually regulated ecosystem.

In hunter-gatherer studies the ecosystem approach is exemplified by Lee's input-output study of Dobe Ju/'hoansi subsistence (1969). Lee quantified the energy procured by Ju/'hoansi foragers by weighing the meat, mongongo nuts, and other plant foods harvested during July and August of 1964. Given the caloric content of these resources, Lee computed how much energy was brought into camp each day (2,355 kcal/person). Lee then estimated the energy expenditure of men, women, and children using standard tables of body size and activity levels. He found that, on average, an individual Ju/'hoansi required 1,975 kilocalories per day. Thus, for the time period involved, the Ju/'hoansi acquired more energy than they needed. The excess was used to feed dogs, to perform trance dances, or was stored as body fat to be metabolized during lean periods of the year. Betty Meehan made a similar study of shellfish collecting among the Anbarra of northern Australia (Meehan 1977a,b, 1982, 1983). Cultural ecology stimulated subsistence studies among many other hunter-gatherer peoples, especially those of central Africa's Ituri Forest, the Kalahari, Australia, and the Arctic.[3]

Studies conducted under the rubric of cultural ecology have increased our knowledge of hunter-gatherer societies immeasurably. Nonetheless, in many ways cultural ecology suffered from some of the same problems as the culture-area concept. Many cultural ecological studies are only "anecdotal ecology" that provide plausible accounts of how well adjusted hunter-gatherers are to their environments, but are subjective, post hoc explanations (Wilmsen 1983). For example, Yengoyan's important paper on Australian section systems mentioned above included no data to show that marriages actually did provide people with affines who provided assistance in times of stress (see chapter 7). Nor did Piddocke demonstrate that differences in subsistence security accounted for differences in village prestige and rank (see chapter 8; Bettinger 1991:54–57). To know whether the potlatch in fact was a response to resource variability requires data covering a long time span, documenting specific relationships between potlatching villages. Quantitative data, if they could be gathered (and this is not always possible), could test and refine the ideas proposed by cultural ecologists and determine whether they are or are not successful in explaining human behavior.

Take, for example, Damas's discussion of Inuit winter camp size and breathing-hole seal hunting. Damas says only that "a large number of hunters offers great advantages in this type of hunting" (1969b:51). But it is not clear what the advantages are: an increase in foraging efficiency (a greater per capita harvest rate), minimization of variance in per capita hunting success, or a minimization of variance in how much seal meat the average individual eats. Years after Damas's study was published, Eric Smith collected quantitative data on winter camp size and seal hunting (1981, 1991; although for a different Inuit group, one far removed from Damas's study area). He found that large hunting parties do not maximize per capita return rates, nor do large groups reduce foraging risk, that is, variance in seal harvest (which instead is correlated with return rates; 1991:323–30). Instead, he found that a camp containing about seven foraging groups with three to eight hunters each *who share their kills* might minimize variance in per capita consumption rates. Assuming that active hunters make up about 25 percent of the population (E. Smith 1991:327), seven foraging groups of three to eight members each implies a residential camp population of 120—within Damas's range of 50–150.

In addition to vague measures of success, cultural ecology also lacked a common language of structure and organization, that is, a common theoretical framework (Thomas, Winterhalder, and McRae 1979). This made it difficult to see the relevance of one study to another, as individual studies focused on specific variables without reference to a wider framework. This was most clearly exemplified in characterizations of the environment. For example, it was (and still is) often said that modern hunter-gatherers cannot be used as analogues for prehistoric ones because modern hunter-gatherers live in marginal or restrictive environments, whereas many prehistoric hunter-gatherers lived in more benevolent or permissive ones (e.g., Keene 1981). There may be common ecological structures underlying the diverse plants, animals, and climates of the so-called benevolent environments that make it easy to get food in these places (which is what benevolent seems to mean, rather than referring to weather or topography), and hard to get food in "marginal" ones. But these structures are never delineated and the causes of cultural variability among the peoples who inhabited presumed benevolent or marginal environments is unknown. Although many prehistoric hunters did live in environments that modern hunter-gatherers do not occupy, categorizing environments with subjective, generalizing terms does not help measure the complex relationships between societies and their environments.

Moreover, cultural ecological studies found it necessary to draw a spatial boundary to each society, to put limits on energetic input-output analyses, just as culture-area theoreticians had to draw boundaries through continuous distributions of cultural traits. Drawing boundaries at some level is, of course, a necessity for model building—and a perennial problem of any ecological approach, since few systems have natural boundaries. But the result in cultural ecology was to treat human societies (variously defined according to the ethnographic case) as if they were pristine, isolated, self-sufficient units.

This encouraged an ahistorical approach to hunter-gatherer studies, and also directed researchers away from taking interactions with other societies into account (Winterhalder 1984). Cultural change was attributed to disruptive forces from outside (primarily colonial powers, when they were mentioned at all), population growth, or environmental change; it was not attributed to internal sociopolitical structure (as the Marxist critique pointed out). Consequently, cultural ecology tended to continue the nineteenth-century view that hunter-gatherers were relic Pleistocene populations, people who had had no reason to change over the millennia.

These are important problems, but cultural ecology's fatal flaws lay in (1) a neofunctionalist concept of *adaptation,* and (2) an implicit reliance on group selection (Bettinger 1991). Cultural ecologists treated hunter-gatherer societies as though they were at equilibrium. The term adaptation consequently came to refer to any behavior that seemed a reasonable way to maintain the status quo. Adaptation was seen as a state of being rather than a continual process of becoming (see Mithen 1990:8–9).[4] This led to an important tautology: behavior is adaptive because it exists—otherwise, it would not exist. But this Panglossian view of life held an important contradiction, for it assumed that if a behavior exists because it accomplishes a goal more effectively than previous techniques or strategies, then, presumably, at some time those former nonadaptive techniques had existed. This contradicts the fundamental premise of cultural ecology. In this regard, cultural ecologists seemed to be like culture-area theoreticians in that they assumed that societies went through changes in the past, but were, at the time of study, best adapted to their environment. How societies change was not their concern, consequently, change and stasis could not be accounted for in the same theoretical framework.

The implicit reliance on group selection comes from the assumption that people do what is best for the group, not necessarily what is best for themselves or their kin. This idea was drawn primarily from the work of ethologist V. Wynne-Edwards (1962). Wynne-Edwards argued that as population density rose and competition for food increased, the resulting stress affected various behaviors (such as mating displays) that acted to curtail reproduction, eventually bringing population back into line with the food supply and thus permitting the species to exist. In restricting their own fertility, organisms allegedly act altruistically to do what is best for their species or population.

The idea of group selection can be seen in cultural ecologists' view of hunter-gatherer demography. Hunter-gatherers are frequently said to hold their population below carrying capacity, an environment's maximum sustainable population at a given technological level (but see chapter 6). Conventional wisdom after "Man the Hunter" was that hunter-gatherers maintain their population at 20–30 percent of carrying capacity through a variety of cultural means, including infanticide, breastfeeding, and intercourse taboos. In so doing, they prevent overexploitation of food supplies and remain in homeostatic balance with the environment (e.g., Lee and De-Vore 1968:11; Birdsell 1968). From this vantage point, hunter-gatherers altruistically sacrifice their own reproductive interests, including, when needed, their own offspring, for the good of the population. Cultural ecologists assumed that somehow a system could impose its will upon people (see discussion in Lee and DeVore 1968:243). In so doing, they attributed to the population a decision-making capacity that can only reside in the individual (a practice known as *methodological collectivism*). The notion that group members could have different, even conflicting goals did not surface in cultural ecology. For example, in the generalized foraging model, flexibility in group membership was portrayed as either an intentional or subliminal consensus adaptation to resource fluctuation. Bettinger, however, suggests that flux in band membership could also be produced by tension between differing needs and goals of a group's current members (1991:162).

The concept of group selection as it was originally proposed met with considerable criticism. Biologists demonstrated that selection at the level of the gene could produce the altruistic behaviors that were the focus of group selection if the altruist and benefactor were genetically related. Others showed that altruism could be selected for if the altruist stood to gain through reciprocity. And, if a population contained a large number of altruistic individuals, nonaltruistic ones could enter it, exploit the altruists' behavior to their own advantage, and outreproduce the altruists, becoming more and more common. Thus, communities of altruists should not be common in nature. While more complex models of group selection (usually at the level of the deme, or breeding population) have been developed, most biologists would say that selection at a group level is far less significant than selection at the individual or genetic level.

Additionally, self-limitations on reproduction can be interpreted as the product of individual reproductive maximization rather than as a sacrifice performed for the benefit of the group. In the nonhuman world, field studies indicate that animals often produce fewer offspring than they are capable of producing. This is not to hold population down, but because producing many offspring can actually result in a smaller number surviving to adulthood than if few offspring were initially produced. Animals that limit their reproduction may actually maximize the number of offspring they raise success-fully (i.e., to reproductive age).

Such a pattern may hold true for many human populations as well (Cronk 1991). Ju/'hoansi women, for example, produce a child about every four years, a fact that is often used to demonstrate that hunter-gatherers intention-ally hold their populations below carrying capacity to prevent resource over-exploitation (we will discuss this case in more detail in chapter 6). Nicholas Blurton Jones, however, demonstrated that Ju/'hoansi women who produce a child every four years raise more children to adulthood than women who have babies at closer intervals (1989). If Ju/'hoansi women limit their fertility it is probably to maximize their reproduction, not to altruistically do their share to hold group population below carrying capacity.

Cultural ecology's emphasis on homeostasis and its adherence to an out-dated group-selectionist perspective caused many anthropologists to turn to alternative theoretical frameworks such as Marxism, structuralism, and sym-bolism. Others, however, recognized that while cultural ecology was not entirely correct, neither was it entirely wrong. Missing from it was a Dar-winian evolutionary component.

If humans are animals, albeit cultural animals, then to a certain extent they are susceptible to the same evolutionary processes that govern the nonhuman world. Evolution can be defined as the differential persistence of variability over time, and adaptation as the process of selection and differential repro-duction. Cultural ecology, therefore, was not evolutionary in the Darwinian sense since it deemphasized the potential for conflict between members of a group and hence the importance of behavioral variability within groups. Instead, it was a "theory of consequences" (Bettinger 1991:113–220), where the end result, the consequence of adaptation, defined the process rather than vice versa. Cultural ecology did not specify how adaptive change oc-curs. When external circumstances changed, people seemed to decide that this or that way of doing things was better for the group in the face of changing conditions. But the way in which these decisions were made re-mained nebulous, and what was meant by *better* was not clear (avoid extinc-tion? increase tribal size? more offspring? stronger offspring? psychological satisfaction?).

Take our example of population regulation. While it was assumed that hunter-gatherers keep their populations below carrying capacity, at the same time we were told that the origins of agriculture, an artificial increase in an environment's carrying capacity, was a product of population growth. Appar-ently, some hunter-gatherers were not so adept at controlling growth. Why should some populations grow and some not? Why should some respond to the potential for growth by limiting reproduction and others by permitting growth and augmenting production? We cannot answer these questions by asserting adaptation in each case.

To overcome the theoretical paradox of cultural ecology some anthropologists in the 1970s turned to a range of research paradigms that we shall here call behavioral or evolutionary ecology. This is a relatively new field, and, like any system of knowledge, it contains many different and sometimes opposed perspectives and assumptions. In the following section we cover only the highlights of current discussions to provide background for research discussed in succeeding chapters (see Smith and Winterhalder 1992b for extended discussions).

BEHAVIORAL ECOLOGY

A fundamental difference between behavioral ecology and cultural ecology is that the former makes explicit use of evolutionary theory. Where cultural ecology sought functional connections between normative descriptions of a society and its environment, behavioral ecology seeks to know how evolutionary processes, in particular natural selection, shape human societies. Smith and Winterhalder argue that explaining what a behavior does (e.g., hunting in a particular way) does not fully account for how that behavior, rather than another potential variant, became common in a society (Smith and Winterhalder 1992a; Winterhalder and Smith 1992). Functional explanations, in other words, depend on causal explanations. Cultural ecology could only appeal to rational choice to explain behaviors that appeared to be efficient: what would a rational human do under a given set of circumstances with an assumed set of goals? But rational choice presupposes not only a set of general goals (e.g., foraging efficiency) but preferences for strategies with a high degree of probability of meeting those goals. A process of natural selection must be responsible for fixing, maintaining, and altering these goals and preferences.

How does behavioral ecology treat variability? Evolution occurs due to differential survivorship and/or reproduction of particular phenotypes; it therefore presupposes variability and it requires some means whereby different traits are passed from generation to generation. Given that no two individuals in a society are exactly alike, either biologically or culturally, and given that most human behavior is socially transmitted, evolutionary forces are potentially at work. Therefore, variation both *within* and *between* populations is foregrounded in behavioral ecology. This does not radically alter the subject of ecological anthropology since behavioral ecology still analyzes choices with respect to their impact on reproduction, health, and survival—subjects that have long been the concern of ecological anthropology. Behavioral ecology does not replace cultural ecology. Instead, it makes it more complete by adding the concept of natural selection.

Natural selection

Human populations change in their genetic composition through several mechanisms including genetic mutation, recombination, genetic drift, and natural selection. Natural selection changes the frequency of genotypes in a population but operates directly on phenotypes—the visible properties of organisms that are produced by the interaction of the genotype with its environment. A phenotype is judged to be more or less adaptive *relative* to other phenotypes by whether it contributes more or less genetic material than other phenotypes to succeeding generations (by an individual bringing more offspring to reproductive age than other phenotypes and/or by assisting genetically close kin to do the same).

For humans, a phenotype includes cultural behaviors. The nature-nurture controversy of anthropology breaks down in behavioral ecology since human behaviors are seen as part of the phenotype produced by both genetic and environmental factors (including the natural and social environment). For humans, therefore, the question arises: what is the link between behavioral and genetic variation?

Proponents of the "strong sociobiological thesis" argue for a close link between genetic and behavioral variation (see review in Cronk 1991). If a behavior is genetically controlled, and if that behavior endows its bearers with greater reproductive success, then it is easy to see how that behavior could become more prevalent in a population relative to other genetically programmed behavioral variants. The problem in applying this principle to humans, of course, is that the vast bulk of human behavior, certainly that of traditional concern to anthropologists—differences between human populations—is clearly not genetically determined.

The majority of behavioral ecologists, therefore, adhere to a "weak sociobiological thesis" in which people tend to select behaviors from a range of variants whose net effect is to maximize their individual reproductive or inclusive fitness. People need not be aware of the reproductive consequences of their behavior. Though specific behaviors are not genetically selected for, weak-thesis proponents argue that the evolutionary process nonetheless "endowed our species with psychological predispositions, mental capacities, and physical abilities that have tended to be adaptive in the environments of human evolution, with 'environments' understood to include individuals' cultural and social situations" (Cronk 1991:27). The weak thesis does not argue that behavior is genetically controlled; there is not, for example, a hunting gene, or a gene for matriliny. It does argue that humans have the ability to evaluate the reproductive consequences of behaviors subconsciously. Behaviors that are linked to greater fitness in a particular natural and social environment and that are heritable (through culture or genes) should, therefore, tend to become more prevalent in a population. This assumption, however, is still undergoing empirical tests and debate.

Central to this debate is the concept of *fitness*. Most generally, fitness is an organism's "propensity to survive and reproduce in a particularly specified environment and population" (Mills and Beatty, in Smith and Winterhalder 1992b:27). As Smith and Winterhalder point out (1992a), this focuses attention on adaptive design and the potential number of descendants, rather than on actual reproduction, since the number of offspring produced (or the percentage that survive to adulthood) can be affected by numerous factors apart from the phenotype. Thus, behavioral ecologists are interested in the mean fitness of some class of organisms. In anthropology, these classes are sometime referred to as *behavioral variants,* since we are concerned with the mean fitness of particular behaviors rather than the fitness of particular individuals. This is because for humans a large part of the phenotype consists of culturally rather than genetically transmitted behavior. Behavioral ecology assumes that selection favors traits with high fitness, and that people evaluate the available phenotypes and adopt those with high fitness payoffs. To test hypotheses, behavioral ecologists may have to measure the fitness of individuals within different behavioral classes. A proxy currency, such as mean foraging efficiency, is often used to measure or keep track of the fitness consequences of different behavioral variants (see below).

Opponents of sociobiology argue that cultures establish their own standards of success, standards that are highly variable from one society to another. Where one society values material wealth, another values prestige; where one values pigs, another values gold. Behavioral ecologists recognize this but argue that while different natural, social, and cultural environments result in different standards of success, individuals who meet these standards should also manifest a behavioral variant that achieves greater fitness than other variants. People who live under different conditions are expected to make different decisions, but decisions which, nonetheless, should tend to maximize an individual's fitness, even though their particular behavior is in all likelihood not genetically controlled. Reproductive fitness in this case is a scorecard, a basis on which to judge the selective value of behaviors. However, as we shall see below, this initial assumption of behavioral ecology may be confuted when we add human culture to the picture.

To accomplish its goals, behavioral ecology makes two simple but far-reaching assumptions: methodological individualism, and optimization.

Methodological individualism.   As we have already noted, evolution sees the individual, rather than the group, as the primary (but not sole) locus of selection. Stated most generally, selection operates on variability within a population and favors individuals whose behavior enhances the opportunity to achieve goals (Foley 1985). Critics claim that behavioral ecology assumes that people act independently of their culture, but this is fallacious. The specific content of an individual's goals comes from both biological and cultural information. That is, the drive to "succeed" probably entails not only biological directives (to reproduce) but cultural directives as well (e.g., bring home as much meat as possible, spend time with offspring, produce many children, produce few children, acquire prestige, acquire wealth, be good to your relatives, etc.). Behavioral ecological analyses require that goals be defined, but there is no reason to assume a priori that all goals will be identical. Behavioral ecology only requires the legitimate assumptions that people be capable of storing knowledge, that they be capable of understanding (or at least thinking that they understand) the relationship between their actions and goals, and that they attempt to maximize opportunities to achieve their goals.

Optimization.   The optimization assumption focuses on (1) the behavior of individuals making decisions about (2) the available set of behavioral options using (3) some currency (energy, measured as calories, dominates current studies) that permits the costs and benefits of each option to be evaluated, within (4) a set of constraints that determines the options and their benefits. In hunter-gatherer studies, optimization approaches focus on several questions relevant to foraging—when, where, and how long to forage? how many should forage together? how many should live together? which food items should be selected? which should be shared? Behavioral ecological studies focus on an individual's foraging behavior because it is likely that foraging behavior is directly related to survival of individuals and their families (E. Smith 1991:24). A common working assumption is that foraging efficiency is a proxy measure of reproductive fitness. It bears pointing out, however, that this assumption is rarely tested in empirical studies (Hill and Kaplan 1988a,b).

Expressed in more specific terms, evolutionary theory suggests that the goal of a forager should be to forage optimally, that is, to maximize the net *rate* of food intake (E. Smith 1979). This does not mean that foragers actually do maximize foraging efficiency or that researchers assume that they maximize it, but only that behavioral adaptations will tend toward—have as a goal—a maximization of foraging efficiency. This can result in a minimization of the time spent foraging or a maximization of the food gathered (see below). Some argue that hunter-gatherers will maximize their rate of food intake only under the threat of starvation. However, there are at least four other conditions that could produce optimizing behavior (E. Smith 1983:626; 1987, 1988):

(1) when specific nutrients are in short supply (maximizing the net rate of return of those foods providing the limited nutrients increases the probability that the forager will acquire the necessary amount of the scarce nutrients);

(2) when time for necessary nonforaging activities is scarce (the forager must maximize the net rate of energy capture so as to secure enough food while maintaining sufficient time for nonforaging activities essential to fitness, e.g., reproductive behavior, but also religious activities, prestige competition, etc.);

(3) when foraging exposes the forager to risks such as predation, climatic extremes, or accidents (the forager maximizes the rate of return to insure that adequate energy is acquired while spending as little time as possible foraging and thus reducing the risk associated with foraging);

(4) when excess food can be used to enhance reproductive fitness, for example, through sharing extra food a forager could in some circumstances increase (a) mating opportunities, (b) the attention others devote to his or her children, or (c) the potential for reciprocation in the future when he or she has foraged unsuccessfully.

These conditions will vary in importance. Some environments will be more severely limited in certain nutrients than others. In some areas of the world humans face few predators or environmental dangers; in others (e.g., the

Arctic in winter), foraging can be extremely dangerous. In some societies, nonforaging activities, such as instructing children or protecting a village from raids, can be important selective factors. Nonetheless, while taking specific constraints into account, behavioral ecologists still argue that all hunter-gatherers live under one or more of these conditions, and therefore that optimization is a reasonable working assumption.

The optimization assumption is integral to behavioral ecological studies that direct themselves to how people allocate their time among competing activities. There are many demands on the time of any forager: food must be gathered, children raised, social obligations met, and so on. How do people decide how to spend their time? The contrasting cases of the Ache of Paraguay and the Efe Pygmies of Zaire illustrate the issue. The Ache are a recently settled group of hunter-gatherers who today live in a mission horticultural settlement, but occasionally go on hunting treks in the forest.[5] The Efe, one of four major groups of BaMbuti, live symbiotically with Lese (Bantu) horticulturalists in the Ituri rain forest. The Efe hunt for themselves, and to acquire meat to trade with the Lese. The Efe also work in the fields of Lese villagers, exchanging their labor for food.

Among the Ache, good hunters tend to stay out all day, hunting as long as possible, even after acquiring game (an Ache's hunting skill is not tied to the number of hours he hunts, that is, a man is not a good hunter because he stays out late each day). Good Efe hunters, on the other hand, spend less time hunting than poor Efe hunters. Good Efe hunters make a kill quickly and then return home. Efe hunting is an example of a *time-minimizing strategy*, while Ache hunting is an example of an *energy-maximizing strategy*. Why is there a difference? What is it that Efe hunters do in nonforaging time that Ache hunters apparently do not need to do? What difference in goals makes it more important for an Ache to acquire a large supply of meat, than to maximize time spent on nonforaging tasks?

While the answer is undoubtedly complex, one important factor may lie in the difference between the relationships of husbands and wives. Efe men apparently run a large risk of losing their wives (or potential wives) to Lese horticulturalists. Among the Efe, 13 percent of marriageable women are married to Lese villagers; this increases the competition for wives among Efe men since they cannot marry Lese women (R. Bailey 1988).[6] Robert Bailey shows that, although hunting success is not directly correlated with marital status (1991), it appears to be indirectly related through material wealth (pots, pans, knives, machetes, etc.). Men with many material possessions are more likely to be married than men with few material possessions, and many of these goods are acquired through trade with the Lese. While good hunters want to acquire meat to trade, they must also allocate time to cultivating exchange partnerships with villagers and to exchange itself.

Ache men, on the other hand, apparently trade meat for sexual favors (not uncommon among Amazonian groups; Siskind 1973). Among the Ache, good hunters have more children than poor hunters, counting legitimate and illegitimate children (Hill and Kaplan 1988a,b; Kaplan and Hill 1985a,b; see chapter 5). According to Kim Hill and Hillard Kaplan, the Ache get more utility (that is, maximize their fitness) out of maximizing their catch than from minimizing their hunting time. On the other hand, since Efe men must trade with Lese to acquire the material goods that make them more attractive as husbands, Efe men have a constraint on their time that Ache men do not. Thus, Efe men probably get more utility from spending time cultivating trade relationships than by acquiring more meat.

So Efe and Ache men both try to maximize their foraging efficiency, although for different purposes. This does not mean that either group of men are foraging in the most energetically efficient way possible. In fact, there are several reasons to expect individuals to fall short of this goal. Some of these reasons include: a time lag between ecological change and behavioral change, the effect of other selective forces which may be directing the behavior under study toward different objectives than those being measured (such as balancing foraging efficiency with predator avoidance, or seeking resources that bestow prestige rather than calories), and the effects of a highly variable and fluctuating environment (see Stephens and Krebs 1986:128–50; Winterhalder 1986a,b; Foley 1985).

Most important, however, since cultural evolution is a process that transmits *existing* biological and cultural information differentially from generation to generation, natural selection does not necessarily result in the single best strategy, but rather selects a strategy that achieves goals better than other existing ones (E. Smith 1987). Again, it is assumed that behaviors will only tend toward optimization, not that all behaviors in a society will be optimal. Optimization analyses provide a way to model the abstract predictions of selection theory and make them amenable to tests, but they do not assume that people will always behave in the most absolutely efficient way possible (see Smith and Winterhalder 1992a).

Many optimization models are applied to situations where the consequence of a behavior is not affected by its frequency in a population (this is what Elster, in Winterhalder and Smith 1992, calls *parametric* environmental contexts.) Most optimal-foraging analyses take human interactions with the environment to be of this type. Here, the choice of which seeds to gather or which animal to hunt is based on current perceived characteristics of those seeds or that animal (e.g., caloric content, time to locate, time to harvest), but not on how many people are going after those seeds or animal or what resources others have decided to seek out (although the number of people may indirectly affect choices by directly affecting the abundance or behavior of the resources being sought). Interaction with the physical environment therefore is normally considered amenable to analysis with the optimal-foraging models we will discuss in chapter 3.

But oftentimes a decision to pursue a particular strategy is affected by the frequency of that strategy and its variants in a population. This is typical of most social interactions (and is what Elster calls *strategic* environmental contexts), where the consequences of a behavior are dependent on the frequency of that behavior and other variants in a population. One individual may, for example, choose to maximize hunting success *because* many others are already pursuing other prestige-seeking behaviors. These situations are best analyzed through game theory (see Smith and Winterhalder 1992a). Game theory predicts the frequency of different behavioral variants in a population given known fitness consequences of interaction *between* the different variants. A description of game theory is beyond the scope of this book, but suffice it to say that it predicts the frequency at which different behavioral variants (e.g., different parenting techniques) can be expected to exist within a population (given certain initial conditions) as a function of the outcomes of each variant's interaction with other behavioral variants and with its own type. This can result in a stable mix of behavioral variants that differ in their energetic efficiencies (e.g., in terms of net resource returns from foraging—see chapter 3 for an example) which is labeled an *evolutionarily stable strategy*. The point here is that applications of game theory show that situations can arise in which none of the behavioral variants is as optimal as would be predicted by a simple optimal foraging model (see Hawkes 1990, 1992, 1993), and that behavioral ecological models do not expect everyone in a society to behave the same.

In sum, behavioral ecology offers the best *learning strategy* for understanding the mechanism linking environment and society—the mechanism that Wissler sought but found elusive, that Kroeber thought too complex to study, and that Steward started to uncover. And, by incorporating evolution, the differential transmission of information from generation to generation, into our understanding of the relationship between environment and human society, behavioral ecology necessarily leads us away from its own family of simple optimization models toward more complex models that take culture into account.

What about culture?

The weak sociobiological thesis is sometimes justified by claiming that the biological capacity for culture must have been selected for in the distant pre-*Homo sapiens* past. Therefore, proponents of the weak thesis argue, cultural behavior should be an extension of biological adaptation and should operate in similar terms and in similar ways.

However, while the *capacity* for culture has a biological base and therefore most certainly arose through (and continues to maintained by) natural selection, there is no reason to presume that cultural evolution is a simple extension of or a parallel to biological evolution. Once hominids became cultural the rules of the evolutionary game changed. (It is not clear when humans became cultural, although it was certainly by the Upper Paleolithic, or even if our ancestors became fully cultural, as we understand the term, at a single point in time.) Cultural information, after all, is not encoded in genes but in symbolic communication, and is passed on through enculturation, rather than reproduction. We receive our genes from only our biological parents, but we acquire our culture from many people. By being an influential role model, it is possible for a single individual to alter phenotypic frequencies in a human population and yet have few or even no offspring. That a single individual or group of people has more or fewer offspring than another does not necessarily (that is, though genetic transmission) alter the frequencies of behavioral phenotypes in a society (Dunbar 1988). For humans, changes in genotype frequencies probably have no *direct* effect on cultural change.

Humans pass on information between generations about kinship, subsistence, religion, morals, aesthetics, and so on. Since cultures change through time, some information is obviously not passed on, while some new information (brought in through diffusion, independent invention, or errors in the enculturative process) is retained. In other words, information is selectively passed on from generation to generation, making culture analogous to genetics, in that information, encoded in symbols rather than in DNA, is "inherited" by one generation from another. One might assume, then, that it operates according to a set of principles of inheritance (Boyd and Richerson 1985; Bettinger 1991).

As we noted above, some anthropologists argue that diversity in human behavior is the manifestation of various cultural values that can only be understood within particular historical contexts. We can accept this perspective without hesitation. However, not all members of a culture share exactly the same set of values, and societies display different ranges of variation. In any given culture, at any given time, each individual represents slight variations on a cultural theme. Some individuals, for example, may value work a bit more than others, or some may hold to religious canons more enthusiastically. Culture change is change in the frequency of these variants, for example, a change from a generation in which few people take land issues seriously to one in which many do. The question we face is how do behavioral variants within a society change in frequency over time? What determines whether new behaviors or ideas are accepted or rejected? whether existing behaviors become more or less prevalent?

The study of culture from the perspective of neo-Darwinian evolutionary theory is just beginning and a complete description of it is beyond the scope of this book (Cavalli-Sforza and Feldman 1981; Durham 1991). We will only give a very brief overview of one theory, Robert Boyd's and Peter Richerson's "dual inheritance theory" (1985; see also Bettinger 1991). Our purpose is only to point out that the biological and cultural processes of inheritance are often, perhaps usually, asymmetric, and to note the effect that this observation has for the subject of behavioral ecology.

Boyd and Richerson identify two major evolutionary forces, *guided variation* and *biased transmission,* that affect the transmission of cultural traits and the amount of cultural variation present in a society. The force of guided variation operates in situations where individuals acquire behaviors initially by mimicking those around them and, later, by experimenting and learning on their own, making decisions based on a set of rules. (Boyd and Richerson suggest that these "rules" are most likely genetic in origin and very general in nature; Bettinger [1991:186] gives pleasure and pain as two examples. Since pleasure and pain can themselves be culturally defined, however, I cannot see why the rules must be genetic in origin, or even, if they are, why they could not still be passed on culturally. To be genetic, the rules must be extremely general—such as the pain associated with hunger.)

For example, a man may learn how to hunt from his relatives and then experiment on his own, always with a culturally shaped goal in mind, such as spending as little time as possible hunting. Assuming that other hunters are doing the same, this learning process will move the hunters' population as a whole (at least, its male members) toward a single type of hunting behavior. Behavior that becomes more frequent within a generation through learning also becomes more frequent in the following generation since it will be a more common role model. At the same time, however, the learning process generates errors and invents new behaviors that also become potential role models. Each generation therefore reduces variation in its initial set of role models, but creates new variants for the next generation. Through the errors produced by the learning process, guided variation continually produces behavioral variation, but, through rule-guided experimentation, variation that tends in a particular direction. The effect of guided variation is strongest when initial behaviors—in our example, basic hunting techniques—are difficult to master on one's own.

The force of biased transmission recognizes that people do not imitate role models at random and therefore that cultural transmission of information can favor some behavioral variants over others. Boyd and Richerson describe three kinds of biased transmission. *Direct bias* entails the ability to select a behavior from a range of behavioral choices by evaluating those choices rationally, perhaps through experimentation, rather than by modifying, through learning, an initially selected behavior. As in guided variation, the alternative behaviors are evaluated using criteria that are generalized (maximize foraging returns, minimize foraging time, etc.). Returning to our example, a hunter may be exposed to several different stalking techniques, experiment with each, and then select the one that meets his criteria.

Guided variation acts to continually produce variation through errors and invention; direct bias acts to continually reduce variation through selection. Direct bias is favored where the cost of experimenting is low relative to the amount of behavioral variance in the population. (Bettinger notes that this might occur most often when migration brings many locally maladaptive behaviors into an area and where the cost of experimenting with them is fairly low [1991:189].) Where people select a behavioral variant from a range of choices, the rate of change in the frequency of the different variants depends in large measure on their initial frequencies; direct bias has its greatest effect when variants occur in roughly equal frequencies.

Boyd and Richerson argue that guided variation and direct bias are likely to promote genetic fitness even though they may not be genetically controlled. This would seem to support the weak-thesis school of behavioral ecology, but Boyd and Richerson give us reasons to think that in many situations, cultural behavior need not result in maximization of fitness.

Guided variation and direct bias operate where behavioral techniques are relatively easy to learn or experiment with, and/or where individuals can see a direct relationship between goals and behaviors. However, many behaviors are often difficult to master, or mistakes in the trial-and-error process can be extremely costly. Imagine trying to master on one's own the hunting of seals through their winter breathing holes, or to learn a body of religious or medicinal knowledge without an apprenticeship. Likewise, relationships between goals and methods are not always apparent, as where there is a time lag between cause and effect (Bettinger 1991:191), or when what one does as a youth dictates how one will be treated in old age.

Where these situations hold true—and it is likely that they hold true for most human behaviors—Boyd and Richerson argue that two other processes of biased transmission, *frequency-dependent bias* and *indirect bias* may prevail since they are less costly than guided variation or direct bias. In frequency-dependent bias, individuals being enculturated select from a range of behaviors on the basis of frequency, selecting either those that are most common (conformist transmission) or those that are least common (nonconformist transmission) depending on the specific circumstances. Individuals who immigrate into another band, for example, might do best if they were predisposed to what the majority of others are doing (e.g., how the majority of women gather seeds, or how the majority of men hunt). If individuals select the most common behavior, the end result can be the same as direct bias but there is an important difference in that by simply mimicking the majority an individual avoids the potential cost of experimentation. By creating conditions in which one group can have a significantly different range of behaviors than another, frequency-dependent bias can theoretically establish conditions for group selection (Bettinger 1991:195–96).

Where the relationship between particular kinds of behavior and success (however culturally defined) is not clear, indirect bias may take on a selective advantage. Three cultural traits are important here: preference traits (e.g., cultural ideals, such as "good hunter"), indicator traits possessed by role models (hunting ability), and other behavioral traits (also possessed by the role model but not necessarily related to the indicator trait, e.g., particular clothing, songs, magic, etc.). Here, individuals attempt to achieve a cultural goal by copying other behavioral traits displayed by members who also display the indicator trait. This may occur where it is not entirely clear what gives the model his or her abilities (is he a good hunter because of his stalking abilities, or because of the magic he uses?). This is a low-cost way of obtaining very complex cultural information and results in traits being passed on as blocks, rather than separately, so that a whole complex of traits can be passed on as attributes of a good hunter, a good gatherer, a good father or mother. In other words, and as anthropologists well know, some behavioral acts or elements of material culture take on symbolic meaning and will be adopted for their meaning rather than their function. Through mathematical models, Boyd and Richerson give us reason to suspect that many behavioral traits can be passed on regardless of whether or not they actually increase an individual's genetic fitness. Through indirect bias, for example, a woman who is a good gatherer can pass on her behavioral attributes to many others, even though she may produce no children herself.

This perspective on cultural and genetic transmission of information places two requirements on anthropological research. First, it is essential that we document variation *within* communities. To test models of genetic and cultural transmission, we must begin with an understanding of how much behavioral variation exists in a society. Unfortunately, the greater part of the ethnographic record on hunter-gatherers was developed under a theoretical paradigm in which ethnographers recorded normal or average behaviors (or more commonly what informants claimed to be the normal or acceptable behavior). New ethnographic investigations are now being conducted to collect the data necessary to evaluate behavioral ecological models (e.g., R. Bailey 1991; E. Smith 1991).

Second, it is essential that we not stop with understanding how interaction with the environment affects the lives of adult men and women. To understand cultural change we must know how changes in adult activities affect enculturation, the process whereby children learn their culture. For example, Barry Hewlett notes that poorer male hunters among the Aka spend more time with their children than do good hunters (1991b). What the poor hunters cannot bring home through hunting they make up for by spending more time in childcare. How does this affect the development of the two sets of children? More generally, how does a society's range of values shift as a function of changes in the way children are raised? What role does change in intrasocietal variation in enculturation play in cultural change? Does it alter the range of behaviors presented to a generation and/or the criteria used to select a behavior from this range? Although the connection between enculturation studies and behavioral ecology has not been fully explored, we might expect that ecological factors affecting adult activities that in turn affect child rearing could play a large role in cultural change. We will speculate on the relationship between adult foraging, enculturation, and cultural change in several places in this book.

CONCLUSIONS

Interaction with the physical and social environment is an inescapable fact of human life—for hunter-gatherers as for anyone else. Anthropologists have recognized this for many years, but have focused on patterns between the conceptual monoliths of environment and culture or society, leaving the links between the two unspecified. Cultural ecology relied on the ambiguous and tenuous assumption that all societies try to maintain homeostasis. It set aside the fact that individuals, not societies, make decisions, and that these individuals' decisions can conflict with one another.

Behavioral ecology offers a perspective and a methodology that helps us understand how hunter-gatherers make decisions about interacting with their environment and how those decisions affect the transmission of cultural traits. It forces us to examine behavioral variation within societies. It focuses on foraging behavior because foraging is obviously critical to survival among hunter-gatherers.

Behavioral ecology begins with the assumption that people's behavior is aimed at maximizing reproductive success. But based on current thinking of the relationship between biological and cultural inheritance, reproductive fitness is not the sole criterion we need to understand differences in human behavior, especially those differences between populations that anthropologists have traditionally recognized as cultural ones.

As it is defined here, behavioral ecology offers a conceptual framework with which to understand the relationships between the abundance and distribution of food resources, decisions about how to allocate time to foraging and other activities (e.g., mate selection, prestige competition, reproduction, and child rearing), and the effect these have on the transmission of cultural information. It is a conceptual framework with which we can build theory that accounts for change as well as stasis in human societies, and, since it foregrounds the relationships among human activities, reproduction, and enculturation, the best framework we have to understand humans for what they are: biological and cultural beings.

Behavioral ecology also offers a way out of the argument that modern hunter-gatherers are not analogous to prehistoric ones. Behavioral ecology sees environments as made up of resources whose acquisition entails costs and benefits. Behavioral ecology does not make and does not have to make assumptions about the pristine nature of modern hunter-gatherers. Whether food is acquired through direct procurement, or by trading a nonedible forest product for it, or whether it is acquired with a spear and throwing board or a shotgun and pickup truck does not matter; both kinds of activities can be evaluated in the same terms (e.g., see E. Smith 1991:chap. 6). This does not mean that behavioral ecologists can ignore the ways in which hunter-gatherers are affected by their agricultural or industrial neighbors, or the extent to which they are involved in cash economies. Instead, the availability of new technologies, such as the introduction of shotguns to tropical forest hunters, or the availability of new resources, such as processed flour or wage labor, can actually be used to test the predictions of models (see chapters 3 and 6).

Informed by new models of cultural transmission, behavioral ecology could take a very different ecological approach to hunter-gatherers (and others) than that taken through most of the twentieth century. But it is a direction that does not leave behind its concern for the place of humans in their environment. As we will show in the succeeding chapters, the environment figures prominently in how hunter-gatherers decide what to eat, whether to move or stay, to share or to hoard, to let someone into their territory or not, to have children or not, to participate in prestigious feasts or not. Understanding how these decisions are made and how they affect the transmission of cultural information between generations is necessary to building an evolutionary anthropology.

FORAGING AND SUBSISTENCE | 3

I would like to say a few words about this land. The only food I like is meat.
Inuk man (Brody 1987:62)

Why should we plant, when there are so many mongongos in the world?
/Xashe, a Ju/'hoansi man (Lee 1979)

Subsistence studies have long been prominent in hunter-gatherer anthropology, but especially so since the "Man the Hunter" conference. Before that conference, meat was seen as the primary constituent of diet. But ethnographic data presented at the conference revealed the importance of plant food to many groups; in some cases nuts, seeds, or roots provided more daily calories than meat. Especially persuasive were data on the Ju/'hoansi's diet, 85 percent of which was made up of plant food. Paradoxically, while the conference emphasized the role of the environment in forager lifeways, Lee nonetheless concluded that "latitude appears to make little difference in the amount of hunting that people do," although he had to leave Arctic groups aside to do so (Lee 1968:42).[1] He went on to point out that the mean contribution of meat to foraging diets at all latitudes is 35 percent. The patrilineal-band model, with its emphasis on hunting, was overturned. In the minds of many anthropologists at the time, meat was a constant, but less important component of the classic forager's diet than plant food. Some even replaced the term *hunter-gatherer* with *gatherer-hunter* (e.g., Bender and Morris 1988).

At the time, recognition of the role of plant food in hunter-gatherer subsistence was an important step, exposing bias in hunting-focused models of human evolution and opening the eyes of archaeologists to erroneous assumptions about prehistoric diet. Nonetheless, switching the emphasis from hunting animals to gathering plant food repeats the error of stereotyping and deflects attention from understanding differences among hunter-gatherer diets. In this chapter, we first establish that hunter-gatherer diets are systematically related to their environments by demonstrating simple correlations between gross dietary and environmental variables. We then examine optimization models that have been used to account for the composition of foraging diets.

ENVIRONMENT AND DIET

While many hunter-gatherers do depend primarily on plant food, table 3-1 shows the range of variability in hunter-gatherer diets. The methods used to estimate the relative importance of gathering, hunting, and fishing in this table are admittedly often vague. Gathered food, for example, consists mostly of plant food, but can include small mammals and shellfish. In some cases, the relative values are based on weight, in others they are estimates of the actual calories contributed by each category, and some are simply the ethnographers' impressions. There is also some discrepancy between these data as indicators of economic activities and as actual diet. For example, some tropical forest groups have high ratings under the category of hunted food, yet much of this hunted food is traded for horticultural produce—the high hunting values reflect trade activities, not diet. Nonetheless, the size of the errors is small enough when viewed on a global scale that these data still demonstrate that hunter-gatherer diet is highly variable around the globe and cannot be readily generalized.

These data can also be used to show that hunter-gatherer diet is systematically related to environmental characteristics. To see this relationship, we must first introduce the two variables of effective temperature (ET) and primary production (PP). Developed by H. Bailey (1960) and introduced to the anthropological literature by Lewis Binford (1980), ET provides a simultaneous measure of the intensity of solar radiation as well as of its annual distribution. ET is derived from the mean temperatures (°C) of the warmest and coldest months (W and C):

$$ET = \frac{18\ W - 10\ C}{(W - C) + 8}$$

Table 3-1. Environment and Diet

Group	ET (°C)	PP (g/m²/yr)	Hunting (%)	Gathering (%)	Fishing (%)
Polar Inuit	8.5	45	40	10	50
Taġiuġmiut (Tareumiut)	8.7	59	30	0	70
Yukaghir	8.9	89	50	10	40
Ona (Selk'nam)	9.0	401	70	10	20
Angmagsalik	9.0	333	20	0	80
Sivokakhmeit	9.0	195	15	5	80
Copper Inuit	9.1	115	40	0	60
Iglulingmiut	9.5	90	50	0	50
Nunamiut	9.8	115	87	3	10
Yahgan	9.9	706	20	10	70
Caribou Inuit	10.0	144	50	10	40
Naskapi (Innu)	10.0	278	70	10	20
Alacaluf	10.0	535	20	10	70
N. Tlingit	10.0	633	30	10	60
Chipewyan	10.3	283	60	0	40
Tutchone	10.3	209	45	10	45
Kaska	10.4	206	40	10	50
Gilyak	10.4	482	30	20	50
Tanaina (Dena'ina)	10.4	464	40	10	50
Bella Coola (Nuxalk)	10.5	828	20	20	60
Bella Bella	10.5	828	30	20	50
Chugach Inuit	10.5	323	20	0	80
Kutchin (Gwich'in)	10.5	144	40	10	50
Slavey (Dené thá)	10.6	327	50	10	40
Ojibwa	10.7	699	40	30	30
Mistassini Cree	10.8	555	50	20	30
Ingalik (Deg Hit'an)	10.8	245	40	10	50
Nunivak	10.9	209	30	10	60
Tanana	10.9	217	70	10	20
S. Tlingit	10.9	633	30	10	60
Tsimshian	11.1	862	20	20	60
Haida	11.1	837	20	20	60
Chilcotin	11.2	354	30	20	50
Tahltan	11.2	245	50	10	40
Carrier (Dakelne)	11.2	350	40	20	40
Makah	11.3	757	20	20	60
Sarsi	11.3	283	80	20	0
Blackfoot (Siksika)	11.4	472	80	20	0
Quinault	11.5	871	30	20	50
Plains Cree	11.5	397	60	20	20
Aleut	11.6	283	10	30	60
Montagnais	11.6	456	60	20	20
S. Kwakiutl (Ft. Rupert)	11.6	822	20	30	50
Ute (Uintah)	11.7	278	35	40	25
Saulteaux	11.7	533	35	20	45
Assiniboine	11.7	432	70	20	10
Uncompahgre	11.8	583	50	35	15
Ainu	12.0	661	20	30	50
Wind River Shoshone	12.0	307	50	30	20
Flathead	12.1	369	40	30	30
Klamath	12.2	320	20	30	50

Table 3-1. Environment and Diet (*continued*)

Group	ET (°C)	PP (g/m²/yr)	Hunting (%)	Gathering (%)	Fishing (%)
Washo	12.3	235	30	40	30
Puyallup–Nisqually	12.3	820	20	30	50
Twana	12.3	720	30	10	60
Wadadika (Ruby Valley)	12.4	161	30	50	20
Shuswap	12.4	450	30	30	40
Agaiduka (Lemhi)	12.5	181	30	30	40
Nootka (Nuuchahnulth)	12.6	943	20	20	60
Alsea	12.7	925	20	10	70
Coast Yuki	12.7	671	20	40	40
Sanpoil	12.7	283	20	30	50
Micmac	12.7	772	50	10	40
Sinkyone	12.8	692	30	40	30
Timpanogots (Utah L.)	12.9	432	30	40	30
Tubatulabal	12.9	391	30	50	20
Gosiute	12.9	172	40	50	10
Kidütökadö (N. Paiute)	12.9	186	20	50	30
Crow (Apsáalooke)	13.0	354	80	20	0
Yurok	13.3	713	10	40	50
Nez Perce	13.3	259	30	30	40
Tolowa	13.3	804	20	40	40
Kuyuidökadö (Pyramid L.)	13.3	135	20	50	30
Achumawi	13.3	464	40	30	30
Tenino	13.3	464	20	30	50
Cheyenne	13.3	408	80	20	0
Umatilla	13.3	285	30	30	40
Modoc	13.3	318	30	50	20
W. Mono	13.4	303	40	50	10
Maidu	13.5	584	30	50	20
Atsugewi	13.5	550	30	40	30
Kaibab (S. Paiute)	14.0	425	30	70	0
Shasta	14.0	539	30	40	30
Kiowa-Apache	14.3	1,045	80	20	0
Comanche	14.4	706	90	10	0
Botocudo (Kaingang)	14.4	1,844	40	50	10
Kiowa	14.6	717	90	10	0
Wintu	14.6	812	30	30	40
Diegueno (Tipai-Ipai)	14.6	26	40	50	10
≠Kade G/wi	14.8	476	20	80	0
Sierra Miwok	14.8	699	30	60	10
Panamint	15.0	45	40	60	0
Cahuilla	15.0	487	40	60	0
Kawaiisu	15.0	67	30	50	20
Luiseño	15.1	415	20	60	20
Walapai	15.1	144	40	60	0
Moapa	15.2	47	40	60	0
Borjeno (Baja Calif.)	15.8	67	18	57	25
Dieri	15.9	85	30	70	0
Aranda	15.9	202	40	60	0
S.E. Yavapai	16.0	134	40	60	0
N.E. Yavapai	16.0	134	40	60	0
Aweikoma	16.5	1,286	60	40	0

Table 3-1. Environment and Diet (*continued*)

Group	ET (°C)	PP (g/m²/yr)	Hunting (%)	Gathering (%)	Fishing (%)
Karankawa	16.6	976	30	40	30
Hadza	17.7	1,508	35	65	0
Kariera	18.0	323	50	30	20
Seri	18.3	212	25	25	50
Walpiri (Walbiri)	18.4	209	30	70	0
Ju/'hoansi (Dobe)	18.8	459	20	80	0
G/wi	19.3	476	15	85	0
Groote Eylandt	19.5	1,755	10	30	60
Wikmunkan	19.6	2,164	40	40	20
Siriono[a]	20.6	2,358	25	70	5
Chenchu[a]	20.8	1,482	10	85	5
Aeta	21.2	3,800	60	35	5
Anbarra	21.6	2,890	13	22	65
Tiwi	22.6	2,450	30	50	20
Vedda[a]	23.0	2,800	35	45	20
Gidjingali	23.0	2,892	30	50	20
Murngin	23.5	2,617	30	50	20
Semang[a]	23.7	4,622	35	50	15
Mbuti	23.7	2,624	60	30	10
Andamanese (Onge)	24.4	3,884	20	40	40
Penan	24.9	5,128	30	70	0

Note: The ET and PP figures were computed from climatic data given by an ethnographer or listed in climatic-data compilations and maps. Diet is listed in terms of the rough percentage of food derived from hunting, gathering (including small game and sometimes shellfish), and fishing (including shellfish and sea mammals). Diet estimates are either taken from Murdock 1967 or are taken from ethnographies. (See chapter 1, note 18 for comments on ethnographic-atlas data.)
[a]Some reliance upon horticulture.

ET varies from 26 at the equator to 8 at the poles; low ET values are associated with cold, seasonal environments with short growing seasons while high ET values are associated with tropical, nonseasonal environments (in terms of temperature, not precipitation) with long growing seasons.

Primary production (PP) refers to annual net above-ground plant production (g/m²/yr), and is a more direct indicator of the amount of food available to herbivores than ET. A product of effective precipitation and solar radiation, primary production is computed from evapotranspiration (E) values (UNESCO 1974; Thornthwaite Associates 1962, 1963, 1964) using Sharpe's equation (1975):

$$\text{Primary Production} = .0219 \ E^{1.66}$$

Holding solar radiation constant, primary production increases with increasing precipitation until the solar-energy threshold is reached (at which point additional rainfall has no effect). Holding precipitation constant, primary production is a function of solar radiation.

Included in table 3-1 are estimates of the primary production and effective temperature of the environments of 123 hunter-gatherer societies. (This is not a random sample, and is biased toward nontropical environments, with 80 percent of the cases coming from places in the *ET* range of 8–15. It is also geographically biased, with 77 percent of the cases coming from North America.)

Not all primary production is edible by humans. One hundred grams of primary production in the Arctic is mostly in the form of lichens or moss, while a larger fraction of the same 100 grams of production in a temperate desert is edible seeds. In a tropical forest, a large percentage of primary production is in inedible primary biomass—stems and leaves. In general, a larger percentage of production may be humanly edible in tropical and temperate deserts—places where a number of ethnographically well-documented hunter-gatherers, such as the Ju/'hoansi, live. Thus, the generalization that hunter-gatherers rely primarily on plant food is the result of differential ethnographic documentation. Understanding the relationship between hunter-gatherer diet and the environment requires that we seek systematic relationships between dietary and environmental variables, rather than generalizations.

The amount of plant food in a foraging diet should be related to the amount of humanly edible plant food that is available in an environment (Belovsky 1987). Given the above argument, this amount can be roughly predicted by a combination of primary production and effective temperature. A multiple linear-regression analysis shows this to be true. For the 123 groups in table 3-1, *ET* and *PP* predict the dependence on gathering quite well ($df = 120$, multiple $R = .75$, $p < .01$); however, *ET* and *PP* do not predict dependence on hunted foods very well ($df = 120$, multiple $R = .14$, $p > .05$). (Neither *ET* nor *PP* alone are correlated with dependence on gathering or hunting at $p < .05$.) Apparently, other factors are involved that result in some hunter-gatherers hunting more and some hunting less than one would expect based on environmental data alone (as measured by *ET* and *PP*). Since *ET* and *PP* only characterize the terrestrial environment, two possible intervening factors are the use of aquatic resources—fish, shellfish, and marine mammals—and the effects of trade with neighboring peoples (e.g., other hunter-gatherers, horticulturalists).

We can develop a rough model to predict dependence on hunted foods independent of aquatic resources by constructing a regression equation using the variables of ET and PP for those groups that are not heavily dependent on fishing. For groups with less than 25 percent dependence on aquatic resources, PP and ET predict the dependence on plant food and hunting quite well (for plants, $N = 54$, $df = 51$, multiple $R = .66$, $p < .01$; for hunting, $N = 54$, $df = 51$, multiple $R = .60$, $p < .01$).

Let's assume that aquatic resources are used in lieu of gathered or hunted food. Using the multiple linear regression equation describing the relationship between ET, PP, and dependence on gathered food (for groups with less than 25 percent dependence on aquatic resources), we can predict the dependence on gathering for all 123 societies in table 3-1. Likewise, we can use the regression equation relating dependence on hunting to ET and PP to predict dependence on hunted foods. If aquatic resources are used in place of gathered or hunted foods, then the dependence on aquatic resources should correlate with the difference between the predicted and actual dependence on gathered or hunted foods, respectively.

Dependence on aquatic resources is correlated with the expected minus actual dependence on gathering in this sample, although dependence on aquatic resources does not account for much of the variance ($df = 121$, $r = .32$, $p < .01$). The use of aquatic resources tends to be higher in colder than in warmer climates (as Lee also found to be true [1968]). In general, northern waters are relatively more productive than the adjoining terrestrial environment (a difference between surface and deep-water temperatures creates upwelling coastal currents that bring up nutrients [see Yesner 1980]), perhaps making the former more attractive than the latter. Hunter-gatherers in cold climates also rely more heavily on stored food than those living in warmer climates; in fact, food storage dramatically increases, in general, in environments with ETs below 14 (Binford 1980). Is the need for stored food related to the difference in productivity between the aquatic and cold terrestrial environments? For those groups in ET settings of less than 14, dependence on aquatic resources only accounts for a small amount of the difference between the expected and actual dependence on gathered food ($n = 80$, $df = 78$, $r = .24$, $p < .05$). Some dependence on aquatic resources may replace storable plant food (Binford 1990; Pálsson 1988), but other factors must be involved.

Dependence on aquatic resources accounts for more of the variability in the expected minus actual hunted food for the entire sample ($df = 121$, $r = .79$, $p < .01$) as well as the low-ET sample ($df = 78$, $r = .38$, $p < .01$). The higher the dependence on fishing, the less hunting a group is actually doing relative to the predicted amount (figure 3-1). Therefore, the use of aquatic

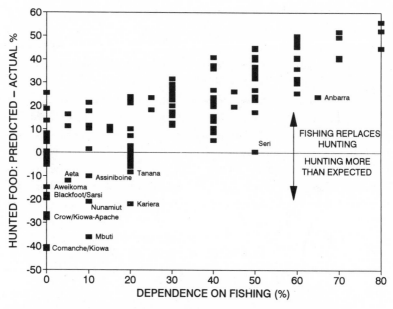

Figure 3-1. Relationship between dependence on fishing and the difference between the expected and actual dependence on hunting.

resources may in general be a function of an inability to hunt as much as is needed. In the ethnographic sample, groups dependent on aquatic resources frequently live under very high population densities within small territories at high latitudes (Binford 1990; Keeley 1988; Yesner 1980). This may restrict how much a society can depend on hunting since hunting in cold environments requires large territories (see chapter 4).

Those groups that lie below the horizontal line in figure 3-1 hunt *more* than expected. Many of these are tropical groups who trade meat for carbohydrates (Mbuti, Aeta, possibly Aweikoma), northern groups who do not have direct access to substantial aquatic resources and who cannot turn to plant food as a substitute (Nunamiut, Tanana), and Plains hunters who, like tropical forest groups, trade meat for carbohydrates (in this sample, corn grown by Pueblo or other horticultural peoples) and who live in interior grasslands where much of the primary production cannot be eaten by humans and where aquatic resources are not abundant (Kiowa, Comanche, Cheyenne, Crow, Kiowa-Apache, Sarsi, Blackfoot). The Kariera (northwest Australian coast) and Seri (northwestern Mexico) also hunt more than expected; these may be coding errors or cases where people turn to aquatic resources in place of gathered foods (where the tropical aquatic environment provides better foraging than the plant foods in a group's desert terrestrial environment).

There are many more patterns in these data that we cannot explore here. This brief analysis does, however, point out that stereotypes of hunter-gatherer diets are not very useful, for these diets are clearly variable. Moreover, the fact that forager diets are systematically related to a few simple environmental variables that measure the gross abundance of terrestrial foods suggests that hunter-gatherer diets are the products of a decision-making process that takes the cost of acquiring resources into account, whether this means hunting, gathering, fishing, or exchanging for them. Informed by the theory of evolutionary ecology, microeconomic optimization models provide one approach to explaining how foragers arrive at subsistence decisions given their choice of resources. We will examine three simple models here: linear programming, the diet-breadth model, and the patch-choice model.

OPTIMAL-FORAGING MODELS

Optimal-foraging models were developed by ecologists interested in understanding the factors affecting nonhuman foraging behavior. Their utility to students of human foragers rapidly became apparent, especially since diversity in human diets cannot be attributed to differences in physical perceptual abilities, prey-capturing appendages, or predator size—all potential sources of diversity in the nonhuman world.[2]

Optimal-foraging models include a *goal*, a *currency*, a set of *constraints*, and a set of *options*. The goal is normally maximization of foraging efficiency (food gathered per unit time), but it need not always be. The currency most often used is calories, but again, it need not be. Constraints include such things as the maximum amount of time which can be spent foraging or the forager's capacity to digest certain foods. Options include the potential food resources and other choices about how to spend time (e.g., childcare). Given a set of resources with specified characteristics (e.g., nutritional content, harvest and processing times), optimal-foraging models propose how those resources will be used.

Linear programming

Linear programming gained popularity in the 1970s because it provided the mathematics needed to model diet in intricate detail (Reidhead 1979, 1980;

Table 3-2. Diet Characteristics in Linear-Programming Example

Diet element	Amount per 100-g portion		Daily requirement
	Food X_1	Food X_2	
Kilocalories	60 kcal	30 kcal	2,000 kcal
Protein	1 g	2 g	60 g
Vitamin W	2 mg	1 mg	20 mg
	Cost of acquiring 100-g portion		
	40 kcal	15 kcal	

Keene 1979, 1981). Linear programming is a method for solving multiple linear equations for any number of variables. While many optimal-foraging models use only energy (calories) as their currency, linear programming can simultaneously evaluate diets in terms of an array of dietary elements. Proponents, of linear programming argue that this gives a more realistic analysis since humans require a variety of vitamins and minerals to survive in addition to calories. A simple example will demonstrate how the method works.

Imagine that a forager needs to acquire 2,000 kilocalories (kcal), 60 grams of protein, and 20 milligrams of vitamin W each day. Two hypothetical food resources, X_1 and X_2, are available to the forager containing the postprocessing amounts of the dietary elements shown in table 3-2. The caloric cost of acquiring 100 grams of each resource (to search for it, harvest it, and process it) are also given in the table (these would be derived experimentally, or taken from ethnographic data). We will assume that the forager's objective is to obtain a sufficient amount of calories, protein, and vitamins while spending the least amount of energy. The question is: how many 100-calorie portions of each resource should the forager gather to meet the minimum daily requirements at the least cost? In other words, the solution to the equation, cost $= 40X_1 + 15X_2$, must be minimized. The linear constraints are:

$$X_1, X_2, \geq 0$$

and,

$$60X_1 + 30X_2 \geq 2,000 \text{ kcal}$$

$$1X_1 + 2X_2 \geq 60 \text{ g of protein}$$

$$2X_1 + 1X_2 \geq 20 \text{ mg of vitamin } W$$

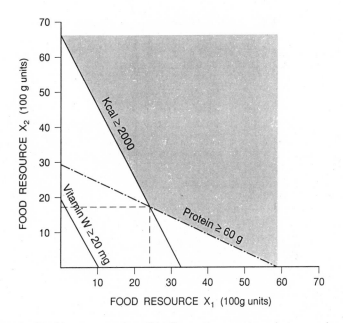

Figure 3-2. Graphic representation of the linear-programming solution to a hypothetical diet, given two resources and three linear constraints. Drawn by Dan Delaney.

The solution in this case can be portrayed graphically (figure 3-2) and is found by solving each of the inequalities. The optimal solution lies where the kilocalorie and protein inequalities intersect, about 24 100-gram units of resource X_1 and 19 100-gram units of resource X_2. At this point, the minimum daily requirements are procured at the least cost (cost = 40(24) + 15(19) = 1,245 kcal). Any dietary composition in the shaded area (e.g., 50 units of resource X_1 and 20 units of resource X_2) is a potential diet, since at least the minimal amount of each resource will be acquired, but the least-cost solution is where the lines intersect. Note that as long as adequate protein and calories are acquired, a more than adequate amount of vitamin W is also acquired. Thus the vitamin is not a constraining element in the diet, and could be dropped from analysis.

Arthur Keene used linear programming to predict the precontact and postcontact diet of the Arviligjuarmiut band of the Netsilingmiut (1979; postcontact the Netsilingmiut used rifles). Keene reconstructed the diet month by month for twelve resources and ten dietary requirements (plus one nonfood requirement, hides), that included energy (kcal), protein, fat, carbohydrate, calcium, vitamin A, thiamine, riboflavin, ascorbic acid, and iron.

Keene did not use direct energetic measures of the caloric cost of exploiting a resource. Instead, using an approach developed by Michael Jochim (1976), he estimated from ethnographic data the cost of acquiring food resources using measures of each resource's mobility, density, degree of aggregation, and the maximum distance at which a resource could be acquired. Keene computed the cost of searching for a resource as mobility divided by resource density, and the cost of pursuing a resource as the maximum distance to a kill divided by the resource's degree of aggregation. Added together, and multiplied by a risk coefficient, the search and pursuit costs became the cost coefficient. Keene did not take resource-processing time into account, but since he considered only fauna (the Netsilingmiut environment offers inconsequential plant foods) the inclusion of processing time would not have altered the relative differences between resource-cost coefficients, since the processing time of game is generally correlated with animal body weight.[3]

Keene used the analysis to predict the times of the year particular food resources should be used and then compared the predicted diet to the actual diet as reconstructed from ethnographic data. While he found some correspondence between the predicted and actual diets, the model was not perfect. Keene found that both energy and protein were available in abundance, and that a Netsilingmiut who obtained a just-sufficient amount of protein and energy would be deficient in calcium, ascorbic acid, and possibly other nutrients.

Gary Belovsky made an alternative use of linear programming, trying to predict only the proportions of plant food and meat in Ju/'hoansi diet (1987). From Lee's field data, Belovsky derived average costs of acquiring plants and hunted food (including tool-preparation and maintenance times), and average caloric contents of plants and hunted foods. Belovsky developed several linear equations describing a temporal constraint (the time that can be devoted to foraging), a digestive constraint (the amount of food that can be consumed in a day—the amount of food collected in a day does little good if the stomach cannot process a sufficient amount of it to meet daily caloric needs), an energy constraint (the combinations of plant and hunted food that can be obtained to provide the minimum amount of energy needed), and a protein constraint (the combinations of plants and hunted foods that can be obtained to provide the minimum amount of daily protein).

By altering the model's constants, Belovsky modeled situations in which the Ju/'hoansi collect only for themselves and those in which they collect for themselves plus dependents (the latter is the more realistic situation). Additionally, he modeled diets that minimize the amount of time spent searching for food, and diets that maximize the amount of energy acquired each day. Belovsky found a near-perfect fit between the actual Ju/'hoansi diet and the energy-maximization model, assuming adults forage for themselves and dependents. Altering the model's parameters for environmental differences, Belovsky also accurately modeled the diets of two bands of G/wi (other Kalahari hunter-gatherers), and of the Ache.

There are difficulties in operationalizing linear-programming analyses. The parameters used by Belovsky require accurate estimates of such things as resource processing, digestion rates, and tool-manufacture and maintenance times. These are important. Belovsky found that a change of as little as 10 percent in some of the model's parameters dramatically altered the predicted dietary proportions. Furthermore, the more nutrients included in a linear-programming model, the more accurate must be information on resource attributes and human nutritional needs. Keene pointed out (1981), for example, that the thiamine content of cooked foods in his analysis may have been underestimated, and that even a 25 percent reduction in calcium and ascorbic acid needs does not substantially change the model's predictions.[4] In sum, this means that the parameters of a linear-programming model have to be very precise in order to be accurate (although it also means that different situations can be modeled and their test implications generated).

This is a difficult requirement of linear-programming models because human nutritional requirements are affected by a number of variables, including activity level, age, and body size; the particular nutritional values selected, therefore, could be misleading. Linear programming also assumes that the cost of acquiring a resource is a constant and thus creates a linear function between cost and return (Bettinger 1980:220–21). Optimal-foraging analyses demonstrate that cost is a function of density. As a resource is harvested, its density decreases and the cost per unit harvested increases (see the marginal-value theorem below). Thus, the relationship between cost and return is often curvilinear, not linear.

Finally, applications of linear programming have served more as elegant descriptions of hunter-gatherer diet than as tests of hypotheses of behavior. Hill points out that Belovsky adds dimensions to his linear-programming model (e.g., number of dependents) until he achieves a good fit between the model's predictions and actual Ju/'hoansi diet (1988). And, by separating out the cost of searching for each resource, linear-programming models assume that resources are sought one at a time. While this is sometimes the case, it is not always true. Belovsky gets around this issue by examining only plant versus game resources, rather than individual food types. Since plants are harvested predominantly by women and game by men, each set of resources is searched for singularly. But Belovsky cannot address the important issue of dietary diversity. Other optimal-foraging models try to overcome this limitation of linear programming.

The diet-breadth model

Borrowed from ecology (MacArthur and Pianka 1966; Emlen 1966), the diet-breadth model has been applied to several modern and prehistoric hunter-gatherer societies, although thorough tests of the model are few in number and limited in scope (e.g., E. Smith 1983, 1991; Hill and Hawkes 1983). The diet-breadth model specifically predicts only whether a resource will be taken by a forager when he or she encounters it while foraging.

Whereas linear-programming analyses lump the costs of acquiring resources into a single measure, the diet-breadth model requires that resource acquisition be broken into *search costs* (or *encounter rates*) and *handling costs*. Search cost is the time it takes to locate a resource; the handling cost is the time it takes to harvest (or to pursue and kill, in the case of game) and process the resource. These are normally expressed in a measure of return per unit time (e.g., kcal/hr), and are based on ethnographic field data (figure 3-3), or experimental research with reconstructed technologies (e.g., Simms 1987).

A simple example will show the difference between search and handling costs. Let's say that a forager could expect to encounter a field of ricegrass (*Oryzopsis hymenoides*) containing an average of 1,000 kilograms of seeds for every 3 hours of searching. This means that the search cost is .003 hours per kilogram of seed. The handling cost is the time it takes to process the ricegrass after locating the plants. Using aboriginal technology, Steve Simms found that after harvesting and processing Indian ricegrass for 41 minutes he had procured 98 grams of edible food for a handling cost of .68 hr/.098 kg = 6.97 hr/kg (1987:119). Resources are normally ranked in terms of their *postencounter return rate,* the amount of energy gathered per unit time after encountering a resource. This is similar to the handling cost, but differs in being dependent on the caloric content of a unit of the resource. For example, since ricegrass contains 2.74 kilocalories per gram, its return rate in Simms' experiment is 2.74 × 98 g/41 min = 6.55 kcal/min or 393 kcal/hr. Experimentally or ethnographically derived return rates of various resources

Figure 3-3. Alice Steve, a Paiute woman, demonstrating traditional piñon-pine-nut processing; she is winnowing the cracked hulls from the seeds. Search and processing costs are best determined through observation of such ethnographic situations. Photograph by Margaret Wheat or Laura Mills, about 1958. Margaret Wheat Collection, Special Collections, University of Nevada-Reno Library.

from around the world are provided in table 3-3. This table shows that there are some classes of foods that tend to have lower or higher return rates than other classes. Seeds and roots, for example, normally have lower return rates than small, medium, or large game. But within any one class there is still considerable variability and some classes overlap one another.

Search costs will change with changing resource densities or with the techniques used to look for food, for example, by using horses, or new tracking techniques, or by acquiring more accurate information on the location of food. Handling costs and return rates can change, often quite dramatically, as a result of different technologies—for example, by using woven paddles to beat seeds from plants rather than stripping them by hand (Simms 1987), by using a net rather than a leister or hook and line to catch fish, or by using a shotgun in place of a spear or bow and arrow. Return rates can also depend on whether we include the cost of manufacturing the necessary equipment in the pursuit cost (Bailey and Aunger 1989a), or whether the resource is to be prepared for storage (increasing the handling cost). Resource return rates can also change with seasonal changes in resource composition, for example, seasonal changes in animal body fat, or in animal behavioral characteristics that alter search or handling costs. Note, for example, the seasonal difference in large-game return rates in the boreal forest in table 3-3. Return rates can also differ from person to person, depending on their skill, or even from day to day for the same person. In Australia's Western Desert, return rates of several Kukadja-speaking foragers searching for lizards varied from 114 to 8,580 kilocalories per hour per person; even for the same individual, return rates varied from 1,030 to 8,580 kilocalories per hour (Cane 1987:table 22). Experimentally derived return rates must be considered only as relative measures, and, where possible, averages of numerous observations should be used.

The separation of search from handling costs is an important characteristic of the diet-breadth model since it allows us to evaluate the effects of changes in a resource's density or in search techniques independent of changes in a resource's handling, (e.g., changes in processing or procuring technology). It is important that both aspects of resource acquisition be considered when evaluating a resource's utility. For example, Lee's data on mongongo-nut use suggests a return rate of 1,900 kilocalories per hour. But Hawkes and O'Connell point out that Lee did not take into account the time required to break open mongongo nuts and pound the nut meat into a digestible form (1981, 1985). When handling time is accounted for, the return rate for mongongo drops by nearly two-thirds, from 1,900 to 670 kilocalories

Table 3-3. Post-Encounter Resource Return Rates

Name/location	Type	Return rate (kcal/hr)
Australia		
Panicum australiense and		
Fimbristylis oxystachya	grass seed	261
Panicum australiense	grass seed	1,226
Fimbristylis oxystachya	grass seed	405
Panicum cymbiforme	grass seed	668
Chenopodium rhadinostachyum	grass seed	652
Vigna lanceolata	tubers	255
Ipomoea costata	tubers	1,769
Cyprus rotondus	roots	848
Solanum chippendalei	fruit/bush tomato	9,380
Cossidae sp.	larvae/witchetty grub	2,834
various species	lizards	2,975
Ipomoea costata	tubers	6,252
Sandhills		
Solanum centrale	fruit	5,984
Acacia coriacea (unripe)	tree seed	4,333
Varanus sp.	lizard	4,200
Vigna lanceolata	tuber	1,724
A. Coriacea (ripe)	tree seed	<676
A. aneura	tree seed	580
Grass seeds	seeds	575
A. cowleana	tree seed	552
Other acacias	tree seeds	538
Mulga woodland		
Amphinolarus/Varanus sp.	lizard	4,200
Vigna lanceolata	tuber	1,724
Cossid	larvae	1,486
A. Aneura	tree seed	580
Grass seeds	seeds	575
Floodplain		
Cyperus sp.	tree seed	4,435
Grass seeds	seeds	575
Great Basin		
Anabrus simplex	grasshoppers	41,598–714,409
Odocoileus hemionus	deer	17,971–31,450
Ovis canadensis	sheep	17,971–31,450
Antilocapra americana	antelope	15,725–31,450
Lepus sp.	jackrabbit	13,475–15,400
Thomomys sp.	gopher	8,983–10,780
Sylvilagus sp.	rabbit	8,983–9,800
Typha latifolia	pollen, cattail	2,750–9,360
Spermophilus sp.	squirrel	5,390–6,341
Citellus sp.	squirrel	2,837–3,593
Anas sp.	waterbird, ducks	1,975–2,709
Quercus gambelli	seeds, gambel oak	1,488
Descurainia pinnata	seeds, tansymustard	1,307
Pinus monophylla	seeds, piñon pine	841–1,408+
Lewisia rediviva	roots, bitterroot	1,237
Elymus salinas	seeds, salina wild rye	921–1,238
Atriplex nuttalli	seeds, shadscale	1,200
Atriplex confertifolia	seeds, shadscale	1,033
Scirpus sp.	seeds, bulrush	302–1,699
Echinochloa crusgalli	seeds, barnyard grass	702
Lepidium fremontii	seeds, peppergrass	537
Helianthus annuus	seeds, sunflower	467–504

Table 3-3. Post-Encounter Resource Return Rates (*continued*)

Name/location	Type	Return rate (kcal/hr)
Great Basin *continued*		
Poa sp.	seeds, bluegrass	418–91
Elymus salinus	seeds, wild rye	266–473
Oryzopsis hymenoides	seeds, ricegrass	301–92
Phalaris arundinacea	seeds, reed canary grass	261–321
Muhlenbergia asperifolia	seeds, scratchgrass	162–294
Hordeum jubatum	seeds, foxtail barley	138–273
Carex sp.	seeds, sedge	202
Typha latifolia	roots, cattail	128–267
Scirpus sp.	roots, bulrush	160–257
Distichlis stricta	seeds, saltgrass	146–60
Allenrolfea occidentalis	seeds, pickleweed	90–150
Sitanion hystrix	seeds, squirreltail grass	91
Gila bicolor	minnow (with nets)	750–7,514
U.S. Plateau[a]		
Lomatium hendersonii	roots, lomatium	3,831
Lewisia rediviva	roots, bitterroot	1,374
Lomatium cous	roots, biscuitroot	1,219
Lomatium canbyi	roots, Canby's lomatium	143
Perideridia gairdneri	roots, yampah	172
Malaysia		
Dusky leaf monkey	medium fauna	1,620
Banded leaf monkey	medium fauna	1,550
White handed gibbon	medium fauna	1,490
Binturong	medium fauna	1,290
Giant squirrels	small fauna	1,060
Macaques	small fauna	480–780
Squirrels	small fauna	330–480
Birds	small fauna	230
Boreal forest		
Moose and Caribou	large fauna	
Winter		6,050
Spring		11,950
Summer/Fall		5,920
Fall (rut)		11,280
Net fishing	fish	
Winter		1,060
Spring		3,180–9,680
Summer		2,260–5,320
Fall		6,390
Hare snaring	small game	1,900
Muskrats	small game	
Spring trapping		250–2,500
Fall hunting		1,330–2,370
Beaver	small game	
Winter trapping		1,640–5,280
Waterfowl	small game	
Pre-breakup		720
Post-breakup		1,980
Pre-freezeup		1,190
Blueberries	berries	250

Sources: Cane 1987; O'Connell and Hawkes 1981; Simms 1987; Kuchikura 1987; Couture, Ricks, and Housley 1986; Winterhalder 1981; Madsen and Kirkman 1988; Raymond and Sobel 1990 (see also table 3-5).
[a]Processing not included for U.S. Plateau.

per hour. This makes mongongo look less attractive than Lee originally suggested.

The diet-breadth model assumes that a forager will decide on which foods to take based on a knowledge of the quality of different foods and on a knowledge of resource densities (hence search costs) and handling costs (hence return rates). When a forager encounters a resource, he or she must decide either to harvest that resource, or to bypass it and search for something better. This is similar to deciding whether to buy food in the corner convenience store, or to drive to a large supermarket to see if there is a better buy. The diet-breadth model approximates the decision-making process that a forager makes based on the assumption that the goal of foraging is to maximize the overall energy-return rate. The model also assumes that time spent pursuing (harvesting) precludes searching for other resources so that there is an *opportunity cost* to each resource as well, namely, the potential loss of energy or time entailed in choosing to pursue a resource when another resource offering a higher rate of return (or some other nonforaging activity) may be available. The decision to harvest a particular resource depends on the probability (or rather the forager's perception of the probability) of encountering something with a higher return rate. Due to its simplicity and generality, the diet-breadth model has successfully predicted hunter-gatherer diet in a number of instances although at varying levels of precision.[5]

Two applications of the diet-breadth model show how it predicts change in dietary breadth. The first uses four hypothetical resources to show the relationship between search costs and foraging efficiency (table 3-4). The resources in table 3-4 are ranked, *A* through *D,* in terms of their post-encounter return rates (kcal/handling time). If a forager is searching only for resource *A* then his or her net foraging-return rate is 25 kilocalories per

Table 3-4. Search and Handling Costs and Optimal Diet

Resource	Search time (min)	Handling time (min)	Kcal/ unit resource	Post-encounter return rate (kcal/min)	Units encountered in the time it takes to encounter one unit of resource *A*	Net return rate (kcal/min)
A	30 (120)	10	1,000	100	1 (1)	for *A*: 25.0 (7.7)
B	20 (30)	20	800	40	1 (4)	for *A* + *B*: 30.0 (20.0)
C	20	30	800	26	1 (6)	for *A* + *B* + *C*: 28.9 (23.1)
D	10	40	400	10	3 (12)	for *A* + *B* + *C* + *D*: 18.1 (15.9)

minute (1,000 kcal/[30 min search + 10 min handling]). If the forager includes resource B in the diet, then the net foraging-return rate increases to 30 kilocalories per minute ([1,000 kcal for resource A + 800 kcal for resource B]/[30 min search time for both resources + 10 min handling resource A + 20 min handling resource B]). Since resource C provides a lower post-encounter return rate than that achieved by taking only resources A and B, it should not be included in the diet. As the table shows, if it were added, the net foraging efficiency would actually decrease to 28.9 kilocalories per minute ([1,000 kcal for resource A + 800 kcal for resource B + 800 kcal for resource C]/[30 min search + 10 min handling for resource A + 20 min handling for resource B + 30 min handling for resource C]). Resources C and D should be ignored even though they will be encountered more frequently than resources A and B.

Decreasing the search costs of resources C or D (i.e., making these resources more abundant) has no effect on the predicted diet breadth. But increasing the search costs of resources A and B, making them rarer, increases diet breadth. In table 3-4 the numbers in parentheses reflect changes in the number of units of a resource that are encountered and in the net foraging-return rate if the search costs of resources A and B are increased to 120 and 30 minutes, respectively. For example, where previously only one unit of resource C was encountered in the time it took to locate one unit of resource A, now six units of it are encountered in the time it takes to find one of resource A. Maximum foraging efficiency is now achieved when resource C is included in the diet (23.1 kcal/min). As expected, when high-ranked resources become rarer, diet breadth expands.

A second example shows the application of the diet-breadth model to an ethnographic situation, that of the Ache (Hawkes, Hill, and O'Connell 1982). As pointed out in the first example, maximizing the rate of energy acquisition means that the forager adds encountered resources to the diet until the return rate of the nth resource (E_i/H_i) and its handling cost is equal to or greater than the overall return from foraging (E/T); that is, different resources are added to the diet as long as $E/T \leq E_i/H_i$, where:

E = total kcal acquired while foraging
T = total foraging time (search, gathering, and processing)
E_i = kcal available in a unit of resource i
H_i = handling time per unit of resource i

Table 3-5. Ache Diet over Two Months

Resource	μ_i (kg)	E_i (kcal/kg)	H_i (hr/kg)	Return rate (kcal/hr)	Total handling time ($\mu_i \times H_i$)	Rank
Peccary[a]	232	1,950	.03	65,000	7.0	1
Deer	300	819	.03	27,300	9.0	1
Paca	307	1,950	.28	6,964	86.0	2
Coati	351	1,950	.28	6,964	98.3	2
Armadillo	386	1,950	.33	5,909	127.4	3
Snake	10	1,000	.17	5,882	1.7	3
Oranges	1,283	355	.07	5,071	89.8	4
Bird	35	1,240	.26	4,769	8.7	5
Honey	57	3,037	.93	3,266	52.5	6
Peccary[b]	457	1,950	.71	2,746	324.5	7
Palm larvae	43	3,124	1.32	2,367	56.8	8
Fish	189	975	.46	2,120	86.9	9
Palm heart	171	595	.39	1,526	66.7	10
Monkey	533	1,300	1.07	1,215	570.3	11
Palm fiber	1,377	120	.10	1,200	137.7	11
Palm fruit	249	350	.37	946	94.6	12

Source: Hawkes, Hill, and O'Connell 1982:table 3.
[a]Collared peccary.
[b]White-lipped peccary.

The overall return from foraging changes as different resources are added to the diet:

$$E/T = \frac{\sum \mu_i - E_i - T_s}{T_s + \sum \mu_i - H_i - T_s} = \frac{\sum \mu_i - E_i}{1 + \sum \mu_i - H_i}$$

where T_s is the total search time for all resources and μ is the amount of the *i*th resource. If an encountered resource provides a lower return rate than that being experienced by the forager, it should be ignored.

The characteristics of sixteen resources consumed by Ache on sixty-one foraging days are shown in table 3-5. These data were recorded from a total of 3,673 hours of search time and 1,024 hours of carrying time (carrying food back to camp). In figure 3-4, the upper curve plots the return rate (E_i/H_i) for each of the resources assembled along the *x*-axis by their rank. The lower curve plots the changing values of the overall foraging-return rate (E/T). For example, the foraging-return rate for collared peccary and deer is (232 × 1,950 = 452,400) + (300 × 819 = 245,700) divided by (3,673 search hr + 1,024 carrying hr + 16 handling hr) = 148 kcal/hr. Adding paca and coati to the diet, kilocalories increase by 1,283,100 to 1,980,800;

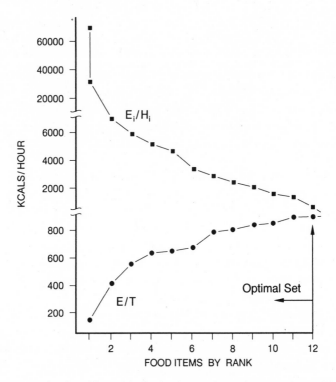

Figure 3-4. A diet-breadth model of Ache diet. Redrawn from Hawkes, Hill, and O'Connell 1982 by Dan Delaney. Reproduced by permission of the American Anthropological Association from *American Ethnologist* 9(2), May 1982. Not for further distribution.

likewise the cost increases by 184.3 handling hours which produces an overall foraging-return rate of 405 kilocalories per hour. With incremental additions of the remaining resources to the diet we find that the curves intersect at about 870 kilocalories per hour. The Ache should not take any resource with a return rate below 870 kilocalories per hour, and do not appear to do so. The diet-breadth model predicts the Ache's choice of food items while on foraging treks in the forest.

The diet-breadth model suggests several nonintuitive conclusions, the most important of which is that a resource's abundance alone cannot be used to predict whether it will be utilized. No matter how frequently the Ache encounter a resource with a return rate below 870 kilocalories per hour they would not be expected to use it. More specifically, the model points out that the decision to include a resource depends on the abundance of higher-ranked resources. An increase in the search costs of a higher-return-rate resource decreases overall harvesting efficiency and results in a diet expansion, *regardless of the abundance of the lower-ranked resource*. At the "Man the Hunter" conference, Birdsell wondered why it was that hunter-gatherers do not concentrate on resources such as mice, which in terms of sheer biomass are more abundant than deer (Lee and DeVore 1968:95). The answer should now be clear: the return rate of harvesting a tiny, burrowing animal is so low that there are many far more efficient resources to be used even if they are less abundant.

Conversely, if a higher-ranked resource becomes available, a lower-ranked resource will be dropped from the diet, regardless of its abundance. This may account for why the Ju/'hoansi occasionally leave mongongo nuts rotting on the ground (Lee 1968:33). Do the Ju/'hoansi have so much food that they do not need the nuts? Given mongongo's low return rate (once processing time is taken into account, as we noted above), the Ju/'hoansi may ignore mongongo not because it is abundant, but because of the availability of another resource with a higher return rate.

The diet-breadth model also forces us to consider the actual return rates of different resources, and can thus point to circumstances in which we can predict use of a resource despite what our ethnocentrisms may predispose us to believe. Take the use of insects, for example. Some hunter-gatherers consume a significant number of insects during particular times of the year (Hayden 1981b). Western Desert Aborigines of Australia relished the witchetty grub, and Aborigines living in the southeastern Australian highlands collected the fat-rich bogong moth (Flood 1980). The Mono and Paiute of the southern Sierra Nevada in California harvested caterpillars (Fowler and Walter 1985), while elsewhere in the Great Basin, Paiute and Shoshone gathered fly larvae (*kutsavi*) and grasshoppers from the shores of lakes where they washed ashore forming long windrows (Heizer 1950; Madsen and Kirkman 1988; Sutton 1985). Some Shoshone, Paiute, Cheyenne, and Assiniboine held grasshopper drives. Only a few experimental studies have been conducted with these resources, but they suggest that at times, insects can provide remarkably high return rates; grasshoppers, for example, can provide over 270,000 kilocalories per hour (Madsen and Kirkman 1988)—certainly placing them, at these times, high above other food resources.

The diet-breadth model predicts diet diversity, but it does not explicitly predict how frequently an item will be in the diet. For example, though collared peccary is the highest-ranked resource in the Ache's menu (while on treks in the forest), it does not make up the bulk of Ache diet. And Winterhalder found that the overall amount of a resource harvested by the Cree in the boreal forest did not correlate with the total biomass of that resource (1981). The diet-breadth model only proposes that all high-ranked items will be taken *when encountered,* but if they are encountered rarely they will make up only a small portion of the diet. How frequently a resource is encountered, of course, depends largely on its actual density, but its encounter rate can be affected by other factors. For example, in the boreal forest, heavy snow, especially if it has a crust, reduces moose mobility, making them easier to pursue, but making them harder to find since they move less and do not leave long trails. Since hunters search for tracks, rather than the moose itself (Winterhalder 1981:73), heavy snowfall can reduce the encounter rate for moose without altering the actual density of the resource itself. (However, given a known encounter rate, the value of a food item, and the total amount of time spent foraging, it should be possible to predict the amount of each resource in a diet.)

The diet-breadth model appears to be sufficiently simple and general to be a powerful explanatory model, but it is not without its difficulties and limitations. The Ache case study described above points to one of its methodological difficulties. To test the diet-breadth model, the researcher needs data on resources that may not be in the diet. But if a resource is not used, information on that resource's search-and-handling costs will not be available. A diet-breadth model could then appear to be accurate when in fact it is not. Consider the Ache case. If there are resources in the Ache environment that provide return rates higher than 870 kilocalories per hour, but are for some reason not taken (perhaps because they are tabooed), then the Ache could violate the optimal diet model without the researcher being aware of it (Hill et al. 1987:4).

This dilemma can be overcome in two ways. The first is to obtain return rates for all reasonable food resources. This would be beyond the limits of practicality in most cases. However, experiments can be set up under field conditions to answer questions about the trade-offs between specific resources. Hawkes, O'Connell, and Blurton Jones used this approach in a study of Hadza subsistence. Hadza men normally hunt or scavenge large game for an average post-encounter return rate of about one kilogram per hour. Do they maximize their return rate by ignoring small game? Since they do not normally take small game, the question cannot be confidently answered with data from routine Hadza foraging. Therefore, Hawkes, O'Connell, and Blurton Jones asked some experienced Hadza men to spend some time *only* taking small game (1991). The data from this experiment showed that the average return for most small game was significantly below one kilogram per hour: Hadza hunters do appear to maximize the return rate from hunting by ignoring small game.

A second approach is to use the models to predict behavior under different circumstances so that the models predict changes in diet breadth. While some criticize the analysis of foraging trips that make use of shotguns or a researcher's vehicle (Dwyer 1985a), such forays can provide the researcher with tests of foraging models. A researcher's vehicle, for example, can reduce search or travel time. Assuming that the nonvehicle search time was already known, the researcher should be able to predict which resources will fall out of the diet as a function of decreased search or travel time, thus testing the foraging models. Likewise, a change in weapons can alter pursuit time and thus the predicted diet breadth. Hill and Hawkes show that Ache diet breadth changes when shotguns are used instead of bow and arrows (1983). Since shotguns kill more quickly and do not require as uncluttered a line of sight as does an arrow or blowgun in the forest, they should decrease pursuit time, increase harvest efficiency, raise the E/T curve (refer to figure 3-4) and reduce diet diversity. As expected, the Ache do indeed decrease their diet breadth when shotguns are used, ignoring monkeys and small birds (Hill and Hawkes 1983). Hill and his associates also found that they could predict how the Ache would respond to particular hunting situations given an understanding of how a particular situation (e.g., weather conditions) alters a resource's search cost or return rate (1987:24–26). Ache diet also changes in predictable ways from season to season as the abundance of specific resources (and thus their search costs) changes (Hill et al. 1984). Winterhalder shows that as search time decreases with the use of snowmobiles, Cree diet becomes more specialized (1981); resources that would have been pursued while hunting on snowshoes are ignored when snowmobiles permit rapid travel to, for example, good moose-hunting areas. Similarly, O'Connell and Hawkes used the diet-breadth model to predict that seeds should drop out of Australian Aboriginal diet as soon as commercial flour becomes available due to the high processing costs of the indigenous seeds (1981, 1984). They also predicted that seeds should enter and leave the diet as droughts alter the availability of higher-ranked resources. Their predictions have received some support by John Altman, who found that seeds and other plant foods dropped out of Gunwinggu diet as soon as flour and sugar became available (1984), and by Pate (1986), who found that seeds entered and left Ngadadjara diet as a result of climate-induced changes in the availability of higher-ranked resources. (Although he found that the relationship between drought and resource availability was not quite as O'Connell and Hawkes expected, their prediction was nonetheless upheld.)

Where the diet-breadth model falls short in its predictive power, it is probably because human foraging often violates one or more of the model's conditions. The model's most important condition is a *fine-grained encounter* foraging pattern, that is, that a forager encounters food items in proportion to the density of those resources. If a resource makes up 25 percent of all resources in an environment, then foragers should encounter it 25 percent of the time they are foraging. There are actually two assumptions made here, one about the environment and one about the forager. First, the model assumes that resources are homogeneously distributed. This is rarely true, for the distribution of food resources is controlled by microclimatic and topographic conditions, resulting in a patchy distribution. Second, the model assumes that hunter-gatherers search their environment randomly. This, too, is rarely the case. Foragers normally set out with a particular goal in mind. Random, "let's see what's out there" forays also occur, but it is unlikely that hunter-gatherers would frequently take this kind of risk unless they were unable to predict their environment well (and the degree to which foragers can predict the location of food is not a constant). However, a particular foraging goal is probably based on the likelihood of encountering a resource—the higher the probability of encountering a resource (given a forager's knowledge of current conditions and resource characteristics), the higher the likelihood that the forager will go after that resource. Thus, the diet-breadth model's condition of a fine-grained encounter may approximate the end result of a forager's decision-making process over the long term. (This could make the diet-breadth model useful to archaeologists, who always deal with long-term aggregates of data.)

Nonetheless, since the diet-breadth model is best applied to circumstances where the condition of fine-grained encounter is clearly valid, another approach is needed to model other conditions.

The patch-choice model
The patch-choice model assumes that resources are dispersed in patches rather than homogeneously across a landscape. Like the diet-breadth model, it assumes that patches are encountered sequentially and randomly, in direct proportion to their frequency in the environment. The model also assumes that a forager does not return to a patch until its resources are rejuvenated, and

that travel time between patches is nonproductive. The patch–choice model asks, which resource patches (as opposed to resources) should be included in a foray? The patch–choice model is similar to the diet-breadth model in that patch types can be ranked in terms of the energetic return per unit time. It differs from the diet-breadth model in that the time spent searching a patch for resources is included in calculating a patch's overall return rate.

Thus, linked to the patch-choice model is the question of when a forager should quit searching in one patch and move on to another. In the simplest case, when a forager first enters a patch, net resource-harvest rate is high. But as the resources are gathered, the encounter and net harvest rates decrease; eventually the forager reaches a point of diminishing returns (Charnov 1976; Winterhalder 1987:323). Moving to another patch returns the forager to a higher rate of resource harvest. Moving on, however, takes time and energy. Therefore, the cost of moving and encountering another patch must be balanced against the benefit of continuing to forage in the current patch. To maximize their net rate of resource harvest, the *marginal-value theorem* predicts that foragers will move out of a resource patch when the rate of harvest in that patch falls below the average rate for the entire environment (the entire population of potential resource patches, with travel time included), rather than when the return rate in the current patch has fallen to zero.

Although the actual solution is derived mathematically, figure 3-5 gives an idea as to how the marginal-value theorem predicts when a forager should leave a patch. In the figure the slope of line R, the *Mean Environmental Return Rate,* is the average of the resource-return rates for all patches in the environment, taking travel time between patches into account. (This line theoretically intersects the x-axis at a point that is the mean travel time between resource patches.) The two concave-downward curves show the change over time in the net returns in two patches with different overall return rates. The return rate of any point along these curves is the slope of a line tangent to the curve at that point (Charnov 1976). The point of intersection between a line parallel to line R but tangent to a net-resource-harvest curve indicates the length of time a forager should spend in a patch. Thus, the dotted lines indicate (on the x-axis) the length of time a forager should stay in patch *A* or *B*. We can see that foragers would remain longer in patch *B* (up to T_b) than patch *A* (leave after only T_a length of time); but in either case they would leave before complete resource depletion occurs.[6]

The curves shown in figure 3-5 describe a simple case of diminishing returns; other patch types will have different net-resource-harvest curves (see figure 3-6). In some foraging patches, open-ocean fishing, for example, the

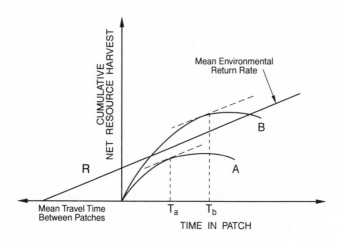

Figure 3-5. Graphic representation of the marginal-value theorem. Line R, the Mean Environmental Return Rate, is the average net return rate for the environment (including travel time between patches). The two concave-downward curves (A and B) show the change in returns for two foraging patches, one more productive than the other. The marginal-value theorem predicts that a forager should spend less time in A than in B. Drawn by Dan Delaney.

net resource harvest could increase linearly with length of time spent in the patch as the fisherman may not have a significant effect on the density of fish (case A in figure 3-6). Alternatively, net resource harvest could increase linearly with time spent in the patch until a point is reached at which the net rate of return drops immediately to zero, and no further gain in net resource return is made (case B in figure 3-6). This may be a fairly common situation in human foraging. Consider a forager collecting seeds from a single stand of grass of constant density, the limits of which are visible to the forager when he or she comes upon it. The forager could collect all the grass seed and work all the while at a constant rate of intake, and a steadily increasing net resource harvest until the field is depleted. The marginal-value theorem is applicable only in the case of diminishing returns (case C in figure 3-6). We will return to the difference between these cases in chapter 4.

There are no true anthropological tests of the patch–choice model largely because foragers do not encounter patches randomly, but instead choose where they will forage before leaving camp. Nonetheless, the model suggests that foragers should choose the highest-return-rate patches given their environmental knowledge. E. Smith found some support for this version of the patch-choice model in that the Inujjuamiut tend to use the resource habitat

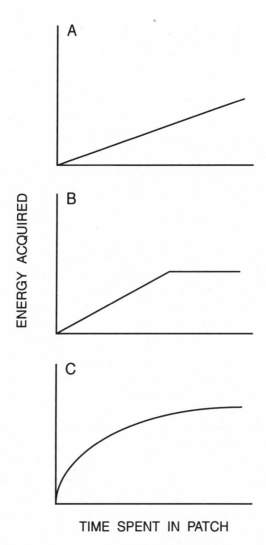

Figure 3-6. Three simple resource-harvest curves: (A) indefinite linear, (B) limited linear, and (C) diminishing returns. The marginal-value theorem applies only to (C). Redrawn from Kaplan and Hill 1992 by Dan Delaney. Used with permission from E. Smith and B. Winterhalder, eds., *Evolutionary Ecology and Human Behavior* (New York: Aldine de Gruyter), copyright © 1992.

or patch (saltwater, freshwater, sea ice, inland) that provides the highest return rate at a given time of the year, whether data are aggregated by season
or by month (1991). However, these tests were not conclusive, as the correlation between time spent in a habitat or patch and mean seasonal or monthly
return rate was not very strong. Rather than selecting patches or habitats,
Smith argued, the Inujjuamiut allocate their time to hunt types (ocean netting, summer canoe hunting, rod fishing, winter caribou, etc.). Hunt types
can be considered different resource patches since a decision to conduct a
certain kind of hunt limits the range of resources by limiting where a hunter
goes and the equipment he carries. Aggregating the data by season, and considering hunt types to be patches, Smith found some support (although the
pattern was not strong) for the hypothesis that the Inujjuamiut allocate more
time to hunt types that provide the higher return rates.

Likewise, there are no true tests of the marginal-value theorem. This is
partly because of the data needed, such as return rates for all potential resource patches and the mean travel time between patches. But it is also
because the central assumption is that travel time between patches is nonproductive. This is not always true, and may in fact be true only rarely. Winterhalder found that the Cree, who hunt for moose in particular patches, do not
search their environment patch by patch but, where possible, travel between
potential hunting patches searching for moose tracks, which they then follow into a patch (1981). Additionally, the absolute density of game in different forest patch types is not adequate for predicting Cree use of the patch
types because other characteristics of a patch type affect the density of prey
in a patch. Patches with thick brush in them are ignored because, while
moose may be present there, the Cree cannot move through them without
making much noise and scaring the moose away. For all intents and purposes,
these patches contain no game. Consequently, Winterhalder found that the
Cree did *not* make as generalized a use of different habitat patches as was
predicted. This did not, however, point to a deficiency in the patch-choice
model as much as it pointed to the difficulty of making the model realistic
for a particular situation. Tentative support for the marginal-value theorem
can be found in the fact that Cree hunters leave patches before depletion
occurs.

Hawkes, Hill, and O'Connell made a different use of the marginal-value
theorem (1982:391–92). As Smith had done for hunt types, Hawkes and her
associates considered individual resources as patches. The Ache often cease
to collect or pursue a resource that is theoretically part of the diet in order
to search for something else. That is, the pursuit of one resource does not
preclude the possibility of searching for others and changing plans accord-

ingly—a violation of the diet-breadth model, but a common feature of human foraging. Thus, Hawkes and her co-workers asked under what conditions the Ache should continue pursuing a resource if they encountered another during the pursuit. As we might expect, while pursuing a peccary or monkey, the Ache continually decide whether the resources they pass by will provide greater returns than that which they are pursuing given the amount of time they have already put into the pursuit.

This situation can be modeled by treating hunting as if it were a patch (Hill et al. 1987). A nongame resource is expected to be taken while searching for game if its return rate is not below that expected from hunting. In their initial study, Hawkes, Hill, and O'Connell determined the average return from hunting (i.e., for the hunting patch) to be 1,115 kilocalories per hour, including search, pursuit, and processing costs (1982). Resources such as oranges (4,438 kcal/hr), honey (3,231 kcal/hr), or palm larvae (1,849 kcal/hr) should be and are taken by the Ache while searching for game (in patch returns here take search and handling time into account, thus the overall return rates are lower than those in table 3-5 where only handling time is taken into account). Once a collared peccary is sighted, however, no other resources are sought or pursued since the potential return from the peccary (65,000 kcal/hr) is higher than that of other resources. However, the longer the pursuit continues, the lower the return rate will be if the peccary is captured and, consequently, the greater the probability that other resources will be taken if encountered late in the hunt. Thus, the patch-choice model as used by Hill and his co-workers may be a more accurate predictor of behavior the longer the actual pursuit and thus the higher the opportunity costs of a resource (Hill et al. 1987:18). Nonetheless, this use of the patch-choice model duplicated the results obtained using the diet-breadth model (see above).

This exercise points to three ways in which human foraging is different from the nonhuman foraging behavior that was the original focus of foraging models:

(1) Human hunters often pursue game for a longer time than do non-human predators (Hill et al. 1987:17). Nonhuman carnivores seem to make "decisions" as to whether or not they will capture prey very soon (often within moments) after beginning pursuit. Human hunters, on the other hand, not being very fast or capable of bringing down large prey physically, use poison or bleeding to kill prey slowly. Most bows and arrows or spears do not kill large animals quickly, but only weaken them, over time, to the point where they can be dispatched.

Therefore human hunting involves techniques that require longer pursuit times and hence higher opportunity costs than anticipated by the
diet-breadth model.

(2) Among humans, resource processing often occurs at times when resources cannot be sought, for example, after dark, or during inclement
weather (Hill et al. 1987:17). Processing costs in many cases should not be
included in determining the comparative opportunity costs of resources.
Additionally, resource processing may be done by someone other than
the one who is searching for and pursuing food. It is not uncommon, for
example, for hunters to make a kill, then send someone back to camp to
call others to do the butchering and carrying (whether they do this or not
depends on the size of the animal, the distance back to camp, and the
number of potential bearers there). This effectively raises a resource's return rate (by lowering its handling time) vis-à-vis the hunters since, as far
as they are concerned, the processing time is almost zero.

(3) While the rate of food acquisition is important, the total amount of
food obtained is also relevant. Hill and his co-workers pointed out that
armadillos yield higher individual return rates than peccaries (17,520 vs.
5,514 kcal/hr; 1987: 21–22). However, a very high return rate does not
matter if the sought-after resource does not result in the acquisition of
sufficient calories. Recovering a peccary results in a higher net return
than an armadillo (29,040 vs. 3,504 kcal). In addition, searching for
peccaries yields higher daily return rates, since other resources can be
searched out and possibly pursued while tracking pigs. Understandably,
Ache men prefer to encounter peccaries rather than armadillos (but see
below and chapter 5 on the importance of large game for sharing).

The patch-choice model and marginal-value theorem may predict behavior when balancing one resource against another rather than one resource
against the average for the environment. Foragers know (with varying degrees of probability) when and where particular resources are available. They
balance what they are currently doing against the costs and benefits of alternatives. To give a hypothetical example, imagine a group of foragers collecting bulrush seeds in a marsh. At first, they can collect many seeds quickly,
and their return rate can be quite high. As the denser stands of bulrush are
harvested and they turn to less dense stands on the edge of the marsh, the
return rate declines. While collecting the seeds, the foragers notice that there
are quite a few minnows in the water which they can catch if they go back
to camp and get their net. The foragers also know that they can travel into

the foothills and collect ricegrass seeds. The patch-choice model predicts that when the return rate from bulrush collecting is equivalent to that of netting minnows (adding in the time to go back to camp to get the net) or ricegrass seeds (adding in the travel time to the foothills), then the foragers should quit collecting the seeds, get their net and go after the fish or travel into the foothills and collect ricegrass (assuming that the highest return rates for minnows and ricegrass are each below that of bulrush seeds).

It should be clear that optimal-foraging models are ultimately aimed at reconstructing the on-the-ground decision-making process of foraging (Mithen 1989, 1990). The patch-choice model and the diet-breadth model may be profitably used for this purpose to model diet in a hierarchical fashion, with the former used to predict which areas should be targeted for foraging and the latter to predict which resources in those patches should be used (assuming there is more than one resource type in a patch). While optimal foraging provides anthropology with a powerful first generation of models, it is also clear that assumptions made by the models require that they be modified to take into account what we know to be true of human hunting and gathering.

The role of information

The patch-choice and diet-breadth models both assume that foragers search the environment randomly and simultaneously for all food resources. But foragers usually have some idea of where they are going and what they are going to do during the day before they leave camp; they rarely move at random. While foraging, men and women note the presence of plants, animal tracks, spoor, water sources, burrows, and nests, later sharing this information with others.[7] In northern Australia's Arnhem Land, men out hunting took account of "trees with bee hives in them, and those bearing fruits or nuts. They told the women about these later" (McCarthy and McArthur 1960:153). Adrian Tanner was once told by Mistassini Cree hunters "the sex and age of [an] animal and where it would be found two days before the hunt occurred" on the basis of various signs seen around camp (Tanner 1979:55).

However, the ability to predict the environment on a day-to-day basis is not a constant. A distinction can be made between *perfect* and *complete* information (see E. Smith 1991:58–61). With perfect information a forager knows *exactly* what the outcome of a particular strategy will be. Complete information is knowledge that is sufficient to allow one to predict with a certain *probability* the outcome of a particular choice, for example, the chance that caribou will be in a particular valley, or the chance that salmon will be running during a particular week of the year (this is the kind of information with which gamblers work). It is most likely that foragers operate with complete information about their environment and thus are normally acting in terms of strategies that they think have a high probability of success (or at least a higher probability than alternative strategies).

As a simplifying assumption, informational constraints are usually relaxed in optimal-foraging models, but we can see that when they are included they will have an effect on model predictions. The locations of plant foods, for example, can usually be predicted more easily than those of animals. Information obtained today about plants will be useful tomorrow, while today's information about game may help direct a hunter's foray tomorrow but may not guarantee success. In general, as dependence on hunting increases, women spend more time in camp tending to food processing and material repair (since they are probably not hunting—see chapter 7) and men's forays will depend more on their own knowledge of the environment, or may become more random, depending on the degree to which game locations can be predicted. It is not uncommon, therefore, for Arctic and subarctic hunter-gatherers to make specific information-collecting trips to determine the location of game. In the spring the Nunamiut search widely to determine the movement of caribou (Binford 1978:169). The Chipewyan and Cree make trips specifically to search for signs of large game to determine when and where to move camp (Heffley 1981; Winterhalder 1981), and where to hunt in years to come (Tanner 1979:133).

The degree to which resources can be predicted requires that more or less effort be put into information-gathering (thus, a trade-off is made between procuring food now and collecting information to ensure the collection of food later). Some variability in hunter-gatherers' diets is probably a function of the degree to which perfect versus complete information can be gathered about the potential food resources. None of this contradicts optimal-foraging theory, but it does mean that the patch structure of an environment is to be measured not only in terms of the physical distribution of food resources but also in terms of foragers' knowledge of those resources.

Individual versus aggregated data

The Ache diet-breadth data presented earlier were from both men and women, old and young; yet in an evolutionary framework, the individual should be the unit of analysis. Foragers' capabilities are a product of a number of factors: their age and physical/mental condition, whether they have children with them on a foray, whether women are breastfeeding infants, and so forth (Hill et al. 1985; Hurtado et al. 1985; Mithen 1989; E. Smith 1983). Middle-aged Ache men, for example, have higher return rates than either young or old men (Hill et al. 1987; see also Dwyer 1983; Ohtsuka 1989). Individuals within a foraging group may have different strategies for different purposes (creating the potential for evolutionarily stable strategies). What is the unit of analysis for assessing the validity of optimal-foraging models? What would happen, as E. Smith asks (1983), if the Ache data were analyzed in terms of individuals?

Jochim argues that optimal-foraging studies should always at least separate male from female foraging strategies since the effective environment of each sex is different (1988). Female foragers tend not to hunt, and instead focus on highly reliable resources such as plants, shellfish, and small game; men tend to seek out riskier large game (see chapter 5 for discussion). Data could also be aggregated in terms of other groups of foragers (e.g., old versus young, married versus unmarried) depending on the type of questions being asked. An a priori decision (on the part of a group of foragers) to limit foraging activity by certain members to certain resources means that it would be inappropriate to model one sex or age group with all resources actually available since some of them will, for all intents and purposes, not be available.

We must also ask, over what time period should data be analyzed, or, in other words, how long does it take a forager to obtain an optimal diet? There will always be variance in the kinds and amounts of resources harvested from day to day, season to season, and year to year. Hunter-gatherers frequently gorge on certain resources, especially meat and honey. Over the course of a year a group may eat a diversified diet, but at any one time people may consume a very limited number of food items. What should be the time period studied? We have few data to guide us here, although Smith's analysis of Inujjuamiut diet pointed out that the diet-breadth model was a more accurate predictor of diet over fine as opposed to coarse temporal (and spatial) scales.[8]

Risk

In recent years, the concept of risk has assumed prominence in anthropological studies of hunter-gatherer peoples, since no environment is constant from season to season or from year to year.[9] Winters may be mild one year and severe the next; summers may be wet one year and dry the next; migratory species such as salmon or caribou may arrive late, or not at all. Risk is usually defined as unpredictable variation in some ecological or economic variable (over time and/or space). Hunter-gatherers respond to risky situations by altering their diets as the range of resources and conditions change. As a consequence, a hunter-gatherer lifeway is not static, but variable, even over short periods of time.

To respond to conditions of risky resources, Brian Hayden argues (1981a,b), hunter-gatherers diversify their resource base and in so doing make it more stable and reliable. With a variety of resources in the diet, if one fails, another will be available. Hayden sees the appearance in prehistory of broad-based economies as a product of our species' continual struggle to increase subsistence reliability through technology that permits diversification (e.g., seed grinding, fishing technology, storage). The diet-breadth model, however, argues that diversification does not result from a conscious desire to reduce risk, but from a reduction in the availability of high-ranked resources. Moreover, optimal-foraging simulations conclude that under some conditions energy-maximization diets (those predicted by the diet-breadth model) are the same as risk-minimization diets (Winterhalder 1986a), although empirical tests are still needed.[10] The sharing of resources may also reduce variance in foraging returns more effectively than diet diversification (see chapter 5).

But risk does play a role in the decision-making process that optimal-foraging models try to approximate. Humans rarely have perfect information (as defined above) about their environment, which means that they never really forage optimally, but base decisions on their best guesses. Depending on conditions, foragers may want to minimize the time spent foraging, maximize net returns from a day of foraging, or reduce the risk of coming home empty-handed; in some circumstances, foragers may even seek risk (see chapter 5 for a further discussion of subsistence and risk).

Steven Mithen uses a simulation that contains elements of the diet-breadth model but includes the conflicting demands of increasing long-term returns and reducing the risk of going without any daily return (1989, 1990). In his simulation, the ability to make decisions about food selection is affected by the forager's own expertise and knowledge of local conditions combined with the knowledge of others. The individual forager is the unit of analysis in Mithen's computer simulation, and activities are modeled on a minute-by-minute basis. The forager's goals can change as the day goes by depending on what has happened earlier in the day and depending on how the forager sees the place of the day's activities in achieving some long-term goal. The model simulates the activities of several individuals who share information among themselves, and all of whom try to increase long-term return rates while reducing the risk of going without any food on a daily basis. Therefore, a forager in the model decides to harvest a resource based on (1) how much food has already been acquired that day, (2) whether the resource can be procured given the amount of time remaining in the day and the forager's knowledge of the energetic cost of pursuing the resource (as opposed to searching for and possibly pursuing others in the time remaining), and (3) a desire to bring back at least a minimal amount of food each day. Applying his model to the Valley Bisa of east Africa, Mithen found a close agreement between the ethnographic data and a model containing both a long-term goal of increasing individual foraging efficiency and a short-term goal of reducing the risk of going without food completely.

It is important to remember that risk can refer to several different phenomena. Resources can vary in their *intensity* (how much variance over time there is in a resource's abundance), *frequency* (how frequently a resource's abundance fluctuates below or above a given level, e.g., two standard deviations from the mean abundance), *spatial extent* (how large an area is affected by a particular resource's fluctuations), and *predictability* (how much can be known in advance about a resource's future condition); this last dimension could be broken down into both temporal and spatial categories. When many authors refer to *risk* or *stress* they often are using an amalgam of these different dimensions. Usually, *risk* is taken to mean the chance of going without enough food, and *stress* refers to periods when this happens. But since resources can vary in different ways, there are also different kinds of risk and stress (see Cashdan 1992 for a review). The effect of risk on optimal-diet models is just beginning to be studied (see Stephens 1990).

Should energy be the currency?

There has been considerable debate over the utility of energy as a currency in foraging models.[11] As noted in our discussion of linear programming, some think that a range of nutrients should be included in the modeling process, especially if energy is easy to come by. Applying Occam's razor, others insist that energy is a sufficient dietary currency.

To survive, humans need certain amounts of five basic nutrients: carbohydrates, lipids, proteins, minerals, and vitamins. However, it is by no means clear how much of various nutrients are required by human populations. Many human populations are consistently deficient (or overindulging) in cal-

Table 3-6. Adult Caloric Consumption and Mean Body Size

Group	Males		Females		Per person kcal consumption	Reference
	Ht.(m)	Wt.(kg)	Ht.(m)	Wt.(kg)		
Ache	1.61	59.6	1.50	51.8	3,827	Hurtado and Hill 1987, 1990
Hiwi	1.54	59.0	1.45	48.0	2,043	Hurtado and Hill 1987, 1990
Ju/'hoansi	1.60	49.0	1.50	41.0	2,355	Hurtado and Hill 1987, 1990
Anbarra	1.70	59.9	1.60	47.4	2,150	Meehan 1977
Onge[a]					1,740	Bose 1964
Efe[b]	1.45	42.9			2,848	Bailey and Peacock 1988
Efe[b]			1.36	37.8	2,509	Bailey and Peacock 1988
≠Kade G/wi	1.59	54.6	1.49	49.6	1,800–2,300	Tanaka 1980

[a] For entire population of 41 over a one-month period.
[b] For dry season only, based on mean caloric intake per kg body weight for population as a whole.

ories or certain minerals or vitamins, according to standardized measures, such as the U.S. recommended daily allowance or those of the World Health Organization (WHO). According to WHO standards, the Efe consume 26 percent more calories and 138 percent more protein than needed (Bailey and Peacock 1988). Hunter-gatherers also often consume large quantities of one particular resource, especially meat or honey, and the long-term physiological consequences of this is unknown. For the most part, a reasonably diverse diet of sufficient calories probably provides a sufficiency of necessary nutrients.

Given these difficulties, calories might be the most parsimonious and realistic dietary currency. However, human daily caloric requirements are not known with certainty; 2,000 kilocalories per day is often used as a basic adult requirement, but the actual amount depends on age, sex, body size, activity level, pregnancy or lactation, and environmental parameters such as average daily temperature. Caloric intake can vary seasonally as well, sometimes quite dramatically (Hurtado and Hill 1990; Lee 1979; Meehan 1982; Wilmsen 1982). Table 3-6 provides some idea of the variability in hunter-gatherer mean daily caloric intakes.

Humans know when they are not getting enough calories—they become hungry. We might expect, therefore, that where plant food provides the bulk of calories, that only a shortage of plant food would lead people to talk of starvation, but we would be wrong. Even in plant-dependent societies, hunter-gatherers still refer to the lack of meat in camp as a time of hunger and starvation (see Silberbauer 1981b:494; Shostak 1981). Even though hunting frequently provides very meager returns (see table 3-7), all foragers value the act of hunting highly (Dwyer 1985b). Despite the importance of plant

Table 3-7. Meat Consumption and Hunting Success

Group	Consumption kg/day/person	Kg/hr/ hunter	Kg/day/ hunter	Success rate (%)[a]	Reference
		Return rates			
Etolo	1.23	.2–.3			Dwyer 1983
Ache	1.78		1		Hill et al. 1985; Hurtado et al. 1985
Ache (bow)		.53			Hill and Hawkes 1983
Ache (shotgun)		1.60			Hill and Hawkes 1983
Ache (hands)		.27			Hill and Hawkes 1983
Yanomamo (bow)	.21–.49	.48	3.9		Hames and Vickers 1982
Yanomamo (shotgun)		1.35			Hames and Vickers 1982
Ye'kwana			13.3		Hames and Vickers 1982
Siona–Secoya			16.8	85	Vickers 1989
Bisa			25	9–33	Marks 1976
Hiwi			3.6		Hurtado and Hill 1987
Ju/'hoansi	.46	.66	2.6	23	Lee 1979, 1982
≠Kade G/wi (snares)			.48	20	Wilmsen and Durham 1988
≠Kade G/wi (archery)			2.9	16	Wilmsen and Durham 1988
≠Kade G/wi	.30				Tanaka 1980
Kutse Bushmen				38	Kent 1993
Efe (monkey hunts)	.42[b]			30	Bailey 1991
Efe (ambush hunts)	.20[c]			11	Bailey 1991
Efe (group hunts)	.26[d]				Bailey 1991
Efe (archery)			.33		Terashima 1983
BaMbuti (nets)		.12–.39			Ichikawa 1983
BaMbuti (nets)		.12			Terashima 1983
BaMbuti (archery)		.11			Terashima 1983
BaMbuti (nets)	.45	.22			Hart 1978
BaMbuti (archery)	.11–.17			52	Harako 1981
BaMbuti (nets)		.37		61	Harako 1981
BaMbuti (nets)	1.06	.38	2.6	100	Tanno 1976
BaMbuti (spears)	.22	.63			Harako 1981
Anbarra	.55				Meehan 1977b, 1982
Ngadadjara	.56				Gould 1980
G/wi	.29				Silberbauer 1981a, 1981b
Agta (male)				17	Estioko-Griffin and Griffin 1985; Goodman et al. 1985
Agta (female)				31	Estioko-Griffin and Griffin 1985; Goodman et al. 1985
Agta (mixed)				41	Estioko-Griffin and Griffin 1985; Goodman et al. 1985
Batek	.2			59	K. Endicott 1981
Semaq-Beri (villages)		.41	3.3	43	Kuchikura 1987, 1988
Semaq-Beri (camps)		.5	2.8	33	Kuchikura 1987, 1988

Note: These are only averages over varying lengths of time. There is also seasonal variability in meat intake. The daily per capita meat intake of the G/wi, for example, varies from only .06 kg in September to .57 kg in January (Silberbauer 1981b).

[a] The percentage of hunting trips during which any kind of kill is made, regardless of size.

[b] Standard deviation = .464; mean return is .319 if time to manufacture arrows is taken into account.

[c] Mean return is .185 if time to build hunting perch is taken into account.

[d] Standard deviation = .274; there is a 70–96 percent chance that a man will not kill an animal while hunting communally.

Figure 3-7. A Kua Bushman near Mosetlharobega butchers the rib portion of a scavenged eland. Meat can be sought after—through hunting or scavenging—as a source of calories, protein, and/or fats. Photograph taken in April 1978. Courtesy of Robert Hitchcock.

foods to Bushmen diet, for example, the Dobe Ju/'hoansi "eat as much vegetable food as they need, and as much meat as they can" (Lee 1968:41; figure 3-7). In some Australia societies, young men acquire religious knowledge from older men by exchanging meat for it. Men cannot become full-fledged adults and marry if they do not acquire sufficient ritual knowledge; thus they are motivated to hunt. Hunting success correlates with quantity of ritual knowledge as well as with secular status in Australia (Altman 1984, 1987; Sackett 1979). Gunwinggu men are divided into *maihmak* (men good for animal flesh) or *maihwarreh* (men rubbish for animal flesh; Altman 1987). In fact, hunting among many foragers often takes on strong symbolic meanings since it takes the life of beings who are, as the Cree point out, "like humans" (Tanner 1979). An ecological approach to diet, however, must initially assume that an activity's value is related to its material consequences. Why is meat so highly desired in all hunter-gatherer societies?

One obvious reason is that meat contains high-quality protein, the nine essential amino acids that the human body cannot synthesize. (Meat also provides some essential minerals such as iron and zinc, vitamins such as B_{12}, and some glucose—all in an easily digested form. Meat is also more nutrient-dense than plant food.) High-quality proteins are essential for normal metabolic function. However, while ethnographic accounts abound with references to the importance of meat, they equally convey the importance of fat in assessing the quality of game (Abrams 1987; Jochim 1981:78–87; Hayden 1981b; Speth and Spielmann 1983). Among the Kaska, for example:

Meat itself is ranked in order of preference. . . . Fat is greatly relished and all meat is improved if it contains fat. From October, when the moose begins to run, and throughout the winter, bulls are tough and their meat contains little fat. They then are regarded as "no good eating," in comparison to the cow, which is rich and succulent with fat. (Honigmann 1949:104)

Animals that generally have little body fat are often considered secondary resources, or even starvation food. During a time when no large, fat-rich game was available in the Canadian subarctic, for example, a Hare man wearily moaned that it was "back to choking rabbits" (Savishinsky 1974:25). It may therefore be fat rather than protein that drives the desire for meat in many foraging societies (note, for example, that the protein constraint was unimportant in Belovsky's analysis of Ju/'hoansi diet). Animal fat is important as a source of linoleic acid (although not as good a source as oil-rich seeds) and is important for the absorption, transportation, metabolism, and storage of fat-soluble vitamins. There is, therefore, a physiological reason for humans' preference for fatty foods.

Are protein and fat the reason that meat is so highly preferred by hunter-gatherers? Both protein and fat can serve as a source of energy. At four kilocalories per gram, the protein in meat provides the same amount of energy as carbohydrates, and fat provides twice that amount. To derive energy from protein, the human body must raise its metabolic rate by 10 percent over that required to process energy from carbohydrate or fat (Noli and Avery 1988:396). The rate of oxygen uptake by the liver limits the proportion of an individual's energy need that can be derived from protein to about 50 percent. Safe protein intake is about 20 percent of total caloric intake (at present, the American Dietetic Association recommends .8 g protein/kg body weight/day). Experimental studies show that consuming large amounts of lean meat leads to clinical symptoms of protein poisoning: nausea, a sense of uneasiness, dehydration, and diarrhea, signs that the kidneys and liver are overloaded. Excessive use of protein as an energy source can also lead to toxic levels of ammonia in the blood, calcium loss, and lean-tissue loss, even over the short term (and it may be especially damaging to pregnant women; see Spielmann 1989; Speth 1990; Speth and Spielmann 1983).

In addition, human energy needs must be met before protein needs. A diet high in protein and low in carbohydrates or fat results in the body using protein as energy, rather than as protein, meaning that a diet high in lean meat could actually result in a protein deficiency (Speth and Spielmann 1983:13). Carbohydrates and fat spare protein from being used as a source of energy. All things being equal, a hunter–gatherer should want a certain amount of carbohydrate or fat in the diet so that an appropriate amount of protein can be acquired from the meat consumed. Researchers may be justi-fied in using calories as the only currency in foraging models if the caloric and protein contents of foods are correlated, as Hawkes and O'Connell show to be true for the foods consumed by the Dobe Ju/'hoansi (1985). If not, then analyses may overemphasize the importance of protein.

This perspective on calories, protein, and fat makes some sense out of the so-called fat and grease obsessions of maritime hunter–gatherers such as those of the Northwest Coast, where eulachon oil was highly prized (see Noli and Avery 1988). It also accounts for meat gorging among Plains hunter–gatherers (Speth and Spielmann 1983), and the trading of meat for plant carbohydrates between foragers and horticulturalists (as noted in chapter 1; see also Spielmann 1991). This discussion also sheds some light on the nature of tropical-forest subsistence. Certain facets of tropical (especially Amazo-nian) hunter–gatherer and horticulturalist behavior—including intervillage warfare and hunting taboos (see review in Sponsel 1986)—have been attrib-uted to the difficulty of acquiring sufficient animal protein.[12] A growing number of studies suggest, however, that hunter–gatherers in the tropical forests acquire a substantial proportion of calories from meat; the Hiwi, for example, receive 68 percent of their calories from game (Hurtado and Hill 1990). Tropical hunter–gatherers often have an excess of protein, and are more often deficient in carbohydrates (Hill et al. 1987; Milton 1985; Sponsel 1986). The Efe, for example, trade meat for Lese agricultural produce con-taining two to five times the meat's caloric content (Bailey and Peacock 1988; Hart 1978). Tropical horticulturalists, however, may display the oppo-site pattern. Keegan found that the manioc and maize gardens of the Machi-guenga of southeastern Peru provide sufficient amounts of calories at return rates above those of forest carbohydrate sources but fall short of meeting protein needs (1986). Protein, rather than calories, provides more accurate predictions of Machiguenga use of forest resources. It appears that, though energy is the limiting factor for hunter-gatherers in tropical forests, protein (or fat) may be the limiting factor for horticulturalists.

Finally, we can consider an apparent paradox in Ache foraging behavior. As we saw above, optimal-foraging models appear to be good predictors of Ache diets. However, the researchers noted that men eschew easily collected resources such as palm pith in order to pursue game. Ache men hunt at a rate of 1,340 kilocalories per hour while Ache women collect about 2,630 kilocalories per hour from palm fiber and shoots. Since an Ache man passes within fifteen meters of a palm every eight minutes while hunting (Hill et al. 1987:11; Kaplan and Hill 1992), why don't men ignore hunting, focus on palms, and thereby double their daily caloric return rate?

There are two possible explanations for this. Hill argues that the use of one resource rather than another may be a product of the forager switching the criterion for choosing resources from calories to protein or lipids (1988:165). Since Ache men know that women are collecting carbohydrates, they may select resources for protein or lipids, rather than calories, to complement food gathered by their wives. The diet-breadth model only evaluates resources along a single scale (usually energy). Evaluating resources along more than one scale requires a different approach. Hill borrows the technique of indifference curves from microeconomics as a way to permit prediction of the mixes of different but complementary and substitutable resources. Unfortunately, the data needed to use this approach in a satisfying manner have not been collected for the Ache; initial analyses suggest that the Ache do make such trade-offs while foraging, switching to a different resource-ranking scale as sufficient amounts of one nutrient are acquired (although the effect of protein versus lipids cannot be distinguished). Nonetheless, future foraging models will have to consider trade-offs between carbohydrate, protein, and lipid acquisition, and direct effort toward predicting when one of these factors will take precedence.

Hawkes offers an alternative explanation for male Ache foraging strategies that focuses on risk rather than nutrition (1990, 1991, 1992, 1993b). She suggests that while men could increase their long-term average net energy-return rates by gathering instead of hunting, hunting lets men occasionally bring home large caloric packages of food (which are also rich in protein and lipids). They trade off higher energetic returns by actively seeking risk. This provides men with the ability, as Hawkes puts it, to "show off." The meat acquired by these men is shared throughout a foraging band so everyone receives some value from the show-offs. These men may acquire more sexual partners as a result, and raise their fitness (we return to this case in chapter 5). A similar pattern may hold true for the Hadza in Tanzania as well (see Hawkes, O'Connell, and Blurton Jones 1991), and Gragson shows that the Venezuelan Pume also seek risk in their hunting and fishing strategies (1993). Through the use of game theory, Hawkes argues that a male focus on hunting can be an evolutionarily stable strategy even if it lowers mean return rates (but see Bettinger 1991). While it is still not clear why Ache men hunt so much, this case suggests that decisions about which foods to eat are not made solely in terms of food or food-getting activities, but in terms of other goals and activities as well. We may begin by analyzing subsistence strictly in terms of nutritional needs and foraging constraints, but it invariably cannot be fully understood outside of its social context.

CONCLUSIONS

This chapter began by considering global patterns in gross diet categories which revealed that hunter-gatherer diet cannot be stereotyped and that it is related in a fairly straightforward fashion to gross environmental characteristics. We saw that the use of aquatic resources may be related to low hunting returns or the inability to store an adequate amount of plant food or meat for a lean season. But these are only speculations based on patterns. Explanations of variability in subsistence lie in the economic decision-making process of hunter-gatherers as they are confronted by a set of resources, a process that enables them to choose between resources depending on their goals. The optimal-foraging models described here aspire to model that process, and have had some success in doing so. Expressed in the terms of optimal foraging, we could say that when the return rate from hunting is lower than the return rate of fishing, then foragers will forgo hunting for fishing. In areas where plant collection provides low return rates, such as the tropical forests or grasslands, and there are no fish resources, foragers may devote more time to the hunting of meat to be traded with horticulturalists for carbohydrates (or kept for their fat content) as a way to obtain sufficient calories.

The characteristics of food resources themselves set the initial conditions of the subsistence decision-making process. It is likely that at times, foragers select resources in terms of energy, and at other times in terms of protein or lipids. In extreme cases, they may even select resources in terms of specific nutrients, but this is unlikely to be a factor in explaining large-scale dietary patterns. Current applications of the diet-breadth and patch-choice models demonstrate that human hunting and gathering can be modeled fairly well with slightly modified models borrowed from economics and evolutionary ecology. These models assist in understanding the variables important to human foraging and in modeling foraging as an explicitly human decision-making process (see Mithen 1990).

A frequent criticism of optimal-foraging models is that what constitutes food is culturally defined, and that optimal-foraging models cannot cope with resources that are taken or excluded for nonenergetic reasons, or resources that are collected for their nonfood value (e.g., feathers or furs). Men can be motivated to go hunting to seek prestige (Dwyer 1974, 1985a,b); some resources may be tabooed, perhaps because they are sacred, or considered inedible. How can optimal foraging account for resources that are either not taken or are taken in larger-than-expected numbers for nonsubsistence reasons?

Foraging models do not claim to duplicate reality; instead, they claim to model reality at some level of specificity *if hunter-gatherers are behaving according to a model's set of goals and conditions*. Optimization models are heuristic; they do not provide a priori answers and explanations. By predicting which resources a forager will take if resources are ranked only in terms of their search costs and post-encounter return rates, for example, optimal-foraging models flag those resources that are treated for reasons other than energetics. We have noted that some resources may be taken for their nutrient value, but there could be other reasons for taking or ignoring them that have nothing to do with subsistence per se. For example, when Mithen applied his foraging model to Africa's Valley Bisa, he originally predicted that zebra should be included in the diet (1989). Yet, in actuality, zebra are rarely taken. It is unclear whether this is for legal reasons or because zebra fall outside what the Bisa deem edible resources. (Coincidentally, the G/wi in Botswana do not hunt zebra either, a fact that Silberbauer also found inexplicable [1981a:293].) In either case, the fact that the model predicts zebra to be in the diet, when in fact they are not, suggests that the decision not to eat zebra probably has little to do with energetic factors.[13]

Foraging models also offer an explanatory framework in which to test theories of technological change, such as the change from atlatl to bow and arrow, or the use of poisons as opposed to shock weapons. Different food-getting technologies can produce substantially different search-and-handling costs of the same food resources (see Hurtado and Hill 1989). We should be able to use hypotheses about diet to predict changes in technology, or vice versa; these could both be especially useful tactics for archaeology. Consider, for example, the use of dogs, one of the earliest and most widespread of domesticated animals. Besides being food themselves and beasts of burden, dogs can assist in foraging, helping to cut down both search and pursuit time (Dwyer 1983; Goodale 1971:167; McCarthy and McArthur 1960:150). The cost of having dogs around is often minimal since they can scavenge for themselves or be fed on garbage. In some cases, however, especially in the Arctic, dogs must be fed and so they are costly to keep (Schnirelman 1994). Models could be constructed to predict the effect of dogs on diet—as both food and food-getters—and the conditions under which the increase in foraging efficiency is worth the cost of having dogs.

Similarly, we could develop foraging models to predict the use of traps or mass-capture devices. On the one hand, traps permit hunter-gatherers to do two things at once, since a forager can search and pursue other food resources while the trap is "pursuing" another; mass-capture devices such as weirs or hunting nets permit groups of people to collect large numbers of fish or game at one time. On the other hand, traps, weirs, and hunting nets can require large investments of time in their initial construction and maintenance (Bailey and Aunger 1989a). Some large Australian hunting nets required many months for their manufacture (Satterthwait 1987; this study did not include the time required to gather the raw materials). Foraging models could predict the conditions that would make this initial labor investment and that of continued maintenance worth the benefit of double use of foraging time or mass capture.

In sum, the optimal-foraging models of behavioral ecology open many productive avenues of thought as they allow us to model the relationships of foraging strategies, diet, and technology, and can generate empirical expectations that are amenable to testing. And, as the Ache case suggests, the use of foraging models to analyze subsistence will ultimately lead us away from strict issues of diet toward nonforaging activities, such as childcare and reproduction, and thus add an evolutionary component to the economic analysis of foraging behavior.

FORAGING AND MOBILITY 4

> When I'm a kid we're always moving. Never stay around one place for
> long. We got to move, otherwise we find no food. Even then sometimes
> there's no food for a while, so people in camps go hungry. Wherever
> there's food, well, we got to move to that place.
> Kutchin man (Nelson 1986:273)
>
> [We do not like] sitting one place all the time like white men.
> Kaska man (Honigmann 1949:102)

There is hardly a more romantic image in anthropology than that of a small
band of hunter-gatherers setting off through the dunes and scrub, their few
belongings on their backs. Mobility, in fact, has long been considered one
of the distinguishing characteristics of hunter-gatherers. At the "Man the
Hunter" conference, Lee and DeVore assumed that all hunter-gatherers
"move around a lot" and that this was a strong determinant of the foraging
way of life (1968:11). In one sense they were correct; mobility does exert a
strong influence over other elements of hunter-gatherers' lives. Anthropologists have recognized this for some time. Marcel Mauss, for example, related
the Eskimos' seasonal mobility to their moral and religious life (Mauss and
Beuchat 1906). Sahlins saw mobility as conditioning cultural attitudes toward
material goods (1972).

Yet hunter-gatherers move in different ways. Some do indeed "move
around a lot," but others move hardly at all. (And hunter-gatherers are not
the only ones who move; many horticulturalists, and virtually all pastoralists,
are also mobile.)[1] As in subsistence, there is considerable variability in how,
and how much, hunter-gatherers move (see table 4-1). Many students of
anthropology think of hunter-gatherer movement in terms of a systematic
seasonal round, wherein hunter-gatherers move between different locations as

Table 4-1. Hunter-Gatherer Mobility

Group	Primary biomass (kg/m²)	Residential moves/yr	Average distance (km)	Total distance (km)	Total area (km²)	Logistical mobility (days)	Reference
Baffinland Inuit	low	60	12	720	25,000		Hantzsch 1977
Ona (Selk'nam)	17.8	60					Gusinde 1934; Stuart 1972
Netsilingmiut	low	14	16.8	237	6,000		Balikci 1970
Nunamiut	low	10	69.5	725	5,200–20,500		Amsden 1977; Binford 1978
N. Tlingit	19.1				2,500		Schalk 1978
Chilkat	18.4	>2		8–80			Mitchell and Donald 1988
Bella Coola (Nuxalk)	20.3				625		Schalk 1978
Owikeno Kwakiutl	20.5				639		Schalk 1978
Mistassini Cree	18.7	10		510	3,385		Rogers 1963, 1967a,b, 1972
S. Tlingit	20.1	3			1,953		Schalk 1978
Berens River Ojibwa	18.7				320		Rogers 1967, 1969b
Grand L. Victoria Cree	19.8				2,890		Rogers 1967, 1969b
Pikangikum (Ojibwa)	18.5				650		Rogers 1967, 1969b
Haisla	20.7				4,000		Schalk 1978
Tsimshian	20.5	3–5		290–450			Schalk 1978; Mitchell and Donald 1988
Haida	20.3				923		Schalk 1978; Langdon 1979
Makah	19.8	2	7.3	15	190		Schalk 1978
Quileute	20.0				185		Schalk 1978
Blackfoot (Siksika)	18.3		16–24				Ewers 1955
Quinault	20.6				110		Schalk 1978
S. Kwakiutl (Ft. Rupert)	20.3	3–4+	13.6	35 252–276	727		Schalk 1978 Mitchell and Donald 1988
Waswanipi Cree	19.0				4,870		Rogers 1967, 1969b
Aleut	low	1				32	Coxe 1804; Laughlin 1980
Montagnais	18.2	50	64		2,700		Tanner 1944; Leacock 1954
Chinook	20.4				118		Schalk 1978; Kroeber 1939
Ainu	19.4	2	4.3	8.6	171	48	Watanabe 1968, 1972
Klamath	.6	11	7.5	84	1,058	27	Gatschet 1890; Spier 1930; Barrett 1910
Twana	19.6	4		48–70	211		Mitchell and Donald 1988; Elmendorf 1960
Puyallup-Nisqually	20.2				191		Schalk 1978
Upper Skagit	19.9				203		Schalk 1978

Table 4-1. Hunter-Gatherer Mobility (*continued*)

Group	Primary biomass (kg/m²)	Residential moves/yr	Average distance (km)	Total distance (km)	Total area (km²)	Logistical mobility (days)	Reference
Nuuchahnulth (Nootka)	21.0	>3	10	30	370.5		Drucker 1951; Mitchell and Donald 1988
Squamish	20.5	0–4					Mitchell and Donald 1988
Other Gulf Salish	18.7	3	34.9	77	631		Schalk 1978
Straits Salish (E. Saanich)	19.2	4–5		75–110	58		Schalk 1978; Mitchell and Donald 1988
Straits Salish (W. Saanich)	19.2	3–5		165–320			Schalk 1978; Mitchell and Donald 1988
Nooksack	20.4				356		Schalk 1978
Micmac	19.9		56		1,000–5,200		Wallis and Wallis 1955; Denys 1908; LeClerq 1910; Speck 1921
Sanpoil	.7	10					Ray 1932
Tasmanians, N.W.	20.7			400	376		Jones 1974
Wiyot	19.5	0–2			32		Schalk 1978
Kidütökadö (N. Paiute)	.7	40				29	Kelly 1932
Crow (Apsáalooke)	1.5	38	19.2	640	61,880	32	Nabokov 1967
Tasmanians, S.W.	20.8			400	476		Jones 1974
Nez Perce	18.3		16–24		2,000		Haines 1955
Cheyenne	.7	33	12	396			Gussow 1954
Tolowa	20.1	2?			91		Schalk 1978; Cook 1976
Yurok	19.6	0–2			35		Schalk 1978; Cook 1976
Maidu	18.8				455–3,255		Dixon 1905; Beals 1933
Tasmanians, Oyster Bay	20.8			160	572		Jones 1974
Karok	18.1				30		Schalk 1978
Tasmanians, Big River	20.8			480	1,114		Jones 1974
Kaibab (S. Paiute)	1.1				706		Leland 1986; Kelly 1964
Kiowa	2.0		16–24				Kroeber 1939
≠Kade G/wi	1.2	17	25	300	906	10	Tanaka 1980
Kua (mobile)	1.0	11			990	6	Hitchcock and Ebert 1989; Hitchcock 1982
Walapai	.6				588		Kroeber 1935
Pitjandjara	.6					5–6	Tindale 1968, 1972
Ngadadjara	.6	37	43	1,600	2,600	8–16	Gould 1968, 1969a,b; Pate 1986

Table 4-1. Hunter–Gatherer Mobility (*continued*)

Group	Primary biomass (kg/m²)	Residential moves/yr	Average distance (km)	Total distance (km)	Total area (km²)	Logistical mobility (days)	Reference
Borjeno	.5					26	Aschmann 1959
Aranda	.6	10			260		Spencer and Gillen 1927
Worora	2.6				743		Peterson and Long 1986
Guayaki	71.7	50	5.9	295	780		Clastres 1972
Hadza	10.4	27	8	216	2,520	3–4	O'Connell, Hawkes, and Blurton Jones 1988; Woodburn 1968, 1972
Seri	.7			248			McGee 1898
Ju/'hoansi (Nyae Nyae)	1.2					6–10	Hitchcock and Ebert 1984
Ju/'hoansi (Dobe)	1.9	6	23.6	142	260–2,500	10	Hitchcock 1987a,b; Lee 1979
/Aise (sedentary)	1.9	0			2–10		Hitchcock and Ebert 1984
Kua (sedentary)	1.9	0				7–46	Hitchcock and Ebert 1984
Alyawara	.8				1,500	7	O'Connell, Latz, and Barnett 1983;
Dorobo (Okiek)		6					Huntingsford 1929
G/wi	1.2	11	25	275	782	8–24	Silberbauer 1972, 1981a,b
Mlabri (Mlabrai)	45.1	24	19	196	2,826	1	Pookajorn 1985, 1988
Birhor	32.4	8	10.3	90.3	130	5–6	Williams 1974
Mardudjara	.6					15	Cane 1987; Tonkinson 1978
Siriono	32.1	16	14.4	230	780		Holmberg 1950; Stearman 1984
Chenchu	24.6	4	11.2	39.5			Furer-Haimendorf 1943
Nesbitt R. (Cape York)	26.8				35–70		Chase and Sutton 1987
Hill Pandaram	22.3	45	4	144	79.8		Morris 1982
Aeta	49.4	22	12.8	281.6	3,265		Vanoverbergh 1925
Agta	49.4	20	5	107			Rai 1990
Batak	56.7	17–26					Eder 1978; 1987
Anbarra	37.6	3	3.2	7	56	1–4	Meehan 1982
Aka	42.5	8	7	60	250		Bahuchet 1988; 1979
Glyde River	37.6	5	3.5	14.2			Peterson 1973
Vedda	36.6	3	11.2	36.3	41		Seligmann and Seligmann 1911
Mbuti	34.7	11	5.2	57	150–780		Bicchieri 1969b; Tanno 1976; Harako 1976; Turnbull 1972
Semang	63.2	26	11.3	203.8	2,475		Schebesta 1929

Table 4-1. Hunter-Gatherer Mobility (*continued*)

Group	Primary biomass (kg/m²)	Residential moves/yr	Average distance (km)	Total distance (km)	Total area (km²)	Logistical mobility (days)	Reference
Andamanese (Onge, inland)	50.6	8	2.4		40	8	Radcliffe-Brown 1922; Cooper 1990
Andamanese (coastal)	50.6				25		Cooper 1990
Penan	73.5	45	8.5	384	861		Harrison 1949
Shasta	18.6				3,255		Dixon 1907
Owens Valley Paiute	.5				1,964		Steward 1933
Washo	17.0				2,327		Downs 1966

Note: It is difficult to acquire these data from ethnographic sources. A residential move in the original study (Kelly 1983) was defined as any change in the residential locus made during the seasonal round. Even if a single location is seasonally reoccupied (such as winter villages on the Northwest Coast), the group is considered to be residentially mobile as long as *most* of the group leaves the location seasonally. To insure comparability, fine-grained data must often be made more coarse-grained, e.g., a residential move was sometimes counted as a single move, although on the way the group may have stopped for two or three days in an intermediate spot (e.g., Williams 1974; Clastres 1972; Kozak et al. 1979). This could raise estimates for tropical, boreal forest groups, and horse-equipped Plains hunters. Many of the data in table 4-1 were not given explicitly in an ethnography, but were derived by piecing together indirect references to when or how far a group moved. Many cases describe an entire seasonal round, but some of the data are normative, inferential, or extrapolated from one season to another where I thought it appropriate.

Most of these data are derived from a specific band for a specific year. No case should be taken to be representative of all years for all bands within an ethnographically defined group. For example, the Ngadadjara data come from Richard Gould's fieldwork, and they are not necessarily identical to other foragers of Australia's Western Desert, or even to that of other bands of Ngadadjara.

resources come and go with the seasons. The Great Basin Shoshone, for example, spent the winter in villages in the piñon and juniper forests of the mountains (figure 4-1). As spring came, they moved down to the valley floors, where seeds had begun to ripen, later moving upslope as seeds began to ripen there. In the late summer, they might move to a river where trout were running, or to a marsh where waterfowl were passing through on their way south or where bulrush seeds could be harvested. Later still, in the early fall, they might move back into the mountains to collect piñon nuts and hunt deer or bighorn sheep, and establish their winter camps again.

But our purpose in this chapter is not to document variability in seasonal rounds but to describe variation in the organization of movements and the relationships between environment, individual foraging, and camp movement. We first discuss concepts and ethnographic data that point to relationships between mobility and the environment. We then present a simple foraging model that considers how different foraging environments could result in longer or shorter individual forays, and more or less frequent group movement. Following this, we discuss sedentism and, finally, the relationship between foraging and enculturation, and how foraging studies shed light on whether hunter-gatherers manage or conserve resources.

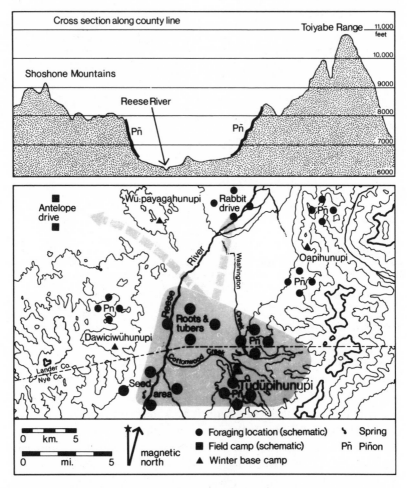

Figure 4-1. Settlement pattern of the Tüdüpihunupi, the Reese River Valley Sho-shone. From Steward 1938 (figure 8) as redrawn by Dennis O'Brien, in Thomas 1981. Courtesy of the American Museum of Natural History.

MOBILITY AND THE ENVIRONMENT

Variability in hunter-gatherer mobility has not gone unrecognized. One early scheme that received wide attention divided hunter-gatherers into four categories: *free-wandering* groups, which have no territorial boundaries and are characteristic of colonizing populations; *restricted-wandering* groups, which live under higher population densities and are constrained by territorial boundaries; *central-based wandering* groups, which seasonally return to a spe-

Table 4-2. Biotic Zones and Murdock's Settlement Patterns

		Settlement pattern				
Zone	ET range	Fully nomadic	Semi-nomadic	Semi-sedentary	Sedentary	Mean
Tropical forests	26–21	9 (75)	2 (16.7)	1 (8.3)	0 (0)	1.33
Tropical/ subtropical deserts	20–16	9 (64.2)	4 (28.5)	1 (7.1)	0 (0)	1.42
Temperate deserts	15–14	3 (9.3)	21 (65.6)	3 (9.3)	5 (15.6)	2.31
Temperate forests	13–12	4 (7.5)	32 (60.3)	12 (22.6)	5 (9.4)	2.33
Boreal forests	11–10	5 (11.1)	21 (46.4)	12 (26.6)	7 (15.4)	2.46
Arctic	9–8	5 (41.6)	4 (33.3)	2 (16.6)	1 (8.3)	1.91

Source: Binford 1980:table 2.
Note: Numbers in parentheses are row-wise percentages. The mean is the mean score of the values given to the four settlement-pattern categories (Fully nomadic = 1, Sedentary = 4).

cific village; and *semipermanent sedentary* groups, which occupy a village year-round but move it every few years (Beardsley et al. 1956).

Murdock later modified these categories into fully nomadic, semi-nomadic, semisedentary, and fully sedentary, respectively (1967). Binford used these gross categorizations to demonstrate that mobility is related to the environment, and ushered in a renewed round of interest in hunter-gatherer mobility, especially among archaeologists (1980). Using ET as a measure, Binford showed a systematic relationship between environments and Murdock's settlement types (table 4-2). Hunter-gatherers in the tropical forests and extreme Arctic tend to be very mobile. In temperate forests and deserts, mobility is seasonally constrained, especially as the use of stored food during the winter becomes more important, or as the distribution of water sources constrains the movements of desert foragers.

Binford described the variability he saw in hunter-gatherer settlement systems with two settlement types, *foragers* and *collectors*. These types rested on the concepts of *residential* mobility (movements of the entire band or local group from one camp to another), and *logistical* mobility (movements of individuals or small task-specific groups out from and back to a residential camp). Foragers move consumers to food resources, and thus map onto a region's resource locations (figure 4-2), while collectors move residentially to key locations not necessarily defined by food (e.g., where water or firewood are available) and use long logistical forays to bring resources to camp (figure 4-3). *In general,* Binford suggested that foragers have high residential mobility and invest little effort in logistical movements, while collectors make few residential moves and frequent, often lengthy logistical forays.

But not all foragers (as Binford defined them)[2] are highly mobile, nor are

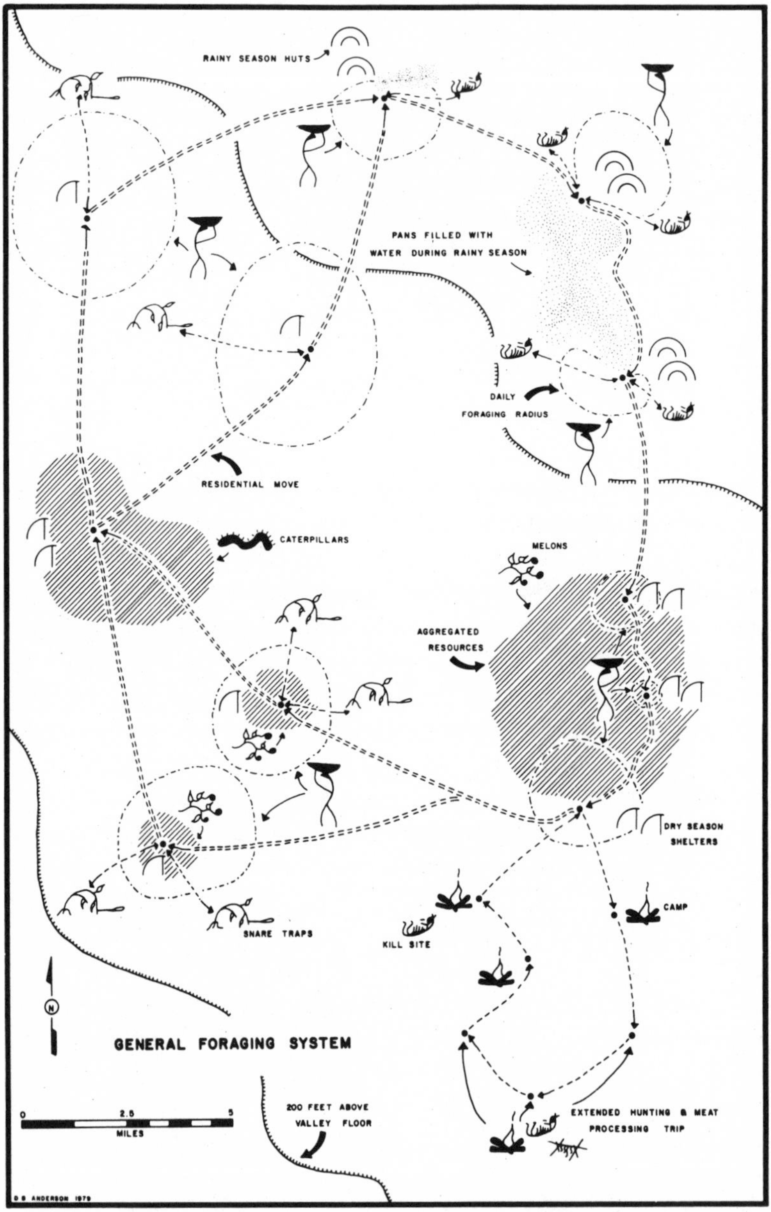
RAINY SEASON HUTS
PANS FILLED WITH
WATER DURING RAINY SEASON
DAILY
FORAGING RADIUS
RESIDENTIAL MOVE
CATERPILLARS
MELONS
AGGREGATED
RESOURCES
DRY SEASON
SHELTERS
CAMP
KILL SITE
SNARE TRAPS
GENERAL FORAGING SYSTEM
0
2.5
5
MILES
200 FEET ABOVE
VALLEY FLOOR
EXTENDED HUNTING & MEAT
PROCESSING TRIP
D B ANDERSON 1979

Figure 4-2. Characteristics of a foraging subsistence-settlement system. From Binford 1980, drawn by Dana Anderson. Reproduced by permission of the Society for American Archaeology from *American Antiquity* 45(1), 1980.

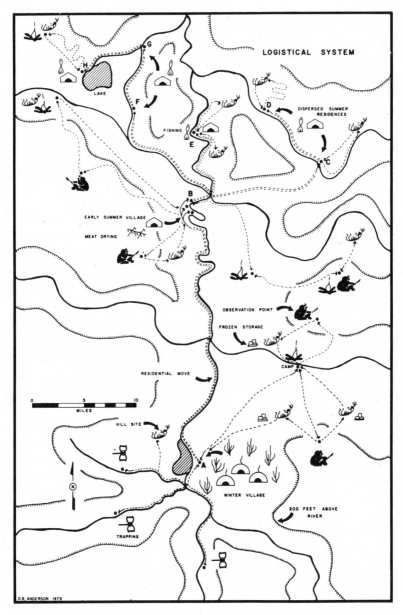

Figure 4-3. Characteristics of a collector subsistence-settlement system. From Binford 1980, drawn by Dana Anderson. Reproduced by permission of the Society for American Archaeology from *American Antiquity* 45(1), 1980.

all collectors nearly sedentary. Binford's typology focuses not on the frequency of movement but on the *organization of camp movement relative to food-getting activities*. The Anbarra of North Australia, for example, move only a few times a year, but make frequent, relatively short forays to hunt and fish, and to collect shellfish, roots, and water (government rations provide about 50 percent of their calories). The Semang of Malaysia make frequent residential moves, but they too usually make only daily forays from camp. Both, however, are foragers in Binford's sense because they move consumers to resources. The difference in the frequency of movement is related to the food density of their respective environments, but the relations between the individual forager and group movement remain the same.

Binford did not intend that his two settlement-system types be used to pigeonhole ethnographic or archaeological cases (although they have been used for such purposes). Instead, he saw these types as a simple way of describing a continuum of settlement forms and possibilities. Foragers and collectors were the extreme ends of a continuum that Binford saw as generally paralleling other scales of seasonal differentiation and patchiness of food resources. Where resources are homogeneously distributed and where food is available more or less year round, a forager pattern is more likely; where the opposite conditions hold true, a collector pattern can be expected. As we will see in chapter 6, this simple pattern is not unexpected, for where resources are patchily distributed, maximum foraging efficiency is obtained by aggregating in a central place and sending out foraging parties. Where resources are more homogeneously distributed, maximum foraging efficiency comes from group dispersion to resource locales. In general, resources become more aggregated in space and more constrained in their seasonal availability from the equator to the Arctic, except for the high Arctic, where there are some groups who do not have access to migratory fish or large migratory caribou herds (see below). Therefore, the pattern Binford observed in Murdock's categories and *ET* shows the expected parallel between the forager-collector continuum and resource distribution.[3]

Binford's forager-collector continuum makes the case that mobility is related to the environment. Ethnographic data also demonstrate this point.

ETHNOGRAPHIC DATA ON MOBILITY

Rather than rely on a typological scheme, I have used five separate variables to measure dimensions of mobility: (1) the number of residential moves made each year; (2) the average distance moved; (3) the total distance moved each year; (4) the total area used over the course of a year; and (5) the average length of a logistical foray (Kelly 1983; table 4-1).

I analyzed these five dimensions of mobility in relation to the gross abundance and distribution of food, using effective temperature and primary biomass for their measurement. We defined effective temperature in chapter 3. Here we introduce primary biomass as the total amount of standing plant matter in an environment. For the most part, humans eat the reproductive parts of plants (nuts and seeds) or their stored carbohydrates (tubers). In areas of high primary biomass, plants invest more energy in structural maintenance and the capture of sunlight than in reproductive parts or storage, resulting in primary production that is largely inedible or difficult to reach (i.e., at the tops of trees or at the ends of branches). In areas of low primary biomass, plants invest less energy in structural maintenance and growth and more in reproductive tissue (seeds). In addition, many plants of dry, low-primary-biomass environments have large subsurface tubers (an adaptation to droughts and range fires). Therefore, primary biomass is, in general and within limits, inversely correlated with the effective abundance of edible plant food. It is also inversely related to faunal abundance and distribution since animals in high-primary-biomass settings tend to be small (so they can feed in tree tops) or, if large, few in number and widely spaced. Coupled with effective temperature, primary biomass provides a rough relative measure of the potential return from foraging in a given environment.

Primary biomass is calculated from two regression equations utilizing the primary production and biomass of major biomes that are grouped into arid and humid categories (Kelly 1983). Humid environments are those with more than 400 millimeters of precipitation per year and either ET values from 8 to 12.5 or from 19.5 to 26 degrees centigrade. Arid environments are those with ET values of 12.5 to 19.5 degrees centigrade, as well as those within the ET ranges of humid environments which have less than 400 millimeters a year of precipitation (tundra and Arctic environments excluded):

Arid Environments:

$$\log_{10} \text{Primary Biomass (g/m}^2\text{)} = 2.66 + .0009X$$

Humid Environments:

$$\log_{10} \text{Primary Biomass (g/m}^2\text{)} = 4.2 + .00013X$$

where X = net above-ground primary production (g/m²/yr). In a few bor-

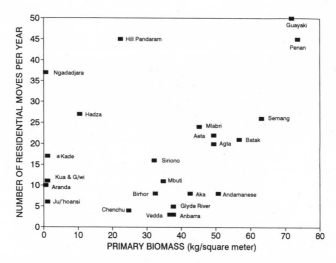

Figure 4-4. Number of residential moves per year plotted against primary biomass as a proxy measure of resource density for tropical and subtropical foragers. This figure shows both tropical forest and desert cases (Hill Pandaram, Ngadadjara, Hadza, ≠Kade, Kua, G/wi, Aranda, and Ju/'hoansi).

derline cases I choose to ignore the equation determined by the climatic data and to use the other if I thought it would describe a group's environment more accurately.

Number of residential moves per year

In high-primary-biomass areas the number of residential moves per year should increase as overall food density decreases as measured by primary biomass. Figure 4-4 shows this to be true for our largest data set, the tropical forest ($N = 16$, $df = 14$, $r = .86$, $p < .01$). Those dependent on aquatic resources (e.g., Anbarra, Andamanese), state-provided rations (e.g., Anbarra), or horticulture (e.g., Mbuti; the Chenchu and Vedda also do some agriculture and are linked to villages) would probably move more frequently were these resource not available (perhaps turning the linear relationship into a concave-downward curve).

For many tropical hunter-gatherers, camp movement also serves as a foraging trip. This often limits group movement, reducing the distances between camps. Among the Malaysian Semang, "A whole troop, with children, cannot, of course undertake long marches in the day, for the group is com-

Figure 4-5. A family of Penan walking through the Sarawak forest in 1985, moving their campsite to a better sago-palm-foraging area, about a three- or four-hour walk from their last camp. The men had gone out the day before to locate a camp and blaze the trail. Photograph courtesy of Peter Brosius.

pelled to look for food en route. Sometimes they stop by the river bank to fish, sometimes in the forest to search for edible roots" (Schebesta 1929:150). Among the Philippine Agta, "travel is leisurely unless a game animal is encountered to provoke a hunting spree. Frequent stops are made to chew betel nut, fish, gather or cook and even to nap" (Rai 1990:59).

Although most of our data come from tropical forest groups (figure 4-5), boreal forest groups, such as the Ona, Micmac, and Montagnais also move frequently (figure 4-6). The Micmac "remained encamped in a place only so long as they found the means of subsistence for their families" (LeClerq 1910:100). LeJeune, wintering with a group of Montagnais in 1633–34, noted that the group moved twenty-three times between 12 November and 22 April, or about once a week (Leacock 1954; see also Rogers 1972; Turner 1889; Helm 1972). The Tasmanians, living in a temperate, evergreen forest "daily removed to a fresh place," at least during part of the year (Backhouse, in Roth 1890:104; see also B. Hiatt 1967, 1968). Among the Ona (Selk'nam)

Figure 4-6. An Ahtna camp in central Alaska. The ephemeral shelter indicates high residential mobility, although the Ahtna lived in substantial pithouses in villages during the winter. Photograph by the Miles Bros., probably 1902. Courtesy of the National Anthropological Archives, Smithsonian Institution, no. 75-5658.

of Tierra del Fuego's interior forests, "the family hastens restlessly after the game animals [guanaco] and settles down for a few days at just that spot at which booty fell to it. After using up the supply, it again moves on and constantly changes its dwelling site" (Gusinde 1934:276). Where game is not abundant, it is worth the effort to move camp frequently since foraging in cold, northern climates can be exhausting:

The first day a hunter without food starts out with a fair prospect of being able to kill a moose. He is able to travel twenty or thirty miles and has a good chance of finding the track of a moose, which he may follow to success. The second day the chances are considerably less and by the third or fourth day the exertion and cold without a supply of food has completely worn him out. (Goddard 1917:215)

In nontropical high-primary-biomass environments, the number of residential moves per year does seem to be correlated with primary biomass, as

Table 4-3. Mobility among Temperate and Boreal-Forest Groups

Group	Primary biomass (kg/m²)	Dependence on fish (%)	Annual residential moves
Kidütökadö	0.7	30	40
Cheyenne	0.7	0	33
Crow	1.5	0	38
Ona	17.8	20	60
Montagnais	18.2	20	50
Mistassini Cree	18.7	30	10
Aleut	low	60	1
Klamath	0.6	50	11
Sanpoil	0.7	50	10
Chilkat	18.4	high	>2
Other Gulf Salish	18.7	high	3
Straits Salish (E. Saanich)	19.2	high	4–5
Straits Salish (W. Saanich)	19.2	high	3–5
Ainu	19.4	50	2
Wiyot	19.5	high	0–2
Yurok	19.6	50	0–2
Twana	19.6	60	4
Makah	19.8	60	2
S. Tlingit	20.1	60	3
Tolowa	20.1	40	2?
S. Kwakiutl (Ft. Rupert)	20.3	50	3, >4
Tsimshian	20.5	60	3–5
Squamish	20.5	high	0–4
Nuuchahnulth	21.0	60	>3

long as a group does not depend heavily on aquatic resources (table 4-3). Dependence on aquatic resources is almost always associated with low residential mobility (Yesner 1980); in fact, the few available data suggest that if a group is heavily dependent on aquatic resources, the number of residential moves is *inversely* correlated with primary biomass (Kelly 1983:292). In chapter 3, we suggested that aquatic resources may be used in lieu of terrestrial game. In temperate, and especially in cold settings, where primary production is lower than in the tropics, game become more important to diet and a more important determinant of mobility. But in the same environments, large game become more dispersed and less abundant as primary biomass increases and/or temperature decreases. Dependence on aquatic resources should increase along a gradient of increasing primary biomass as the cost of hunting increases. Note that in table 4-3, dependence on aquatic resources does increase with increasing primary biomass for those groups less than 50 percent dependent on aquatic resources. For groups heavily dependent on aquatic resources, those living in lower-primary-biomass settings (e.g., Klamath) are more mobile than those in high-primary-biomass settings. All groups with heavy dependence on aquatic resources and low residential mobility live in high-primary-biomass settings. (Most of the cases, however, come from a single culture area, the Northwest Coast of North America, and thus are not conclusive.)

While hunter-gatherers frequently do choose campsites on the basis of foraging conditions, they must also take into account such things as firewood, tree boughs for bedding, shelter, water, and how dirty the present camp has become. The location of other groups of hunter-gatherers (or non-hunter-gatherers) can also condition movements, either by attracting or repelling foragers, depending on the nature of the relationship.

Deserts present a special problem in this regard. Given humans' almost daily need for water, the location of water is often more critical than foraging considerations as a determinant of residential movement in deserts. Meehan describes how tension and anxiety permeated Anbarra camps in northern Australia as water became more scarce and had to be carried from longer and longer distances; movement of camp was often predicated upon the severity of these arguments (1982). Taylor labels groups whose movements are restricted by water sources as *tethered foragers* (1964, 1972). In desert settings, the relationship between residential movement and primary biomass is conditioned by the availability of water. Since a number of local factors can determine the availability of water (springs, subsurface geology, topography, etc.), we could expect a fair amount of variability in subtropical mobility with no correlation to primary biomass (figure 4-4).

The Dobe Ju/'hoansi and G/wi demonstrate the effect of water on desert mobility. One of the key differences between these two groups is that the Ju/'hoansi have access to extensive pans that hold water during the dry season. The geomorphology of the G/wi's habitat prevents the formation of water pans. The Ju/'hoansi are less mobile during the dry season, preferring to make long individual foraging trips from campsites near water pans. Data in table 4-4 show the nature of Ju/'hoansi movements during the late wet and early dry seasons. During the wet season, however, families become more mobile, making foraging treks from Dobe since surface water is more available (Yellen 1976; villages near Dobe also encourage the Ju/'hoansi to remain at the water hole). Conversely, the G/wi are mobile during the dry season and obtain water from the rumens of game animals and *tsama* melons (Silberbauer 1972, 1981a,b; Tanaka 1980). To insure a constant supply of these items, the G/wi must move camp more frequently than the Ju/'hoansi during the dry season.

Where water sources are localized in deserts, we could expect foraging

Table 4-4. Tethered Foraging Trips of the Dobe Ju/'hoansi

Trip	Days	Camps	Mean duration of camp occupation (days)	Days at Dobe upon return
1	24	6	4	17
2	22	10	2.2	11
3	17	4	4.25[a]	26
4	16	6	2.6	14
5	19	6	3.1	—

Source: Yellen 1976:table 3.
Note: Period covered is from 27 January to 11 July 1968. Trips 3 and 4 were 35 and 40 km in length (Yellen 1976:map 5), respectively, for an average move distance of 7 and 5.7 km per move.
[a]One camp occupied for 12 days.

efficiency to be sacrificed in favor of remaining close to a water source. Consider Australia's Western Desert, where several thousand square kilometers may contain only a handful of water sources (e.g., Cane 1990:157). Here, people such as the Ngadadjara tend to stay at a water hole until it dries up before moving on to another. They also tend to use water sources in increasing order of reliability (Gould 1991; personal communication, 1989), so that they always know that the next water source is more dependable than the one they are currently using in case the dry season should be hotter and drier than expected. Water-tethered foragers may make full use of all exploitable resources within foraging distance of the water source, leaving only when net returns reach zero. It is my impression that water-tethered foragers forage farther from their camps for resources (including plant food) than do non-water-tethered desert foragers. The Ju/'hoansi, for example, forage 10 or more kilometers from camp, while the G/wi tend to forage no more than 5 kilometers from a campsite. Diet may also be affected by water-tethered foraging. Among the Bororo of the central Baja California desert, "as water sources dried up, forcing the concentration of population at a few springs, hunting on most of the game ranges was reduced to the vanishing point. The accessible districts would be essentially hunted out before exhaustion of the vegetal resources were evident" (Aschmann 1959:96). In this case, as game became scarce, men turned their efforts to collecting plant food alongside the women. Bororo diet as well as mobility was affected by the need to reduce the energetic cost of acquiring water.

Most contemporary hunter-gatherers follow a pattern of tethered foraging. Along with water, however, living hunter-gatherers are frequently tethered to agricultural plots (their own or those of sedentary neighbors), sources

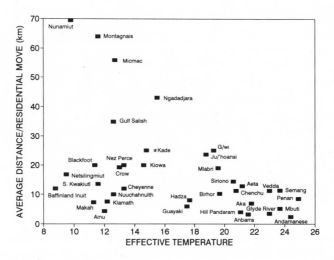

Figure 4-7. The average distance moved per residential move plotted against effective temperature as a proxy measure of the distance between resources.

of wage labor, cigarettes and alcohol, government agencies and welfare rations, or mission posts. In this respect, many contemporary hunter–gatherers are very similar to tropical horticulturalists, such as those in the Amazon, who periodically make treks into the forest that last from several days to several weeks in order to collect forest products and food, especially meat (see papers in Hames and Vickers 1983).

Average distance per residential move

We have discussed how residential mobility enables hunter-gatherers to position themselves relative to food and other resources. We could deduce that the average distance moved between residential locations should be closely related to the distribution of food resources. In general, resources tend to become more spatially segregated along a gradient of decreasing temperature; therefore there should be an increase in the average distance per residential move with decreasing *ET*. The relationship between the two variables is depicted in figure 4-7.

This figure, however, shows a second pattern in addition to the expected one. This consists of groups that do not move very far residentially on average although they live in environments with low to medium *ET*. These exceptions fall into three groups: the extreme Arctic (Netsilingmiut and

Baffinland Inuit), equestrian bison hunters (Crow, Cheyenne, Kiowa, Nez Perce, Blackfoot), and coastal fishers (Nuuchahnulth, Klamath, Ainu, Makah, Southern Kwakiutl).

Unlike many other Arctic groups, neither the Netsilingmiut nor Baffinland Inuit have access to large herds of caribou.[4] Instead, they hunt solitary animals, fish small streams, or, during the winter, live on the frozen surface of the ocean and hunt seals through breathing holes in the ice. The resources they exploit are dispersed, and their distribution resembles more that of resources in the tropical forest than that of other Arctic regions. Like hunter-gatherers in the tropics, those of the extreme Arctic exploit dispersed resources around their camp, then move so that they are at the center of a new foraging area. While hunting seals in the winter, the Copper Inuit, for example, hunt an area 8 kilometers in radius. After the area is depleted, the group moves about 16 kilometers to a new hunting area (Damas 1969a,b, 1972), that is, a move of twice the foraging radius. It is not surprising, then, that the Netsilingmiut and Baffinland Inuit have short residential moves like tropical foragers.

Plains bison hunters used horses to move camp frequently, but not always very far in a single move. Larocque's 1805 journal (Ewers 1955:147), for example, shows that the Crow moved 47 times in only 76 days, moving a median distance of 15 kilometers, but with a range of 5 to 38 kilometers per move. Dunbar traveled about 644 kilometers with the Pawnee during a winter hunt of 1834–35 that lasted 156 days. During this time the Pawnee made 33 camps for an average of 20 kilometers per move (Roper 1991). By taking resources that were mobile and dispersed, Plains hunters were in one respect similar to Arctic and tropical forest foragers: they must have experienced rapid drops in foraging returns soon after occupying a camp. Consequently, Plains groups moved short distances frequently. Factors other than bison distribution, such as the availability of firewood, plants, forage for the horses, or the presence of enemies undoubtedly affected camp movement, but the horse probably lowered the cost of moving sufficiently so that Plains groups could afford to move more frequently and for shorter distances than we might otherwise expect.

Many northern fishing societies move short distances because they are territorially constrained and cannot move very far without trespassing. Living in small territories with high population densities, they move from winter villages, often located near the coast at the mouths of rivers, to nearby spring/summer fishing, shellfishing, or plant-gathering camps, then back to the winter village. Figure 4-7 suggests that if these coastal societies were not territorially constrained or relying upon aquatic resources, they would move very long distances, perhaps especially in winter.

These three sets of exceptions show that whereas *ET* is not a perfect measure of resource distribution, it nonetheless points to foraging considerations as significant factors in structuring hunter-gatherer residential mobility.

Logistical mobility and territorial coverage

To this point, we have only discussed movements of the residential camp. Yet, if we were to track an individual's movements, we would find that the majority of the time he or she spent moving was not spent in moving camp, but in logistical forays to hunt or to gather plant food. Though foragers also make trips to procure raw materials or firewood, to visit, or to gather information, these tasks are often embedded in food-getting forays (Binford 1982; Lee 1979:211; O'Connell and Hawkes 1981). We will assume that food collection is the primary purpose of logistical forays from camp.

Given the general trophic pyramid of any environment, carnivores must normally use larger territories than herbivores. Holding other factors constant for the time being, we would expect to see an increase in the area of land exploited by hunter-gatherers as dependence on hunting increases. Figure 4-8 shows that there is a strong relationship between the relative dependence on hunting and the total area exploited ($N = 36$, $df = 34$, $r = .66$, $p < .01$). The equation describing this relationship, $\log y = .024x + 2.06$, is actually curvilinear: as dependence on hunting increases, the size of the territory increases very rapidly. The same factors which act on the average distance per residential move affect the total area exploited since hunting becomes more important toward the poles and since fauna need large territories to support themselves in cold latitudes. Additionally, although our data are not adequate for analysis, group size could also factor into the equation, with larger groups needing larger ranges. However, as we shall see in chapter 6, both empirical data and theoretical argument suggest that there is an upper limit to foraging group size of not much more than twenty-five people. And, where local group size is large, as it is, for example, on the Northwest Coast, territories are often small and subsistence focuses on aquatic resources. As a group grows in size it may fission or if this is not possible, it may alter its settlement and subsistence strategy. Thus, group size may be a less significant factor than the food source in directly determining range size.

Hunter-gatherers heavily dependent on fauna may use a large range annually, but they do not necessarily cover their range as thoroughly through

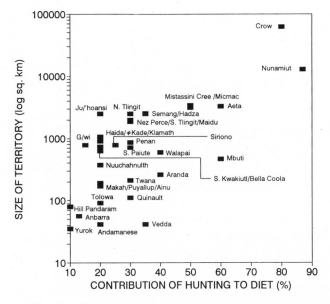

Figure 4-8. The size of foragers' annual ranges plotted against the percent dependence on hunting (from chapter 3, table 3-1). As the dependence on hunting increases, so must the size of the exploited territory.

residential mobility as groups heavily dependent on plant food. As we will see below, the distance at which a resource can be gainfully procured is related to the resource's return rate (and its transportability). High-return-rate resources can be procured at a longer distance from camp than low-return-rate resources. In general, large game provide high return rates once they are sighted. In economies dominated by gathering, foragers cannot gather resources at long foraging distances, and therefore should move shorter distances than in societies dominated by hunting. Hunters should use long logistical forays and cover less of their large territories through residential mobility. Gatherers can be expected to cover their territory more thoroughly through residential mobility. A rough coverage index can be calculated from table 4-1 by dividing the total distance moved residentially by the total area exploited each year. These indices are grouped according to the dominant subsistence category (hunting, gathering, fishing; from table 3-1) with the following results: for groups dependent on gathering, mean = .54 (N = 10; mean = .65 if Hadza and Semang are excluded), for groups dependent on hunting, mean = .05 (N = 6). These figures support the argument that gathering groups cover a greater percentage of their range through residential mobility than do hunting groups.[5] Conversely, hunters probably cover more of their range and spend more time moving individually about the landscape. Hunter-gatherers who rely heavily on aquatic resources also do not cover their ranges through residential mobility (mean = .08, $N = 6$) but make long logistical trips, although, since many are made in boats, these are not directly comparable to terrestrial forays.

Residential and logistical mobility are not mutually exclusive. Investing energy in residential mobility does not exclude the use of extensive logistical mobility as well. Both boreal forest hunter-gatherers and horse-equipped bison hunters, for example, invest a great deal of energy in both residential and logistical mobility. In general, hunter-gatherers heavily dependent on large game (especially in high-primary-biomass settings), have the potential for both high residential and logistical mobility.

This brief overview of ethnographic data only demonstrates patterning between environmental and mobility variables. It assumes that the nature of foraging in a particular environment affects the movements of groups. We now need to examine this assumption in more detail.

INDIVIDUAL FORAGING AND GROUP MOBILITY

In *Stone Age Economics,* Sahlins pointed out that the day-to-day economy of hunter-gatherers is

seriously afflicted by the *imminence of diminishing returns*. Beginning in subsistence and spreading from there to every sector, an initial success seems only to develop the probability that further efforts will yield smaller benefits. This describes the typical curve of food-getting within a particular locale. A modest number of people usually sooner than later reduces the food resources within convenient range of camp. Thereafter, they may stay on only by absorbing an increase in real costs or a decline in real returns: rise in costs if the people choose to search farther and farther afield, decline in returns if they are satisfied to live on the shorter supplies or inferior foods in easier reach. The solution, of course, is to go somewhere else. (Sahlins 1972:33; emphasis in original)

Ethnographic literature demonstrates the link between individual foraging and camp movement quite clearly. In the central Kalahari, for example, ≠Kade women

begin to gather food near the campsite [and] they can complete their work in a trip of 1 to 2 km during the first few days of their stay. Then, gradually, as they consume the plants near camp, they must go farther. If the round trip for gathering food plants exceeds 10 km or so, convenience dictates that they move themselves with all their belongings to virgin territory. (Tanaka 1980:66)

The Mbuti also move when foraging becomes difficult within 5 kilometers of camp (Harako 1981:535). Williams found that 91 percent of Birhor movements were for foraging reasons; specifically, a camp moved when hunting within a 5- to 6-kilometer radius fell below acceptable levels (1974:74). The Australian Pitjandjara move when women complain of walking too far to forage (Tindale 1972:244–45). Although the Hadza can forage for roots up to 8 kilometers from camp, they generally do not go beyond 5 kilometers (Vincent 1984). They move

primarily because food and water are less readily available than they would like; and even where some other motive is present, they will of course at the same time try to improve their access to food and water. However, movement normally takes place long before shortages have become in any way serious. (Woodburn 1968:106)

For the G/wi, "migration to the next campsite is timed to occur before the resources of the last become depleted to the stage at which interhousehold competition might arise to threaten cooperation and dislocate coordination" (Silberbauer 1981a:250–51). When Malaysian Batek women find themselves walking an hour to find yams, they consider it time to move camp (Endicott and Endicott 1986:149). Agta move before all local resources are used (Rai 1990:59). (All of these cases could, of course, have been predicted by the marginal-value theorem; see chapter 3.) A 20- to 30-kilometer round trip appears to be the maximum distance hunter-gatherers will walk comfortably in a day in a variety of habitats.[6] Thus, the distances walked by many hunter-gatherers in daily food-collecting trips are frequently less than the maximum possible walking distance. Since these distances clearly affect when and how far camp is moved, what conditions how far a person will walk in daily foraging?

The distance from a residential camp at which a forager can procure resources at an energetic gain is limited by the return rates of those resources. Figure 4-9 shows the results of a simple central-place foraging model (Kelly 1990, 1991). In this model, two foragers collect food for their family each day. We will assume that the family requires about 14,000 kilocalories per day, that the forager walks at a leisurely pace of three kilometers per hour at a cost of 300 kilocalories per hour, and that the cost of walking increases by 30 percent when returning home with food (Jones and Madsen 1989). We

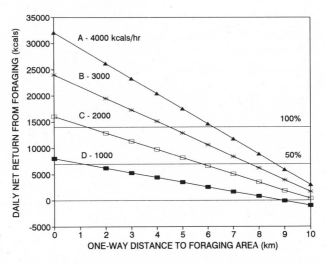

Figure 4-9. The relationship between the daily net return from foraging and distance to the foraging area as a function of the mean foraging-return rate. The horizontal lines indicate the calories that a forager must provide: 50 percent if a family has two foragers, 100 percent if only one. As foragers expend more time and effort in traveling to a foraging area, the mean daily return declines. As a forager provides for more of the family's food needs, and/or as the return rate from the environment declines, the distance at which he or she can forage from camp becomes shorter.

will also assume that foraging activities, including the time to travel to foraging areas as well as the time to harvest and process the food resource, are confined to eight hours a day.[7] The daily return to foraging is simply:

$$\text{Net Return} = [(8 - 2T)R] - (300T + 390T)$$

where:

T = travel time to foraging patch (distance/3 km/hr)
R = mean environmental return rate (varied here from 1,000 to 4,000 kcal/ hr for four different environments).[8]

For any of the four environments, the net return from foraging decreases farther from camp as the forager spends more time and energy traveling to and from the foraging area relative to the time spent collecting and processing food resources. As could be expected, the net return also decreases with a concomitant decrease in an environment's return rate. The two horizontal lines indicate the amount of energy needed on a daily basis by the family depending on whether the forager is gathering 50 or 100 percent of the total caloric intake. The distance at which the forager brings home at least a day's worth of food, the intersection between the sloping net-return lines and one of the horizontal caloric-needs lines, becomes shorter as the return rate decreases or as the individual forager's workload increases. Let's say that our forager lives in local environment C, providing a mean return rate of 2,000 kilocalories per hour. Another resource located more than 10 kilometers from camp is collected by another family member (this is not an atypical division of labor in which the wife collects resources near camp while the husband hunts at longer distances). We will also stipulate that the forager collecting the 2,000-kilocalories-per-hour resource is responsible for 50 percent of the diet. This forager, therefore, can collect food up to about 5.75 kilometers from camp. If for some reason the need for the resource increases, so that it makes up 100 percent of the diet (e.g., if the other forager becomes ill), then it can only be collected at a net gain up to about 1.5 kilometers from camp. The *effective foraging radius,* therefore, is largely a product of the return rates of the available resources and the degree of dependence on them (which, in turn, is a function of how many people are foraging for each family, family size, and per capita caloric needs). As average resource-return rates decline (as would happen if lower-ranked resources are added to the diet) and/or as the amount of food a forager must bring back increases, the effective foraging radius becomes shorter and the family will probably move more frequently and for shorter distances.[9]

The relationship between return rate and the effective foraging radius has an effect on diet. Central-place foraging models suggest that the further a forager travels from camp, the more restricted his or her choice of resources must become. Only high-return-rate resources can be taken at long distances from camp; a wider diversity of food can be taken close to camp (Kaplan and Hill 1992; see Vickers 1989 for an ethnographic example and Speth and Scott 1989 for an archaeological one). However, a resource's transportability also figures in here. If a resource is bulky compared to its caloric value, it cannot be transported easily and this will offset its high return rate. We noted in chapter 3 that under the right conditions grasshoppers can be collected at very high return rates. However, Kevin Jones and David Madsen demonstrate that grasshoppers cannot be carried long distances at an effective return rate, since a relatively small weight takes up a rather large volume (1989).[10]

So far we have discussed foraging as if the decision to move or not is based

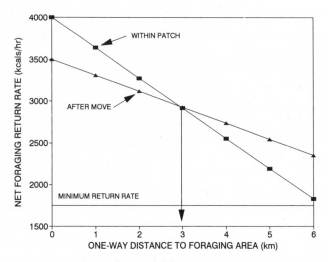

Figure 4-10. The relationship between the return rate experienced within a foraging area relative to that which could be expected if the foragers moved to a new area. The model predicts camp movement at the point at which foragers are traveling about 3 kilometers from camp in order to find food.

only on the nature of foraging around the immediate camp. However, as Sahlins pointed out, hunter-gatherers must weigh the cost of remaining where they are and foraging farther out (or using progressively lower-return-rate resources nearby) against the potential benefit of moving to a new area.

Imagine a foraging family living in an environment where a 4,000-kilocalories-per-hour resource is homogeneously distributed across the landscape. For the sake of simplicity, let's say each family has one active forager who must, therefore, collect 14,000 kilocalories per day to feed the family. Assuming an eight-hour workday, this means that the forager must gather the resource at a minimum overall daily return rate of 14,000/8 = 1,750 kilocalories per hour. Making the same assumptions as above, the net return rate (RR) decreases with increasing one-way foray distance (figure 4-10):

$$RR = \frac{4000\,(8 - 2T) - (300T + 390\,T)}{8}$$

This gives an effective foraging radius of 6 kilometers; the area encompassed with this 6-kilometer radius of camp is the effective foraging patch.

We can also compute the return rate if the family were to move to a new foraging area after exploiting the resources within a given radius of the site. Since food is homogeneously distributed, we initially will assume that they move the minimum distance to position themselves in a pristine foraging area, that is, twice the current foraging radius. The after-move return rate of the individual forager, allowing an hour for camp breakdown and setup (more on this variable below) is figured as:

$$RR = \frac{4000 \ (7 - 2T) - 300 \ (2T)}{8}$$

The after-move line in figure 4-10 shows the daily return rate if the forager were to move camp after foraging within 1, 2, 3 . . . kilometers of camp. Note that at a return rate of just under 3,000 kilocalories per hour (achieved at a foraging distance of about 3 kilometers), the net after-move return rate is equal to the within-patch return rate. After foraging within about 3 kilometers of camp, the family would do better to move to the center of a new foraging area (6 kilometers away). Even with the move, the forager would achieve a higher return rate for that day (and would return to a 4,000-kcal/ hr rate the following day) than if they had not moved. This simple model and the ethnographic cases cited above suggest that if maximization of foraging efficiency is the general goal of foraging behavior, then central-place foragers should try to minimize travel time (Orians and Pearson 1979).

At the heart of the relationship between daily foraging and group movement are the perceived costs of camp movement and foraging. In the above model, we assumed that the location of the next camp was a function of the foraging radius of the current camp. But campsites can be determined by many different factors, such as water sources, firewood, shade, shelter, insects, and so on. In figure 4-11, the distance to the next patch is not a function of the current foraging radius, as it was in figure 4-10, but is held constant at 5 and, for comparative purposes, 7 kilometers; thus the slope of each after-move line is zero, since the cost of moving is now constant rather than being a function of the size of the foraged area. As we would expect, if the next camp is 5 kilometers away, a forager should forage within 3.9 kilometers of camp before moving; if the next camp is 7 kilometers away, he or she should forage within 4.9 kilometers of camp before moving (creating some overlap in foraging areas and decreasing the amount of food available at the next camp). The predicted differences in foraging distance may seem to be minor. But note that increasing the effective foray distance from 3 to 4 kilometers (a 33 percent increase) increases the foraging area, and the length of time a camp can be occupied, by 77 percent (assuming homogeneous resource distribution).

Distance to the next patch, however, is only one variable affecting the

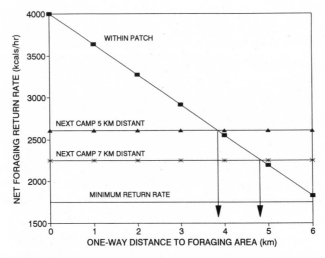

Figure 4-11. The relationship between the return rate experienced within a foraging area relative to that which could be expected if the foragers moved to a new area 5 or 10 kilometers away. As the distance to the next patch increases, we could expect the current foraging patch to be occupied for longer and longer periods of time (as the marginal-value theorem also predicts).

cost of moving. The difficulty of traversing the terrain also figures into the calculations (figure 4-12). For example, 10 kilometers of muskeg in the spring is harder to cross than 10 kilometers of prairie. Increasing the moving cost to 1,200 kilocalories per hour in the model while leaving the foraging cost at 300 kilocalories per hour predicts camp movement after foraging a 4- rather than a 3-kilometer radius. If the walking cost of both foraging *and* moving is 1,200 kilocalories per hour, then the group should move after foraging within only about 2.25 kilometers of camp. Thus, group mobility responds to the cost of group movement and foraging effort. This will be affected not only by the terrain to be crossed, but also by whether draft animals and transportation technology are available (e.g., dogsleds or horses; see Binford 1990). A moving cost of 1,200 kilocalories per hour is excessive but we have chosen it to make a point: as the cost of moving increases relative to the cost of foraging, residential mobility is expected to decrease. The cost could include other factors in addition to those affecting the physical movement of belongings. For example, if the anticipated next campsite is already occupied, the cost of moving would have to include the cost of displacing current residents, perhaps through warfare.

Figure 4-12. A band of Tree River (Agiarmiut) Copper Inuit move across the tundra; women and dogs pull the sleds. The cost of moving is affected by the terrain to be crossed, the weather, the amount of material to be carried, and the type of housing. Photograph by J. J. O'Neill, October 1915, courtesy of the Canadian Museum of Civilization, no. 38571.

Housing also affects the cost of moving. The time required to break down and set up camp is seldom discussed in the literature. The models as first developed used a one-hour camp breakdown/setup time based on what little information was available (Robert Hitchcock, personal communication, 1989; Peter Brosius, personal communication, 1989). Camp breakdowns may be quicker for many tropical groups, but could be slower for Arctic peoples due to differences in the amount of goods carried (see Burch 1988:107 for an example of a one-hour camp-setup time for an Arctic group).[11] We can see, however, that increasing or decreasing this time greatly alters the mobility solution by changing the length of the working day (figure 4-13): a camp-breakdown time of two hours means that it is not worthwhile to move before exhausting nearly all food within a 6-kilometer radius, while a breakdown/setup time of one-half hour predicts movement at a 1.5-kilometer foraging radius. It appears, then, that as the movement of camp itself becomes more difficult and time consuming, hunter-gatherers may remain in their current foraging area for longer periods of time. Conversely, if

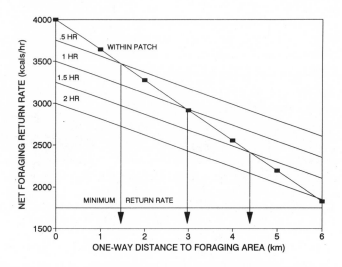

Figure 4-13. The relationship between the return rate experienced within a foraging area relative to that which could be expected if the foragers moved to a new area at different camp-move times, from one-half hour to two hours. As the cost of camp breakdown and setup increases, so does the predicted foraging radius and length of time the current camp is occupied.

a group must be mobile for energetic reasons (low return rates that result in a short effective foray distance), their housing should be tailored to their mobility needs. Obviously, housing and mobility are expected to be systematically related to each other (Binford 1990).[12]

This simple model assumes only that hunter-gatherers move as families, not necessarily as bands. From ethnographic data we know that some hunter-gatherer social units can have extremely fluid composition, with individuals and families moving at different schedules. Anthropologists frequently attribute this fluidity to the need to relieve social tension. Though this may be the proximate cause, subsistence can often be the ultimate source of this tension. Agta band members intensely debate for hours or even days whether to move or not, with foraging effort playing a prominent role in these debates (Rai 1990:59). Large families could have higher camp move costs (see below), and thus may wish to remain in a current camp longer than small families. On the other hand, foragers with large families need higher minimum daily returns than those with small families, and thus have shorter effective foraging radii. If a large family has remained in camp out of a social need or obligation, the foragers of this family may forage past the point at which they could forage more efficiently by moving, and even reach the edge of their effective foraging radius before the foragers of smaller families, resulting in tension and possibly group fission. Therefore, large and small families should move on different schedules. Family size will not be important in determining camp movement, however, where everyone's subsistence is tied to the same resource (e.g., fish runs, communal hunting).

We should also point out that since many plant foods provide returns lower than those of large game—but are much more reliable resources— the effective foraging distance for plants is shorter, in general, than it is for large game. Since large game is usually procured by men (with some exceptions; see chapter 7), women's foraging should by and large determine when camp is moved. Among the Agta, "[since] hunting depends on mobile animals, it is not an important consideration [in determining moves]. Men and women freely voice their opinion on residence change, but women, who must carry out the most gathering, have the final say" (Rai 1990:59). This is important when considering the effect of reduced residential mobility on women's and men's nonforaging activities (see below).

Other variables: return rates

The effects of alterations in the return rates used in figure 4-10 can be easily computed. If the return rate of the resource to be used in the next camp is lowered relative to that of the resources used at the current camp, the forager is predicted to remain at the current camp for a correspondingly longer period of time. However, if the return rate of the resources of both the current and potential camp is changed, but held constant, the within-patch and after-move return rates always equal one another at a foraging radius of about 3 kilometers. They do not alter the predicted outcome even if, as is true for a return rate of 1,000 kilocalories per hour, it is not possible to forage at an energetic gain at a distance of 3 kilometers. Under circumstances of low return rates, camp-breakdown time and the amount of material possessions would have to be extremely low (and/or family size would have to be very small). In these cases, some people may set out before others, using the camp move as a foraging trip as well. In some tropical forest cases, men head out immediately for the new camp, hunting along the way, while women pack, move camp and gather plant food as they travel (e.g., Morris 1982:176; Hill and Hawkes 1983).

This leads to an intriguing contradiction between the marginal-value theorem and the foraging-radius model used here. In chapter 3 we introduced

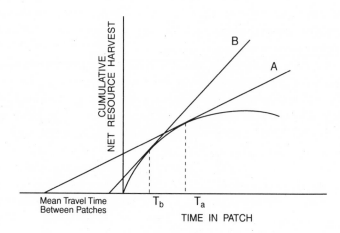

Figure 4-14. The curve in this illustration depicts a general depletion curve: the net return decreases the longer a forager stays in a patch. Recalling the MVT, where mean environmental return rates are low (the slope of line A) the forager should remain in the current patch longer (T_a) than when return rates are high (Line B, T_b). Drawn by Dan Delaney.

the marginal-value theorem (MVT) to predict when a forager should leave one foraging patch and move on to another. To review the most general case, a forager enters a patch and collects resources at a net gain initially, but slowly depletes the resources, lowering the net gain over time (figure 3-5). The MVT states that the forager should leave the patch when the rate of return in the patch equals the mean environmental rate of return (taking travel time into account). Figure 4-14 shows how different mean environmental return rates produce different patch-residency times. Line A represents an environment with a low return rate while Line B, with a steeper slope, is an environment with a high return rate. Holding other variables constant, and though it may seem counterintuitive, in the environment with the higher mean return rate the forager would leave the patch sooner than if overall return rates were low (E. Smith 1991:255). In either case, they would leave before patch depletion occurs. The foraging-radius model suggests that under low return rates (and holding other factors constant) foragers will reach their effective foraging radius before reaching the moving-on threshold and could completely deplete a patch before moving on.

There are several reasons for this. The MVT does not hold, strictly speaking, in the case at hand since in the present foraging-radius model resources are homogeneously rather than patchily distributed. Moreover, the foraging-radius model assumes that foragers are aware of the resource distribution and are more or less vacuuming up resources close to camp, then those further away, then those still further away, and so on until they reach their effective foraging radius or the point at which they would do better to move camp. The MVT assumes random search and encounter. Also, the model used here does not use resource density. Resource density is central to the MVT since the diminishing-returns curve is based on gross returns over time that decrease as a function of increased search time that is in turn a function of decreasing abundance. Finally, the foraging-radius model is a central-place model, in which foragers go out from camp, procure resources, and then return, rather than consuming resources as they encounter them while foraging. In the foraging-radius model, a decline in return rates results from investing time in traveling to and from the foraging area. In the diminishing-returns case to which the marginal-value theorem is applicable a decline in return rates results from increasing search time. Foraging situations could fall under the conditions of the central place or MVT conditions. This raises the question of whether the pattern of increasing residential mobility relative to primary biomass depicted in figure 4-4 is a product of decreasing return rates (as measured by the proxy variable of primary biomass) and decreasing net per capita gains, or a product of increasing return rates (since primary production increases with primary biomass) and higher consequent opportunity costs. The ecological perspective taken above argues for the former situation, but hard data on foraging returns for a diversity of groups along a similar environmental gradient are needed for a test.

We might also note that the rate of decrease in a resource's net return correlates with the slope of the net-return line. That is, in figure 4-9, net returns from collecting in a 4,000-kilocalories-per-hour environment decrease more rapidly relative to foraging distance than in the 1,000-kilocalories-per-hour environment. Simms also found that the returns from high-ranked resources decrease more rapidly with decreases in abundance than do returns from low-ranked resources (1987:50–55). This means that hunter-gatherers are likely to perceive and respond to changes in the availability of high-ranked resources before they respond to changes in lower-ranked resources. This makes sense in light of the central prediction of optimal-foraging theory's diet-breadth model discussed in chapter 3: that inclusion of low-ranked items in a diet is a function of changes in the availability of high-ranked items.

Time frames

In the model, we assumed that some foraging is done on the day of the move. But this may not be true in many cases. Where no foraging is done on the day of the move, the after-move return rate of the day of a move would be zero. According to the model used here, this would mean that the forager should not move until eating everything within the 6-kilometer radius of camp. In other words, the effective foraging patch should be completely depleted before moving. This is clearly not supported by the ethnographic data cited at the beginning of this section.

The answer may lie in the time frame used. In the model used here we assumed an hourly return-rate maximization, a common assumption, as we noted in chapter 3, of simple foraging models. However, is an hour the time period over which hunter-gatherers evaluate resource returns? Or, recognizing that there is always some daily variance in returns and that food may not be gathered every day, do they respond to the environmental return rate averaged over several days, or even weeks? Moving before exploiting everything (in our model) within a 3-kilometer radius of camp may result in return-rate depression for a single day, but hunter-gatherers may accept this temporary loss knowing that the day after the move the return rate will be 4,000 kilocalories per hour.

Let's assume that the forager achieves a 4,000-kilocalories-per-hour return rate for several days after moving, but does not forage on the day of the move. As figure 4-15 shows, depending on the time period over which rates are averaged, the forager stays for different lengths of time than those predicted by a model assuming foraging on the day of the move. For example, if after-move returns are averaged over only two days (0 for the day of the move + 4,000 kcal/hr for the next/2 = 2,000 kcal/hr), the forager should remain at the current camp until consuming everything within 5.5 kilometers of camp. If a four-day average is used, then the mean return is increased to 3,000 kilocalories per hour, and the forager would remain in the current camp for a much shorter period of time. Ethnographic data, unfortunately, are not sufficiently detailed to provide much guidance on what time frames may be used under different conditions but it is likely that the relevant period is several days in length.

Risk

The model used here also assumes that hunter-gatherers have a perfect knowledge of the environment and can know the state of anticipated re-

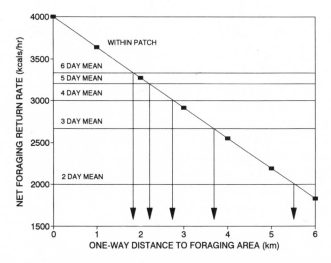

Figure 4-15. The relationship between the return rate experienced within a foraging area relative to that which could be expected if the foragers moved to a new
area with after-move return rates averaged over two- to six-day periods. As the
period over which after-move return rates are averaged increases the predicted foraging radius and camp-occupation time decreases.

sources. This is rarely true, and so the cost of moving must include a risk
factor. If the anticipated resource is not a certain one, then the cost of
moving will, in effect, be higher, and we could expect hunter-gatherers
to stay longer in their current camp. Many desert hunter-gatherers elect
to remain at a water source at the expense of decreasing foraging-return
rates because they are uncertain of the condition of other water holes;
they may remain at the current water hole either until it runs out or
until the status of other water sources is ascertained. Some Australian
Aborigines, in fact, will accept extremely low caloric intakes and forage
up to 15 kilometers from camp rather than move from a secure water
source (Cane 1987; Gould 1969a).

One way to look at risk is in terms of return-rate variance. As noted in
chapter 3, holding resource type, density, and even forager capabilities constant, there can be a great deal of variance in day-to-day return rates. How
might this affect foragers' decisions to move?

First, this is a question about perception. Given that hunter-gatherers do
not carry notebook computers, how low must an average return rate be
before the foragers decide to move, knowing that variance in the after-move

return rate can also be expected? At what point would foragers perceive that they can do better (maximize foraging efficiency) by moving? Figure 4-16 shows the within-patch and after-move return rates depicted in figure 4-10, but with a ±200-kilocalories-per-hour variance limit around the within-patch line and a ±400-kilocalories-per-hour variance limit around the after-move line. In this case, there is greater variance in the after-move return rate than in the within-patch return rate, although the average returns are equal. Note that at a foraging radius of just over 4 kilometers, the lower variance limit of the within-patch return rate is about equal to that of the after-move return rate. It is at this point, after using everything within 4 kilometers of the current camp, that the foragers may move, knowing that they are guaranteed to do better than their current average effort. The higher the variance in the after-move return rate, the *longer* foragers are predicted to remain in the current camp.

However, variances and means are normally inversely related to one another; a low mean return rate will normally have a high variance. As we have already seen, if the return rate of a resource to be exploited at the next potential camp is lower than that of the current camp, the foragers should remain in the current camp for longer periods of time than if the resource return rates were the same. It may not be possible, or necessary, therefore, to separate the effects of mean return rates from variance.

Second, there is a question about goals. We know very little about whether hunter-gatherers judge resources in terms of mean return rates or variance (see Gragson 1993 for a recent effort). But if foragers wish to go for a resource that can occasionally provide very high returns, they may elect to seek out resources with high variances intentionally. For reasons we will discuss in chapter 5, some hunter-gatherers (perhaps especially male hunters) do indeed seek out riskier resources. If a forager wished to try and maximize his foraging return, he might move when the highest *possible* return after moving is higher than the highest possible return of foraging from the current camp. Referring to figure 4-16, this would be at a foraging radius of less than 2 kilometers, implying a *shorter* occupation time than our original model predicted. Unfortunately, foragers' perceptions of resources in terms of variables that we, as anthropologists, consider important is not well known and merits further field study.

Linked to the issue of resource variability is the issue of storage. Storage obviously results in the accumulation of food at one or more locations, increasing the patchiness of an environment, and could encourage decreased residential mobility. Food storage among hunter-gatherers may principally

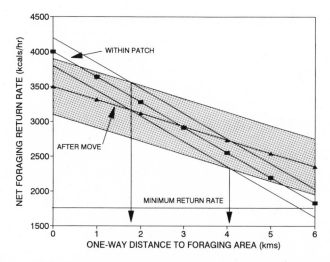

Figure 4-16. The effects of return-rate variance on decisions to remain in the current camp or move. To maintain as high a return rate as possible, the forager should remain in the current patch until the lower variance limit of the after-move rate equals the lower variance limit of the within-patch rate. Alternatively, to seek risky resources, the forager may move much sooner, when the upper variance limit of the after-move rate exceeds that of the within-patch rate.

be a way to cope with resource seasonality: data show that the volume of stored resources increases with decreasing *ET* (Binford 1980; see also Keeley 1988). The decision to reside at the location where food is stored or to transport the resources to another location, however, depends on the return from moving one set of resources versus the return rate expected from each location's resources (Jones and Madsen 1989; Rhode 1990). Thus, food storage does not necessarily cause a reduction in residential mobility. The decision to move also depends on the variance of the return rate of the next anticipated resource. Figure 4-16 suggests that, given a choice of several resources with similar return rates, hunter-gatherers may move from their current foraging area to that of the resource with the least variance. If resource variability increases over the long term, hunter-gatherers could be expected to invest more in storage, and decrease mobility, since there is no variance in the acquisition of food once it is stored (see Rowley-Conwy and Zvelebil 1989).

As noted above, not all residential movements are directly controlled by subsistence. People may move to gain access to firewood, raw materials, or because insects have become intolerable at the current camp. Movements can be socially or politically motivated as well, as people seek spouses, allies, or shamans, or to distance themselves from sorcery, death, or political forces. People may move to relieve social tension, to visit friends and relatives, trade, gamble, participate in rituals, or just catch up on news.[13] However, some movements made for social reasons can ultimately be related to foraging. For example, during a period of drought-induced food stress, /Xai/xai Bushmen stated that they were going elsewhere to trade, but this decision followed two weeks of bickering over food (Wiessner 1982b). While the model presented here is limited to the extent that it is based only on considerations of foraging efficiency, as we pointed out in chapter 2, this permits analysis to determine when factors other than foraging efficiency are at work in a particular case.

SEDENTISM

To this point we have discussed the factors that keep hunter-gatherers moving. Yet we know from archaeology that at certain times and in certain places, hunter-gatherers settled down, and ceased to move residentially. The origins of sedentary communities is an important question in anthropology, for it is with the appearance of sedentary communities that we find evidence of nonegalitarian sociopolitical organization—social hierarchies and hereditary leadership, political dominance, gender inequality, and unequal access to resources, as well as changes in cultural notions of material wealth, privacy, individuality, and cooperation (Wilson 1988). We examine the possible relationship between sedentism and sociopolitical organization in chapter 8. In this chapter we are concerned with understanding the cause(s) of sedentism.

The term *sedentism* means different things to different people.[14] For the most part, sedentism refers to the process "whereby human groups reduce their mobility to the point where they remain residentially stationary year-round" (Hitchcock 1987a:374) or as settlements where "at least part of the population remains at the same location throughout the entire year" (Rice, in Rafferty 1985:115). Sedentism is usually thought of as a relative difference rather than a static condition, thus sedentary settlement systems are "less mobile than previously" or become "increasingly sedentary over time" (Kelly 1992). Frequently, definitions conflate several dimensions of mobility, including seasonal movement of the residential base camp, movement of individuals around and between residences, movement of a group's yearly range or aggregation site (e.g., winter villages on the Northwest Coast or wet-season villages in seasonal tropical forests), and the permanence of facilities such as houses and fish weirs (Eder 1984; Ingold 1987; Rafferty 1985; Stark 1981).[15] In conflating these different dimensions there is a tendency to think of mobility in terms of a single scale of residential mobility and sometimes to think of societies as either mobile or sedentary. But it should be clear by now that mobility is not an all-or-nothing affair. Nor is there a single scale of mobility, for as we have seen, mobility varies along several potentially independent behavioral dimensions.

Ethnographic data show the interplay between group and individual movements as residential mobility decreases. Formerly nomadic, the Batak now maintain a central settlement at which someone is almost always present throughout the year (Eder 1984). They move this central settlement, however, every seven to ten years. An individual family spends only about 25 percent of the year in the central settlement. The rest of the time is spent in field houses and forest camps. Moving among a limited number of locations, a Batak family changes location about ninety times a year, moving about 3 kilometers each time for a total yearly residential mobility of about 270 kilometers. Individuals make foraging trips into the forest from these camps, adding to overall individual mobility. In other words, the Batak "shifted the burden of that [residential] mobility off of the local group as a whole and onto lower levels of social organization" (Eder 1984:851). It appears to be generally true that as residential mobility is reduced, logistical mobility increases (Binford 1980). This process occurs among many hunter-gatherers who, for one reason or another, have become sedentary in recent decades (see Hitchcock 1982, 1987a,b; Hitchcock and Ebert 1984, 1989). As Bushmen become sedentary (due to government coercion or the attractions of wage labor) men make longer logistical forays (Hitchcock 1982). The Kalahari's residentially mobile Kua, for example, might not travel more than 6 kilometers from camp, while members of sedentary Kua villages make trips of up to 50 kilometers.[16]

In brief, there is a constant trade-off between the costs and benefits of group movements on the one hand, and individual logistical movements on the other. Sedentism does not save energy, but it does reorganize it. Why should this happen?

For many years, the reigning view in anthropology was that a nomadic lifestyle was not something any right-thinking individual would want. "We have taken for granted," wrote the participants in a 1955 seminar in community patterns, "that in general sedentary life has more survival value than wandering life to the human race, and that, other things being equal, whenever there is an opportunity to make the transition, it will be made" (Beardsley et al. 1956:134). The opportunity was thought to be either plant domestication or resource abundance. The former was assumed to be the more likely cause, and sedentary hunter-gatherers, such as those of the Northwest Coast, were considered anomalies. However, we now have many archaeological cases where agriculture preceded sedentism or where sedentism preceded agriculture (see Kelly 1992; Price and Brown 1985b). Ethnographically, there are many horticulturalists who are seasonally mobile (e.g., the Raramurí of Mexico; see Hard and Merrill 1992), who make long treks (e.g., many Amazonian societies), or who shift residence every few years in response to soil depletion or a decline in hunting returns (see Vickers 1989). Thus, the relationship between agriculture and mobility is by no means straightforward.

Binford challenged the resource-abundance argument—what he called the Garden of Eden perspective—by raising the issue of seasonal and yearly resource variability (1983). Hunter-gatherers remain mobile, Binford argued, not because they don't have the opportunity to settle down, but in order to maintain information about resources in order to have backup options in case an expected resource is not available. Maintaining knowledge of current and potential future states of resources—the status of a water hole, signs of game and plant food—is critical for group planning. In the early spring Nunamiut men, for example, "travel widely attempting to find moving caribou . . . [and] to gather information as to the number of animals and the probable timing of movement so they may plan their intercept strategy" (Binford 1978:169). The Arctic's Netsilingmiut and the Australian Aranda do much the same thing (Balikci 1970; Horne and Aiston 1924). Hunter-gatherers use this information to assess various alternatives, much as a chess player does:

in assessing the cost of exploiting resources, the band considers not only its next move but the whole series of migrations in the foreseeable future . . . the aim is not to plot the coming season's itinerary in detail but to work out a series of moves that will permit the band the widest choice of subsequent sites. (Silberbauer 1981a:249)

Consequently, many hunter-gatherers feel compelled to maintain knowledge of enormous areas. The Nunamiut maintained knowledge of nearly 250,000 square kilometers (Binford 1983:206); the Australian Pintupi have knowledge of over 52,000 square kilometers (Long 1971).[17] No one in either of these groups uses all of his or her territory in a single year—a Nunamiut, in fact, may personally use only one-tenth of it in his or her lifetime. Nonetheless, mobility does help individuals maintain knowledge of enormous areas.

Others point out that mobility also helps hunter-gatherers to maintain social ties that form insurance networks of affinal kin, trading and religious partners, and instructs children in the resource geography of a region.[18]

However, the extent to which hunter-gatherers must maintain information about and ties to other areas is related to the degree of temporal and spatial variation in resources. Whereas no environment is perfectly constant, environments fluctuate on different scales. We could expect some variability in the need and ability to maintain information or social ties relative to the degree of resource fluctuation (see chapter 5). Where resources are constant and reliable, mobility will not be needed to gather information. Also, maintaining knowledge of other areas does not *require* residential movement— sedentary horticulturalists maintain information networks without moving their villages. Leaving aside the issue of information, then, we return to the relationship between foraging and residential mobility and ask: is sedentism a product of resource abundance?

Recall the foraging model discussed above (figure 4-10). Exactly how long a forager could remain in the 6-kilometer-radius patch depends on the density of food within the foraging area. Assuming a homogeneous caloric yield of .25 kilocalories per square meter, the 6-kilometer foraging area could potentially be occupied for upwards of 673 days by a band of 25 people. But if the foragers leave after eating everything within about 3 kilometers of camp, the camp is occupied for only 167 days. Even though they could remain where they are and forage at an energetic gain for nearly two years, this band of hunter-gatherers should leave after a few months *if* they wish to maintain as high a daily return rate as possible.[19] It would seem that even in a Garden of Eden, and leaving aside other factors that could encourage movement, foragers should still move. In fact, this model suggests that in an environment of homogeneously distributed resources, the only apparent reason hunter-gatherers would not move is if there is no place to move to— that is, if population density rises to the saturation point, packing foraging groups into a region. As population density rises, residential mobility would involve the additional cost of displacing a group already using a region. Since this could involve physical violence, it may tip the scales in favor of remaining in place and thus encourage sedentism. Where resources are dense and return rates high, hunter-gatherers may be very mobile initially; but high per capita return rates (or high rates of recovery; see Winterhalder and Goland 1993) could result in rapid population growth that could quickly constrain residential movements (see chapter 6).

What about environments where resources are not homogeneously distributed? In our discussion above (refer back to figures 4-10 through 4-16), we saw that as more energy or time was needed to move camp, relative to the cost of foraging at the current camp, the camp would be occupied for longer periods of time. The frequency of residential movements decreases as resource patches become more spread out, while the length of logistical forays increases. We have already discussed several factors that are important here: the distance to the next camp, the terrain to be crossed, the amount of material that must be carried, the time required to construct housing, and the anticipated return rate (and variance) of resources at the next location. Nonetheless, these variables all converge on the single question raised by Sahlins and reiterated by behavioral ecology: what is the cost (and benefit) of staying in one place versus the cost (and benefit) of moving somewhere else? From our models we can deduce that hunter-gatherers should stop moving residentially if the anticipated return rate of the next patch minus the cost of moving is greater than the anticipated return rate of the patch currently occupied. Stated more generally, sedentism can be a product of local abundance in a context of regional scarcity. This is different than saying that resource abundance results in sedentism. While it is clearly necessary that resources be continuously available year round, or be available in sufficient bulk to be stored for a seasonal lean period, in order for hunter-gatherers to be sedentary (and continue to hunt and gather, rather than farm), it is also likely that the decision to become sedentary is based on regional, not just local, resource conditions.

Sedentism may also have a domino effect. If there is some overlap in groups' ranges (as frequently appears to be the case ethnographically) when one group elects to become sedentary, for example at the mouth of a productive salmon stream, they in effect remove a resource patch from others. This makes the environment more patchy, and increases the cost of moving to an occupied resource area (since it would require displacing the now-sedentary group). Once established, then, a single sedentary village could encourage neighboring groups to become sedentary. Therefore, sedentism may be a regional phenomenon, with sedentary communities occurring in batches, rather than singly.[20]

FORAGING, MOBILITY, AND SOCIETY

The mobility ethos

Among many hunter-gatherers, mobility is highly valued; there are even a few cases of hunter-gatherers, such as the Australian Anbarra, who move despite the fact that they could be sedentary (Meehan 1982). Members of modern or formerly mobile hunter-gatherer societies often express a strong desire to move around in order to visit friends, to see what's happening elsewhere, or to relieve boredom. In the subarctic, traveling is "something of an end in itself" (Savishinsky 1974:120), and "to travel to see new things is good in itself" (Slobodkin 1969:84; see Boas 1888:166–67). Though Australian Aborigines prefer to travel where they have relatives (as many people do), they too consider it good to see "a bit of the world" (Beckett 1965:19; see Myers 1986:44; Gould 1969b:87). Among the Hare, traveling is a metaphor for freedom (Savishinsky 1974:120), and the Kaska did not like "sitting one place all the time like white men" (Honigmann 1949:102).[21] Though unlikely to account for large-scale evolutionary changes, cultural ideals that value movement might encourage mobility even where it is possible to be sedentary. They may help perpetuate cultural and niche differences between populations of horticulturalists and hunter-gatherers/pastoralists, since mobility can be a strategy to maintain cultural autonomy.

We cannot claim that hunter-gatherers are mobile because they value mobility, however, for this only raises the question of why they value mobility. We pointed out above that mobility helps in (but is not essential to) maintaining knowledge of large areas, as well as maintaining social ties. But the first forager quoted at the beginning of this chapter points to the primary cause of a mobility ethos among hunter-gatherers: from a purely energetic standpoint, they know they have to move to find food, even in an area of abundant resources, so they have come to value movement. If selective pressures have anything to do with the evolution of human society, and if foraging efficiency is a proxy measure of fitness, then there should be tremendous pressure upon foragers to be residentially mobile, at some level, for residential mobility permits foraging efficiency. Though we could expect variability in the strength of a mobility ethos as the need to move to gather food and/ or information changes, it should not be surprising that residentially mobile foragers value a mobile lifestyle.[22]

Foraging and enculturation

Foraging, of course, is not all that hunter-gatherers do. They also spend considerable amounts of time in religious activities and prestige competition, in fostering and maintaining family life, in socializing, trading, defense, and tool manufacture. Spending time foraging means that one or more of these activities is not being done. The amount of time an individual devotes to foraging represents a balance between the costs and benefits of foraging and nonforaging activities. Research into evaluating how hunter-gatherers decide to forage or to do something else has just begun (Winterhalder 1983, 1987; Hill 1988). It is a difficult topic, for though we can reduce assorted food resources to a common set of measurements—return rates, net returns, density, and so forth—it is much more difficult to develop a common set of measurements of the utility of activities as various as foraging, childcare, tool manufacture, and socializing.

Nonetheless, we should consider the potential impact of adult foraging decisions on one especially important area, the rearing of children. The study of child rearing has a lengthy history in anthropology, but it has not figured prominently in hunter-gatherer studies despite recognition of its importance.[23] Given that there is variability in how much time foragers devote to getting food, we can expect there to be variability in how much time they devote to their children. (The greatest variability may be in fathers' attention to children given a child's need for the mother's breast milk. Hewlett, for example, shows that 22 percent of the time that Aka fathers are in camp they are holding an infant, but Ju/'hoansi fathers devote only 2 percent of their camp time to infant care [1992a].) How much time adults devote to children is significant in that it affects enculturation and thus cultural evolutionary change. Here we are especially concerned with the effect that changes in adult foraging activities that occur with the inception of sedentism have in conditioning the dramatic cultural changes that often occur as a mobile people become sedentary (see also chapter 8).

There are two basic forms of enculturation, *parental* and *peer group* (see review in Draper and Harpending 1987). In the first form, a child's primary caretaker is its parents, especially the mother. The mother is a predictable and consistent provider of resources, beginning obviously with breast milk, but including affection, attention, and protection. The child learns that desirable things, such as food, are held by one or two individuals. As a child grows and can fend more and more for itself, its parents become less giving. Though its demands may become more insistent, the child is eventually cut off by its parents. Pat Draper and Henry Harpending argue that in this situation the child learns that resources and desirable goods are limited and hard to obtain (1987:220). This may lead the child to become more assertive and independent, which could lead to a proclivity to select foraging activities largely on the basis of return rate, and perhaps to depend on technology rather than social favors to acquire goods (Schlegel and Barry 1991). Barry, Child, and Bacon found such training to be common among hunter-gatherers as opposed to agriculturalists (1959). In mobile as opposed to sed-

entary societies, boys appear to deemphasize male–male competition and fo-
cus more on manipulation of the natural world through technology
(Schlegel and Barry 1991). Additionally, where children learn their culture
primarily from their parents, there may be a large amount of intracultural
variation in beliefs, behaviors, and so on (Cavalli-Sforza and Feldman 1981).
Barry Hewlett finds evidence in support of this hypothesis in the ways that
Aka fathers interact with their children (Hewlett and Cavalli-Sforza 1986;
Hewlett 1991b).

In the case of peer rearing, at about two years of age a child is placed in
the care of an older sibling (often an older sister) and becomes a member of
an age group. The peer group becomes the child's primary locus of social
interaction. Status and power differences between its members, however, are
not as large as between a child and its parents. As the children move among
a village's residences, children learn that there are many sources of food and
desirables other than their parents. Children raised in a peer group learn to
network and learn that resources can be acquired by manipulating social
relations. "What is important is who the individual knows, who these people
are, what they have, and how they are disposed toward the child" (Draper
and Harpending 1987:223). These children grow up with the idea that resources are not scarce, and can be acquired through persuasion. Additionally,
since children acquire their culture from each other more or less simultaneously, there could be less intracultural variation among adults who were
peer-reared than among adults who were parent-reared.

The decision to raise children in peer groups may be related to the activities of parents. If these activities change as hunter-gatherers become sedentary, then child rearing may also be altered, and will be responsible for some
of the ensuing cultural change. The longer a camp is occupied, the greater
the distance foragers must go to procure resources. They may also use lower-
return-rate resources, and therefore spend more time in resource acquisition
and processing. Assuming that men hunt, and that women gather lower-
return-rate resources, sedentism probably means that men will generally
spend more time away from children, and that women will invest more time
in resource acquisition and processing. This has been shown to be true for
some Bushmen groups as they have become sedentary (e.g., Hitchcock 1982,
1987b; Draper and Cashdan 1988). Where parents, especially young mothers, devote much time to foraging and resource processing, or where fathers
are away on long foraging trips, even six-month-old children may be passed
to an older sibling for care, setting up peer-group rearing. This change in
the mode of cultural transmission may help account for why sociocultural

change seems to occur so quickly once hunter-gatherers become sedentary (see chapter 8).

While we have been discussing children in general, it is likely that parental versus peer-group rearing has a differential effect on girls and boys (Draper 1985). In societies where children are peer-reared, girls may more frequently be the assigned caretakers of younger children than boys, and this has been identified as a factor that contributes to gender differences in behavior and attitudes favoring nurturance, prosocial behaviors, and restricted spatial range on the part of girls (see Draper and Cashdan 1988:340; Draper and Harpending 1982). In such societies fathers may be away from children for extended periods of time. It has been suggested that in families where the father is absent, boys tend to develop poor attitudes toward females, to be aggressive and competitive toward other males and, when grown, to give little attention to their offspring, insuring a continuation of peer rearing (Draper and Harpending 1982). One cross-cultural study of adolescence found that the importance of boys' peer groups was higher in sedentary than in mobile societies (Schlegel and Barry 1991). These competitive groups defined a boy's success in life more than in mobile societies where, presumably, fathers, in general, are more often present. Sanday also found in a cross-cultural survey (not limited to foragers) that where men spend a lot of time with their offspring, and cooperate in child rearing, there is little cultural emphasis on competition (1981:60–64, 67, 90). Where men spend time away from children (which is associated with a general physical separation of male and female tasks), competition, especially among men, is encouraged (see also chapters 7 and 8). Partially as a response to male behavior, peer-reared girls show expression of sexual interest and assumption of sexual activity early in life, while also showing negative attitudes toward males and a poor ability to establish long-term relationships with one male (Draper and Harpending 1982, 1987). There are obviously many other factors involved in determining modal personality than whether children are parent- or peer-reared, and no clear division exists between parent- and peer-reared cohorts. The subject merits far more attention than we can give it here, but it is introduced in order to suggest how a change in foraging and individual mobility can affect cultural transmission and hence produce cultural change.

Foraging and resource conservation

Prior to the "Man the Hunter" conference, foragers were seen as giving no thought to the future, as unconcerned about what impact today's actions might have on tomorrow's food. A significant result of Sahlins' portrayal of hunter-gatherers as "affluent" at the conference, however, was to overturn this perception. By the late 1960s, foragers were seen to manage their resources through an ethic of resource conservation (see papers in Williams and Hunn 1982; Feit 1973). Foragers would altruistically forgo an opportunity to take a resource, it was commonly assumed, if taking the resource meant endangering the food supply of future generations. There is some truth to this. Some foragers managed their resources through a variety of means including the intentional sowing of wild seeds, simple irrigation of wild stands of seeds, and burning to stimulate new plant growth and intentionally attract game.[24] They may also

control their food supply by culling game animals selectively, by operating restrictions on hunting which have the effect of providing a closed season, by using vegetable resources with discretion and replanting portions of the root so that the plants regenerate, by extracting only part of the honey from wild bees' nests so that the sites are not deserted and by many similar techniques of conservation. (Woodburn 1980:101)

Conservation ethics are reflected in spiritual beliefs as well. The G/wi believe that N!adima (God) will be angered if they do not leave enough plants behind for regeneration. The Waswanipi Cree look upon animals as *chimiikonow*, or gifts, because animals are "like persons," who act willfully and intelligently, and who give themselves over to a hunter who has lived up to standards of reciprocity (Feit 1973:116, 1994:433). Improper acts toward the environment and its inhabitants, such as killing more animals than needed or ignoring obligations to share, could result in retaliation by game, who might not allow themselves to be captured by the Cree.

Of particular importance to this chapter is the role mobility might play in the conservation of resources. In our discussion so far, we have covered only dimensions of mobility that pertain to a single seasonal round. However, there is another dimension to movement: long-term mobility, or shifts in the annual range. Many hunter-gatherers shift the size of their annual range or territory every few years. The size of Nunamiut annual territory, for example, can shift from 4,000 square kilometers to over 6,000 or even as much as 22,000 as a result of fluctuations in the size of the caribou population (Binford 1980, 1982; Amsden 1977). Likewise, the area used by the Dobe Ju/'hoansi can change from as little as 260 square kilometers to over 2,500, and that of the G/wi from 700 to 4,000. Ranges can shift in location as well as size. The Nunamiut shifted their annual range about every eight years. In a study of Cree hunting-territory use,

Harvey Feit found that of twenty-two territories, only six were used both winters of his study (1973). These patterns of land use permit plant and animal populations to periodically reestablish themselves.

In recent years, however, some have asked whether the behaviors that allegedly conserve resources are intentionally directed at resource conservation, or if conservation is an unintentional (although nonetheless real) consequence of optimal foraging by low-density human societies (Smith 1983; Alvard 1993). Optimization models predict that hunter-gatherers will stop using a patch before, and sometimes long before, depletion occurs. Feit points out that the Cree change their hunting territory when a drop in sightings, animal signs, and success rate all indicate that the territory is being overhunted (1973:122). Both the marginal-value theorem and the foragers-as-altruistic-conservationists model predict the same behavior but for different reasons: switch patches when the return rate drops below an acceptable level because hunting has now become inefficient, or switch patches because harm is about to be done to the environment. Discovering which principle guides foragers' behavior is not easy (Hames 1987).

Assuming that foraging peoples have some knowledge of the reproductive capacities of their food resources, we might expect them to avoid overexploiting those that have low rates of increase if they do intend to conserve resources. Michael Alvard approached this issue by asking whether an optimal-foraging model or a resource-conservation model best accounts for the game hunted by the Peruvian Piro (1993). He argued that the resource-conservation model predicts that game with low maximum rates of increase (the rate of increase under ideal conditions) should be periodically eschewed even if encountered while hunting in order to permit the population to survive. Alvard used a diet-breadth model to predict what resources should always be taken based only on their caloric yields and search and handling costs. A resource-conservation model implies that hunters would be willing to take a short-term loss in their foraging return rates for a long-term gain; the diet-breadth model implies that foragers will always try to maximize their short-term foraging return rate no matter what the consequence. In brief, Alvard found that the diet-breadth model predicted Piro hunting behavior better than a resource-conservation model. The Piro took some game that have low rates of increase whenever they were encountered.

But hunted game made up less than 14 percent of the Piro's diet. Would the Piro exercise greater selectivity if they were more heavily dependent on game? We don't know. But it is clear that many modern foragers do indeed think about the connection between today's actions and tomorrow's consequences. One has only to look at the feelings foragers and former foragers have toward the many development projects on their ancestral lands. Seeing hunting territory disappear beneath mammoth dams and reservoirs, the Cree today are puzzled, and saddened, by what they see as the wanton and irreversible destruction of resources that belong to future generations (Feit 1994).

It is hard to accept, as some might argue, that the appearance of a conservation ethic in these indigenous cultures is a product of contact with Euroamerican society (the culture that brought us Love Canal). But the question is not whether all foragers conserve their resources. Apparently, some do and some do not. The question is: under what conditions would we expect to see behaviors that intentionally manage and conserve resources, as well as cultural concepts that encourage such behaviors? Robert Brightman, for example, suggests that a widespread ethic of resource conservation among North American boreal forest peoples is a post-fur-trade phenomenon, replacing an ethic in which to *not* kill an animal whenever encountered would result in a lack of game in times of need (1987). Could the fur trade, as a new element in the economy, or the ensuing geographic restrictions brought on by European colonization, or depopulation brought on by disease, have altered the nature of foraging such that cultural ideas reinforcing conservation-related behaviors became more prevalent? Restrictions on mobility, brought about by a desire to stay near fur-trade posts or by the loss of land to European settlers, could have encouraged resource management and conservation among many foraging peoples. This is certainly a subject that deserves greater attention than we can give it here. Our objective is only to point out that mobility, diet, resource-conserving behaviors, and cultural notions of proper resource use are interrelated. Resource conservation cannot be understood outside of its foraging context.[25]

CONCLUSIONS

We began this chapter by considering some concepts that have been used in classifying hunter-gatherer societies. Through this discussion we saw that mobility is a property of individuals who may move in many different ways: alone or in groups, frequently or infrequently, over long or short distances. Some sorts of individuals may move more than others (e.g., men vs. women, parents vs. nonparents, young vs. old, good vs. poor foragers); these movements occur on daily, seasonal, and annual scales. It is not useful to think of mobility in terms of either a single dimension of group movement or as a dichotomy (mobile versus sedentary). Ethnographic data demonstrate that residential and logistical movements are related to the environment in sys-

tematic ways that point to the importance of the relationship between foraging and group movement.

We then developed a simple model of foraging in order to determine the
effect of different variables on foragers' decisions either to remain in the
current camp or to move themselves and their dependents to a new camp.
The cost of moving (which is related to the terrain to be crossed but includes
the nature of housing), the distance to the next camp (which can be affected
by nonfood variables such as water and firewood), the difference between
the mean and variance of the current and anticipated return rates, storage,
and the time frame over which foraging rates are averaged and decisions are
made, all enter into decisions to move.

We then examined the issue of sedentism. We argued that no society is
wholly sedentary in that a reduction in movement as groups requires increased movement as individuals. Returning to the foraging model, we saw
that even in those instances where it is possible to remain in a single location,
optimization theory and foraging models predict that a forager should still
move a residence if he or she wished to maximize his or her daily return
rate. There appear to be two major contexts for the appearance of sedentary
communities. First, they appear in areas where population growth has resulted in group packing, such that the costs of moving entail the cost of
gaining access to the resources controlled by those already residing in a location. Second, they appear, even under low population densities, where the
cost of moving is high relative to the cost of remaining in the current camp.
This may play a role in some instances of sedentary settlement along Arctic
coasts (e.g., see Renouf 1991). Though there are many more factors involved
in the origin and development of sedentary communities, it is likely
that local resource abundance is a necessary but not sufficient condition for
hunter-gatherer sedentism.

Ethnographers who have lived with nomadic hunter-gatherers quickly see
the effects of mobility on these societies. Although these are many and varied, we have only touched upon two effects in this chapter, enculturation
and resource management. In succeeding chapters we will discuss others—
demography, land tenure, and sociopolitical organization. Our brief discussion in this chapter of the relationships between mobility and child rearing,
and mobility and resource management, points to the importance of further
research on the impact of changes in mobility on changes in other aspects
of hunter-gatherer society. It is especially important as the world's few
remaining mobile peoples are forced to become sedentary and undergo
dramatic changes in their lives.

SHARING, EXCHANGE, AND LAND TENURE | 5

My country is the place where I can cut a spear or make a spear-thrower
without asking anyone.
Western Desert Aboriginal man (Tindale 1974:18)

You know we are not /xai/xai people. Our true n!ore is East at /dwia and
every day at this time of year we all scan the eastern horizon for any sign
of cloud or rain. We say, to each other, "Has it hit the n!ore?" "Look, did
that miss the n!ore?" And we think of the rich fields of berries spreading
as far as the eye can see and the mongongo nuts densely littered on the
ground. We think of the meat that will soon be hanging thick from every
branch. No, we are not of /xai/xai; /dwia is our earth. We just came here
to drink the milk.
Ju/'hoansi man (Lee 1976:94)

During fieldwork among the Mistassini Cree, Eleanor Leacock found herself
and her informant some distance from camp with very little food. They
encountered two acquaintances in the forest who were very hungry and
who asked for something to eat. Leacock's informant gave away the last of
his flour and lard to them:

This meant returning to the post sooner than he had planned, thereby reducing his
possible catch of furs. I probed to see whether there was some slight annoyance or
reluctance involved, or at least some expectation of a return at some later date. This
was one of the very rare times Thomas lost patience with me, and he said with
deep, if suppressed anger, "suppose now, not give them flour, lard—just dead in-
side." More revealing than the incident itself were the finality of his tone and the
inference of my utter inhumanity in raising questions about his action. (Leacock
1969:13–14)

Experiences such as this helped to establish sharing as the sine qua non of
hunter-gatherer culture in the minds of contemporary anthropologists (figure 5-1). It is said that "generosity is almost universally valued, inculcated in

Figure 5-1. A group of Ju/'hoansi in the Tsodilo Hills, Ngamiland, resting, work-ing, and cooking near a hearth. One man prepares a bow and arrow. The food in the pot came from a nearby Mbukusku (agricultural) group. Scenes such as this helped establish sharing as an essential characteristic of the foraging lifeway. Photo-graph taken in April 1976. Courtesy of Robert Hitchcock.

the young, and sanctioned by myth and tradition" among hunter-gatherers (Dowling 1968:503), that they "give things away, they admire generosity, they expect hospitality, they punish thrift and selfishness" (Service 1966:14). Sahlins proposed that generalized reciprocity, nonimmediate gift exchange with no systematic effort to insure that gifts are equivalent, was the primary mode of exchange among hunter-gatherers (1972). Participants at "Man the Hunter" repeatedly emphasized the importance of sharing within hunter-gatherer bands. Reconstructions of hominid evolution have long assumed that evidence of sharing and especially the sharing of meat was critical in establishing the first appearance of humanity among Plio-Pleistocene hominids.

However, hunter-gatherers vary along a continuum, from treating re-sources as if they were common property, to individual ownership (Hayden

1981b; E. Smith 1988:245–46). Although in the Cree language there may be no term equivalent to the English term *property* or the verb *to own* (Scott 1988:37), in Australia, "notions of material and intellectual property are well developed . . . in the one case associated with land and in the other with rights in songs, myths, paintings, dances and esoteric knowledge" (Altman and Peterson 1988:76). Burch finds that generalized sharing only occurs within families among northwest Alaskan Eskimos, not between families, where different forms of exchange exist (1988). Burch also suggests that some unforeseen ethnographic bias may have helped crystallize the idea of sharing as the primary mode of exchange among hunter-gatherers:

> The north-west Alaskan data also suggest why it is so easy to conclude that sharing was ubiquitous in traditional times. "Everyone in the village used to share" is a view that is often expressed by native elders today. But of course everyone in most villages used to belong to a single local family, which is the precise context in which generalized reciprocity (or diffused ownership) did occur. (1988:109)

Hunter-gatherers also share the use rights to land in different ways and to varying extents. The Great Basin Shoshone, for example, had vague territorial boundaries, and individual movement was quite high in general (Fowler 1982), although some Great Basin hunter-gatherers were more territorial than others, with some more territorial during some seasons than others (Thomas 1981). The Ju/'hoansi and many desert Australian Aborigines related specific individuals to specific tracts of land, and had social mechanisms, often quite elaborate ones, to regulate access to one another's territories. Among the northwest Alaskan Eskimos there were rigid social controls on group membership and reciprocal access to resources (Burch 1988). Still tighter group control is found among Northwest Coast hunter-gatherers, where Kwakiutl *numayms* controlled specific hunting grounds and berry fields, and Tlingit and Tsimshian matrilineal households owned stretches of beach, halibut- and cod-fishing grounds, and berry fields (see chapter 8; Boas 1966; Codere 1950; Richardson 1982). In northern California, Yurok or Tolowa individuals owned specific trees or even particular branches (Richardson 1982; Gould 1982). We will use the term *land tenure* here to refer to these different ways of regulating people and land. The term more commonly used is *territoriality*, but since that term specifically means the exclusive use of a defended area, it focuses attention on only one aspect of a range of behaviors differentially implemented to regulate resource use under different conditions.

The giving of gifts and the granting of rights are such an integral part of the hunter-gatherer lifeway that it is often hard to separate these behaviors into the categories of sharing, exchange, or land tenure. But it is precisely this difficulty that leads us to analyze them in the same terms. Stated simply, land tenure, exchange, and sharing are all forms or part of the *permission-granting behaviors* whereby hunter-gatherers regulate access to resources, and all may be responsive to similar selective pressures. They operate on different scales, entail individuals acting sometimes on behalf of themselves and at other times as representatives of groups, and incorporate different kinds of exchange, but we will attempt to show that they can be understood within the same theoretical framework.

SHARING

The ways of exchanging food, material goods, and prestige are various and intricate. Among the Dobe Ju/'hoansi, for example, credit for a kill goes to the owner of the arrow that killed the animal. Since Ju/'hoansi trade arrows, a man could intentionally choose someone else's arrow from his quiver, and in so doing give him a claim to some of the meat. In Australia, young men hunt and give their kills to older men, who distribute the meat (e.g., Altman 1987:142); in return, the young men receive religious knowledge, and have their marriages arranged. In North America's boreal forest, while Chipewyan men hunt, the meat is distributed by their wives. Men do not directly take meat from another's kill, but instead send their wives to acquire meat from the successful hunter's wife (Sharp 1981).

Students new to anthropology, however, are often disappointed to learn that these acts of sharing come no more naturally to hunter-gatherers than to members of industrial societies. Children in hunter-gatherer societies are enculturated into the idea of sharing at an early age; Ju/'hoansi children, for example, are taught to trade at the age of six months, and by the time they are five years old, they give gifts on their own. The importance of giving gifts and sharing is reinforced throughout life until it becomes deeply embedded in a person's personality, as Leacock's Mistassini informant testifies. The act of sharing is often valued as much, if not more, than what actually is shared (Bird-David 1992b; Myers 1988a), and is important in maintaining an egalitarian social order (Gardner 1991; Kent 1993), or at least the appearance of an egalitarian order (see chapter 8). The failure to share among many hunter-gatherers, in fact, results in ill feeling partly because one party fails to obtain food or gifts, but also because the failure to share sends a strong symbolic message to those left out of the division.

However, acts of sharing among foragers are often preceded by one person's insistence that another share with him or her. This "demand sharing" is common among hunter-gatherers (Altman and Peterson 1988; Peterson 1993). Lee (1979:372) and Marshall (1976) describe the Ju/'hoansi as masters of verbal abuse and jesting, much of it intended to encourage adequate reciprocity and meat distribution. When a game animal is being butchered in a ≠Kade camp, a senior man may "shout out directions like: 'You should cut a little off that rib meat over there and add it to this pile'" (Tanaka 1980:95). Anthropologists who work among the Bushmen quickly become exhausted by the constant dunning for gifts (Draper 1975; Tanaka 1980:97). The Ju/'hoansi themselves feel that their friends and relatives "kill them" for gifts and trade items (Wiessner 1982b:80; see Altman 1987:147 on the Gunwinggu). Once someone gives a gift, he or she has the right to make demands, to ask for particular things in return. The Ju/'hoansi accept a certain amount of dunning as reasonable behavior. "Most !Kung [Ju/'hoansi] agreed that it was bad to have too many or too few [trading] partners, the former causing a person to be g//akwe, a poor person, and the latter leading to many squabbles over giving and sharing" (Wiessner 1982a:656). Within a social system that is predicated upon giving and sharing as a primary mode of social interaction, pleas of hunger and even starvation are legitimate idioms in which to ask for food (Bird-David 1992b); they also forcefully insure sharing (who could deny food to a "starving" person?).

Sharing, therefore, strains relations between people. Consequently, many foragers try to find ways to avoid its demands. When possible, members of one Gunwinggu band in northern Australia lie to members of another band about how successful they have been at hunting and thus deflect demands for sharing (although at other times they will go to lengths to share surplus food with kinsmen in other bands; Altman and Peterson 1988:88–89). Hunters will sometimes consume game at a hunting camp, ignoring ideal sharing regulations (e.g., Altman 1987:131). Pintupi men hide cigarettes so that they will not be asked to share them (Myers 1988a), for if a man clearly has cigarettes, and does not share when asked, he will be regarded as stingy. But if he does not appear to have cigarettes, he will not be asked, and cannot be labeled stingy.

Besides pointing to efforts to limit sharing, ethnographic data also demonstrate that there is variability in how much, what, and with whom hunter-gatherers share. The meat of large game, for example, is always shared, but

Table 5-1. Meat Sharing

Society	Description of meat sharing
Ache	Families keep about 10 percent of game whether the game is large or small; remainder is shared equally to other families taking family size into account
Mamainde	Meat is equally distributed among the families in a band after controlling for family size
Yanomamo	Large game shared more than small game; families of hunters receive about twice the amount of meat from a kill as others; strong kin bias in meat distribution
Yora	Hunters keep for their families about 40 percent of the game they acquire
Hiwi	Families keep about 60 percent of small game; 40 percent of medium-sized game, and 20 percent of large game
Gunwinggu	Hunters keep for their families about one-third of game they acquire

Source: Hill and Kaplan 1993.

it is not always shared equally. Table 5-1 lists some of the differences in the ways meat is shared among some foraging and horticultural societies. Recall also from chapter 3 that hunter-gatherers are as much interested in animal fat as in the meat itself. Yet many game animals are divided according to specific cultural rules, with certain parts always going to certain relatives of the hunter. Among the Gunwinggu in Northern Australia, for example, the head and one of the forequarters of macropods (kangaroos, wallabies) goes to the hunter, the other forequarter to the hunter's companion or brother. The rump and tail go to the hunter's mother's brother's son or his mother's mother's brother's daughter's son. Each hindquarter goes to a senior man, while the heart, liver, tripe, and other internal organs go to the hunter and senior men, or other men present at the kill (Altman and Peterson 1988; Altman 1987). This sort of codified sharing of macropods is not uncommon in Aboriginal Australia, although several factors such as the number of people present, the status of the hunter, the number of animals killed on a particular day, and the relationship of the hunter to the owner of the hunting weapons and the land on which the animal is killed can alter the ideal sharing regulations (Gould 1968; Altman 1987:136–37; White 1985).

In any case, since fat is differentially distributed on an animal, some people may receive more of it than others. Speth makes the case that rules of meat division in Australia prevent women from obtaining as much meat, and especially fat, as men (1990; see also White 1985; Hetzel 1978; Walker and Hewlett 1990; see also chapter 8). Among the Ju/'hoansi and Hadza, men often eat the fatty parts of a kill, including the marrow, at the kill site before returning to camp where the remainder is distributed (in some parts of Australia, however, a man may receive the least desirable portions of his own kill). Among the Tlingit, the elders and household heads (*yitsati*)—all men— received the most desirable portions, probably the fattiest pieces (Oberg 1973). These different sharing patterns could create gender inequality in nutrition by decreasing the amount of fat women receive (see chapter 3). However, we do not know how much effect, if any, differential sharing has on the physiology and nutritional well-being of women and infants.

Other cases show the limits to sharing. In Arnhem Land, for example, food is shared after much demanding, but "there are limits to the demand for generosity. These limits are found at the household level" (Altman and Peterson 1988:93). Large game is shared more than small game, and young unmarried men are required to give more away than married men since unmarried men have fewer familial obligations. Food is shared beyond the family only when possible, and people know what resources can be shared in such a way and therefore which resources can be successfully obtained through demands. These limits to sharing depend very much on context. South American Yora share more while on treks in the forest than at their central settlement (Hill and Kaplan 1993). For other foragers, sharing varies with season, group size, and the particular resource.

Following the "Man the Hunter" conference, the standard wisdom was that sharing is a way to reduce the risk involved in foraging by building up social bonds of reciprocal obligation and by defining some resources as public goods. Sharing was seen as a way to pay back past acts of generosity, but also as a way to create indebtedness. Indeed, it is a banking strategy, although it is favors and obligations, rather than food and goods, that are stored— what some call "social storage" (O'Shea 1981). Marcel Mauss described gifts as containing power that compelled the receiver to return a comparable gift in the future ([1924] 1990). In 1875, John Simpson noted that among the Inuit in northwest Alaska "it is not too much to say that a free and disinterested gift is totally unknown among them" (Burch 1988:109); another Inuk man put it more bluntly: "with gifts you make slaves just as with whips you make dogs!" (Freuchen 1961:109).

So a balance sheet of sorts is kept; sharing is not a product of the innate generosity of hunter-gatherers. Within any given society, some resources are more widely shared than others, some individuals share more than others, and not all persons have the same claim on another's resources. If sharing is a way to reduce the risk of foraging, and since different societies use different resources, then we should expect there to be differences between societies in the amount and kind of sharing that occurs. Richard Gould, for example, argues that sharing exists only in highly variable environments, where it builds the social bonds that can be called upon in times of need (1982). Thus, the Ngadadjara of Australia's austere Western Desert share extensively. Where these environmental criteria are relaxed, Gould suggests, sharing is restricted to a much smaller social radius. As an example, he points to the Tolowa of North America's western coast, who shared less than the Ngadadjara due to the fact that they live, according to Gould, in an environment where resources are reliable and abundant. Gould argues that "the more suitable a given habitat is for maximization of resources based upon strategies of individual family exploitation, the smaller and more restrictive [the social network] will be, with aggrandizement of resources at the heart of a system based upon increasing degrees of familial self-sufficiency" (Gould 1982:88; rather than share excess resources, Tolowa men use them in prestige competition and to acquire wives through bridewealth payments; see chapter 8). Though Gould is correct to note variation in sharing behavior, I suspect that the differences between the Tolowa and Ngadadjara are not due to the presence or absence of the need to share but are part of a range of behaviors responding to both the need as well as the ability to share and to demand. What is needed is a theoretical framework within which variability in sharing can be anticipated.

Variance- (risk-) reduction models of sharing

Daily returns from foraging are never constant, and there is always the risk that a person or family could go hungry. Potential shortfalls in daily foraging can be avoided by increasing diet breadth, storing, exchanging, or sharing food. Each of these strategies has costs and benefits. By increasing diet breadth, for example, foragers could increase the probability of finding food, but could also decrease their overall foraging efficiency (chapter 3). Through storage, resource blooms can be exploited and their utility extended over time, but the forager must put in the extra labor to prepare food for storage and accept the risk that the stored food might spoil. Through sharing, a forager could take advantage of someone else's windfall, but will have to repay the favor in the future. Foragers also might have to risk sharing with someone who might not reciprocate. Exchanging one kind of resource for another (e.g., meat for carbohydrate) requires balancing the cost of acquiring the one relative to the benefit of the others, and the cost of maintaining the relationships that permit exchange to occur (see discussion of Efe trade in chapter 2). How do foragers balance these costs and benefits?

Using a computer simulation of stochastic foraging, Winterhalder compared the costs and benefits of sharing versus diet diversification (1986a,b). This model has implications for these two options as well as storage and exchange. In brief, his simulation showed that expanding diet breadth by a single new food item results in only an 8 percent reduction in the standard deviation of the net rate of food intake, a small reduction in the risk of going hungry, and a 6 percent reduction in foraging efficiency. On the other hand, two foragers with the same diet breadth who pool resources can maintain their high foraging efficiency while reducing their pooled variation in the rate of food intake by 58 percent. Winterhalder concluded that to reduce daily variance in food resources without decreasing foraging efficiency, it is better to share resources than to increase diet breadth.

Winterhalder then argued that the extent of sharing should be related to environmental factors affecting variance in an individual's average return rate and the degree of correlation in daily returns among a co-residential group of foragers (Winterhalder 1986a,b; E. Smith 1988), that is, in the amount of day-to-day variability in a forager's net returns from foraging and the day-to-day similarity in how well each forager does. If there is no variance in a forager's day-to-day return rate, then there is no need to demand resources of one another. Alternatively, even if there is variance in returns, if each forager does just as well or just as poorly as all others, then there is no ability to share since when one forager needs food, no one else will have surplus to share. From this observation Winterhalder speculated on how foragers might respond to four different scenarios defined by high versus low variance in individual forager returns and a high versus low correlation between the returns of individual foragers (figure 5-2). The four scenarios are:

Case A. In this instance, foragers have highly variable daily returns—they gather more than needed some days, less than they need on others—but all foragers do the same each day. Foragers' return rates may be correlated where all depend on the same resource, such as salmon runs, where all those finding food will be equally successful. There is little incentive to share in this case, for when a forager has an abundance of food, so does everyone else; when a forager has a shortfall, so too does everyone else. Instead, Winterhalder suggests that foragers can be expected to store resources at the household level (as the Tolowa do) to tide them over in times of need, or, if possible, to migrate to areas where food is available when shortfalls occur. The choice would probably depend on how long the short-

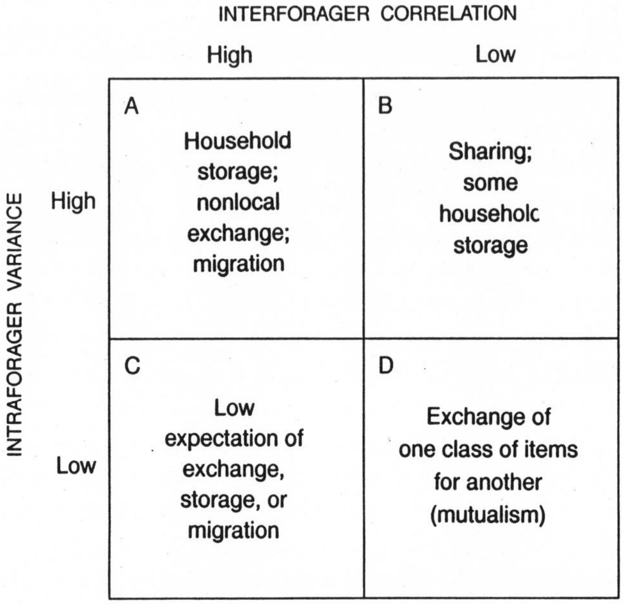

INTERFORAGER CORRELATION

	High	Low
High	**A** Household storage; nonlocal exchange; migration	**B** Sharing; some household storage
Low	**C** Low expectation of exchange, storage, or migration	**D** Exchange of one class of items for another (mutualism)

INTRAFORAGER VARIANCE

Figure 5-2. Four sets of relationships between foragers defined by different combinations of interforager correlations in return rates and intraforager variance in day-to-day return rates. Redrawn from Winterhalder 1986a by Dan Delaney. Reproduced courtesy of *Journal of Anthropological Archaeology.*

fall is expected to last and the cost of moving to a new foraging area (see chapter 4).

Case B. Where there is high variability in returns, but where some foragers do well on days when others do poorly, sharing should occur. Winterhalder demonstrated that as the degree of correlation between foragers' returns decreases, sharing results in a larger reduction in variance of the group as a whole. However, a limit is reached at about seven to eight foragers, after which there is no significant reduction in net-return-rate variance. Thus, the limits to sharing are realized at fairly small group sizes. This case accounts for why meat is shared more than plant food, since hunting is usually a riskier venture than plant collection, and, in the case of large game, produces more food than is immediately needed.[1] It also explains why large game is shared more than small game, since the latter is less risky (Hayden 1981b).

Case C. Where there is low variance in individual returns and a high correlation between foragers' individual returns, and assuming that the population is in balance with foraging returns (see chapter 6), Winterhalder expects there would be little reason or incentive to share, since no one currently needs or will need someone else's food. The social implications of this situation are not clear (what happens when there is no sharing to enforce equality?).

Case D. Finally, when both the variance in individual returns and the degree of correlation between forager returns is low, differentiated exchange (sharing) might occur between foragers if they are specialized collectors of different products. If, for example, hunting and gathering each require specialized activities, then those specializing in hunting would share with those specializing in gathering. If there are reasons for one gender to focus on one or the other activity (see chapter 7), then sharing can be expected between the genders. This case may also describe mutualistic relations, for example, between hunter-gatherers and agriculturalists, where meat is exchanged for carbohydrates (Spielmann 1986).

What is to prevent people from hoarding, from simply saying no to demands for reciprocity? In other words, when is the cost of reciprocal sharing (reducing one's gain when one does well) worth the benefit (an expectation of an increase in gain when one does poorly)? Sharing appears to be advantageous for the entire group, but we must avoid the neofunctionalist mistake of assuming that what is best for a group is what individuals will choose to do. From an evolutionary point of view, there must be some payoff to the individual for sharing.

E. Smith approached this question using game theory (1988; Smith and Boyd 1990). It will come as no surprise that he found that if a few foragers hoard while others share, the hoarders come out best, that is, they gain the most utility from resources since they keep all that they collect, plus some of the sharers' returns. The sharers, of course, fare worst under these conditions since they give while receiving nothing in return. Smith also found that when all individuals hoard, individual outcomes are the same, although no one, obviously, does as well as the hoarders did when sharers were present. When everyone shares, all do better than when everyone hoards. But if even one individual decides to hoard, that hoarder will do better than the others. The sharing foragers have two options in this case: to continue sharing (in which case they continue to fare worse over time) or to switch to a hoarding strategy. Smith showed that hoarding will eventually become the dominant strategy, *even when sharing provides the greatest good for the greatest number* (Smith 1988:240). Smith's simulation implies that all foraging systems will tend toward communities of hoarders over the long run. But this is contrary to the ethnographic record. What is it, then, that holds hoarders in check?

Smith's initial model is what might be called an instantaneous model. When it is run over time, and human memory of debts and obligations are added to it, the sharers soon learn not to share with hoarders, and eventually the tables are turned. Hoarders find themselves left out in the cold, socially speaking, and a hoarding strategy is replaced by a sharing one. Therefore, "the existence of collective goods is . . . dependent on a system of monitoring, ongoing expectation of reciprocity, and costly sanctions against free-riders" (Smith 1988:240). Constant tension between a desire to hoard and a need to share produces the anxiety of sharing so often recorded by ethnographers—the assertions by the Ju/'hoansi, for example, that trading partners often demand too much, and the constant dunning for gifts and accusations of stinginess.[2] There are also limits to how far sharing can go. Winterhalder showed that the benefits of sharing are maximized at small group sizes. As group size increases, demands cannot be met, the potential for continued face-to-face interaction between two individuals decreases, and free-riding as a strategy becomes possible (Smith and Boyd 1990). At the same time, as group size increases there is no further reduction in foraging variance, but there is a continual reduction in mean returns due to depletion (Winterhalder 1986a). As groups increase in size hoarding can potentially increase while food supply will decrease; the result is increased social tension. For example, Fred Myers found that as Australian Pintupi group size increased in settlements, so did the perceived stress on the sharing networks—too many people asking for too much, with too little pressure to reciprocate, and too few resources to go around (1988a:58–59).[3]

Is variance reduction sufficient to explain sharing?

Variance reduction would seem to readily account for sharing. However, though sharing may indeed help reduce variance in foraging returns, some data point to additional reasons for sharing, as in the sharing of meat from large game. Since some difference in hunting success is due to inherent differences in ability (e.g., eyesight), some men always provide more meat to the communal pot than others. Do these good hunters get back what they put in, as the variance-reduction hypothesis would suggest?

Apparently not, argues Kristen Hawkes (1990, 1991, 1992, 1993a,b). She claims that among the Ache, Hadza, and Ju/'hoansi, a few men contribute considerably more to the sharing network than they and their families receive in return. Men who contribute less—free riders—continue to receive shares from the good hunters. Ache men, for example, keep only about 10 percent of the meat they acquire from large or small game while on treks in the forest. These good hunters could provision their families with more food if they concentrated on collecting plant food and small game. As we saw in chapter 3, an exclusive focus on hunting large game does not necessarily result in the highest average daily rate of return, and certainly does not result in low variance in returns. Why, then, do men continue to hunt?

Hawkes argues that the resources themselves dictate that they be shared—because large game is acquired sporadically and comes in quantities larger than immediately needed by the hunter (see discussion of tolerated theft below). In effect, she argues, large game is a "public good." Hawkes points out that Ache men always target the riskier resources; even during the rare times when men gather food normally collected by women, they still gather those resources that are shared more (1991). Poorer hunters may contribute to a sharing network because they gain from it, but why do better hunters do so?

To answer this question Kaplan and Hill examined Ache sharing patterns in terms of four hypotheses: kin selection, tolerated theft, reciprocity, and cooperative acquisition (1985a,b).[4]

Kaplan and Hill argue that under conditions where the individual on the receiving end of an act of sharing receives more benefit from the item than the giver loses by giving it away, and where there are limitations on reproductive opportunities, natural selection favors *kin selection,* or sharing among genetically close individuals. In evolutionary theory, one is expected to favor those relatives where the fitness benefit to the receiver of the resource given divided by the cost to the giver is greater than the reciprocal of their genetic relatedness. Since one's biological children (sharing half a parent's genes) are one's closest relatives, and since the cost of acquiring a resource is certainly higher for a child than an adult, parents should share resources with their children before sharing with adults or the children of others.[5] Although it will surely come as no surprise that parents share food with their children, there is variability among foragers in how long parents provide food for their children. Hadza children, for example, begin collecting upwards of half their own daily food by the age of five. Ju/'hoansi children are fed by their parents until they are much older (Blurton Jones, Hawkes, and O'Connell 1989; see chapter 6). The ease and safety of foraging, the size of resources harvested, and the types of mating and child-rearing systems could all have an effect on the amount and duration of parent-to-children sharing.

A second hypothesis is known as *tolerated theft* and tries to make sense out of the ethnographic fact that much sharing occurs as the result of badgering and solicitation ("Give to me because you have some and I do not") rather than from reminders of the requester's past generosity (Blurton Jones 1983). The hypothesis of tolerated theft predicts that food sharing can be expected to occur when the cost of defending a resource exceeds the benefit of keeping it. Assuming no storage or exchange, the benefit of the twentieth kilogram of a resource is less than the first kilogram. And if the cost of defending the twentieth kilogram is the same as that of the first, any portion beyond the needs of the forager are likely to be shared. Tolerated theft therefore is likely to be found when food resources occur in large packages (e.g., large game) such that a forager acquires them in an amount larger than immediately needed.

The third hypothesis, which covers the same ground as Winterhalder's model, is *reciprocity* or reciprocal altruism and entails the exchange of resources. When the value of a resource received is greater than the value of a resource to be given at some future time, and when nonreciprocation will result in a cessation of sharing, *tit-for-tat reciprocity* is expected to occur. The value of a resource is relative to the individual; what is important to one person may be of less benefit to another. Though this may seem similar to tolerated theft, in this form of sharing future reciprocity is *expected,* whereas in tolerated theft the decision is based on the cost of trying to keep a resource (relative to its benefit) and not on an expectation of future sharing. In tit-for-tat reciprocity, the likelihood of future exchanges determines whether a resource is given or not. The potential donor may know the petitioner's past record and the future probability of reciprocation. Thus, it is more to create than to repay debts (as the Inuk man observed above). Like tolerated theft, tit-for-tat reciprocity is expected to occur where resources are acquired in large packages, but also when they are sporadic in their occurrence.

In a second form of reciprocity, *trade,* resources of different types are exchanged, for example, resources high in protein for resources high in carbohydrates. Here the expectation of future reciprocation is not necessary if the exchange is immediate, making this more like tolerated theft. However, here the issue is not defending a resource, but whether what is to be given is of greater or lesser benefit than what is being offered in exchange. This may cover instances of exchange between foragers and horticulturalists. Many

Table 5-2. Ache Food Sharing

Resource/ consumer class	N	Acquirer (%)				
		Self	Spouse	Sibling	Parent	Other
Meat						
Men	1,376	5.7	0	6.8	0	87.5
Women	998	0	14.8	2.8	0	82.4
Children	787	0	0	0	16.9	83.1
Honey						
Men	454	16.5	.6	5.7	0	77.2
Women	408	2.5	14.7	1.5	0	81.4
Children	232	0	0	0	11.6	88.4
Collected						
Men	888	22.0	13.4	3.8	0	60.8
Women	959	39.4	6.5	1.6	0	52.5
Children	549	0	0	3.3	25.5	71.2
Mission-brought						
Men	85	0	40.0	0	0	60.0
Women	93	59.2	0	3.2	0	37.6
Children	94	0	0	0	50.0	50.0
Totals						
Men	2,803	12.4	5.6	5.5	0	76.5
Women	2,458	18.0	11.0	2.1	0	68.9
Children	1,662	6.0	0	1.1	20.9	78.0
All	6,923	11.4	6.2	3.2	5.0	74.2

Source: Kaplan and Hill 1985a.

foragers today, and undoubtedly some of the past, are specialized hunters, who exchange with horticulturalists. For those foragers who can procure large amounts of meat (e.g., Plains bison hunters), even a small amount of a carbohydrate such as corn is worth more than a little extra meat in the diet. Likewise, horticulturalists may fall short of producing sufficient protein (see discussion of tropical hunting in chapter 3); for them, it makes sense to exchange some excess garden produce for even a small amount of meat.

Finally, in *cooperative acquisition,* resources acquired through group actions are shared among the participants. This could be, however, to insure future participation in communal hunts (if communal hunts are necessary to acquire a particular resource) as tit-for-tat reciprocity also predicts, or because the amount acquired through cooperative hunting is large enough that tolerated theft comes into play (in which case cooperative acquisition may not be necessary to acquire the resource).

Kaplan and Hill recorded a large sample of food-consumption events, noting whether the food being eaten was acquired by the individual or was given to them (table 5-2). The Ache data demonstrate the tremendous amount of sharing that can occur within a hunter-gatherer band (although other foragers may not share quite so much; see Hill and Kaplan 1993). Well over half of the food eaten by any Ache man, woman, or child was acquired by someone other than the consumer. The majority of food eaten by an adult was given to that person by someone other than his or her spouse; for example, on average 88 percent of the meat eaten by a man was hunted by someone else. The majority of food eaten by a child was given to him or her by someone other than his or her parents. The Ache data indicate, in fact, that *all* food resources, not just meat, were widely shared. Even plant and mission-brought foods (foods brought on the forest trek from the mission settlement) were shared. Meat was, however, the most widely shared food.

Examined more closely, there are patterns in the Ache's sharing habits that shed light on the four proposed hypotheses. The cooperative-acquisition hypothesis did not receive much support, as Kaplan and Hill found no difference in the way resources acquired cooperatively versus those acquired individually were shared.

The tolerated-theft hypothesis also did not receive much support even though the resources that come in the largest caloric packages—meat and honey—were also the most widely shared. In contrast to the hypothesis's predictions, there were no visible contests over food. Such contests are indeed rare among foragers, but their lack of visibility does not mean that there are no bad feelings about the division of a particular resource (see Altman 1987:147; Tanaka 1980:109 for examples). Also, in contrast to the hypothesis's predictions, Ache individuals often gave up food that was of greater value to themselves than to those with whom they shared, even reserving food for people who were not present.[6]

In support of the kin-selection hypothesis, plants and mission-brought food were shared primarily within nuclear families from parents to immature children. Meat and honey, however, and some plant and mission-brought food, were shared beyond the nuclear family. Kaplan and Hill suggest that in small groups, such as the Ache, the sharing radius must increase beyond the confines of close kin if one is to maintain a sufficient number of trading partners. As an example, they point to the difference between the Netsilingmiut and Copper Inuit (see Damas 1975a). The Netsilingmiut live in large extended families and have few meat-sharing partners, whereas the Copper Inuit live in small nuclear families and have several extrafamilial seal-sharing partnerships. Thus Kaplan and Hill suggest that in small groups reciprocity may be favored over kin selection.

The amount of food a nuclear Ache family acquires through sharing is correlated with the number of dependents in that family. Meat and honey are the primary resources received from outside the nuclear family. One might expect that married men do the most foraging since they have more dependents than single men. However, this is not the case: single Ache men produce the most and are the most consistent in their production. They share the most and receive the least in return. What do they gain from this?

One possible explanation is that reciprocity balances out over the long term. The Ache analysis only includes data from foraging treks that average eight days in length. Do men's foraging efforts even out over the long term? Kaplan and Hill have only two years' data to examine in this regard, but they find no evidence that reciprocity balances out over this period; there were, instead, real and consistent differences in individuals' production (related, no doubt, to differences in skill). Additionally, if men were only sharing meat to insure that they received something when they had a run of bad luck, they would only bring back the average amount hunted by all men. But this is not the case: men who are skilled at hunting and have high return rates also spend the most time hunting, contributing far more to the pooled meat supply than other men. Thus, Kaplan and Hill conclude that tit-for-tat reciprocity or variance reduction was not entirely supported by these data.

Kaplan and Hill look to trade to explain resource sharing, specifically the exchange of meat for sex (trade here is similar to Winterhalder's category D). As we noted in chapter 3, Ache men could maximize their caloric returns by gathering palm starch instead of hunting, yet men devote much of their time to hunting, especially men who are skilled hunters (Hill and Kaplan 1988a,b; Hill et al. 1987). Since they eat little of their own meat, and since some men consistently bring in more meat than others, Kaplan and Hill argue that men must achieve some other fitness benefit from hunting and sharing meat. In support of this idea they present data showing that males who are good hunters also have significantly more surviving children, when extramarital children are included, than men who are not good hunters (Hill and Kaplan 1988a,b; Hawkes 1990). (Good hunters' wives, however, do not have more children than the wives of poorer hunters.)

Assuming that the paternity data are accurate,[7] why would other men tolerate the extramarital sexual activity of good hunters? In essence, Kaplan and Hill suggest that they are bribed. Since men eat far more meat from others' kills than from their own, poorer hunters tolerate the extramarital affairs of better hunters in order to keep them and the meat they acquire in the band.

However, though meat is commonly exchanged for sexual favors among Amazonian cultures (Siskind 1973), it is not so common outside this culture area (at least, it has not been documented), although the extensive sharing of large game is common. It is possible that sexual favors may indeed be given as a result of the sharing of excess meat among the Ache, but it is not clear whether this is driving the system, or is an epiphenomenon of it (see Bettinger 1991:201–2; Hill and Kaplan 1993:706). If these good hunters could provide more food to their families by collecting rather than hunting, why would they not be selected against by women preferring "providers" rather than "show-offs," that is, men who seek resources that will provide their families with the most food, rather than men who seek resources that will automatically be shared with others (Hawkes 1991, 1993b)? Good hunters among foraging societies do indeed acquire prestige from being good hunters. Even if their efforts are lampooned and ridiculed, and even if "the hunter may end up with no control over the distribution of game, he will always acquire prestige. People are acutely aware of who the successful hunters are and of the frequency of their success" (Altman and Peterson 1988:80). Among other foragers, the social attention that accrues to good hunters may have fitness benefits of kinds that could be more valuable in some circumstances to a show-off's spouse than the increased food a "provider" husband could acquire, for example, increased attention to the children of a good hunter by others in a residential group, lessening the wife's workload.

Hill and Kaplan have backed away somewhat from their previous explanation of Ache sharing for several reasons but especially because large game is not always shared in the same fashion (1993; see table 5-1), meaning that the nature of a resource does not entirely dictate how that resource will be used. Large game need not always be a public good; it need not always be something that anyone can place a claim on. It is possible that since we have a very small sample of reliable quantitative data on sharing, and since large game is usually also a risky resource, we may be unable at present to sort out the effects of resource size and resource reliability. What would happen, for example, if large game could be procured with the same reliability as, say, roots? It might be worthwhile to reconsider, then, to what extent variance reduction or reciprocal altruism could account for the apparent paradox noted by Hawkes.

Anthropologists have offered two suggestions here. First, some argue that if data covering a sufficiently long period of time were available (and there is no such data set yet) we would see an averaging-out of returns—good hunters would eventually get back what they contribute. However, Hawkes argues that (1) computer simulations suggest that individuals who remember past acts for long periods of time are not as successful as those who only remember the most recent event because they avoid the cost of reprisals (in other words, it does not pay to bear a grudge); (2) people discount the value of future reciprocity in direct proportion to the length of time between one exchange and the anticipated one; and (3) ethnographic data show that good hunters (over the short term) continue to share with men whom they have already put in their debt (1993a). Long-term data are needed before we can respond to these observations.

Second, others argue that good hunters use their apparently uncompensated contributions to the sharing network to bank against their old age, when they are no longer good hunters. Foragers go through a period of proficiency at their subsistence tasks (however they may be defined by the society) and then enter a period of time as they age when they are not so proficient. For male hunters, hunting success decreases over the age of forty due to eye problems and arthritis. Women's foraging efforts, on the other hand, may decrease much less in old age. Elderly Ju/'hoansi and Hadza grandmothers continue to gather after equally aged men have ceased hunting, although they, too, eventually retire from foraging.[8]

Over their lifespan, therefore, individual foragers (and perhaps especially male foragers) will have high variance in their overall return rates. Returning to Winterhalder's model (figure 5-2), this means that cases C and D do not apply, and the forager is left with two options: either store resources for one's old age, an unrealistic option, or store up favors through sharing to be repaid in old age. Hunter-gatherers' social-security networks may very well be the relationships they establish through sharing when young. Much of the behavior that is recorded in ethnographic accounts, accounts that by their nature record only short-term behavior, may reflect behavior that anticipates what people know will happen in the future. Hunter-gatherers may plan for retirement, in part, through the sharing networks of their youth and middle age. Among the Ju/'hoansi, for example, older individuals "who have carefully tended their kin-based webs of trading and mutual-aid relationships have ensured that favors and gifts are owed to them as they grow old and can no longer provide for themselves" (Biesele and Howell 1981:93). Draper and Buchanan found strong associations for both Ju/'hoansi women and men between surviving into old age and having two or more children surviving to adulthood; however, the correlation was only significant for women (1992). Men may rely more on networks beyond the family.

Good Ache hunters may hunt a great deal in order to share and build up sentiments that will improve their position in old age. Women, on the other hand, who generally collect plant food that does not have to be shared, may use sex as a way to build support networks (see chapter 7 on division of labor). Jane Collier and Michelle Rosaldo argue that in brideservice societies (a form of marriage said to be common among hunter-gatherers; but see chapter 7) "women are most likely to use sexual skills in an attempt not to win power from men but, rather, to escape constraining marital bonds and build the networks of affection and support that will assure them considerable freedom throughout life" (1981:317; see also Goodale 1971:131). Extramarital affairs are as much a female as a male strategy. However, there are no published data with which to address this issue.[9]

This explanation, however, is problematic for two reasons. First, the elderly in many societies continue to provide important services. They may become storytellers, healers, political leaders, storehouses of knowledge or, perhaps most importantly, caregivers to children (Counts 1985; Lee 1985; Solway 1985). They may exchange their services for food, and thus are not being repaid for the productivity or generosity of their youth. (In fact, I think it is likely that individuals who work hard in their old age are those who worked hard—producing many shared goods—in their youth.)

Second, if the elderly do not produce anything or provide services, then we must ask (though it may seem cruel), within the framework of an evolutionary approach, what cost attaches to *not* sharing with them? Even if they provided many resources in their younger days, what is to prevent younger foragers from ignoring them? As we saw above, sharing occurs where there is the threat of retaliation, something to exchange, and/or the possibility of reciprocation in the future. Hence, there may be no direct cost to not sharing with the elderly. However, there are always feelings of indebtedness between parents and children; it may be *the children* of elderly parents who could retaliate for a young hunter's failure to share with their parents (the strength of culturally instilled notions of indebtedness will play a role here; see Draper and Buchanan 1992). Again, I know of no data with which to address this issue.

We should not expect to find one explanation for sharing. We have very few quantitative data on sharing, but those available do not show the same pattern—not all foragers fit the Ache pattern. Hill and Kaplan show that whereas Ache hunters keep 10 percent of their kills, in other societies, hunters keep considerably more for their families, even from kills of large game (see Hill and Kaplan 1993; Altman 1987). Hadza men, for example, keep the lion's share of their kills for their families (Hawkes 1993a). And it is not clear, since we have little more than anecdotal data or normative descriptions to go on, whether cheaters or free riders are excluded from sharing networks or whether, as Hawkes suggests, they continue to be included (see Tanaka 1980:109 for an instance in which a skilled, generous hunter was initially ignored in a division of meat). Finally, though characteristics of a resource do play a role in defining whether it is likely to be shared, this can vary even within a single society. For tropical foragers who trek, resources are shared more in the forest than in the settlement, where closed houses may constrain sharing by permitting privacy (Bird-David 1992a; Hawkes 1993a; see also Layne 1987).

The degree and kind of sharing found among hunter-gatherers appears to be related to a number of variables and motivated by different factors. In any given case one or two of these may have greater weight than others. Past discussions of sharing have apparently lumped together acts with different motivations, and ones that fall under different selective pressures. We should be prepared for variability in sharing and in the reasons for sharing. Reduction in the variance inherent in foraging (which differs for both resources and environments) probably accounts for much of the sharing that occurs, but not all of it. Tolerated theft explains some. Trade of different resources may motivate some sharing. Men may trade hunting for prestige that can be converted into a number of different resources or services.

In sum, and as the ethnographic record attests, we could expect some hunter-gatherers within a society to share more than others and some societies to value sharing more than others. And, as was true of our discussion of subsistence and mobility, it is difficult to separate and explain sharing independent of other kinds of social interaction and exchange. At present, our ethnographic data are insufficient to provide us with a thorough description of the range of ways foragers share, let alone a thorough account of why this diversity exists. We do, however, have some ideas of the significant variables at play. It is essential that we continue to analyze how these variables condition sharing, given that sharing often plays a crucial role in defining for foragers (and others) where they stand in relation to other individuals and consequently in constructing a shared, group identity.

LAND TENURE

Part of our discussion of sharing can be expanded to shed light on how hunter-gatherers share access to land, a subject linked to the concept of territoriality. To understand where anthropology is today in its understanding of hunter-gatherer land tenure, it is necessary first to review briefly the development of thought on this subject.

In his reconstruction of social evolution, Morgan claimed that the notion of property evolved in tandem with the increase in utensils and tools, and in response to changes in social organization (1877). During the earliest period of "savagery," in which many hunter-gatherer peoples could be placed, Morgan argued that property, including land, was held in common by all members of a tribe.

Frank Speck challenged Morgan's view when he discovered that individual Algonquian families in northeastern North America held exclusive use rights to specific family hunting territories (1915). Trespass on lands was punishable even by death, although use of the land could be granted to outsiders with the expectation that the favor might be returned in the future. Territorial boundaries were not very fluid or negotiable; among the Penobscot, pictorial representations of totems were blazed on trees along boundaries, and natural landmarks were known by all as marking the edge of a family's land.

Like many anthropologists of his time, Speck assumed that the widespread distribution of a trait was indicative of its antiquity. Even in the northeastern United States, Speck observed, land held for generations by Euroamericans, and off-limits to indigenous peoples, was divided into hunting territories by the Penobscot. For Speck, such tenacity indicated very ancient beliefs, and that the "whole territory claimed by each tribe was subdivided into tracts owned from time immemorial by the same families and handed down from generation to generation" (1915:290).

Speck noted that there were differences in the size of these family hunting territories (e.g., territories on the frontiers were larger than those nearer the center of a tribe's range), but he did not propose reasons for those differences. He must have suspected some relationship between the size of the family and food resources, because he argued that one of the primary functions of the territories was to permit resource conservation. (Davidson [1928] and Hallowell [1949] later argued that the size of a territory was a function of game density, and that the area exploited was no larger than was necessary to provide a family with a year's supply of food.)

Speck argued that this territorial system was pre-Columbian in the Algonquian area and took it to be an inherent characteristic of hunter-gatherer societies in general. Speck and others soon discovered hunting territories in other parts of the world (Speck and Eiseley 1939; Davidson 1928; Cooper

1939, although Cooper later retracted his support for pre-Columbian territories [1946]).

Though later research suggested that Algonquian hunting territories were a seventeenth-century adaptation to the fur trade, the idea that hunter-gatherers were territorial became entrenched in anthropological theory.[10] Both Radcliffe-Brown and Davidson saw local patrilineal hordes or clans as owning exclusive cell-like territories (Davidson 1926, 1928; Radcliffe Brown 1930–31; see chapter 1).[11] Likewise, Steward's (1936) construct of patrilineal bands and Service's (1962) patrilocal bands were both predicated on the assumption that hunter-gatherers were territorial, that a specific group occupied and used a specific tract of land exclusively.

The idea that all hunter-gatherers are territorial contributed to the widespread notion that humans are, by nature, territorial. Once this idea entered popular literature, it took on an importance that few anthropologists anticipated: since humans were innately territorial, the argument went, war and national aggression were unavoidable (a point made most famously by the playwright Robert Ardrey in his 1966 book, *The Territorial Imperative*). Participants at the "Man the Hunter" conference reacted strongly against this claim, and in so doing helped revise longstanding anthropological orthodoxy on hunter-gatherer land use.

Before 1966, many anthropologists thought of hunter-gatherers as living in tightly circumscribed areas, suspicious of outsiders. After the "Man the Hunter" conference it appeared that hunter-gatherers went where they pleased, when they pleased, and were welcomed by all. At the conference, Lee and DeVore noted that "all of the hunting peoples we have been discussing have institutionalized means for moving from group to group. So if we find boundaries in a given case, we should not commit the frequent error of assuming that they enclose a defended and exclusive territory" (1968:157). Local groups fluctuated in both size and composition, as individuals moved in and out of the camp to visit relatives and friends, trade with partners, or simply to have a change of scenery (Yellen 1977). Among the Ju/'hoansi, visiting other families is considered to be both enjoyable and necessary (Marshall 1976:180–81; Sugawara 1988), and Ju/'hoansi men often acquire spouses from distant areas (Yellen and Harpending 1972). The annual movements of Dobe Ju/'hoansi families, all of whom consider the land around the Dobe water hole to be their territory, are by no means constrained to what is perceived by them as *the* Dobe territory (figure 5-3).

Following cultural ecological theory, the lenient territoriality of hunter-gatherers was argued to be adaptive since it permitted people to cope with

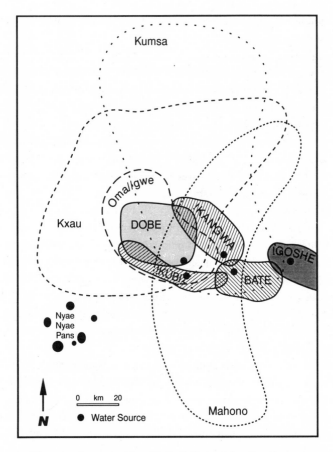

Figure 5-3. The annual ranges of four Dobe Ju/'hoansi families (the areas encompassed by dotted lines) relative to those areas considered to be the Dobe and other
band territories. A composite from Yellen 1977, redrawn by Dan Delaney.

resource fluctuations through movement and thus helped regulate local population density. The social ties such movement encouraged formed security
networks and encouraged a continuous flow of information about people
and resources which in turn permitted a continual adjustment of population
to food resources so as to prevent overexploitation (Lee 1976; Wiessner
1977, 1982b). Sentimental ties to land ensured that groups already spaced
across the landscape would remain that way, but social mechanisms allowed
movement of individuals to other territories in times of need and prevented

overpopulation of desirable areas (Peterson 1975, 1978; Peterson and Long 1986).

But in the 1960s, evidence already existed of hunter-gatherer groups that had distinct spatial boundaries and who maintained exclusive rights to the use of resources contained within them. Many Northwest Coast villages, for example, had exclusive rights to the resources of specific stretches of beach (e.g., Drucker 1951). Maidu village territories had boundaries marked with symbols and were "more or less regularly patrolled to guard against poaching. Even game that had been wounded outside but dies within the territory of a community belonged to the latter people and not to the hunter" (Kroeber 1925:398).[12] Likewise, territorial boundaries among the Vedda of India were marked with a small archer carved into tree trunks. Those passing through a territory were met at the border and escorted across (Seligmann and Seligmann 1911). Among the supposedly nonterritorial Great Basin Shoshone and Paiute, and even the Bushmen, there is variability in the degree of boundary permeability (Barnard 1992; Cashdan 1983; Heinz 1972; Thomas 1981).

Upon reconsideration of ethnographic evidence, we see that no society has a laissez-faire attitude toward spatial boundaries. Instead, all have ways, sometimes very subtle ways, of assigning individuals to specific tracts of land and gaining access to others. Boundaries exist, although at many different levels, and societies vary in their attitudes about defining, maintaining, and protecting them. Many hunter-gatherers do not live their lives on delineated tracts of land that they consider to be their own, but individuals do have specific use rights or statuses as members of a group or band that connect them with a particular area. Myers points out that "bands are largely the outcome of individual decisions, and the actual composition can be explained only through understanding the processes of individual affiliation" (1982:183). Understanding land tenure, therefore, requires recognition of the many different ways that people relate themselves to one another.

The decision-making processes establishing interpersonal relations are very complex and operate on many different levels simultaneously. Yet, though many of these ostensibly only control social affiliation, they also control physical access to land and resources. Among the Eskimo, trading partnerships and spouse exchanges established ties between unrelated individuals, usually men, but also women. For example, Netsilingmiut men's social ties were extended through meat-sharing partnerships established by a man's mother when he was young (Balikci 1970). The Nuuchahnulth's potlatch also sustained social ties between affinal relatives (Drucker 1951). Among the Northern Paiute, use rights to land were associated with named social groups such as Toedökadö (tule-eaters) and Aga'dökadö (trout-eaters). These names do not necessarily indicate the area in which individuals lived, but areas whose resources they had the right to give others permission to use (Fowler 1982). The historic family hunting territories of the North American boreal forest also served to regulate resource use by regulating access to the resident social group and thus to the land (Bishop 1986).

The Australian Pintupi and Dobe Ju/'hoansi provide detailed examples (see also Williams 1982, 1986 on the Yolngu, and Hamilton 1982a on the Pitjandjara). Throughout much of Australia, people identify very strongly with particular sites, and with areas of land which they refer to in English as their "country." In the desert, these countries are frequently defined by dependable water sources. People do not live out their entire lives in their own country, but older Pintupi men often express a great deal of sentiment for their country, and they desire to die in it (Hamilton 1982a; Myers 1982; Peterson 1986).[13] Pintupi tribal members in Australia's Western Desert are related to each other and the land through the concept of *one countrymen* (Myers 1982, 1986, 1988a). This is an individual-centered concept; though two individuals may regard each other as one countrymen, they do not necessarily share all of the same countrymen. One's countrymen are people with whom one could potentially camp and share resources, although at any given time camp partners among the Pintupi are not necessarily all one countrymen.

Being one countrymen with another man can be based on ties of kinship as well as the location of one's birthplace. Myers points out, however, that countrymen relationships are also established by "ownership" of sacred areas, *estates* (see chapter 1). Australian Aborigines have a rich mythological history referred to as the Dreaming or Dreamtime, a period during which mythological beings moved across the land, their paths or tracks memorialized for their Aboriginal descendants via the topographical features they created in their adventures, and by a rich body of mythology, ritual, and songlines. Today, many of these places are considered sacred, and men have responsibility for learning the stories and knowledge associated with those of their country. The Dreamtime also forms the cultural logic through which people negotiate their identity with each other. Men who may not be one countrymen by virtue of kinship or birthplace can become so via shared totemic identities or shared knowledge of a site that lies on the Dreamtime track cutting through their respective countries. A Pintupi man can potentially become one countrymen with another man who is associated with site A: (1) if the man was conceived there, (2) if he was born at a place made by or identified with the same Dreamtime beings as those who created A, (3) if the story line associated with the man's place of conception is associated with the story line of the Dreaming associated with A, (4) if the man is initiated at A, (5) if the man is born at A, (6) if conditions 1–5 hold true for his father, (7) if his mother was conceived at A or if conditions 2, 3, or 5 are true for her, (8) if the man's grandparents were conceived at A or conditions 2–5 are true for the grandparents, (9) if the man lives around A, and/or (10) if the man's close relatives die at or near A. Claims are always open to negotiation and counterclaim, but the multiple criteria of affiliation provide a man with a variety of ways to lay claim to a country or to extend use rights in his country to another (Myers 1986; see Barker 1976 for a more general discussion of the relationship between estate, range, and multiple criteria of affiliation in Aboriginal Australia).

The Ju/'hoansi provide another detailed case of how one group of hunter-gatherers maintains physical access to others' territories by maintaining social access to the resident group. Here, individuals associate themselves conceptually and sentimentally with inherited tracts of land called n!ore. N!ore are centered on a water hole, and vary in size from 300 to 600 square kilometers; n!ore can vary in size from year to year as well (Lee 1979:334). They are associated with a core group of individuals who hold the right to be asked to use the resources of the n!ore. N!ore can be inherited equally through the father, mother, or someone else (Wiessner 1982b), so most Ju/'hoansi hold rights to at least two n!ore. Permission to use resources located on another n!ore must be secured from one of the n!ore's "owners."

Access to the n!ore of another also comes through several social mechanisms including trading partnerships and fictive kin relationships. Fictive kin are established partly through personal names. The Ju/'hoansi name a child after a relative other than his or her parents. According to Lee (1979), a firstborn son ought to be named after his paternal grandfather, and a firstborn daughter after her paternal grandmother; subsequent children are named after the maternal grandparents and parents' siblings. Since names are continually recycled, there are relatively few Ju/'hoansi names for men or women (in 1964, there were only thirty-six male and thirty-two female names in use among the Dobe Ju/'hoansi). Names affirm close kin ties even between distant relatives. For example, if a young man's name is /Tishe and he encounters a distant older male relative who had a son named /Tishe, the older man may call the younger man "son" (it is the older person's prerogative to decide whether there will be a kin relation and what form it will take). The use of names implies social obligations, and the older male relative may now treat the younger man as if he were his son including giving access to his *n!ore*.

Trade networks also establish social ties among the Ju/'hoansi and other Bushmen. From the time they are infants, the Ju/'hoansi participate in a trade network called *hxaro* (Wiessner 1977, 1982a). *Hxaro* entails the giving of goods such as ostrich eggshell beads, blankets, pots, arrows, and clothing (but never food). An adult, especially one over the age of about forty, normally has a dozen or more *hxaro* partners; children and adolescents have fewer. One's direct *hxaro* partners are usually consanguineal relatives, but since spouses trade with each other, a person's *hxaro* network becomes linked with that of his or her spouse. Age and sex of partners matters less than the ability and willingness of a person to trade. Wiessner's data indicate that most *hxaro* partners live within about 40 kilometers of each other, but some individuals have partners living as far as 75 or even 200 kilometers away (1982b).

Hxaro partners expect timely reciprocation for their gifts, and Ju/'hoansi will ask their *hxaro* partners for specific items, often by dropping substantial hints. Gifts are kept for two weeks to two years, but eventually are passed on to yet another *hxaro* partner. In the long run, no one gains materially from the exchange. Arguments over the appropriateness of an item do occur, however, since all items carry symbolic value—giving an "unworthy" item can signal the desire of the giver to terminate the relationship.

People travel intentionally to *hxaro,* and in times of resource fluctuations, *hxaro* provides an ostensible motive for visiting others. For example, in 1974 high winds and rain destroyed the mongongo-nut crop of the /Xai/xai area and made hunting and trapping difficult. Food became increasingly difficult to come by, and sharing eventually broke down. Within two weeks, half the population had gone to visit relatives because "they missed them and wanted to do hxaro with them" (Wiessner 1982b:77), lessening the subsistence pressure on those who remained behind.[14] This Ju/'hoansi example demonstrates a common pattern among hunter-gatherers of moving in with trading partners in times of need (see Spielmann 1986).

In detailing the complexity of Pintupi and Ju/'hoansi group affiliation, we are describing instances of a widespread (although not universal) pattern in hunter-gatherer land tenure: that connections to land are social and permeable, rather than geographic and rigid, and that these connections have social and political in addition to ecological components. In the Pintupi and Ju/'hoansi cases, access to land is controlled through consensual rules that are backed by the threat of social sanctions, normally the realization that violation of someone's right to be asked for permission would result in the withholding of permission in the future (Williams 1982).

The basis for much of the behavior labeled territoriality, then, is the product of individuals making decisions about whether and how to share the right of resource use with others. These decisions are embedded in a complex intellectual process whereby people come to share an identity. Through kinship, trade, mythology, and other cultural mechanisms, people construct ideologies that relate themselves to each other and thus to land. These social relations form the basis for the right to be asked—and to ask—to use resources. Different ideologies give land-tenure systems their particular characters. The focus of research into land tenure, then, should be on the elements that condition permission-giving behavior. The question is not whether hunter-gatherers are or are not territorial, but rather in what ways and to what extent does a group regulate access to land directly versus regulating access to social affiliation and hence to resources?

In the remainder of this chapter we will look at two approaches to land tenure, the economic-defensibility model and the social-boundary defense model. Using insights from these models, we will return to the Winterhalder sharing model, but will apply it to group, rather than individual interaction.

The economic-defensibility model

The economic-defensibility model focuses on the cost and benefit of defending resources. As was true for tolerated theft, Rada Dyson-Hudson and Eric Smith argue that territoriality occurs when the cost of defending a resource is less than the benefit that could be derived from it (1978). If a resource is not very dense and its occurrence (in time and space) is unpredictable, then the cost of defending it could be so high as to offset any gains to be derived from its exclusive use. Where resources are dense and predictable, resources may be worth the effort of defense.

The economic-defensibility model allows us to predict variability in hunter-gatherer territorial behavior in terms of two basic dimensions of environmental variability: effective resource density and resource predictability (figure 5-4). Though variability between cases is continuous, for the sake of simplicity Dyson-Hudson and Smith divide each of the scales into high and low values, creating four land-tenure categories:

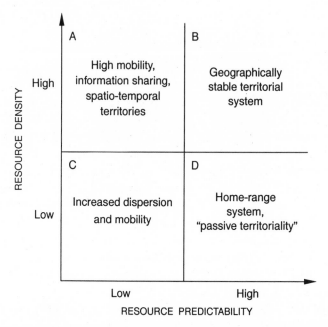

Figure 5-4. Four sets of relationships between foraging bands defined by resource predictability and density. Redrawn from Dyson-Hudson and Smith 1978 by Dan Delaney. Reproduced by permission of the American Anthropological Association from *American Anthropologist* 80:1, March 1978. Not for further distribution.

Case A. Low resource predictability is expected to produce high mobility, information sharing about the state of resources in different regions, and the shifting of territories in response to unpredictable but dense resources.

Case B. Under conditions of high resource density (i.e., high density of food resources relative to population), where resources are predictable, territoriality appears since the cost of defense is worth the benefit of the safeguarded resources.

Case C. Where both resource density and predictability are low, groups are dispersed and mobility is high since the cost of trying to defend an area is low relative to its benefit.

Case D. Where resource density is low, but resource predictability is high, what Dyson-Hudson and Smith call "home ranges" or passive territories develop, probably at low population densities, where

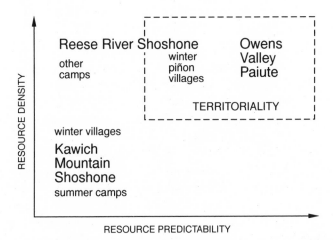

Figure 5-5. The economic-defensibility model applied to three Great Basin foraging societies. Redrawn from Thomas 1981 by Dan Delaney. Courtesy of the
American Museum of Natural History.

groups tend to stay in one region of predictable resources, and do
not need to use other areas.

David Thomas used this model to analyze variability in three ethnographically known Great Basin societies (figure 5-5). Following Dyson-Hudson
and Smith's approach, Thomas did not classify these societies as either territorial or not (1981); instead, they can be more or less territorial at different
seasons depending on the resource(s) being exploited. Thomas suggested
that the Reese River Shoshone are territorial with respect to winter piñon
villages, but not in regard to summer seed-gathering areas because piñon is
a denser, more predictable resource whereas grass seed is more scattered and
less spatially predictable.[15] In the dry Kawich Valley, with almost no piñon,
the Shoshone had few territories at any time of the year. But in the better-
watered Owens Valley, resources were more dense, permitting some
resources such as fish, seeds, and acorns to be gathered in bulk and
stored, resulting in more distinct territories than elsewhere in the Great
Basin (Thomas 1981; see Steward 1933), as anticipated by the economic-
defensibility model. Elizabeth Andrews also shows that where resources are
concentrated and predictable, western Alaskan Eskimo societies are territorial (1994). The Akulmiut, for example, were territorial with regard to river

bottlenecks, where whitefish and pike could be taken in large numbers predictably twice a year.

The economic-defensibility model predicts that territoriality becomes a more viable strategy as resource density increases because the size of the area to be defended, and hence the cost of defense, decreases relative to the benefit of the resources. Though the model's predictions are based on characteristics of the resources themselves, demand for resources should also be considered. The Owens Valley Paiute had denser and more reliable (predictable) resources, but they also had a higher population density than elsewhere in the Great Basin. We can imagine that as local population grew (from intrinsic growth or from immigration), overall resource abundance would have effectively decreased and the costs of defense relative to the cost of *not* defending resources lessened. Dense, reliable, defensible resources are necessary for territoriality to be worth the effort, but the benefit of territoriality "should tend to be in proportion to the intensity of competition" (J. Brown, in Cashdan 1983:54). Increasing competition, which in most cases is related to increasing population density, makes the benefit of trying to take or defend a resource worth the potential benefit. This is not a criticism of the economic-defensibility model, but only serves to point out that to predict territoriality, we need to consider competition as well as characteristics of the resource base. Dense, predictable resources may be a necessary but not a sufficient condition to select for defensive behaviors—intentional monitoring for intruders, the construction of defensive structures, and raiding motivated by revenge for thefts.

Almost all ethnographies note that permission to use resources belonging to another group or individual must be acquired, but it is equally universal that permission is virtually assured *if* asking for permission is considered a culturally legitimate question. Resources may not be there for the taking, but they are apparently there for the asking.[16] The giving of permission is the giving of a gift—and it puts the receiver in debt. As we pointed out above, social relationships are the primary social-security system of hunter-gatherers: the more social relationships, the greater the likelihood that a group or individual will be able to fall back on someone in times of need. As was true for sharing between individuals, land-tenure systems are not instantaneous phenomena, but behaviors that develop in response to the long-term condition of an ecological system and the evaluation of past actions and future possibilities. A strong tendency toward permission-granting rather than active perimeter defense gives human land tenure its own particular character. This observation is at the center of another model of land tenure.

Social-boundary defense

As we saw in the Australian example above, Pintupi men can claim more than one country through their claims to "one-countrymen" status with other men and can therefore claim the right to use the resources of other countries. However, the owners of the country have the *right to be asked* for use of the resources. One-countrymen status can be claimed, but is always open to negotiation. Visitors cannot simply move in and gather foods, but must check with the owners. Permission is almost always granted, but the potential to deny permission is always present. People cannot simply go wherever they want. Even among those hunter-gatherers who do not maintain defended boundaries, social mechanisms control whether another group will be allowed into the territory of another. Among western Cape York Aborigines, ritualized greeting ceremonies allowed a host group the opportunity to decide whether to permit a visiting group to stay with them:

Three men, each carrying a bundle of spears, spear-thrower and fire sticks, appeared out of the scrub to the north of the camp. Although their approach was at once observed, causing an under-current of excitement in camp, no apparent notice whatever was taken of the men, who approached slowly to within about 40 feet of the northern fringe of the camp, where each squatted on the ground a few feet apart, placing his weapons in front of him. . . . Not a word was spoken, and apparently no notice whatever was taken of their presence for about 10 or 15 minutes. Then a 'big' man left the camp unarmed and strolled casually toward the man on the left, scraped a shallow depression in the ground close to him with his foot, as a native does before sitting down, and then squatted on the ground about a yard away from the visitor. . . . Still not a word was spoken. They did not even look at one another, but kept their eyes downcast. After a few minutes had elapsed the old man of the camp spoke a few words in a low tone—inaudible to me where I stood a few yards away—and the other replied in the same casual way. Still neither looked up. . . . At length the old man called the single word *Bat* (fire) and a boy brought out a small piece of smoldering wood which he handed to the old man from the camp. This fire the old man then placed on the ground between himself and the visitor to whom he had spoken. . . . on this occasion a tobacco pipe was lighted and handed to the visitor. A second man now left the camp, strolled casually over and spoke to the man at the other end of the line, making a present, which was reciprocated. A little later all entered the camp, to be followed, in the evening, by a larger party. (Thomson 1932:163–64)

As in our discussion of sharing, there are costs and benefits to allowing visitors into a territory. On the one hand, the visitors may reduce the host group's foraging efficiency. On the other, there is the potential benefit that the visiting group will feel obliged to reciprocate in the future when the host group is in need. The host group's alternative is to patrol the territory's borders, pay the cost of physical retaliation, and find another way to respond to periodic resource failure within the bounds of their own territory (such as long-term storage).

Elizabeth Cashdan argues that the benefits of permitting visitors outweighs the costs when resources are scarce and (consequently) territories are large, making them difficult to patrol (1983). Under these conditions, hunter-gatherers insure reciprocal access to the resources of others by maintaining *social* access to the group or individual(s) holding the right to grant permission for use of those resources. These hunter-gatherers defend their physical resources by controlling their social boundaries. Cashdan refers to this as *social-boundary defense*. The various means through which Pintupi can claim "one-countrymen" status with another man are part of social-boundary defense. For while there are many ways whereby a man can claim one-countrymen status with another man, and thereby make a claim to the resources of another man's estate or range, there are also many grounds on which a man could deny one-countrymen status to another. As Myers pointed out, the process of group affiliation among the Pintupi, and, we might add, many other foragers, is constantly negotiated (1986).

One might ask why, if a region's perimeter cannot be physically defended, should permission even be sought? Why not just trespass? Two reasons may make trespassing a poor decision. First, trespassing can be hazardous to the trespassers, since they may not have sufficient knowledge of the region to make use of it. Second, if a trespassing group intends to use something other than a quickly procured resource (e.g., an animal), they may be detected (through their tracks, smoke from fires, etc.), and risk retaliation (see Tindale 1974:24 for a description).[17] But if permission is sought, why should a host group allow visitors in? As in our discussion of sharing there are two possible answers: first, the tables may be turned next year and the current host group will need a favor from this year's visitors (variance reduction), and, second, the cost of excluding the visitors may be too high relative to the benefit of keeping the resources to themselves (tolerated theft).

Cashdan sees perimeter defense occurring when competition is high and resources are defensible (see also Berkes 1986). (Cashdan says abundant, but the resources must be localized or aggregated; Cashdan would probably agree, since she correlates resource abundance with small territories.) High competition but low resource density (nonlocalized resources) results in social-boundary defense. When competition is low, Cashdan sees neither perimeter or social-boundary defense but something more akin to Dyson-Hudson and Smith's home ranges.

To demonstrate this perspective, Cashdan analyzes the land tenure of four Bushmen groups using mean annual rainfall as a measure of resource abundance and the annual rainfall's coefficient of variability (standard deviation/mean) as a measure of resource predictability (these two variables are usually inversely related). Among these four groups, territory size increases as resource density decreases. The most scarce and least abundant resources are found among the !Ko. According to the Dyson-Hudson and Smith model, the !Ko should exhibit the least territoriality. Indeed, the !Ko do not guard physical boundaries, but the !Ko exhibit the greatest social-boundary defense of the four groups studied.

Cashdan explains that the benefits of territoriality—perimeter defense—decrease as resources become less dense. At some point the benefits are less than the cost of social-boundary defense. For groups such as the Nharo, G/wi, and Ju/'hoansi, social boundaries are highly fluid, and individuals maintain a diversity of relations with members of other groups; little effort is put into controlling who has a social tie to any given group.

Among the !Ko, however, social access is tightly controlled, since they face the greatest competition over their scarce resources; the cost of social-boundary defense is less than the benefits it provides.[18] And the potential threat of expulsion is high relative to the benefit of entry for potential trespassers (since trespassers would need the residential group's knowledge of the region).

There is no neat division of cases into those with social-boundary or perimeter defense. At any moment in time, an individual is affiliated with different kinds of social groupings. A person is simultaneously a member of a family, other kinship groupings, one or more bands, perhaps an age grade, a political group, and a linguistic group, to mention a few. If these different groups have geographic counterparts, then the negotiation of access to land and resources may take on a different character for one set of individuals than for another depending in part on the nature of the resources encompassed by these different levels of society.

Among the !Ko, for example, bands are grouped into what Heinz calls *nexuses* (1972). There is much intermarriage and visiting between bands that make up a nexus, but not between bands of different nexuses. Social-boundary defense is low between the bands that make up a nexus, whereas it is high between each nexus. Cashdan argues that the bands that make up a nexus are bands that can help one another in times of need, but when times are bad for one nexus, they are bad for others as well (1983:55). The case of the !Ko suggests that social boundaries remain fluid between groups that can assist one another in times of need (help reduce long-term foraging variance), but remain more rigid between those that cannot.

Recent changes in G//ana society also demonstrate the process that lies behind the social-boundary defense model (Cashdan 1984). The G//ana are a Bushmen group in central Botswana who in recent decades shifted from a foraging/horticultural base to one relying more heavily on horticulture and wage labor. The availability of steel drums has allowed them to store water, a scarce resource in the central Kalahari. As a result of these changes, the G//ana developed new means of buffering resource fluctuations through agriculture and the storage of food and water (and also goods that could be converted to cash to buy food). In other words, resources became more concentrated and less variable from year to year. As this happened, groups became much more endogamous, and inheritance of *lefatshe* (roughly the equivalent of the Ju/'hoansi *n!ore*) became patrilineal rather than bilateral. Along with these social changes, the G//ana's social-boundary defense increased, and it became harder for others to acquire permission to use G//ana resources. If sufficient demand builds up, we could expect to see territorial behavior between different groups of G//ana.

E. Smith summarizes the conditions under which social-boundary defense can be expected as an alternative to perimeter defense: (1) when residents possess more information about resource location and abundance than visitors, (2) when uncoordinated search produces inefficient foraging through overcrowding, (3) when today's visitors are likely to be tomorrow's hosts, and (4) when residents can impose effective sanctions against those who cheat (1988:250). If reciprocity is a means of establishing social ties with people who could provide assistance in times of need, then choosing exchange partners is a decision based largely on the temporal and spatial parameters of resource fluctuations.

If reciprocity is acting as insurance, it would be expected that an individual would find it beneficial to maintain reciprocity networks with individuals whose eco-

nomic fortunes are independent of his own. If the economic well-being of everyone in the local area is tied to the same source, on the other hand, we might expect
to see people closing off social ties to protect their limited resources. (Cashdan
1985:471)

We can expect to see alliance-forming reciprocal exchanges of one kind or
another between the members of groups living in a region of scarce, unpredictable resources which fluctuate on different temporal and spatial scales.

Finally, in our discussion so far we have assumed that foragers do not acquire more resources than they need for survival, that acquiring more food
than necessary does not confer sufficient benefits to make contests worthwhile. Thus, perimeter defense was said to appear only when population
density had created intense competition over resources. This may be the case
for many ethnographically known foragers, but it need not always be true.
Where the cost of controlling additional increments of a resource beyond
the minimal amount needed is less than the benefits those resources bestow
upon a forager (e.g., greater infant survival rates, more offspring, or achieve-
ment of a culturally defined goal, such as prestige) then we could expect to
see stronger social-boundary defense or, if resources are defensible, perimeter defense, even where population density is not high.

Cashdan suggests that foragers who routinely store large amounts of food
for a lean season may live under these conditions (1983:55). Competition
over resources could occur here even at low population densities. As we will
note in chapter 8, food storage is often associated with social hierarchy. And,
as we will discuss in chapter 6, storage can increase a population's growth
rate. Storage, hierarchy, population density, and territorial competition may
be linked together in a long-term process. It may be left to archaeologists to
address exactly how these factors interact with one another (see chapter 8).

The Winterhalder model reconsidered

We can now return to Winterhalder's model of food sharing and modify it
slightly so that it models intergroup rather than interindividual activity. This
is a long-term model, for, as we have seen, the decision to allow other people
social access to one's group is based on past experiences and future expectations of reciprocity.

Recall that Winterhalder's model focuses on the nature of variance in individual resource returns and the degree of correlation between return rates
of different individuals. Here we substitute the group for the individual so

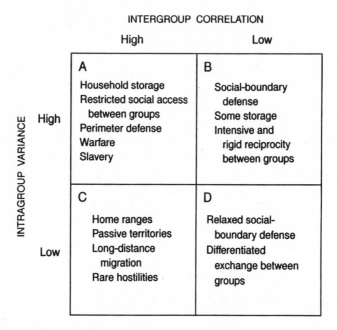

INTERGROUP CORRELATION

High   Low

A	B
Household storage	Social-boundary
Restricted social access	defense
between groups	Some storage
Perimeter defense	Intensive and
Warfare	rigid reciprocity
Slavery	between groups

C	D
Home ranges	Relaxed social-
Passive territories	boundary defense
Long-distance	Differentiated
migration	exchange between
Rare hostilities	groups

INTRAGROUP VARIANCE — High / Low

Figure 5-6. The Winterhalder model of sharing relations between individual foragers translated into relations between groups of foragers. Drawn by Dan Delaney.

that we are looking at variance in the pooled efforts of group members over time and the degree of correlation between returns of different groups.

By saying that the variance in a group's return rate is high, we are saying that the probability of resource failure is high, although there is also the potential for acquiring and storing a surplus—sometimes a group collects a very large amount of food, sometimes it collects far less than they need. Low group variance means that the group always collects about the same amount of food (although this says nothing about how much food is collected by individuals—only how much variation there is in the pooled amount). Assuming that population density is adjusted to some mean resource level, members of groups with a high variance will have to call upon neighbors for assistance more frequently than those in groups with low group variance. High correlation of pooled return rates between groups means that when one group is doing well, the other is also doing well, and when one group is doing poorly, so is the other. As we noted above, under such circumstances, there is no utility to maintaining mutual social access.

With this perspective, we can modify Winterhalder's model (figure 5-6). The four cases below may appear to define a neofunctionalist argument.

They do not, however, because there is no implication that individuals sacrifice their gains for the benefit of others or that the consequence of behavior is the cause of that behavior. Though we outline group responses here, it remains to be seen how these predictions would play out in terms of individual decisions (see chapter 8).

Case A. This case roughly corresponds to Dyson-Hudson and Smith's case C. When high intragroup variance occurs with high intergroup correlation, we can expect to see social access restricted to a few individuals, perimeter defense, and storage of food resources. (The utility of resource storage depends on the time span over which stored resources can be kept and the frequency of resource failure.) Perimeter defense should relax as the periodicity of resource failure decreases, because the frequency of outside attempts to intrude would presumably decrease. Likewise, social-boundary defense should relax as the periodicity of resource failure decreases, but will never be as high as in case B below. Case A could also describe circumstances under which warfare occurs. Some warfare could be directed toward the acquisition of slaves to increase household production. As population density increases, competition for resources also increases and the effective intergroup correlation will become higher. In such cases, we can expect to see warfare aimed at conquest and booty, especially food resources (see chapter 8).

Case B. This is the case with which Cashdan has been most concerned and which probably describes most ethnographically known hunter-gatherers. In this case, the frequency with which a group may need to call upon neighbors may be high, but since intergroup correlation is low, social access will be permitted. Storage may occur during periods of abundant resources, but more energy may be invested in social storage through reciprocal exchanges. We could speculate that as the periodicity of resource failure increases (cases that would fall more to the right-hand side of the cell), the rigidity of the system of reciprocity (with concomitant specificity of the symbolic value of material goods) might also increase since individuals will call upon one another with a greater frequency.

Case C. This describes Dyson-Hudson and Smith's "home ranges" (their case D, figure 5-4). Since intragroup variance is low, the need to call on neighbors for assistance is also low. Regardless of intergroup correlation, we could expect to see passive territories form, that is, groups remaining in a given region not because they cannot move into another group's range, but because there is no need to move out of their own territory. In addition, when resources do fail we could expect to see long-distance migration, since neighbors with high intergroup correlation of net returns could not assist one another. People would have to move to a region that was not ecologically synchronized with their own, or to a group of people utilizing a different suite of resources. Burch, for example, describes a time among the Nuataqmiut when caribou were so low regionally that neighboring groups could not help each other (1972). The Nuataqmiut moved 600 kilometers away to the coast—to a people not dependent on the caribou that the Nuataqmiut hunted. Some amount of hostility could occur during rare resource failures as the mechanisms to permit social and hence physical access to other regions may not exist.

Case D. In this case there will be infrequent need for a group to call on its neighbors, but we could still expect to see social-boundary defense maintained through reciprocity. As population increases and ranges become more restricted, we could expect to see exchanges appear between less mobile populations, depending on the amount of habitat diversity present (Spielmann 1986; Cashdan 1987). Additionally, differentiated exchange may be feasible only where tradable resources are predictable and abundant, and where "a decrease in search, procurement and/or production costs can be gained through a certain degree of specialization" (Spielmann 1986:303).[19]

Deciding which case applies to a given ethnographic or archaeological situation depends on the spatial scale being analyzed, since relations between groups depend to a large extent on the spatial scale of resource fluctuations. In figure 5-7 each pair of local groups lives in an area (A or B) within which resource fluctuations are correlated, but between which resources fluctuate on different time scales. Therefore, intergroup correlation would be high for groups 1 and 2, on the one hand, and 1′ and 2′ on the other, but intergroup correlation between any group in area A and any group in area B would be low. Depending on the density of resources (hence the size and defensibility of the local groups' territories) we could expect to see perimeter or strong social-boundary defense between groups 1 and 2, as well as between groups 1′ and 2′; however, there should be more relaxed social-boundary defense

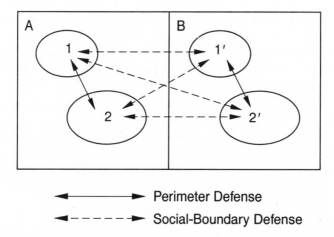

◄──────────► Perimeter Defense
◄── ── ── ──► Social-Boundary Defense

Figure 5-7. Different spatial scales of resource variability create territoriality be-tween some groups, social-boundary defense between others. Drawn by Dan Delaney.

or even mutualism (depending on intragroup return variance and environ-mental heterogeneity) between groups in area A and area B.

This hypothetical situation could become even more complex if one group falls within one category, for example, case B in figure 5-6, and its neighbors fall into case A. Some Kwakiutl villages, for instance, were located on minor streams with small, variable salmon runs; others were located on large streams with large, consistent salmon runs. Here, those living on small streams may occasionally need the resources of those living on large streams, but not vice versa. This creates a situation in which those with dense, defen-sible resources must weigh the cost of defense, and those with variable re-sources must weigh the cost of raiding or penetrating strong social-boundary defense. We return to this situation in chapter 8. Our point here is that for any given case we should be able to translate the interplay between environ-mental and population variables into their significance in terms of intragroup variance and intergroup correlation, and from these predict the specific form of land tenure.

CONCLUSIONS

On the surface, hunter-gatherers appear to share food, goods, and access to land quite readily. Yet a close reading of ethnographic data indicate that this is not simply primitive communism or a reflection of innately kind and generous dispositions (however kind and generous individual hunter-gatherers may be). Sharing is not a product of an evolutionary stage or a subsistence mode, but is the outcome of a decision-making process. There are costs and benefits to sharing resources and it is clear that hunter-gatherers balance these in making decisions to share food or to admit outsiders into their territory.

It is also clear that the costs and benefits of sharing are analyzed over some period of time, taking into account past experiences and future expectations. These costs and benefits are probably analyzed in terms of the degree of correlation between foragers' efforts and the amount of day-to-day variance in those efforts. Individual foragers may share resources to reduce the risk of going without any food in the future, or as an exchange for complementary resources, sexual favors, or support in old age. Given the potential for variability, and the significance anthropologists have given to sharing (especially its alleged role in human evolution), it is important that further research be done on this topic.

If men and women procure different resources, the nature of those resources may affect the way they share. If men hunt large game, then they will automatically come under demands to share since they can acquire more meat than they can use at one time. This also puts men in a position of prestige and may direct their continued attention toward resources and activities that garner prestige (resulting in some men hunting more than is necessary for energetic needs) depending on what one can gain from prestige. If women gather, they can control how much food is collected, perhaps bringing back only enough for their family—food that is not surplus and that cannot be acquired through demand sharing. Women may instead choose to share other things, including sex, as a way to build social bonds and acquire resources.

Land tenure can be analyzed using a similar framework, one that focuses on intragroup variance and intergroup correlation. Where peoples' fortunes are all tied to the same resource, or where resources are synchronized such that when one group does poorly another also does poorly, there is little utility to intergroup sharing of use rights. Territoriality may form under such conditions if resources are defensible. Where the resources of different groups are not synchronized, but where there is variation in resource availability, groups may evolve land-tenure systems whereby people are tied to the land through social processes of affiliation, but ones that leave affiliation continually up for negotiation. Many hunter-gatherers today live under the latter situation, but this may not have been true of many foragers in the past.

Land tenure is as variable as sharing. Evolutionary ecology predicts that territoriality will result when resources are sufficiently dense and predictable to make the cost of defense worthwhile, and where population is high enough that, for someone outside looking in, the cost of trying to acquire a denied resource is worth the potential benefit. But the land that foragers need to survive is often so large, and population density so low, that physical defense of a perimeter is impossible, yet the cost of allowing unregulated visitors in can be too high. In these cases, foragers regulate physical access through social access, the stringency of which is related to the cost of denying visitors the right to use resources versus the potential that visitors have to reciprocate in the future. This makes land tenure much like sharing, with variations predicted by resource density and reliability, intragroup variance, and intergroup correlation in returns. This adds a spatial as well as temporal component to the environmental factors that affect sharing of food and access to land. Both geographic and temporal scales of resource fluctuation must be considered to understand variation in land tenure.

GROUP SIZE AND REPRODUCTION | 6

A woman who gives birth like an animal to one offspring after another has a permanent backache.
Ju/'hoansi saying (Lee 1980:325)

A Dreamtime man died . . . no one knows why . . . and Wirlara the Moon-man, who was traveling with his large pack of dingoes, found the body and decided to try to save the man. He dragged him along by the hand but the body was rotting and pieces of it began dropping off, where-upon the Moon-man, being a clever magician, would stick them back on again. Some people saw him doing this and burst into laughter, ridiculing him for dragging a smelly corpse around. He was very angered by this, and embarrassed, so he scattered the pieces of the body far and wide, say-ing to the people, "From now on you will die and stay forever dead." Had these people not ridiculed the Moon-man in the Dreamtime, human beings would never have to die.
Mardudjara myth (Tonkinson 1978:61)

After the "Man the Hunter" conference, conventional wisdom was that hunter-gatherer bands are made up of about 25 persons and live at low popu-lation densities, holding their population to 20–30 percent of carrying capac-ity. Often, it seemed, anthropologists thought hunter-gatherers *intentionally* held population in check through high rates of infanticide, especially female infanticide, and through the cultural regulation of intercourse, such as prohi-bitions on sleeping with one's spouse before a hunt, after killing a particular kind of animal, or for a time after the birth of a child. This conventional wisdom, however, is an oversimplification of a complex set of biological and cultural processes. Our concern here is with identifying the factors that condition variability in hunter-gatherer group size, rates of population growth, fertility, and mortality. We conclude the chapter with a discussion of the relationships among mobility, foraging, and population growth.

A word of caution is in order. Any attempt to understand hunter-gatherer demography must confront the scanty data at our disposal. Given the impor-tance often ascribed to population as a prime mover of cultural evolution, it is surprising that we have few accurate data on hunter-gatherer demography. Although we can compile a fairly impressive list (table 6-1), the accuracy of

Table 6-1. Hunter–Gatherer Demography

Group	Year	M/100F	m/100f	Ch/Ad	TFR	Reference
World overall					3.6	
U.S.A.	1950	109		0.48	1.8	
Arctic						
Copper Inuit	20th				4–5	Jenness 1922
Bernard Harbor	20th	109	116			Jenness, in Irwin 1989
Greenland Inuit	1950				3.5	Campbell and Wood 1988
Western Alaskan Eskimo	20th				6.0	Brainard and Overfield 1986
Interior Padlimiut	1920	80	145			Birket-Smith 1929
Coast Padlimiut	1920	78	119			Birket-Smith 1929
Qaernermiut	1920	83	218			Birket-Smith 1929
Hauneqtormiut	1920	72	130			Birket-Smith 1929
Harvaqtôrmiut	1920	81	153			Birket-Smith 1929
Qaernermiut	1890	76	141			Boas 1907
Sauniktumiut	1890	79	123			Boas 1907
Sinamiut	1890	100	171			Boas 1907
Avilikmiut	1890	76	178			Boas 1907
Central Inuit	1890	93	105			Boas 1888
Cape Prince of Wales (Alaska)	1920	103	108			Weyer 1932
Cape Smith (Alaska)	1890	87	192			Smith, in Irwin 1989
Utknhikhalingmiut	1920	102	212			Rasmussen 1931
Netsilingmiut	1890	97	208			Boas 1907
Netsilingmiut	1920	98	212			Rasmussen 1931
Copper Inuit	1920	101	270			Rasmussen 1932
Nunamiut	1960	140	108		6.9	Campbell and Wood 1988
Kuskowagamiut					6.2	Driver 1961
Konyags					8.4	K. Taylor 1966
Polar Inuit					4.6	Malaurie 1956
Netsilingmiut					6.4	Schrire and Steiger 1974a
N. Greenland	1920	125	103			Birket-Smith, in Irwin 1989
E. Greenland	1920	90	100			Birket-Smith, in Irwin 1989
E. Greenland	1900	83	77			Hansen, in Irwin 1989
Subarctic						
Kutchin	19th				4.4	Roth 1981
Kutchin	20th				6.6	Roth 1981
Kutchin	1858	67	142	0.45	5.4	Osgood 1936
Kutchin	1858	111	159	0.73		Osgood 1936
Kutchin	1858	103	157	0.68		Osgood 1936
Kutchin	1858	158				Krech 1978
Yahgan					7–10	Stuart 1980
Tanana	1930	120		0.45		McKennan 1959
Tanana		83		0.64		McKennan 1959
Tanana		90		0.79		McKennan 1959
Tanana		86		0.92		McKennan 1959
Tanana		100		0.84		McKennan 1959
North American Northwest Coast						
Central Northwest Coast (not including slaves)						Panowski 1985
Columbia River ($n = 15$)	1825	82				

Table 6-1. Hunter-Gatherer Demography (*continued*)

Group	Year	M/100F	m/100f	Ch/Ad	TFR	Reference
Central Northwest Coast (*continued*)						
Nass R. (*n* = 4)	1846	124	102	0.63		
Tako R. (*n* = 1)	1846	109	109	0.50		
Queen Charlotte Is. (*n* = 3)	1846	101	96	0.92		
Cape Fox (*n* = 3)	1846	97	90	0.81		
Chilkat (*n* = 1)	1846	230	108	0.36		
Cross Sound (*n* = 1)	1846	110	123	0.40		
Sebassas (*n* = 5)	1846	117	126	0.50		
Stekini R. (*n* = 8)	1846	137	125	0.45		
Milbank Sound (*n* = 7)	1846	105	80	0.42		
Skeena (*n* = 2)	1846	183	107	0.61		
Hood's Bay (*n* = 3)	1846	121	109	0.37		
Chatham's Sound (*n* = 10)	1846	95	104	0.61		
Sitka R. (*n* = 2?)	1846	109	109	0.57		
Prince of Wales (*n* = 6)	1846	95	95	0.96		
Temperate deserts						
Paiute/Shoshone						Fowler and Fowler 1971
Central Nevada (*n* = 9)	19th	103		0.28		
S.E. Calif. (*n* = 5)	19th	108		0.27		
Gosiutes (*n* = 5)	19th	105		0.44		
Humboldt River (*n* = 6)	19th	113		0.30		
S. Utah (*n* = 8)	19th	147		0.26		
N. Arizona (*n* = 3)	19th	117		0.35		
Utes (*n* = 7, res.)	19th	104		0.63		
Battle Mt. (*n* = 6)	19th	97		0.39		
Ruby V. Shoshone (*n* = 3)	19th	172		0.33		
S. Nevada (*n* = 15)	19th	115		0.30		
Reese River V. (*n* = 7)	19th	98		0.42		
Pai	1881	113		0.88		J. Martin 1974
Tropical/subtropical deserts						
G/wi	1960	93				Silberbauer 1981a
≠Kade G/wi	1967	68	110	0.85	4	Tanaka 1980
G//ana					0.81	Cashdan 1984
Ju/'hoansi	1960	81			4.08	Harpending and Wandsnider 1982
Dobe Ju/'hoansi	1964	102	78	.43–.5	4.7	Lee 1979; Howell 1979
Ghanzi Ju/'hoansi	1960	91			4.03	Harpending and Wandsnider 1982
Mardudjara	1960	82		0.51		Tonkinson 1974
Pitjandjara		101	94	0.57	4.1	Yengoyan 1981
Hadza					6.2	Blurton Jones et al. 1992
Pitjandjara	1933	116		0.75		Tindale 1972
Seri	1930	96			6.8	Neel and Weiss 1975
Anbarra		100	106			White et al. 1990
Anbarra	1958		124		6.4	Hamilton 1981
Tropical forests						
Onge (Andaman Islands)	1980	110	60		2.6	Pandya, in Hewlett 1991a
Casiguran Agta	1977	83	145	0.53	6.3	Headland 1988; Hewlett 1991a
Palanan Agta	20th				5.9	Headland 1988
Birhor	1960	121	167	0.75		B. Williams 1974

Table 6-1. Hunter–Gatherer Demography (*continued*)

Group	Year	M/100F	m/100f	Ch/Ad	TFR	Reference
Tropical forest (*continued*)						
Asmat	1972	97	114	0.69	6.9	Van Arsdale 1978
Batak	1970	107	107	0.65	3.75	Eder 1987
Batek	1960	117	172	0.98	5.2	Endicott, in Hewlett 1991a
Semai	1960				5.7	Williams 1974
Mbuti (net hunters)	1960	94	120	0.66	5.5	Harako 1981
Mbuti (archers)	1960	119	67	0.29		Harako 1981
Western Pygmies	1965	197	122	0.45	5	Cavalli-Sforza 1986
Efe	1980	109	75	0.31	2.6	R. Bailey 1988
Aka (band)	1976	139		1.02	6.2	Bahuchet 1979
Ache	1970	133	153	0.81	7.8	Hurtado and Hill 1987
Tiwi	1960	88	91	0.64	5.7	F. Jones 1963
Bathurst Island (Tiwi)	20th	91				Peterson and Long 1986
Cape York	20th	81				Peterson and Long 1986
Groote Eylandt	20th	156	128	0.59		Rose 1960
Groote Eylandt	20th	86				Peterson and Long 1986
Arnhem Land, monogamous	20th				6.0	Chisholm and Burbank 1991
Arnhem Land, polygynous	20th				4.6	Chisholm and Burbank 1991
Hiwi	1980	129	165	0.43	5.1	Hurtado and Hill 1987
Paliyan	1960	85	69	0.59		Hewlett 1991a
Hill Pandaram	1960	78	140	1.50		Morris 1982
Hill Pandaram		64	120	0.61		Morris 1982
Hill Pandaram		30	167	1.23		Morris 1982
Hill Pandaram		100	500	0.50		Morris 1982
Hill Pandaram		71	109	1.08		Morris 1982
Hill Pandaram		62	40	0.33		Morris 1982
Hill Pandaram		100	96	0.94		Morris 1982
Pahira	1960				6.3	Basu 1969
Semang	1978				4.5	Gomes 1990
Semang	1988				5.2	Gomes 1990

Note: M/100F is number of adult males per 100 females, m/100f is number of child males per 100 females, Ch/Ad is the ratio of children to adults; TFR is total fertility. Dates of observation are specified as far as possible. Numbers in parentheses indicate that values given are the average of *n* separate groups.

many of these data is unknown for a variety of reasons. It is hard to estimate the ages of people who do not necessarily reckon time by the calendar year, and who physically age at different rates than an anthropologist's home population. Anthropologists have long been the rear guard of colonialism, recording demography after introduced diseases have taken their toll or, conversely, after Western medicines and inoculations have reduced child mortality. Enforced settlement of foragers carries with it a political economy that can have demographic effects independent of those associated with a change in mobility. Also, informants are often understandably reluctant to answer questions about infanticide, paternity, sexual activity, and death. Accurate population enumeration is difficult when people hide their children for fear they will be taken away or when the mention of deceased individuals is culturally prohibited (Hamilton 1981; Rose 1960; Yengoyan 1981). Sampling error also hampers the study of hunter-gatherer demography, for small groups undergo dramatic changes in demographic parameters from year to year as a consequence of chance events. Over a seven-year period, for example, Ju/'hoansi crude death rates fluctuated between four and twenty-six deaths per thousand person-years (Howell 1979). Therefore, a single census of a small population may not be a representative sample of that population's long-term demography (Weiss and Smouse 1976; Winterhalder et al. 1988:320), although that is the sort of data we primarily have. All of these factors mean that we should regard hunter-gatherer demographic data with a healthy amount of skepticism.

GROUP SIZE

The magic numbers 500 and 25

Two legacies of the "Man the Hunter" conference are the magic numbers 500 and 25, respectively the size of hunter-gatherer regional or tribal groups and the size of local hunter-gatherer bands. Steward referred to these as the maximal and minimal bands, the former being "a group with which its members somewhat vaguely identify" (1969b:290). Beginning with the "Man the Hunter" conference, and continuing to today, the figure 500 is cited as the size of maximal bands, as if it had been empirically demonstrated (e.g., Hunn 1994), but it has not. The 500-person figure comes from Joseph Birdsell's effort to construct a gene-flow model for prehistoric populations from Australian Aboriginal data. To do so, Birdsell needed to hold the size of the breeding population constant. Examining relationships between Australian Aboriginal tribal area and density, he concluded that while tribal area varied considerably (as a response to resource abundance as measured by rainfall), tribal size remained constant at about 500 persons. But there are problems in his analysis.

In the first place, he based reconstructions of tribal populations on the *dialectical tribe,* a population unit defined by linguistic boundaries and which Birdsell assumed to be genetically isolated. Leaving aside the question of genetic isolation, later researchers found little support for dialectical tribes in Australia itself (Berndt 1972). Second, the data Birdsell had on tribal areas and populations were also not altogether trustworthy and certainly not numerous. In fact, there were "too few estimates of the population size of aboriginal tribes to work directly with density as a dependent variable" (1953:177). His best estimates of Australian Aboriginal tribes ranged from about 175 to 1,000 persons, and he discarded anomalous cases based on whether they fit his model, not on the quality of the data (1953:178). Third, Birdsell's original argument is fraught with algebraic errors and circular reasoning (K. Kelly 1994). Even though Birdsell attempted to test the validity of the 500-person constant, in actuality he had to assume it: "it becomes crucial for the following analysis to make the intervening assumption that . . . in a statistical sense the population size of the Australian tribe may be considered a constant, in this case approximately 500 persons" (1953:177; see K. Kelly 1994). Birdsell himself even noted that the constant was "clearly not true when applied to a small series of tribes" (1953:172–73).

Sometime later, Martin Wobst used a computer simulation to determine how small a human breeding population could be and still remain viable (1974). He found that the minimal equilibrium size of a population varied within a fairly narrow range of 175 to 475 persons, and was affected by a number of population parameters such as fertility and mortality rates, sex ratio, and cultural rules governing marriage practices. Wobst lent some credence to Birdsell's constant by suggesting that the most realistic assumptions made 475 the likely *minimum* size of a population breeding unit; however, Wobst also noted that additional variables besides strictly reproductive considerations could greatly affect the size of prehistoric breeding populations.

At the "Man the Hunter" conference, Birdsell proposed extending a mean tribal size of 500 back into the Pleistocene. Nonetheless, he was also "inclined to think that the number is probably a little too high" (in Lee and DeVore 1968:246) and concluded that variance in prehistoric breeding population sizes "will be considerable" (Birdsell 1968:233). We would do well to heed this caution.

Data on local or minimal band size are more accurate, and they suggest an average band size of 25 in a variety of different environments, although there is still some variation (table 6-2). Sedentary hunter-gatherers, in particular, appear to live in larger (sometimes much larger) settlements than nomadic hunter-gatherers.

A number of factors may converge to make a group size of about 25 the most desirable for mobile foraging populations. Gregory Johnson argues that group size is limited by decision-making processes (1982). Using a large sample of ethnographic data (not restricted to hunter-gatherers), Johnson argues that when there are more than about six social units (in this case,

Table 6-2. Group Size

Society	Group Size	Reference
Nomadic		
Ju/'hoansi	25 (mean)	Marshall, in Damas 1969c
Hadza	20–60	Bicchieri, in Damas 1969c
Birhor	27 (mean)	Williams 1974
Semang	20–30	Gardner, in Damas 1969c
Andaman Islanders	30–50	Gardner, in Damas 1969c
Athapaskans	20–75	McKennan, in Damas 1969c
Cree	25–50	Rogers, in Damas 1969c
Iglulingmiut	35 (mean)	Damas, in Damas 1969c
Copper Inuit	15	Damas, in Damas 1969c
Cape York (Australia)	10–50	Chase and Sutton 1987
Pai	28	Martin 1973
Hill Pandaram	6–21	Morris 1982
Guayaki	16	Clastres 1972
Ngadadjara	20	Gould 1969a,b
Mistassini	15	Rogers 1972
Paliyan	24	Gardner, in Hayden 1981b
Tiwi	40–50	Hart and Pilling 1960
Sedentary		
Nootka	1,500	Jewitt, in Hayden 1981b
Wiyot	33	Schalk 1981
Yurok	46	Schalk 1981
Tolowa	43	Schalk 1981
Lower Chinook	50	Schalk 1981
Chehalis	110	Schalk 1981
Puyallup-Nisqually	35	Schalk 1981
Quinault	36	Schalk 1981
Makah	164	Schalk 1981
S. Kwakiutl	420	Schalk 1981
Bella Coola	58	Schalk 1981
Haisla	650	Schalk 1981
Tsimshian	389	Schalk 1981
Haida	577	Schalk 1981
S. Tlingit	197	Schalk 1981

families) acting corporately, then a new level of hierarchy must appear to coordinate activities. A group of 25 people could contain about five to seven families, and increasing group size beyond 25 might require the appearance of permanent leaders to coordinate the families' separate efforts. This sets an upper limit on group size. Conversely, Wobst uses a computer simulation to argue that 25 persons (with a mix of women and men) is the minimum group size that can withstand short-term fluctuations in fertility, mortality, and sex ratio for any length of time (1974). That is, groups smaller than 25 persons have a low probability of being reproductively viable. Wobst suggests that 25 is a compromise between reproductive and economic needs: it is sufficiently large to keep the group demographically viable, yet small enough to prevent rapid depletion of local resources. Both explanations, therefore, acknowledge the importance of foraging behavior and the available resources in conditioning group size.

Winterhalder responded to this observation by proposing a model that examines the relationship between group size and foraging. Recall our discussion in chapter 5 of his model of foraging and sharing (1986a). In that model, Winterhalder focused on the relationship between the number of sharing foragers in a group and the mean postsharing variance in individual foragers' returns. However, the model also examined how this variance responded to changes in the number of foragers and the degree of correlation between each forager's presharing return rate. It makes intuitive sense that having more that one forager in a group increases the probability that someone will bring home food. However, the more foragers there are in a group, the more mouths there are to feed, and the more food must be collected every day, increasing the rate of local resource depletion. At some size, a group will fission due to interpersonal tension arising from stress on the local food base and constraints on sharing (see chapters 4 and 5). It is most likely that before reproductive viability and politics become important factors, group size must balance the risk of going hungry with the rate of resource depletion.

Figure 6-1 shows one set of results of the Winterhalder model. This diagram graphs the simulated change in postsharing-return-rate variance (the coefficient of variance, or CV) along the y-axis as the number of independent foragers increases along the x-axis. The curves indicate the relationship between these two variables at different degrees of correlation in the foragers' daily return rates. Where $R = 1$ there is a perfect correlation in return rates—every forager does just as well or just as poorly as each of the others. Where $R = 0$ there is no correlation between foragers' returns—when one does poorly, another may do very well. Note that for each R there is a point at which an increase in the number of sharing foragers does not substantially reduce variance in postsharing return rates. This optimum increases slightly with decreasing correlation between foragers' return rates (smaller R values). Notice that there is rarely an advantage to having more than 7 to 8 foragers in a group.[1] Even where there is no correlation between forager's return rates ($R = 0$), 8 foragers produce a postsharing return rate CV of .12 while at 20 foragers it is only reduced to about .08. Though this is a reduction in postsharing variance, the larger group will deplete the resources around a camp more rapidly than the smaller group and therefore will have to move more frequently. In other words, "at some point the disadvantages to in-

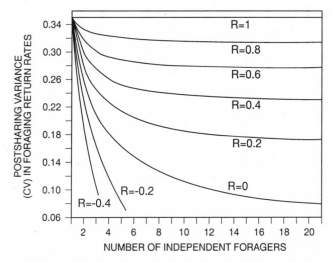

Figure 6-1. Relationship between postsharing variance in return rate and number of sharing foragers at different levels of interforager correlation in daily return rates. Redrawn from Winterhalder 1986a by Dan Delaney. Reproduced courtesy of *Journal of Anthropological Archaeology.*

creasing group size . . . will offset the small marginal increments of benefit gained by sharing" (Winterhalder 1986a:382). According to the simulation, this point appears to be reached, maximally, at a group containing 7 to 8 foragers.[2]

What does this have to do with a mean group size of 25? Not all members of a local group are active foragers. Of a group of 25 foragers, from 30 to 50 percent, 8 to 13 individuals, will probably be under the age of fifteen and contribute little to diet (Hewlett 1991a). Others will be old and infirm, while at any one time, some others may be ill or otherwise unable to forage. A group of 25 people, therefore, probably contains on average about 7 to 8 full-time foragers. In most environments, a group containing this number of foragers probably minimizes daily variance in return rates while also minimizing the rate of local resource depletion. Local groups of less than 25 could be expected where foragers' daily return rates are more highly correlated with one another.[3]

Aggregation and dispersal

While groups of about 25 people are common ethnographically, many foragers seasonally or periodically aggregate into large groups. These aggregations

Table 6-3. Horn's Model

Resource availability	Observed spatial organization
1. Evenly distributed, stable, and predictable	1. Small and dispersed settlements
2. Clumped, mobile, and unpredictable	2. Large settlement in central location
3. Clumped and predictable	3. Large, semipermanent settlement in central location

Source: Vickers 1989, based on Heffley 1981.

are, in fact, a strong element in the lives of many hunter-gatherers. They play an important role in social organization and a people's ceremonial life. The Shoshone, for example, aggregated periodically into large groups and hunted antelope or jackrabbits in communal drives. At these gatherings the Shoshone exchanged information, arranged marriages, traded, and caught up on gossip. There is some debate as to whether such aggregations among hunter-gatherers are a function of resource distribution or of the need to maintain social connections and information. That is, do hunter-gatherers aggregate for social purposes and then hunt communally because they are together, or do they aggregate in order to hunt and gather, and, since they are together, use the opportunity to accomplish social purposes? As we pointed out in chapter 2, foraging models provide a way to predict behavior under a certain set of conditions assuming a certain goal—foraging efficiency. How can we predict when foragers should aggregate only for the purpose of maximizing foraging efficiency?

Horn's model provides one way to answer this question. Developed to explain the nesting patterns of blackbirds (Horn 1968), Horn's model predicts how settlement size and location should change as resources change over the seasons, or over the years (table 6-3). Envisioning the foraging universe as two-dimensional space where food and potential camp locations are defined by x,y coordinates, the model balances the cost of traveling to a foraging location against the probability of finding food there and takes the form:

$$d = 2kT\sum_i\sum_j t(x_i,y_j)\sqrt{(x_i-x_o)^2+(y_j-y_o)^2}$$

where:

d = average round-trip distance between a user and resource points

k = number of foraging trips per unit time

T = total time under consideration

$t(x_i, y_i)$ = proportion of time during which foraging is better at (x_i, y_i) than at any other point in the area

(x_o, y_o) = coordinates of user location

The objective is to minimize the quantity, d, which is taken to be a proxy measure of foraging efficiency.

Horn's model leads to two conclusions. First, when hunter-gatherers depend on evenly spaced, stable resources they are expected to live in small, evenly dispersed groups. Second, when relying on aggregated and mobile resources, they are expected to live in larger, centrally located groups. The model's predictions have been applied to several cases, including Northern Athapaskan camps (Heffley 1981), Siona-Secoya horticultural villages (Vickers 1989), and Mbuti and Andamanese camps (Dwyer and Minnegal 1985).

Applications of Horn's model have required modifications of it in part because measuring the variables used is difficult, and because, whereas Horn argued that d is minimized at a point where the distances to the available resources is balanced against their respective values (the center of gravity), Cashdan points out that the square root in the equation negates this claim (1992). Nonetheless, Dwyer and Minnegal show that the model makes accurate predictions when a resource's size, the technology used to procure it, and storage are taken into account when figuring the degree of resource clumping (1985). Heffley also shows that seasonal changes in resource predictability and distribution predict seasonal changes in Ingalik, Tanana, and Chipewyan group size (1981). However, she also found that Horn's two resource categories did not describe all resource possibilities of the Athapaskans. An additional category of aggregated and predictable resources (e.g., caches of fish) resulted in group aggregation. Horn's model does not separate the effects of predictability from distribution.

In some respects, Horn's model parallels that of Winterhalder. Where resources are predictable, foragers' return rates are likely to be correlated, with a low amount of day-to-day variance. As a result, hunter-gatherers should live in small groups. Increasing the number of foragers in a group decreases variance to an extent, therefore group size could increase when resources are less predictable but aggregated so that the resource-harvest curve is of the limited linear kind (figure 3-7b). In this case, group fissioning would not occur until all resources are harvested. Suitably modified, Horn's model could provide a simple way to predict the conditions under which aggregation should occur solely as a function of characteristics of the resource base. However, though the model assumes that return-rate maximization is the

Figure 6-2. Madjembé, a thirteen-year-old Aka boy, checks a net for rips prior to a communal hunt. Photograph taken in 1984 near the Lobandji River in southeastern Central African Republic. Courtesy of Barry Hewlett.

goal of foraging behavior, it does not deal specifically with the decision-making process that a forager goes through in deciding whether to forage with others or not. Several researchers consider this topic in more detail.

Communal versus individual foraging

Years ago, Colin Turnbull set the stage for a long-running debate in anthropology when he observed that some BaMbuti of the Ituri Forest hunt individually with bows and arrows, while other groups hunt communally with nets (1961, 1965, 1968; figure 6-2). Among net hunters, women and children drive game through the forest undergrowth into an arc of nets where men kill the entrapped animals (although among the Aka it is women who kill and remove the netted game). Archers often take arboreal prey, but also hunt terrestrial animals such as duiker. Net hunters may also shoot arboreal prey (Harako 1981), and archers sometimes hunt communally, driving game into a ring of archers (*motá* hunting). Nonetheless, there is a dichotomy in the frequency of the two different hunting methods among BaMbuti groups.

Turnbull suggested that the rich Ituri Forest itself accounted for the different hunting methods. Because the Ituri was so lush and thick with resources, argued Turnbull, groups could simply pick and choose their hunting methods. The differences were therefore "cultural," and nothing in particular controlled whether BaMbuti foraged individually or communally.

But this conclusion did not sit well with later researchers in the Ituri. Many of these focused on the efficiency of net versus bow hunting. Reizo Harako argued that archery was the primary hunting method of the BaMbuti until the introduction of nets by Bantu horticulturalists (1976, 1981). Net technology spread, Harako opined, because it was more efficient and provided higher rates of return. Accepting that net hunting was more efficient than archery, William Abruzzi argued that net hunting arose as a function of population pressure (1979). As Bantu horticulturalists moved into the forest, they crowded the BaMbuti, requiring that some turn to more efficient net-hunting methods to increase yields. Archers did not have to increase yields, Abruzzi suggested, since they worked as laborers for the Bantu and received some agricultural produce in return. Katharine Milton turned this argument around, suggesting that the net hunters live in a less diverse and less productive environment and therefore must net hunt to increase yields in order to trade with horticulturalists (1985). Like Abruzzi and Harako, Milton accepted that net hunting is more efficient than archery. But, where Abruzzi saw little contact between net hunters and villagers, Milton and Harako saw the opposite. Finally, Paul Roscoe argued that the thick undergrowth of the net hunters' environment makes archery an impractical (low-return-rate) hunting technique there (1990), thus they use nets.

However, through field research and detailed environmental documentation, Robert Bailey and Robert Aunger point out that there are, in fact, no significant differences between the environments of net hunters and those of archers—neither in density of vegetation nor in the abundance of hunted resources (1989a). They also point out that net hunting does not necessarily produce a significantly higher rate of return than bow hunting. In fact, taking the manufacture of nets into consideration (see chapter 3), the start-up costs of net hunting make it less efficient than bow hunting. Why, then, is it used by some groups?

Bailey and Aunger make the important observation that "among net hunters, women participate in hunts; among archers, women rarely hunt" (1989a:273). The issue, perhaps, is not why some BaMbuti hunt communally and others hunt singly, but how women decide whether or not to participate in hunts.

Many of the BaMbuti, especially those who hunt with nets, trade meat with Bantu horticulturalists for produce—often receiving in exchange three or more times the caloric value of the meat (Bailey and Peacock 1988). Some women, however, work as laborers for horticulturalists, receiving produce in exchange. Bailey and Aunger argue that women decide to hunt or to garden depending on which activity gives them the highest caloric return. Bantu gardens in archers' areas tend to be large, and laborers are needed; gardens in net hunters' areas tend to be small, and do not require laborers. In areas where gardens are small, BaMbuti women cannot work in exchange for produce, so they choose to hunt. Presumably, as long as many people are going to go hunting, net hunting is a better way to utilize this wealth of labor than bow hunting.

One reason why it has been difficult for us to understand the difference between communal and individual hunting is the fact that authors make subjective interpretations of often poorly collected data. Satterthwait, for example, argues that communal net-hunting increases catch rates (1987:626), while Hayden concludes that "groups will hunt individually when they can and communally when they have to" (1981b:369). These are not necessarily contradictory conclusions, but neither author has hard quantitative data at his disposal.

Another more significant factor that confounds our understanding of communal hunting is that the question has been framed as a simple dichotomy, communal versus individual hunting. But the BaMbuti case suggests that the issue is understanding how people decide whether to forage alone or with others, and conversely, understanding how an existing group of foragers decides whether to permit others to forage with them. The question is not whether foragers should hunt individually or communally, but what is the optimal size of a foraging party?

The issue has to be examined from the perspective of a single forager looking for a group to join, and from the perspective of those who are already members of a group and are being petitioned by someone else. E. Smith approached this problem using data on the size of foraging parties of the Inujjuamiut of the southeastern coast of Hudson's Bay (1981, 1985, 1987, 1991). Smith predicted that men will join a hunting party if they stand to achieve a higher return rate than if they hunted alone. Group size should maximize the average net return rate per forager for the duration of a foraging period:

$$R = \frac{\sum_{}^{n} (E_a - E_e)}{t \, n}$$

where

R = average net return rate of all foragers
n = total number of foragers for the foraging trip
E_a = total usable energy acquired on trip
E_e = total energy expended on trip
t = total time of trip

Smith analyzed a total of 558 hunting trips of sixteen different hunting types, such as caribou, ptarmigan, goose, and breathing-hole seal hunting. In about half of these hunt types, men sometimes hunted in groups.

It is reasonable to expect that the per capita return rate for a particular hunt type will change with increasing group size (assuming equal sharing of food among all the party's members). Figure 6-3 shows a generalized form of this relationship in which the per capita return rate increases as foraging-group size increases until there are N members; after this point additional group members do not add to hunting efficiency and, if added, will decrease the per capita return rate. At a group size of n the per capita return is equal to that of foraging alone and prospective joiners would do better to forage by themselves (or look to join another group).[4]

If R_x is the group's per capita return rate at size x, current members of the party should allow others to join as long as the per capita return rate will increase (that is, as long as $R_{x+1} > R_x$); Smith terms this the "member's rule." Prospective joiners should try to join as long as R_{x+1} is greater than the return rate for foraging alone ($R_{x+1} > R_1$); Smith terms this the "joiner's rule." Once a group size of N is achieved there will be a conflict of interest between group members and prospective joiners since the joiners stand to increase their individual return rate over that of foraging alone, while the per capita return rate of current foraging-group members will decrease (where $R_x > R_{x+1} > R_1$).

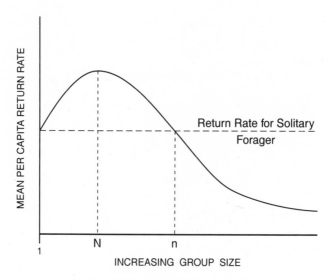

Figure 6-3. Relationship between foraging-group size and per capita return rate. *N* is the optimal size, where per capita return rate is highest; *n* is the group size at which the group per capita return rate is equivalent to that of foraging alone. Redrawn by Dan Delaney and used with permission from E. A. Smith, *Inujjuamiut Foraging Strategies* (New York: Aldine de Gruyter), copyright © 1991.

Smith found that in half the hunt types, foraging efficiency was highest when $N = 1$, and this was the modal group size for these hunt types. Where communal foraging was favored (where $N > 1$), the joiner's rule seemed to prevail (63 percent of cases) because modal group size lay between *N* and *n*. Why? One possible reason is that while foraging-group members lose some foraging efficiency by allowing additional members to join, they are building up social favors and minimizing the risk that they themselves will be excluded from foraging parties in the future (they could be seen as minimizing future risk or as maximizing their long-term per capita return rate; the former is perhaps more likely). Likewise, foraging-group size could also be larger than *N* if resources are pooled by all foraging parties of the residential group (Smith 1985), although this does not appear to be the case among the Inujjuamiut (with the possible exception of breathing-hole seal hunting; Smith 1991:336). Smith also suggests that social factors affect group size, for example, the training of younger hunters, mutual aid, and recreation. Where communal foraging is favored, therefore, the foraging group may be able to accomplish some other nonforaging goals at a slight sacrifice in foraging efficiency.[5]

Smith's study suggests that communal foraging is related to both foraging and social goals. However, communal hunting could be for purely social reasons, for example, to see friends, or to arrange marriages (Riches 1982:51–52). A low return rate may be acceptable given the benefit of the other tasks accomplished at gatherings. Accompanied by much ritual and taboos surrounding the construction of the corral, antelope drives in North America's Great Basin may have been held primarily for social reasons; the same could be said for jackrabbit drives (Steward 1941:220–22, 272, 1943:359; Stewart 1941:367). However, ethnological and archaeological analyses should not assume that an aggregation is for purely social purposes, but should first test foraging-related hypotheses, for current research suggests that foraging conditions exercise a strong influence on residential and foraging-group size, perhaps largely through environmental parameters that affect return rates and their variance.[6]

CARRYING CAPACITY, FORAGING, AND POPULATION GROWTH

To this point we have discussed the size of foraging groups, arguing that the size of these groups may be largely accounted for by the degree to which foragers wish to join an existing group and the degree to which those who are already members will permit others to join. It is likely that as population density and competition for resources rises, there will be increasing tension between current and potential group members which could set into motion a range of responses—for example, a change in foraging techniques, changing rules for membership (e.g., stronger kinship ties, or increased "dues" for joiners), or violence. Although it is commonly assumed that foragers live under low population densities, table 6-4 shows that there is, as the reader can now guess, much diversity in foragers' population densities.

Therefore, we now turn our attention to the factors that affect population density. Initial research in this area focused on predicting population density from food abundance as a way to ascertain the determinants of population growth in a given region. That the population density of hunter–gatherers is related to the abundance of food in their environment makes sense theoretically and can be demonstrated empirically. Although the data used are questionable, Birdsell set the pace in this area by trying to demonstrate that Australian Aboriginal population density increased exponentially with in-

Table 6-4. Hunter-Gatherer Population Densities

Area	Group	Density (persons per 100 km²)	Reference
Arctic			
Greenland	Polar Inuit	0.5	Gilberg 1984
Alaska	Nunivak	30	Kroeber 1939
N. Alaska Coast	Taġiuġmiut (Tareumiut)	4.0	Oswalt 1967
N. Canada	Mackenzie Delta Inuit	3.5	D. Smith 1984
Siberia	Yukaghir	0.5	Keeley 1988
St. Lawrence Is.	Sivokakhmeit	23	Hughes 1984
E. Greenland	Angmagsalik	8	R. Petersen 1984
Canada	Quebec Inuit	0.8	D'Anglure 1984
N. Canada	Copper Inuit	1.2	Damas 1984
N. Canada	Iglulingmiut	0.5	Kroeber 1939
N. Canada	Netsilik	0.5	Boas 1988; Balikci 1984
N. Alaska	Nunamiut	2	Hall 1984
E. Canada	Labrador Inuit	1.7–4	Kroeber 1939
Canada	Caribou Inuit	0.2	Kroeber 1939
N.W. Alaska	Kotzebue Sound Inuit	4.2–19	Burch 1984
Alaska	Bering Strait Eskimo	3.2	Ray 1984
S. Alaska	Chugach Eskimo	18	Birket-Smith 1953
Aleutians	Aleut	65	Kroeber 1939
Subarctic/cold forests			
W. Canada	Lillooet	23.5	Kroeber 1939
E. Canada	Naskapi	0.4	Rogers and Leacock 1981
S. America	Yahgan	4.6	Steward and Faron 1959
Canada	Chipewyan	0.4	J. Smith 1981
Canada	Tutchone	0.6	McClellan and Denniston 1981
Alaska	Ahtna	0.8	de Laguna and McClellan 1981
Alaska	Kaska	1	Kroeber 1939
S.E. Alaska	Kuskowagamiut	3	E. Nelson 1899
Alaska	Tanaina (Dena'ina)	4–6	Townsend 1981
E. Siberia	Gilyak	19.2	L. Black 1973
Canada	Attawapiskat Cree	1.4	Kroeber 1939
Alaska	Kutchin (Gwich'in)	0.5–1.7	Krech 1978
Canada	Dogrib	0.4–0.8	Helm 1981
Canada	Hare	0.3	Savishinsky and Hara 1981
Alaska	Kolchan	0.5	Hosley 1981
Canada	Slave	1.4	Kroeber 1939
Canada	Round Lake Ojibwa	1.7	Rogers 1969a,b
Canada	Ojibwa	3–5	Kroeber 1939
Alaska	Ingalik	2.5–4	Snow 1981
Alaska	Han	1.6	Crow and Obley 1981
Alaska	Nabesna	0.6	McKennan 1981
Canada	Sekani	1	Kroeber 1939; Denniston 1981
Canada	Yellowknife	0.2	Kroeber 1939
Canada	Pikangikum (Ojibwa)	3.2	Rogers 1969a,b
Canada	Berens River Ojibwa	4.8	Rogers 1969a,b
Canada	Grand L. Victoria Cree	0.7	Rogers 1969a,b
Canada	Tahltan	1.1	MacLachlan 1981
Canada	Carrier	7.6	Tobey 1981
W. Canada	Chilcotin	13	Kroeber 1939

Table 6-4. Hunter-Gatherer Population Densities (*continued*)

Area	Group	Density (persons per 100 km²)	Reference
Subarctic/cold forests (*continued*)			
Canada	Beaver	0.5	Ridington 1981
Canada	Waswanipi Cree	0.4	Rogers 1969a,b
Canada	Saulteaux	0.6	Grant 1890
Tasmania	Tasmanians, N.W.	14.5	R. Jones 1974
Tasmania	Tasmanians, S.W.	9.3	R. Jones 1974
Tasmania	Tasmanians, Big River	4.3	R. Jones 1974
Tasmania	Tasmanians, Oyster Bay	8	R. Jones 1974
E. Canada	Micmac	2.3	Kroeber 1939
North American Northwest Coast			
	Tlingit	10–40	Schalk 1981; Keeley 1988
	Haisla	16	Schalk 1981
	Bella Coola	10	Schalk 1981
	Haida	62–96	Schalk 1981; Keeley 1988
	Tsimshian	32–83	Mitchell and Donald 1988; Keeley 1988
	Makah	86	Schalk 1981
	Quileute	64.5	Schalk 1981
	Quinault	33–59	Schalk 1981; Keeley 1988
	S. Kwakiutl (Ft. Rupert)	57	Mitchell and Donald 1988
	Chinook	148.6	Schalk 1981
	Twana	17–33	Elmendorf 1960
	Puyallup–Nisqually	18–195	Schalk 1981; Keeley 1988
	Cowichan	34	Keeley 1988; Kroeber 1939
	Nootka (Nuuchahnulth)	66–77	Mitchell and Donald 1988
	Puyallup	195	Jorgenson 1980
	Alsea	73	Kroeber 1939
California			
	Chumash	843	Keeley 1988
	Serrano	39	Bean and Smith 1978
	Cupeno	39	Kroeber 1953
	Foothill Yokuts	237	Baumhoff 1963
	Kiliwa	33.4	Meigs 1939
	Monachi	190	Spier 1978
	Klamath	25	Keeley 1988
	Washo	28	Downs 1966
	Mattole	210	Elsasser 1978
	Sinkyone	270	Elsasser 1978
	N. Pomo	232	Baumhoff 1981
	C. Pomo	196	Baumhoff 1981
	Coast Yuki	166	Baumhoff 1981
	Tubatulabal	30	C. Smith 1978
	Wiyot	103–430	Schalk 1981; Keeley 1988
	S.W. Pomo	213	Baumhoff 1981
	Achumawi	17.5	Kroeber 1939
	Yurok	180	Schalk 1981
	Tolowa	138	Cook 1976
	W. Mono	40.9	Bean and Theodoratus 1978
	Yana	35	J. Johnson 1978
	Whilkut	214	Wallace 1978

Table 6-4. Hunter-Gatherer Population Densities (*continued*)

Area	Group	Density (persons per 100 km²)	Reference
California (continued)			
	Chimariko	34.1	Kroeber 1939
	Atsugewi	45	Garth 1978
	Maidu	103	Cook 1976
	Hupa	197	Cook 1976
	Karok	98.5	Schalk 1981
	Shasta	74	Cook 1976
	Wailaki	255	Baumhoff 1981
	Lassik	140	Elsasser 1978
	Yuki	232	Baumhoff 1981
	Diegueno (Tipai-Ipai)	18.1	Kroeber 1939
	Wintu	281	LaPena 1978
	S. Yokuts	90	Baumhoff 1963
	Lake Miwok	180	Baumhoff 1981
	S.E. Pomo	431	Baumhoff 1981
	E. Pomo	196–633	Baumhoff 1981; Keeley 1988
	Wappo	176–350	Keeley 1988; Baumhoff 1981
	Sierra Miwok	55	Baumhoff 1963
	Patwin	62.5	Kroeber 1939; P. Johnson 1978
	Nomlaki	71	Cook 1976
	Kawaiisu	11.9	Kroeber 1939
	Cahuilla	39–97	Kroeber 1953; Keeley 1988
	Wappo	163	Cook 1976
	Luiseño	39–257	Kroeber 1953
Temperate deserts			
Great Basin	Sampits Ute	2.7–9	Callaway, Janetski, and Stewart 1986
	Wind River Shoshone	1	Leland 1986
	Wadadika (Ruby Valley)	13.4	Steward 1938
	Agaiduka (Lemhi)	1.5–4	Steward 1938
	Gosiute	1.5	Steward 1938
	Timpanogots (Utah L.)	5.7–15	Leland 1986; Callaway, Janetski, and Stewart 1986
	Reese R. Shoshone	10	Steward 1938
	Tosawihi (White Knife)	15	Steward 1938
	Kawich Shoshone	1.9	Steward 1938; Thomas 1981
	Kuyuidökadö (Pyramid L.)	18	Stewart 1941
	Pahvant Ute (Sevier L.)	6.7–14	Callaway, Janetski, and Stewart 1986
	Kaibab (Paiute)	3–4	Leland 1986
	Owens V. Paiute	19	Steward 1938; Thomas 1981
	S. Paiute (Las Vegas)	1.3	Steward 1938
	Panamint	2.1	Steward 1938
	Kidütökadö	1.1	Stewart 1941
Temperate forests			
Oregon	Modoc	4.8	Kroeber 1939
Plateau	Shoshone-Bannock	1.31	Leland 1986
	Tenino	18	Murdock 1958

Table 6-4. Hunter–Gatherer Population Densities (*continued*)

Area	Group	Density (persons per 100 km²)	Reference
Temperate forests (continued)			
	Thompson	33.2	Kroeber 1939
	Shuswap	4.5–15	Keeley 1988
	Kutenai	2	Kroeber 1939
	Coeur d'Alene	1.5	Kroeber 1939
	Sanpoil	38	Ray 1932
	Nez Perce	8.9	Haines 1955
	Umatilla	4.5	Kroeber 1939
S. Texas	Karankawa	19–42	Keeley 1988
S.E. Australia	Clarence R. tablelands	1.8	Bellshaw 1978
	Clarence R. slopes	5.5	Bellshaw 1978
	Clarence R. coast	13.4	Bellshaw 1978
Plains			
	Blackfoot (Piegan, Blood)	4.3	Kroeber 1939; Ewers 1955
	Plains Cree	1.9	Kroeber 1939
	Assiniboine	5.8	Kroeber 1939
	Crow	2.6	Kroeber 1939
	Arapaho	3	Kroeber 1939
	Cheyenne	3	Kroeber 1939
	Kiowa-Apache	1.4	Kroeber 1939
	Comanche	5	Kroeber 1939
	Kiowa	1.4	Kroeber 1939
Tropical/subtropical deserts			
Australia	Mamu	55	Harris 1978 (c. 1800 A.D.)
	Madjandji-Wanjuru	49	Harris 1978 (c. 1800 A.D.)
	Keramai	29	Harris 1978 (c. 1800 A.D.)
	Idindji	38	Harris 1978 (c. 1800 A.D.)
	Tjapukai-Buluwai	19	Harris 1978 (c. 1800 A.D.)
	Gulngai	60	Harris 1978 (c. 1800 A.D.)
	Kongkandji	200	Harris 1978 (c. 1800 A.D.)
	Djirubal	26	Harris 1978 (c. 1800 A.D.)
	Ngatjan	149	Harris 1978 (c. 1800 A.D.)
	Djiru	125	Harris 1978 (c. 1800 A.D.)
	Wongaibon	19	Yengoyan 1968
	Dieri	1.9	Yengoyan 1968
	Aranda	3	Yengoyan 1968
	Pintupi	0.5	Myers 1986; N. Peterson 1979
	Kariera	7.6	Radcliffe-Brown 1930
	Worora	2	Peterson and Long 1986
	Walpiri (Walbiri)	1	Meggitt 1962
	Alyawara	2.5	O'Connell, Latz, and Barnett 1983
	Mardudjara	0.6	Cane 1987; Tonkinson 1978
	Anbarra	2	White et al. 1990
	Yolngu	.3–.06	White et al. 1990
	Kukadju	.57	Cane 1990
Mexico	Seri	5	Keeley 1988
Mexico	Borjeno (Baja Calif.)	37.3	Aschmann 1959

Table 6-4. Hunter-Gatherer Population Densities (*continued*)

Area	Group	Density (persons per 100 km²)	Reference
Tropical/subtropical deserts (continued)			
Africa	Hadza	15	Woodburn 1968
Africa	Dobe Ju/'hoansi	10–16	Hitchcock 1987
Africa	G/wi	8	Silberbauer 1981a
Africa	Kua (E. Kalahari)	2.1–3	Hitchcock 1982
Africa	≠Kade	5	Tanaka 1980
U.S.	Walapai	4	Kroeber 1935
U.S.	N.E. Yavapai	1.4–4	Kroeber 1939
Seasonal and wet tropical forests			
Philippines	Batak	54	Eder 1987
Australia	Groote Eylandt	11.5	Peterson and Long 1986
Australia	Wikmunkan	18.7	Keeley 1988
Australia	Murinbata	8	Yengoyan 1968
Australia	Nesbitt R. (Cape York)	40	Chase and Sutton 1987
Australia	Yir Yoront	16	Peterson and Long 1986; Yengoyan 1968
Australia	Anbarra	43	Meehan 1982
Australia	Gidjingali	77	Hiatt 1965
Australia	Murngin	5	Warner 1937
S. America	Botocudo (Kaingang)	11	Steward and Faron 1959
S. America	Aweikoma	3.8	Keeley 1988
S. America	Guayaki	3	Clastres 1972
Africa	Mbuti	17	Turnbull 1965
Africa	Aka	28	Bahuchet 1988
Malaysia	Semang	5–19	Rambo 1985
Andaman Is.	Andamanese	86	Keeley 1988
India	Hill Pandaram	69.6	Morris 1982
India	Birhor	22	Williams 1974
India	Paliyan	77	Gardner 1972

creases in rainfall (Birdsell used rainfall as a proxy measure of food abundance; 1953, 1958).[7]

Following Birdsell's lead, others tried to measure food abundance more directly so as to predict population size more accurately and to discover the factor(s) limiting population size. Baumhoff (1958, 1963), Thompson (1966), and Rogers (1969b) all found that hunter-gatherer population size could be predicted by a few simple measures of food density. Baumhoff, for example, determined the abundance of three gross resource categories in California—fish, acorns, and game—by measuring the number of fish-stream miles and the area of different forest types encompassed within the ranges of various ethnographic groups, multiplying these estimates by coefficients to produce resource indices. These were used in a series of regression analyses to see which combination of variables provided the most accurate predictor of population. In the lower Klamath region of northern California, for example, Baumhoff found that the fish index alone was the most accurate predictor of population. Presumably, then, fish was the limiting factor for population density there.

Research into the nature of the relationship between population and resources often utilizes the concept of *carrying capacity*. Carrying capacity has been used in two major ways (Dewar 1984): (1) to refer to the number of people that theoretically can be supported by a given unit of land under a given subsistence technology, and (2) as a density-dependent limit on a population's growth rate (unaffected by environmental parameters). Most studies of hunter-gatherer populations begin with the first of these two definitions (e.g., Casteel 1972, 1979; Hassan 1981; Hayden 1975). To do so, they need to measure edible resource abundance and extractive efficiency (see Dewar 1984 for a more complete discussion). Take, for example, Fekri Hassan's model (1981):

$$Density \ (persons/km^2) = \frac{\sum_{i=1}^{1-n} F_i N_{ij}}{L_j}$$

where:

F_i = the optimum yield to humans for the ith food item/km^2 multiplied by a constant, K, which is a product of four variables: M, the percentage of the yield regularly extracted to allow for a safety margin; E, the edible percentage of live-weight meat; W, the percentage of yield that escapes spoilage; and S, the percentage of animal game selected from the range of game available in their territory

N_{ij} = the nutritional content in calories or some other unit of the jth nutritional element (protein, mineral, etc.) per kilogram of edible portion of the ith food item

L_j = the average consumption requirement per capita of the jth nutritional element

Hassan tested the model with some success against data from the Hadza and Caribou Eskimo. The model requires very detailed information about a local environment—information that is often not possible to obtain in prac-

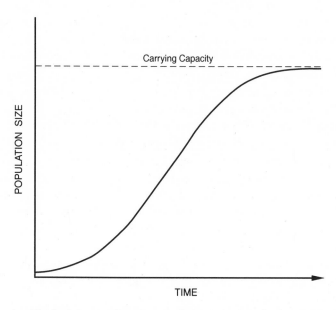

Figure 6-4. The logistic growth curve: population grows rapidly then levels off as carrying capacity is reached. Drawn by Dan Delaney.

tice (Dewar 1984). Its objective is to quantify effective food density very precisely, given human needs for calories, protein, and so on (as we saw in chapter 3, these are not necessarily constants). It then translates food density into population density. Archaeologists are especially fond of such models since it is so difficult to reconstruct prehistoric population size from settlement data.

But carrying-capacity models are fraught with their own difficulties. Like the culture-area studies of Kroeber and Wissler and the cultural ecology of Steward, carrying-capacity models assume that societies are at equilibrium, that they grew very quickly in the past, then reached a plateau at a point below or at carrying capacity, a process described by the classic logistic growth curve (figure 6-4). An assumption of population-environment equilibrium is central to carrying-capacity models, which must then assume that hunter-gatherers consciously or unconsciously recognize the carrying capacity of their environment and implement cultural mechanisms to maintain population below that level. Through postpartum sex taboos, infanticide, abortion, senilicide, and lactation-induced amenorrhea, it is argued, hunter-gatherers keep their population in equilibrium at 20–50 percent of carrying capacity (Hayden 1972; hence, published definitions often conflate both concepts of carrying capacity).

This points to an important flaw in carrying-capacity studies, a flaw that we saw in chapter 2 lies at the heart of the cultural ecological framework within which these studies were conducted: if maintaining equilibrium is a "goal" of hunter-gatherers, and if hunter-gatherers allegedly maintain their population levels below carrying capacity, why did some prehistoric hunter-gatherer populations grow to the point where they needed to augment the productivity of their environment through agriculture and labor-intensive extractive technologies (e.g., irrigation, double-cropping, terracing, etc.)? The answer is that population density is not related to environmental productivity in a straightforward fashion. Other factors that must be considered include interspecific competition for food, the effect human use has on a resource's abundance, and foraging return rates. In a reanalysis of Baumhoff's data, for example, Timothy Gage found that a model including a competitive relationship between humans and deer for acorns gave more accurate predictions of aboriginal population sizes in two California regions (1979). In his model, it is not food density alone or foragers' innate desire that keep foraging populations at 30–40 percent of a carrying capacity predicted solely on the abundance of food, but food density coupled with the effects of interspecific competition.

Two additional models by Belovsky and Winterhalder predict population growth rates from the interaction between foraging behavior, resource density, rates of resource recovery, and human reproduction (Belovsky 1988; Winterhalder et al. 1988; Winterhalder and Goland 1993; Winterhalder 1993). These models are based on the fact that human use of resources affects the abundance of those resources, which in turn, as we saw in chapter 3, affects the human selection of resources to exploit. This in turn affects foraging return rates, the foraging population's reproduction and, ultimately, population growth rates.

Winterhalder uses the diet-breadth model; Belovsky uses linear programming (see chapter 3). Both begin with a human group of known size and with food resources of given densities, return rates, and rates of increase. Population growth rates increase as the net acquisition rate of food increases, and decrease when the net acquisition rate falls. (Population can grow in either case—although faster or slower—only decreasing in size when the net return rate falls below that needed to maintain it.) In this way, static diet-breadth and linear-programming models are made dynamic, and can predict changes over time in human population growth rates as a function of changes in food density, length of the work day, return rates, and rates of resource growth. Both models make simple but not unreasonable assumptions about human energy needs, culling rates, resource-density-dependent growth rates, and population growth rates. Neither model, however, incorporates the effects of nonforaging-related changes in resource populations (e.g., disease, warfare) or interspecific competition. The importance of the models lies in the recognition that while prey affects hunter-gatherer demography, hunter-gatherers affect prey population dynamics as well. Winterhalder and Belovsky demonstrate that "the relationship between foragers and prey biomass is time dependent; it is consistent (that is to say, predictably determined by a few key variables) but it is not proportional, linear, or direct" (Winterhalder et al. 1988:320).

Generally speaking the Winterhalder model makes predictions that follow the classic Lotka-Volterra growth curve: human populations rise from their initial level and eventually plateau, reaching a level at which the human and prey populations are at equilibrium.[8] However, large changes in overall population size and in the nature of population fluctuations over time were produced by relatively minor changes in model parameters such as basal caloric needs, the amount of time spent foraging, or the response of prey to predation.

For example, Winterhalder varied the length of the foraging day, finding that as the work day got longer, the human population increased but reached equilibrium at an increasingly smaller number. The harder they worked, the less the foragers' population grew; at very long work days, in fact, the population quickly crashed. For short work days, the population grew steadily, as depicted in the logistic growth curve. But as the work day lengthened the population exhibited overshoot and damped cycles, climbing above before dropping down to an equilibrium level, or oscillating (in increasingly shorter, less intensive cycles as the length of the work day was increased) about an eventual equilibrium level. The magnitude of oscillations, growth rates, and eventual equilibrium level are sensitive to the density of prey, the net foraging acquisition rate, and the rate at which prey recover from predation. A decline in foraging efficiency can result in a decrease *or* increase in population density depending on resource densities and their rates of recovery (Winterhalder and Goland 1993). Where resources are dense, and (especially) where the rate of recovery is high, population could grow rapidly.

In Belovsky's model, changes in population and food density alter the amount of time spent foraging and produce changes in the dietary ratio of

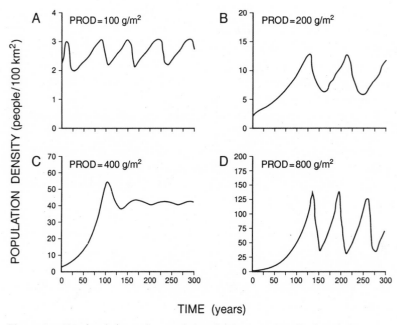

TIME (years)

Figure 6-5. Simulated change in population density over time for four different levels of harvestable primary productivity. Redrawn from Belovsky 1988 by Dan Delaney. Reproduced courtesy of *Journal of Anthropological Archaeology.*

meat to vegetable foods. As this ratio changes, so does the amount of harvestable primary production (given as PROD in figure 6-5). This change in diet composition in turn alters the amount of energy available to the population for conversion into births. The model's most sensitive parameters are the harvestable primary production, the group's nutritional requirements, and the age at which children become active foragers.[9]

Belovsky's model (figure 6-5) predicts more fluctuation in population density than does Winterhalder's over the same time period (300 years). One of the interesting facets of Belovsky's model is that population fluctuates widely when PROD = 200 and 800 grams per square meter, while it fluctuates less at PROD = 100 and 400 grams per square meter. There are limits to population growth in each of the four environments in figure 6-5, but populations do not simply grow and then remain at equilibrium, and the nature of the fluctuations is of greater interest than the upper limits of the cycles. Note that at PROD = 800, population fluctuations are far more dramatic than at PROD = 200 grams per square meter. This suggests that as effective food density increases, populations go through "boom and bust" cycles. If population declines happen over such short time spans that they could be perceived, people may respond to them, perhaps by altering subsistence technologies (e.g., through agriculture) and increase their environment's productivity. The result could be continuous population growth, rather than stable-limit cycles.

These foraging models offer an exciting new approach to the study of foraging-population dynamics. However, both are limited by simple assumptions about how changes in subsistence and foraging are related to birth and death rates. Our understanding of hunter-gatherer demography remains incomplete without understanding the intricate and varied relationships among behavior, diet, physiology, and reproduction.

REPRODUCTION AND CULTURAL CONTROLS

The literature on hunter-gatherer demography is replete with references to conscious controls on fertility. Primary among these are contraception and abortion, postpartum taboos on intercourse, and infanticide. We have relatively little information on contraception and abortion among hunter-gatherers. Herb potions are claimed to either prevent pregnancy or induce abortion in some cultures, but there is no solid evidence that these methods actually work. Abortion is more frequently induced through physical means such as striking the abdomen, but since this could harm the mother, it is doubtful that it was common. Handwerker concludes that hunter-gatherers do not make use of contraception or abortion to any significant extent, and doubts if abortion and contraception ever had an important effect on prehistoric populations (1983; see also Wood 1990).

Postpartum taboos on sexual intercourse are another way in which hunter-gatherers can control fertility. As with contraception and abortion, it is difficult to judge the effectiveness of postpartum sexual taboos since we have only anecdotal data on their effectiveness. Based on analysis of the Standard Ethnographic Sample, Whiting concludes that these rules are more common among horticulturalists than hunter-gatherers (in Cohen 1980:287–88). But even if a rule is in effect, it may not have much impact on fertility. As we discuss below, breastfeeding can reduce a woman's fecundity for many months, even years, after giving birth. Although quantitative data are rare, it appears that postpartum taboos on intercourse permit sexual activity before the effects of breastfeeding on ovulation have been relaxed. Thus, postpartum taboos, even if they exist, may have little effect on controlling fertility (see also Hamilton 1981:123).

This leaves infanticide as the primary conscious control on population size. More has probably been written on infanticide than on any other topic in hunter-gatherer demography, although the volume of literature is inversely related to the amount of good ethnographic information.[10] In one sample of thirty-four foraging groups, for example, just under half are reported to have practiced infanticide (Morales 1987). Birdsell postulated that infanticide occurred at rates of 15 to 50 percent during the Pleistocene (like many others, Birdsell assumed that most of this infanticide was directed at female offspring; 1968). Hassan suggested rates of 15 to 25 percent with a maximum female infanticide rate at the low end of this range (1981). But where the incidence of infanticide has been tabulated from informant interviews, it is substantially lower than has been argued by anthropologists— about 1 percent for the Dobe Ju/'hoansi (Howell 1979), 4 percent for the Hiwi (where female infants were killed more often than males; Hurtado and Hill 1987), and 5 to 11 percent for the Anbarra (Hamilton 1981:123).

These are limited data, however, and could have been affected in unknown ways by colonialism. Given its importance in the hunter-gatherer literature it behooves us to examine both the evidence for and explanations of infanticide. Many ethnographies mention cultural rules requiring that deformed infants and one or both twins be killed at birth, but these make up a relatively small proportion of the total number of births. More important to hunter-gatherer demography are *preferential female infanticide,* and *nonpreferential* or *birth-spacing infanticide.* In the former, female children are the only ones killed, either at birth or through neglect soon after birth. In the latter, an infant is killed regardless of sex because the mother already has a child nursing or for some other reason cannot care for both.

Preferential female infanticide

The idea of female infanticide as a significant population control method can be traced through the anthropological literature to data collected on several Arctic groups, especially the early-twentieth-century Netsilik (Netsilingmiut). These data pertain to the period from about 1880 to 1930; I hope it goes without saying that Arctic peoples do not practice infanticide today.

Data on the Netsilik were collected in the 1920s by the Danish explorer Knud Rasmussen (1931). These consist of interviews of eighteen women and a population census. From the interviews, it appears that 67 percent of female offspring were killed at birth (Rasmussen reported 80 percent, but he either added incorrectly or the published table contains typographic errors; Schrire and Steiger 1974a; Remie 1985). In his census, Rasmussen found far more juvenile males than females. From these data he concluded that the Netsilik were on their way to extinction.

Evidence of female infanticide in the Arctic and subarctic comes largely from sex-ratio data (e.g., Weyer 1932; Irwin 1989; Helm 1980); some censuses show more and some less skewed populations than that of the Netsilik. Informant interviews are a secondary source of information about female infanticide. But just how accurate are informant interviews and census data for a subject like female infanticide? This is important because for all the talk of female infanticide as a way to control population growth, it is rarely reported in cross-cultural surveys—and rarely reported to be of any significance (see Daly and Wilson 1988; Morales 1987).

First, let's think about interview data. Rasmussen interviewed women, but accounts of infanticide from many other foraging groups are based on statements made by male informants to male ethnographers. How accurate are male accounts of infanticide, or accounts given by women to male ethnographers?

In some cases men are responsible for deciding whether a newborn lives or dies. Among some Inuit, life and death decisions were not left entirely to the mother (Balikci 1967:619–20); grandparents, in fact, were often the ones to make the decision (Irwin 1989), although husbands also did (Balikci 1970). Among foragers outside the Arctic, there may be many witnesses to a birth. A Tiwi woman, for example, about to give birth is surrounded by a "big mob of people, [her] father, mother, in-laws, brother, sister," although not the baby's father because "maybe he get too frightened" (Goodale 1971:146).[11] Several people here may influence the decision to keep a newborn.

However, women frequently give birth alone, or with only older female relatives, and since infanticide often occurs soon after birth, sometimes even before the infant has taken its first breath, how does a husband find out about the child's death? Obviously, a man will know that his wife is pregnant and will not miss the fact that she has given birth. Yet, if birthing occurs away from the husband, then the mother could kill a newborn male but tell her husband it was stillborn *or female* so as not to anger him; she may tell the same to a male ethnographer (or may not be interviewed by him—either because he decides not to or because it is culturally inappropriate). Working with the Bolivian horticultural Ayoreo, Paul Bugos and Lorraine McCarthy found that men knew very little about infanticide except for general rules (in the case of twins, deformities, or if the woman felt she could not care for the child); and they knew little about specific women's reproductive histories (1984). Ayoreo women, on the other hand, when interviewed by a female ethnographer, gave very accurate reproductive histories, including accounts of infanticide, of themselves and their neighbors.[12] Thus we must consider that our ethnographic interview data on infanticide could be significantly biased (see also Hamilton 1981:119).

Sex ratios are the other evidence of infanticide. Sex-ratio data can be affected by a number of factors, such as differential male versus female death rates, emigration, immigration, and catastrophes (such as the death of an all-male hunting party). Rasmussen's data, for example, may be affected by the fact that up to one-third of the local population had emigrated before his arrival (Balikci 1984). Some populations may also hide children when census takers arrive out of the fear they will be stolen; where there is informant testimony, female children are said to be the ones most likely to be hidden (e.g., Yengoyan 1981). Unbalanced sex ratios can also be a product of variation in the primary (at conception) or secondary (at birth) sex ratio. Hurtado and Hill (1987), for example, record a secondary ratio of 116:100 (116 males born for every 100 females born) for the Ache and 117:100 for the Hiwi. The Ju/'hoansi, on the other hand, have a secondary ratio of 91:100 (Howell 1979).[13]

These factors can dramatically alter the demography of *small* populations over time; note the diversity in adult sex ratios among local groups of Tanana, Northwest Coast societies, Shoshone/Paiute, and Hill Pandaram in table 6-1.[14] It is difficult to control for these factors systematically. Nonetheless, where multiple censuses show child sex ratios that are consistently biased against females (as in the Arctic) there is probably some level of female infanticide behind them. The rate, however, cannot be determined from simple inspection of census data; the Netsilik case shows us why.

It is now known that Rasmussen and other early Arctic ethnographers, as careful as they were at the time, probably miscounted adult women (Schrire and Steiger 1974a). In the Arctic (and in many foraging groups) it was not uncommon for grooms to be older than their brides.[15] Women tended to marry at about age twelve, while men married later, at about twenty years of age. Like other Arctic explorers (e.g., Mathiassen 1928), Rasmussen used marriage as a way to separate adults from juveniles, and thereby undercounted juvenile females relative to juvenile males.

Schrire and Steiger argue that the differential in marriage ages accounts for most of the apparent discrepancy in the Netsilik's adult sex ratio (1974a). They use a computer simulation to ascertain the maximum rate of female infanticide, finding that a rate of only 8 percent would drive a population to extinction. Questions about the parameters and assumptions used in this simulation (Acker and Townsend 1975), however, led Michael Chapman to propose another (1980). In his model, a simulated foraging group living under Arctic social and physical conditions sustained female infanticide rates of up to 33 percent before evidence of population decline and extinction occurred. Chapman argued that once errors in population enumeration are accounted for, the child sex-ratio data from several Inuit populations suggest a female infanticide rate of about 37 percent. He concluded that many Inuit populations were practicing female infanticide at the maximum possible rate, although this rate is half that predicted by Rasmussen's data.

Making insightful use of life-table models, Eric Smith and Abigail Smith have made the most recent foray into sex-ratio data in the Arctic, analyzing data from ten Inuit societies. They found that the best fit came using life tables that took into account the differential age of marriage and female infanticide. The requisite level of infanticide varied among the groups from 0 to 40 percent, averaging about 21 percent. Marriage age alone cannot account for the Arctic sex-ratio data, but neither can high rates of female infanticide. Schrire and Steiger's dismissal of female infanticide and Rasmussen's fear of the Netsilik's self-inflicted extinction were both unfounded.

Two major explanations for female infanticide in the Arctic are population control and adult sex-ratio balancing. Following a cultural ecological perspective, Milton Freeman suggested that infanticide in the Arctic was a way to insure ecosystem stability by keeping population low and in balance with the food supply. This explanation, however, only purports to account for infanticide; *female* infanticide, Freeman suggested, was a product of male dominance in Arctic cultures. (In support of the interpretation of female infanticide as population control is the fact that population growth rates are more readily curbed by decreasing the number of women rather than men in a population.)

Following an alternative line of reasoning, Asen Balikci argued that female infanticide was a way to maintain adult sex ratios and thus prevent competition over females (1967, 1970). In precontact times, adult Inuit males probably died at a younger age than adult females due to the fact that hunting in the Arctic is dangerous (Weyer 1932; Damas 1975b). By suppressing females at birth, the adult sex ratio allegedly is kept in balance. If this argument is correct, we would expect the sex ratio among Inuit to be biased more in favor of young males in those areas where hunting was most dangerous. Using mean annual temperature as a measure of the danger of hunting (the lower the temperature, the more dangerous the conditions), Colin Irwin demonstrated an inverse correlation between the juvenile male:female ratio and temperature: where temperature is low, there are more boys than girls in the population (1989). Irwin argued that adult male mortality also correlates inversely with temperature—the lower the temperature, the higher the adult male mortality. Thus, female infanticide may help even out the adult sex ratio.

Eric Smith and Abigail Smith evaluated these two arguments (1994). Briefly, they found no evidence to support female infanticide as a population-control mechanism. Indeed, devastating periods of starvation probably reduced population so much that Inuit populations were perhaps always in a growth (recovery) phase. And female infanticide is woefully inadequate as the sort of short-term population-control mechanism that periodic catastrophes in the Arctic demand. As to female infanticide's role in balancing sex ratios, Smith and Smith argued that female infanticide should be higher where the adult mortality rate is not just high, but *higher* than the adult female mortality rate. Smith and Smith found no evidence to support this prediction. Indeed, they found no evidence that female infanticide balanced adult sex ratios. (Which might explain why Inuit men apparently were sometimes forced to raid other camps for wives.) Neither population control nor adult sex-ratio balancing appear to account for female infanticide in the Arctic.

A third explanation concerns the cost and fitness benefits of raising males versus females. Fisher's theory of parental investment (see Smith and Smith 1994) predicts that parents should invest in offspring that "cost" the least to raise to adulthood. Smith and Smith argue that since boys in Arctic societies marry at a later age than girls and have higher mortality rates that they are more "costly" to raise than girls. Since the census data show that girls are not the favored ones, the males may bestow fitness benefits that compensate for their increased cost.

Many Inuit explained to ethnographers that women were not as important as men since women do not hunt (Balikci 1967:622). In the Arctic, a son is crucial to provisioning his parents and his younger siblings years later, when his father's hunting ability has declined. This claim might be countered with the observation that although women may not have directly procured food in the Arctic, they certainly played roles essential to life—making clothing, processing food, and caring for children—and if parents wanted a son to provide them with food later in life, it was not inconceivable to raise a daughter as a hunter (Halperin 1980:394; Schrire and Steiger 1974a). But, since most Inuit societies are patrilocal, women move away to live with their husband's family as soon as they reach their full productive capacity (as young adolescents); even if women are productive, they are not productive for their siblings or parents (Riches 1974). (Rasmussen's interviews with Netsilik women show that it was not just Netsilik men who thought this was important: at least one woman would have urged her daughters to "strangle" a female infant rather than "waste several years" nursing it [Rasmussen 1931:140].)

Insuring that a couple has a son, then, assures the couple that they will have someone to hunt for them in their old age, and someone to look after younger siblings. In support of this hypothesis, Smith and Smith found that adult male mortality was correlated with female infanticide: where adult male mortality was high, so was female infanticide (1994). They conclude that at present the most plausible hypothesis to account for female infanticide in the Arctic is that sons were favored because they could contribute more to the fitness of their parents and siblings than could daughters.[16]

In support of this, Barry Hewlett shows that cross-culturally juvenile male-biased ratios exist where men directly contribute more to subsistence than do women (1991a). He suggests that infanticide in these societies may occur more from neglect than outright homicide at birth, meaning that the effects of female infanticide could occur without the existence of a cultural notion of female infanticide.[17] Hewlett also suggests that where males suffer a higher rate of mortality than females due to warfare, raiding, or dangerous foraging activities (as in the Arctic), female offspring will suffer from neglect.[18] (Although cross-culturally there is only a weak association of female infanticide with warfare; see Hawkes' [1981] critique of Divale and Harris; see chapter 7 discussion of warfare and postmarital residence.)

Despite years of debate, female infanticide among foragers still remains a bit of a mystery, plagued as it is by both theoretical and evidentiary difficulties. Present evidence suggests that while female infanticide did occur, it was probably limited to those populations where men contributed more food directly to the family hearth than did women and, possibly, of these societies, those where male foraging activities were dangerous (these two conditions may frequently occur together). It is probably not very prevalent outside of these conditions; it certainly was nowhere near as common as some published accounts and models suggest since it was not as common in the Arctic as was once thought. Female infanticide was almost certainly not very valuable as a population control mechanism, and archaeologists would be foolish to assume its importance in prehistoric demography without good cause.

Birth-spacing infanticide

An alternative explanation of infanticide is that infants are killed in order to space births a few years apart, so that a mother does not have too many infants to breastfeed or carry at one time. We refer to this as *birth-spacing infanticide* and, if there is an even chance that a birth will be male or female, it should not result in a bias against one sex or the other. (If there is an imbalance in the secondary ratio then presumably birth-spacing infanticide would result in a higher mortality rate of the more frequent sex, balancing the juvenile sex ratio.) In Tom Morales' sample, of those groups that claimed to practice infanticide, 63 percent allegedly performed infanticide to space births (1987). A mother's ability to care for a child is primarily affected by whether she still has a child breastfeeding or otherwise requiring her attention. Since mortality rates in general among children (three to fifteen years old) in foraging populations are lower than those among infants (less than three years old), if a mother produces a child when another is still breastfeeding or not yet able to fully care for itself, she may decide to kill the infant, since it is already at a higher risk than the older child.[19]

Though reductions in offspring would seem to decrease a woman's reproductive fitness and go against evolutionary explanations, the opposite may in fact be true. Nicholas Blurton Jones produced strong evidence that the spacing of births actually maximizes reproductive success for the Ju/'hoansi (Blurton Jones and Sibly 1978; Blurton Jones 1986, 1987). Ju/'hoansi birth spacing is probably a function of diet, breastfeeding, and activity levels (see below), rather than infanticide. But the case demonstrates how having few children at long intervals can maximize reproductive success as well as the conditions under which nonpreferential infanticide could occur (for example, in populations with higher fecundity than the Ju/'hoansi).[20]

Ju/'hoansi women give birth on average about every four years. On foraging trips, Ju/'hoansi women travel quite long distances—up to 20–25 kilometers—carrying their children and equipment with them. Children are carried until they are about four years of age. Citing Lee's research, Blurton Jones pointed out that in the hot, dry Kalahari, carrying more than one child would put an unbearable strain on the mother, and, consequently, on her children.

Through a computer simulation of a "backload model" Blurton Jones showed that the total average weight a woman carries on foraging trips decreases dramatically as birth spacing increases until a birth interval of four years is reached. At birth intervals longer than four years, there is not much of a reduction in total weight carried since the mother only carries one child at a time at such a long birth interval. Thus, spacing births at four years and foraging part-time maximizes the number of children a woman can produce, four to five, while preventing maternal exhaustion. Having children at less than a four-year interval, on the other hand, could affect a child's survival chances by decreasing the mother's ability to provide for him or her by literally working the mother to death (thus the Ju/'hoansi proverb that heads this chapter). (This does not mean that all foragers should have a four-year birth interval, but that the length of the optimal birth interval is related to foraging conditions. Other foragers could have longer or shorter optimal intervals.)

For this pattern to be adaptive, in the strict sense of the term, it must be demonstrated that "women who gave birth substantially more often than once every four years . . . should raise fewer children than those who gave birth at around 4 year intervals. . . . If this prediction is not borne out then wide birth-spacing and 'part time' foraging are not maximizing reproductive success" (Blurton Jones and Sibly 1978:153). Using Nancy Howell's data, Blurton Jones showed that, in fact, those Dobe Ju/'hoansi women who have more than four children (i.e., birth spacing of less than four years) raise fewer of their children to reproductive age than women who have only four children. For the Dobe Ju/'hoansi, a four-year birth interval appears to maximize reproductive success.

In contrast, by analyzing data from a broad survey of Ju/'hoansi (including some of Howell's sample) Renee Pennington and Henry Harpending argued that child survival does not decrease with shortened birth spacing (1988). Contrary to the Blurton Jones model, Pennington and Harpending found that the more children a woman has the more children she has that live to reproductive age. However, Blurton Jones predicted (and measured) the optimal birth intervals, not the number of offspring produced. Pennington and Harpending estimated these intervals from reproductive histories, but the higher fertility could also be a function of a longer period of reproductive viability for the women in their sample, and not necessarily a shorter birth interval. If so, this would not contradict Blurton Jones' conclusion (see Borgerhoff Mulder 1992:349). It may also be that women with shorter birth spacing found some other way to raise their children, one that alters the likelihood of infant survival and which was not available to the Dobe Ju/'hoansi. The key variable in birth-spacing infanticide appears to be the extent to which a mother thinks she can care for her offspring. Two important factors in this regard are the extent to which children can forage on their own, and how much support a woman can expect from others in childcare.

A number of factors affect how much foraging children can do and consequently there is much variability in how hard children work in foraging societies (Hayden 1981b). Among the Tanzanian Hadza, children forage on their own at about five years of age—much earlier than do Ju/'hoansi children (Blurton Jones, Hawkes, and O'Connell 1989). Hadza children, in fact, can provide up to 50 percent of their daily caloric needs by the time they are five years old. Ju/'hoansi children, on the other hand, do not forage until well into their teens. Part of the reason is that Hadza children do not have to walk very far from camp to forage, but Ju/'hoansi children do, placing them at greater risk from predators and heat exhaustion. Additionally, Ju/'hoansi children would have to forage in an expanse of featureless dunes, where there is a greater likelihood of their becoming lost, than in the Hadza's environment of more easily memorized broken hills and gullies (Blurton Jones, Hawkes, and Draper 1994). Therefore, Hadza women do not have to carry children as much as Ju/'hoansi mothers do. According to the backload model, Hadza mothers can afford to have more offspring, and in fact, do so (Blurton Jones, Hawkes, and O'Connell 1989; Blurton Jones et al. 1992). It is not yet clear whether this is due to a shortened birth interval or a longer reproductive period, but the former is more likely.[21]

Children are a double strain on their mothers. Not only does a mother provide a child with its primary nutrition for its first six to twelve months, but the presence of one or more children on foraging trips decreases her foraging efficiency. On the north coast of Australia, small children "drastically inhibited the mother's ability to procure food. Gidgingali women were very much aware of the problem, frequently complaining about having 'too many kin'" (Meehan 1982:137). Thus, children increase a woman's needs but decrease her ability to meet those needs. The two sources of support for a mother are female relatives or friends, and her children's father(s).

Hewlett points out that among the few hunter-gatherers for whom we have data, from 20 to 50 percent of the time an infant is in someone's arms, someone other than the mother is holding it (1991a). Among the Efe and Onge, women other than the mother may breastfeed a child. Where fertility is low, Hewlett suggests, so that there are few children present, and where there is a trusted female cohort freed from other duties (e.g., grandmothers, older sisters), a child will have multiple caretakers. He points out that multiple caretaking is relatively rare among horticulturalists and pastoralists compared to hunter-gatherers. Hewlett argues that where settlements are small and socially "open," multiple caregiving is possible since all members of the band will be familiar with an infant and its parents. However, if a woman lives away from female relatives (as, for example, in the case of patrilocal postmarital residence) there may not be a female cohort she trusts. Or, flux in band membership may not leave a sufficient number of known and trustworthy babysitters (see Draper and Cashdan 1988). This could contribute to cultural child-rearing ideals that emphasize constant maternal care and attention.

A few case studies demonstrate the importance of paternal care for a child's well-being. The reasons most frequently given by Ayoreo women for infanticide is that the husband had left or was unwilling to take paternal responsibilities (Bugos and McCarthy 1984); this is, in fact, a strong cross-cultural pattern (Daly and Wilson 1988). Though Ayoreo women cite the lack of paternal support as the reason for infanticide, Ayoreo men say that women kill a newborn if *she* cannot care for it. Clearly, men and women perceive the costs of raising children differently. (See, for example, the negative response of Nisa's [a Ju/'hoansi woman] father to the news that her mother intended to kill a newborn [Shostak 1981:56], or Van de Velde's account of an Inuk father's decision to kill a newborn female [1954], or Australian Aboriginal debates over family size [Burbank and Chisholm 1992].)

The absence of a child's socially recognized father can also have an unfortunate effect on children. Pennington and Harpending found that among nomadic Ju/'hoansi, children whose mothers were married more than once were twice as likely to die as children of women married only once (1988). Among the sedentary Ghanzi Ju/'hoansi, children of mothers married more than once were almost three times as likely to die during infancy (and evidence suggests that the predominant reason for multiple marriages is the husband's [father's] death). Hill and Kaplan (1988a) and Hawkes (1990) record a similar pattern for the Ache, where children whose fathers die stand a 9 percent chance of dying before age fifteen while those whose fathers live have a less than i percent chance of death. Hill and Kaplan argue that since men provide 90 percent of total calories in the form of meat (while the Ache are in the bush) and since all meat is shared, there is considerable pressure on the group to appease the good hunters by caring for their children (by watching them, providing them with food, etc.). After a man's death, how-ever, his children become only a burden to nonrelatives, and they pay less attention to his surviving offspring. If the hunter's wife remarries, her new husband apparently may even kill her previous children, so as to allow her to care for his own (current or anticipated) children (Hill and Kaplan 1988a,b).[22] On the other hand, father absence appears to have little effect on child survivorship among the Hiwi (Hurtado and Hill 1992).

In general, evolutionary theory predicts two basic strategies for males: invest in parenting and raising offspring, or invest in mating opportunities (although the two are not necessarily mutually exclusive—see Burbank and Chisholm 1992). Men are predicted to invest time in mating as opposed to parenting where additional increments in paternal investment in offspring (which can take many forms—food, protection, education) does not in-crease the probability of offspring survivorship very much. Mating opportu-nities, however, are not the only trade-off. Examining the effects of cultural transmission on behavior, it is not inconceivable that men could perceive that investing time in prestige competition is more important than parenting, regardless of whether the search for prestige results in or is intended to result in more mating opportunities. The end product, nonetheless, is the same: women perceive that they will receive little assistance from their husbands. Consequently, they may be unwilling to keep a newborn if another child still requires their attention.

Where paternal investment in offspring has a significant effect on offspring survival, men should invest in parenting. With the expectation of increased paternal support, women may be more willing to keep a newborn. Hewlett adds to this that the more time husband and wife are together, the more the father will participate directly in childcare (1991b, 1992a). Thus, male labor patterns could have an effect on completed family size. Cross-cultural data on the relationships between fathers and their children among foraging pop-ulations are only now being collected (e.g., Hewlett 1992b).

In sum, female infanticide *may* be a significant factor in those societies where men contribute more to subsistence than women (patrilocal post-marital residence and high adult male mortality may exacerbate this). Birth-spacing infanticide may have been more common cross-culturally, but still may not have affected a sizable number of births. It probably worked to maximize reproductive success, rather than control population size, although its impact on population growth rates is not known. The frequency of birth-spacing infanticide can be affected by the amount of work women must do and the amount of support they can expect from the father and relatives. But rates of infanticide are tied to the rate at which women give birth, which is largely a product of the potential a woman has to conceive and carry a child to term. Before jumping to the conclusion that foragers' growth rates are restricted by cultural controls (be they intentional or not), we must consider the physiology of reproduction, and the variables that control fecundity, the potential a woman has to conceive (for a thorough review, see Wood 1994).

THE ECOLOGY OF REPRODUCTION

It is often claimed that hunter-gatherer populations have systematically lower fertility that other kinds of societies, even without invoking intentional cultural controls. Fertility here refers to a population's *total fertility rate* (TFR). The TFR of a population is the mean number of children that women bear over the course of their reproductive years. This information is acquired by interviewing postmenopausal women (normally defined as women who are at least 45 years old) for their reproductive histories. In general, TFR tends to be low in foraging societies, about five to six children (Campbell and Wood 1988; Bentley, Jasienska, and Goldberg 1993, Bentley, Goldberg, and Jasienska 1993; Hewlett 1991a). Campbell and Wood found no difference between the TFR of hunter-gatherers and other noncontracepting societies (see also Hewlett 1991a). However, Gillian Bentley and her co-workers re-analyzed their data, excluding some problematic cases and reassigning others to more appropriate subsistence categories. They found no difference between foragers and horticulturalists, but they did find that mean TFR was significantly higher for agriculturalists (mean TFR = 6.6 ± .3) than that of the foragers and horticulturalists combined.

As a group, then, hunter-gatherers appear to have lower fertility than agriculturalists, but not horticulturalists. As table 6-1 indicates, however, there is variability in the fertility rates of hunter-gatherer societies. Rather than seek simple generalizations about foragers, we need to understand the biological factors conditioning fertility.

Kenneth Campbell and James Wood divide the factors affecting fertility into exposure and susceptibility factors (1988; table 6-5).[23] The exposure factors are probably less important for our purposes than the susceptibility factors. Campbell and Wood did not find that the proportions of women who are postmenarcheal or postmenopausal predicted the TFRs of nonindustrial populations. However, they did find that age at marriage had some effect on TFR. If sexual relations do not occur until after marriage and if marriage

Table 6-5. Proximate Determinants of Natural Fertility

I. Exposure factors
  1. Proportion of women married or in sexual unions at each age
  2. Proportion of women postmenarcheal at each age
  3. Proportion of women premenopausal at each age
II. Susceptibility factors
  1. Duration of lactational infecundability (the period between birth and regular ovulation and luteal function caused by breastfeeding)
  2. Fecund waiting time to conception (the period between entrance into a fecund period and conception):
    a. Frequency of intercourse
    b. Ovarian cycle length
      1. Length of the follicular phase (preovulatory phase of menstrual cycle)
      2. Length of the luteal phase (postovulatory phase of menstrual cycle; this is an important part of the phase as far as conception is concerned, but most variability in menstrual cycles can be accounted for by variation in the follicular phase)
    c. Proportion of cycles ovulatory
    d. Duration of the fertile period, given ovulation (both c and d can be affected by a woman's nutritional state)
    e. Probability of conception from a single insemination in the fertile period (this can be affected by the male's reproductive capacity as well as by the female's; variability in d and e are virtual unknowns [Campbell and Wood 1988:52])
  3. Prevalence of pathological sterility (e.g., from venereal diseases)
  4. Frequency of spontaneous sterility and abortion
  5. Length of gestation (at 9 months, a constant for human populations)

Source: Campbell and Wood 1988.

Table 6-6. Mean Age at Marriage

	Mean age marriage		
Group	Males	Females	Reference
Nyae Nyae Ju/'hoansi	22–25	14–15	Lee 1982
Dobe Ju/'hoansi	23–30	16–17	Lee 1982
≠Kade	25	17–18	Tanaka 1980
Aka	18–21	16–17	Hewlett 1991b
Tlingit	>16	12–14	Emmons 1991

occurs sometime after menarche, then age at marriage can affect the overall TFR of the population, but this may not be relevant to hunter-gatherers. Our data are limited, but among some hunter-gatherers women are married at or even before menarche (see tables 6-6 and 6-7). Ju/'hoansi women, for example, reach menarche at about age sixteen or seventeen, which is about the age they marry. Many ethnographies allude to premarital or premenarcheal sexual activity of boys and girls, but this may not be significant since a high number of menstrual cycles are anovulatory for two to three years after

Table 6–7. Birth Interval, Menarche, and Reproductive Span

Group	BI	MAM	MAFB	MALB	Reference
Western Pygmies (n = 16)	4.2				Cavalli-Sforza 1986
Dobe Ju/'hoansi	3.7	16.6	18.8	34.4	Lee 1979; Howell 1979
Batak	2.3	15.1	18	26.3	Eder 1987
≠Kade		12			Tanaka 1980
Dobe Ju/'hoansi	2.9	17.1	20.9	37.0	Campbell and Wood 1988
Aka	3.5				Hewlett 1991b
Aka	3.7				Hewlett 1991b
Kutchin (pre-1900)	3.3		22.8	35.0	Roth 1981
Kutchin (post-1900)	3.2		19.8	39.0	Roth 1981
James Bay Cree	2.7		21.9	39.0	Romaniuk 1974
Arnhem Land, monogamous	3.3		19.3	34.1	Chisholm and Burbank 1991
Arnhem Land, polygynous	5.4		19.2	34.3	Chisholm and Burbank 1991
Pitjandjara				35.0	Yengoyan 1972
Anbarra			15.9	35.0	Hamilton 1981

Note: BI is the birth interval in years, MAM is mean age of menarche, MAFB is mean age at first birth, MALB is mean age at last birth. James Bay Cree BI is the mean of trend toward a reduction in BI.

menarche, especially if a woman's diet is low in calories or highly variable. In any case, as Wilmsen argues, in noncontracepting societies marriage is frequently adjusted to pregnancy; that is, by definition, pregnant women are married women (1986:62, citing Howell 1979:232). Therefore, age at marriage may not be an important variable for hunter-gatherers.

Assuming that women are susceptible to becoming pregnant throughout their reproductive years, then, the number of offspring they could potentially produce in a lifetime is a function of the birth interval. Understanding TFR, therefore, means understanding the factors that condition how quickly a woman becomes pregnant after childbirth. Assuming a fairly constant frequency of intercourse, three potentially important factors are interrelated through the endocrine system: breastfeeding, nutrition, and activity regimes.

Breastfeeding and fertility

Campbell and Wood argue that variability in the duration of *lactational infecundability* is the single most important cause of variability in TFR. Without breastfeeding, postpartum amenorrhea may last one to two months. However, the longer a mother breastfeeds a child, the longer the period of postpartum amenorrhea. In fact, the length of postpartum amenorrhea can be accurately predicted from the number of months a mother breastfeeds a child (Bongaarts and Potter 1983:25). Not unexpectedly, then, Romaniuk found that a decrease in the birth interval among the James Bay Cree in the early twentieth century was correlated with a reduction in breastfeeding (1974).[24] And Campbell and Wood's analysis of seventy noncontracepting populations found that lactational infecundability accounts for 99 percent of variation in birth intervals.

How does this happen? Through a chain of hormonal reactions, breastfeeding increases circulating prolactin which in turn decreases estrogen and progesterone production by the ovaries. Decreased estrogen production diminishes ovarian function, resulting in a higher percentage of anovulatory cycles. Decreased progesterone production decreases luteal phase length, the length of time during which the uterus is prepared to receive and implant a fertilized egg, and thus decreases the probability of a viable conception.

The effect of breastfeeding is important because some hunter-gatherers breastfeed children for long periods of time—two to three years is not uncommon (see table 6-8). Where weaning foods are not available, breastfeeding is crucial to infant and even toddler survival. Ju/'hoansi children may breastfeed until six years of age (after three years, male children are more likely to continue to breastfeed than females; Konner and Shostak 1987). However, it is not just the number of months a mother breastfeeds a child, but the intensity and frequency of individual breastfeeding periods as well. Frequent, intense breastfeeding periods have a greater hormonal effect than short, infrequent periods. Ju/'hoansi children can be quite demanding of their mothers and feed for about two minutes four times an hour (Shostak 1981; Konner and Worthman 1980). It is likely that a lengthy period of breastfeeding after birth is associated with intensive and frequent breastfeeding (Bongaarts and Potter 1983), but we should remember that the actual variable at work may be the intensity and frequency of feedings and not simply the number of months a mother breastfeeds her child.

Factors impinging on a woman's ability to provide "on-demand" breastfeeding, therefore, may decrease lactational infecundability and increase the probability of conception, resulting in more frequent births. Breastfeeding could be affected by the availability of appropriate foods that would allow infants to be weaned at an early age.[25] However, the availability of weaning foods may not be sufficient to shorten the breastfeeding period. On-demand breastfeeding continues among the Ju/'hoansi well after a child is capable of eating adult foods (Shostak 1981).

Table 6-8. Weaning Age

Group	Weaning age (months)	Reference
Washo	12–24	Barry and Paxson 1971
Mbuti (net hunters)	12–36	Harako 1981
Montagnais	12–60	Barry and Paxson 1971
Pomo	15?	Barry and Paxson 1971
Micmac	24–36	Barry and Paxson 1971
Slave	24–36	Barry and Paxson 1971
Bella Coola	24–36	Barry and Paxson 1971
Kaska	24–36	Barry and Paxson 1971
Klamath	24–36	Barry and Paxson 1971
Semang	24–36	Barry and Paxson 1971
Eyak	24–36	Barry and Paxson 1971
Yurok	24–36	Barry and Paxson 1971
Yokuts	36+	Barry and Paxson 1971
Andamanese	36–48	Barry and Paxson 1971
Tiwi	36–48	N. Peterson 1976; F. Jones 1963
Siriono	36–48	Barry and Paxson 1971
Dobe Ju/'hoansi	36–72	Campbell and Wood 1988
Ainu	48–60	Barry and Paxson 1971
Hadza	12	Barry and Paxson 1971
Aleut	12	Barry and Paxson 1971
Yahgan	24	Stuart 1980
Gilyak	24	Barry and Paxson 1971
Haida	24	Barry and Paxson 1971
Gros Ventre	24	Barry and Paxson 1971
Kutenai	24	Barry and Paxson 1971
Vedda	24	Barry and Paxson 1971
Paiute	24	Fowler and Fowler 1971
Aranda	36	Barry and Paxson 1971
Yukaghir	48	Barry and Paxson 1971
Murngin	48	Barry and Paxson 1971

The most important factor affecting breastfeeding may be a mother's foraging activities. If children are carried with the mother while she is foraging, then the child can be breastfed throughout the day. If, however, a child is left in camp with a relative, as, for example, Australian Aboriginal women seem to do more frequently than the Ju/'hoansi (McCarthy and McArthur 1960; Rose 1960; Denham 1974a,b), and as Agta women do while hunting (see chapter 7), then the child may only be breastfed by its mother in the morning and late afternoon, reducing breastfeeding's effect on ovulation. As we noted above, the availability of childcare could be a function of the degree of continuity in group membership, postmarital residence, or a cultural emphasis on individualistic child care (Goodman et al. 1985:1208). Thus, social conditions intersect with biological ones to influence fecundity.

Cross-culturally, breastfeeding is probably the single most important control on hunter-gatherer fertility and population growth. However, the effects of breastfeeding can be exacerbated or ameliorated by at least two other factors, maternal nutrition and activity regimes.

Maternal nutrition, activity, and fertility

In the 1970s, biologists observed that female athletes, especially those in endurance sports such as long-distance running, ovulated irregularly, if at all. Rose Frisch hypothesized that this was related to body fat (1978). Briefly, Frisch argued that after menarche, about 22 percent of female body weight must be fat for the maintenance of normal reproductive function; she referred to this ratio of fat to lean tissue as "critical fatness." Following this lead, many researchers suggested that the fecundity of foraging women could be reduced by the hard day-to-day, fat-depleting work of foraging and the nutritional quality of a foraged diet. This idea is supported by evidence that in human populations that manifest seasonal weight changes as a function of seasonal changes in nutrition, births tend to be clustered nine months after the season of highest food availability when maternal nutrition is presumably at its best. This has been shown to be true for Ju/'hoansi, Ache, and Hiwi hunter-gatherers, Turkana pastoralists, and Lese horticulturalists.[26] Additionally, those Ju/'hoansi women who live in settlements and have diets that are higher in calories and that are more constant throughout the year have both higher fertility and births spread more evenly throughout the year than nomadic Ju/'hoansi (Hausman and Wilmsen 1985). However, tests of the critical-fatness hypothesis have produced variable, sometimes contradictory results (Scott and Johnston 1982).

The precise biological relationship between nutrition and fecundity is still unclear. At present, maternal nutrition can be linked to fertility in two ways. First, a decrease in caloric intake could decrease a women's ability to produce breast milk. For lactating women, this could cause an infant to suckle more frequently and intensely, decreasing fecundity through the hormonal mechanism described above (Ellison 1994). Second, a maternal diet low in calories may affect the endocrine system in such a way that it impairs ovarian function. Among the Lese, seasonal changes in ovulatory frequency correlates with seasonal changes in body weight and low progesterone levels. Low progesterone levels directly impact ovarian function by decreasing luteal phase length (Ellison, Peacock, and Lager 1989). Ellison suggests that the key factor here is long-term energy balance, not just nutritional status, so only long-term fluctuations in caloric intake (on the order of several months) have an effect (1990). For the Ju/'hoansi, Wilmsen argues that seasonal fluctuations in a diet that is already only marginally adequate—which appears to be the case, especially for young Ju/'hoansi women (Hausman and Wilmsen 1985; Van der Walt, Wilmsen, and Jenkins 1978)—may decrease a woman's adipose tissue and in particular the cholesterol fraction of that tissue (1982, 1986). Since estrogen may be produced and stored in adipose tissue, decreasing adipose tissue may decrease the availability of estrogen and impair ovarian function. Additionally, since cholesterol may be involved in estrogen production, a decrease in cholesterol alone could decrease the availability of estrogen. A *large* decrease in body weight, therefore, is not necessary for a change in nutrition to affect ovulation. As evidence, Wilmsen notes that the diet of sedentary Ju/'hoansi, besides being high in calories and constant throughout the year, is significantly higher in cholesterol than that of nomadic Ju/'hoansi (1982). As noted above, sedentary Ju/'hoansi have a higher fertility than nomadic Ju/'hoansi.

Female labor patterns, as well as diet, enter into the fecundity equation (figure 6-6). Bentley notes that the season of highest food availability for the Ju/'hoansi is also the season of least demanding female labor (1985). Could activity have other effects on the endocrine system independent of those associated strictly with diet? Bentley describes studies in sports medicine pointing to a correlation between the intensity, frequency, and longevity of the activity regime and fertility. Aerobic exercises such as long-distance running, gymnastics, and ballet appear to have the greatest impact, and, Bentley suggests, closely resemble women's foraging activities in their effects. Work probably lowers fecundity the most when it is combined with weight loss (Ellison 1990).[27] In a preliminary study, Hurtado and Hill found that among the Venezuelan Hiwi seasonal fertility did not correlate with women's weight, work effort, or caloric consumption (1990). Neither did fertility correlate with *differences* in weight or work effort between one season and the previous season. Instead, Hurtado and Hill found that the difference in *net* caloric intake—a product of gross caloric intake *and* work effort—between one season and the previous season accurately predicted fertility.

The relationship between activity and fertility may be analogous to that between breastfeeding and ovarian function in that intense activity regimes performed frequently may decrease progesterone and/or increase circulating endorphins that suppress gonadotropin, just as prolactin does. Perhaps, though, activity and workload are related to fertility through breastfeeding, for women who must work hard may not be able to breastfeed on demand. While the relationship between labor patterns, breastfeeding, maternal

Figure 6-6. Ahtna women carrying camp equipment with tumplines. Women's workload can affect their fecundity as well as determine how much support they will need in childcare. Photo by the Miles Bros., probably 1902. Courtesy of the National Anthropological Archives, Smithsonian Institution, no. 75-5648.

weight, nutrition, and fecundity is not completely clear, it is a promising area of research.

MORTALITY

As we have seen, a number of biological and social factors affect a population's TFR. However, fertility is only one side of the population coin. We cannot understand hunter-gatherer demography without understanding their patterns of death. The rate of population growth may, in fact, be more a product of changes in rates of child mortality than changes in fertility (Handwerker 1983).

In discussing mortality, we are particularly concerned with the death of pre-reproductive-age individuals, what we will label here child mortality (most demographic studies classify individuals over fourteen or fifteen years

Table 6-9. Child Mortality

Group	Mortality (%)		e(0)	Reference
	<1 yr.	<15 yrs.		
Ju/'hoansi (nomadic)	8	12		Harpending and Wandsnider 1982
Ju/'hoansi (sedentary)		6		Harpending and Wandsnider 1982
Efe	14	22		Bailey 1988
Asmat	30	25	25	Van Arsdale 1978
Yahgan		29		Stuart 1980
Ngamiland Ju/'hoansi		34		Harpending and Wandsnider 1982
E. Cagayan Agta		35		Headland 1988; Goodman et al. 1985
Ache	21	42		Hurtado and Hill 1987
Palanan Agta		43		Headland 1988
Greenland Inuit	20	45		Hewlett 1991a
Kutchin (pre-1900)	17	43		Roth 1981
Kutchin (post-1900)	9	20		Roth 1981
Aka (family)	20	45		Bahuchet 1979
Hiwi		52		Hurtado and Hill 1987, 1990
Mbuti (net hunters)	33	56		Harako 1981
Seri		61		Neel and Weiss 1975
Batak	29	52	22	Eder 1987
Dobe Ju/'hoansi	20	49	32	Lee 1979; Howell 1979
≠Kade		28[a]	40	Tanaka 1980
G/wi		7		Silberbauer 1981a
Casiguran Agta	34	49	21	Headland 1989; Hewlett 1991a
Chenchu		49		Hewlett 1991a
Pitjandjara	19			Hewlett 1991a
Tiwi	10			F. Jones 1963; Hewlett 1991a
Anbarra		38[b]		Hamilton 1981

Note: For the Ju/'hoansi, male children have a lower survivorship than female children; 44 percent die before age 15, compared to 30 percent for female offspring. The pattern is the opposite among the Ache, where 47 percent of female offspring die as opposed to 37 percent of male offspring; the same holds true for the Hiwi, where 55 percent of female and 49 percent of male offspring die before age 15.
[a]By age 10.
[b]By age 5 (39 percent of all male offspring and 37 percent of all female offspring).

of age as reproductive). The few good data on childhood mortality suggest that child mortality is very high in hunter–gatherer populations, although Hewlett again found no difference in this variable between hunter-gatherers and horticulturalists/pastoralists (Hewlett 1991a). As shown in table 6-9, child mortality rates among hunter-gatherers can be as high as 60 percent; this is supported by the low child-to-adult ratios in table 6-1. The low life expectancies at birth shown in table 6-9 are largely a product of high infant (less than two years old) mortality.

We have already discussed infanticide as one agent of childhood death. Two other agents are accidents and disease. It is possible that accidental death may contribute more to mortality as one moves away from the equator. In colder environments, seasonality may be a harsher selective force than in more equatorial climates, by making accidents potentially more dangerous. However, among cases for which there are data—and there are few—accidents are of little importance in child and infant mortality.

Instead, the primary causes of death among children in hunter-gatherer societies are infectious and parasitic diseases, including respiratory TB, influenza, pneumonia, bronchitis, and diarrheal diseases resulting in dehydration. Among the Dobe Ju/'hoansi, Howell found that nearly 85 percent of childhood deaths were caused by infectious diseases, especially TB and malaria (1979). Degenerative diseases (e.g., cardiovascular disease) accounted for only 4 percent and violence for 8 percent (with no differences between male and female children). Headland found that 95 percent of Casiguran Agta offspring deaths (zero to fourteen years) between the years 1977 and 1985 were attributable to illness, with 2 percent due to accidents and 3 percent to homicide (1989). (The Casiguran Agta are a special, and unfortunate, case where chronic malnutrition and drunkenness have increased the frequency of childhood diseases while decreasing parental care; the Agta also have a high adult homicide rate—3.26/1,000/year). Among the Aka Pygmies, the primary causes of death are measles, then diarrhea and convulsions; the last two factors account for 26 percent of childhood deaths (Hewlett, van de Koppel, and van de Koppel 1986).

Diarrhea-inducing diseases may be more prevalent among tropical hunter-gatherers than among those living in drier or colder environments that are less conducive to the growth of bacteria and parasites. Based on a sample of only five populations, Dunn shows that there are two to seven times more parasitic helminths and protozoa among tropical forest cases than among tropical desert cases (1968).

Contagious disease is probably not an important factor among small, mobile peoples since their population sizes are too small to support the organisms responsible for such diseases (F. Black 1975). For this reason, some authors suggest that mobility can insure a population's health (Cohen 1989). However, mobility may contribute to other kinds of disease. Though some argue that rates of infant mortality are higher among sedentary as opposed to mobile groups of Bushmen (Hitchcock 1982), quantitative studies by Henry Harpending and LuAnn Wandsnider point out that the infant mortality rate among the mobile Ju/'hoansi is twice as high as among the sedentary Ghanzi Ju/'hoansi (12 percent as opposed to 6 percent; 1982). The more readily available medical care and supply of cow's milk in the sedentary settlement may be largely responsible for the difference. However, Harpending and Wandsnider also attribute the difference in mortality to "traveler's diarrhea" among the mobile Ju/'hoansi. Since different parasites are found in different regions, mobility continually brings highly susceptible infants into contact with new strains of parasites, resulting in repeated bouts of diarrhea and dehydration (analogous to the less dangerous day-care syndrome in industrialized nations) producing a chronic state of poor health that takes its toll. Children of sedentary groups build up resistance to local parasites and are thus less susceptible to diarrhea and dehydration. Although they avoid acute, severe diseases that result in death, children in sedentary villages may, however, suffer more chronic health problems related to the hygiene of a sedentary settlement (Kent and Lee 1992).

In sum, although it is clear that child survival is not necessarily better among nomadic foragers than among sedentary folk, as some may believe, it is also clear that we have a long way to go in understanding the factors that condition variability in child mortality among hunter-gatherers. There is an enormous amount of research to be conducted in this area. And it is important research because it is unlikely that fertility is the only factor that drives the rate of population growth.

MOBILITY AND POPULATION GROWTH

It is often the case that as formerly mobile people become sedentary, the rate of population growth increases (e.g., Binford and Chasko 1976; Ellanna 1990; Hitchcock 1982; Gomes 1982, 1990). Since the sedentization process today is often associated with the availability of Western medicine, this association between population growth and sedentism could be a postindustrial phenomenon. However, archaeologists note that although population increase does occur before the appearance of prehistoric sedentary villages in many parts of the world, dramatic population increase often occurs *after* the appearance of such villages. While there is still much we do not understand about the relationship between behavior, biology, fertility, and mortality, it is possible for us to sketch out a model relating the factors we have discussed in this chapter to mobility. Figure 6-7 depicts how sedentism might affect fertility and child survivorship resulting in an increase in a population's growth rate.

We argued in chapter 4 that sedentism is a trade-off between residential

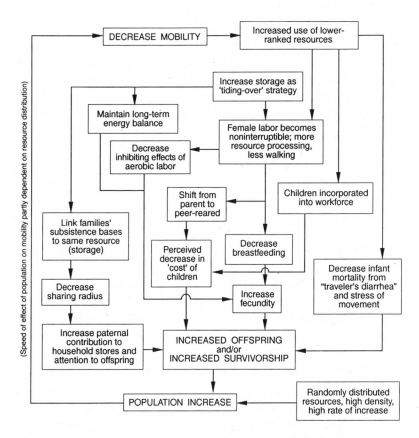

Figure 6-7. Potential relationships between factors that could lead sedentism to produce an increase in the rate of population growth. Drawn by Dan Delaney.

mobility and the use of resources that entailed relatively high harvesting and processing costs. From this we might deduce that both men and women have to work harder in sedentary than in nomadic camps. A change in women's work may be especially important, as it may entail a shift to more time-consuming but less aerobic resource-processing tasks. This could affect fertility in two ways. First, an increase in women's workload might encourage an early cessation of breastfeeding, perhaps through the use of weaning foods (Nerlove 1974), or a reduction in the frequency of breastfeeding episodes. Either might return a woman to regular ovulation quickly after giving birth, and increase fecundity. This receives some indirect support from Sara Nerlove's cross-cultural study (1974). She found that in societies where a child's diet is supplemented before it is one month old (decreasing the need for breastfeeding), women perform more subsistence activities than women in societies where children's diets are supplemented after the child is one month old. Draper and Cashdan also note that the adults of sedentary Ju/'hoansi camps are more busy while they are at home than adults in camps of mobile groups (though we do not know if this is related to sedentism itself, or the particular sociopolitical circumstances of sedentization among the Ju/'hoansi; 1988:343). Finally, Robert Hitchcock observed that sedentary Nata River Bushmen nursed less often and weaned children at an earlier age than the more mobile Kua (1982). As expected, the Nata River group appears to have higher fertility than the mobile Kua.

Second, a reduction in residential mobility may also result, for women, in a reduction in the aerobic quality of their work, as they spend less time walking while foraging or moving camp and more time processing resources. My impression is that this is the case for recently settled foraging groups, but we have no good evidence on whether there is a difference in the aerobic quality of women's work in nomadic versus sedentary contexts. If there is a difference, however, a decrease in women's aerobic activity in sedentary settlements could increase fecundity for reasons we have already discussed.

We also noted in chapter 4 that as mobility decreases, stored resources become the way to tide people over a lean period. Several researchers argue that the diet of recently sedentary hunter-gatherers is poorer than that of mobile groups (Hitchcock 1982), but this generally means that sedentary groups eat less meat and more carbohydrates and sugar, and/or that they have less diversity in their diet. Even if this is a poorer diet, it may still increase fecundity, as Wilmsen argued. Additionally, if sedentary groups store food (or have access to purchased store supplies) their diet may become more constant over the course of the year. Even if the diet of sedentary groups is chronically poorer or less diverse than that of a mobile population in the same region, reducing fluctuations in the diet could reduce fluctuations in the long-term energy balance and remove seasonal fluctuations in fecundity. Along with a decrease in breastfeeding and a decrease in aerobic activity, a constant long-term energy balance could increase fecundity.

As we noted above, children may be less susceptible to debilitating gastrointestinal disorders in sedentary villages and a greater percentage of the increased number of offspring might survive. However, more empirical studies are needed to determine how child mortality relates to changes in mobility.

It may be that child mortality *increases* with sedentism, but is overcompensated for by an increase in fertility. However, current evidence suggests that this is not the case.

There are additional, less directly physiological factors that may come into play as a group becomes sedentary. As women's work efforts increase, children may be incorporated into the work force. Draper and Cashdan, for example, demonstrate a difference in child activities between nomadic and sedentary Bushmen (1988; Draper 1975). By helping care for domesticated animals, by harvesting and processing agricultural produce, caring for other children, and doing tasks such as fetching water, children in sedentary Bushmen villages do substantially more work than children in nomadic camps. Additionally, as we described in chapter 4, when women's labor efforts increase, children may fend more for themselves or be placed under the supervision of an older child. That is, there may be a general shift from parental to peer rearing concomitant with the shift from a residentially mobile to a sedentary lifestyle. When children are peer-reared and do adult labor, the perceived cost of raising children is lowered, and women may be inclined to raise more (Draper and Harpending 1987), since women would not have, as the Ju/'hoansi say, a "permanent backache" even if they had children one after another. (Children may even become an asset to household production. Households of the sedentary Gitksan of North America's Northwest Coast were unable to function if they were below a certain critical size [Adams 1973]; see chapter 8.)

Finally, as we pointed out in chapter 4, as a group of hunter-gatherers become sedentary their subsistence may become tied to the same local resources (especially those to be stored since there are usually only one or two in an environment available in sufficient bulk to make them suitable for storage). Following the discussion in chapter 5, hunter-gatherers who are linked to the same resource would do better to increase family or household stores rather to share. In this case, fathers may contribute more to household stores and pay more attention to their children. As paternal input increases, child mortality due to infanticide or neglect may decrease.

In sum, sedentism can set into motion a number of interrelated biological, behavioral, and psychological changes that can result in increased fertility and decreased child mortality, and an increase in the population growth rate, even if such growth increases work efforts in the long term. The scenario we have outlined here, however, is largely speculative and a large amount of research is left to be conducted on this subject.

CONCLUSIONS

We began this chapter with a review of hunter-gatherer group size—maximal and minimal bands, and foraging-group size. We found that there was little empirical or theoretical evidence to support claims of a maximal band size of 500. However, better empirical data and theoretical arguments support 25 as the average band or residential group size. Allowing for children, elderly, and the incapacitated, a group of about 25 contains about 7 or 8 full-time foragers which, if food is shared, may minimize each individual's return-rate variance while holding the rate of local resource depletion to a minimum. The model holds promise for explaining variation in group size.

We next saw that the argument over communal versus individual hunting is not an either/or question but an issue of optimal foraging-group size. Smith provided a model that predicts foraging-group size assuming that individuals attempt to maximize their own return rates regardless of the consequences for the group or other foragers. An application of the model indicates that sharing and social variables, not just foraging efficiency, condition foraging-group size.

We then considered hunter-gatherer population dynamics, pointing out that carrying-capacity approaches do not model the dynamic relationship between predators and their prey. Theoretical models by Winterhalder and Belovsky suggest that hunter-gatherer population dynamics are much more complex than is suggested by the standard logistic growth curve found in many carrying-capacity models. The amount of harvestable primary production, the length of the working day, resource return rates, and rates of resource response to exploitation all affect the rate of human population growth in computer simulations.

We examined evidence for cultural controls on fertility, finding that infanticide was probably the most significant. However, the evidence for infanticide, and especially female infanticide, is fraught with difficulties. Preferential female infanticide was probably relatively uncommon for many past hunter-gatherers. It may have been present in the Arctic, but the importance of this case for other foragers has been overstated. Nonpreferential infanticide may primarily be a birth-spacing mechanism and its prevalence is related to a population's total fertility rate and several social variables, perhaps the most important being how much assistance a mother thinks she will have with a child.[28]

More important in fertility and population growth may be biological mechanisms, specifically the intensity of breastfeeding, seasonal variance in diet, and female activity levels. Frequent, intense breastfeeding, high seasonal variability in diet, and intense, frequent aerobic activity by women may act together to reduce fecundity. Modeling how women's activities and diet are affected under different circumstances will allow us to model circumstances in which prehistoric populations would have grown quickly.

Infant and child mortality is very high in most hunter–gatherer societies and is related to the degree of paternal input, the harshness of an environment (which increases the potential for accidents), and the amount of disease present, which will be highest in wet/warm environments and lowest in cool/dry ones. By bringing children into continual contact with new parasites that result in diarrhea and dehydration, mobility may also contribute to child mortality.

We then outlined a scenario in which mobility and population growth are interrelated through complex social, psychological, and biological mechanisms. These may act together in such a way that once a system begins moving toward storage and sedentism the rate of population growth may increase, raising the population density and increasing the cost of residential mobility (see chapter 4), which further reduces residential mobility, increasing storage and the population growth rate. Thus, many hunter–gatherers may become caught in an upward spiral of increasing population density once they become sedentary.

MEN, WOMEN, AND FORAGING | 7 |

Women dug roots and men ate them . . . men hunted rabbits
and sat around.
Paiute woman (I. Kelly 1964:132)

Dreams about men are good dreams. . . . I dream like that all the time.
God really tortures me with dreams [laughs]! But when I dream that someone is making love to me, it makes me happy. It means that I have lovers
and I like that. . . . One time, Bo found out about us [Nisa and her lover].
Debe and I had gone with some other people to live in the mongongo
groves for a few days. When we returned to the village, people saw us and
said, "Oh, you're all already dead! Nisa, you and your friend are finished.
Your husbands are going to kill you." Because my friend was also there
with her lover. My heart became miserable. I said, "If that's what's going
to happen, then I'll sit here and when my husband comes, let him
just kill me."
Nisa, a Ju/'hoansi woman (Shostak 1981:329, 331–32)

For many years, models of hunter-gatherer social organization have been
based on the portrait drawn at the "Man the Hunter" conference: bilateral
(or sometimes patrilineal) descent, bilocal postmarital residence, a sexual division of labor, egalitarian political organization, and male-female equality.
It is, in essence, an image of the Ju/'hoansi. As we discussed in chapter 1,
band society was early on defined in social organizational terms, especially
descent and residence. While the stereotype shifted from patrilineal to bilateral descent, patrilocal to bilocal residence, male dominance of women to
male-female equality, variability in all these areas was ignored. As the reader
knows by now, the "Man the Hunter" image does not capture all foraging
societies, and, as a result, it does not fully account for why some social behaviors might be prevalent among ethnographically known foragers. Therefore, we will consider in this chapter variability in the division of labor,
postmarital residence, descent, and marriage. Though stereotyped images of
hunter-gatherer social organization, especially relations between men and
women (equality or inequality), are sometimes taken to be ancient behavior
rooted in Pleistocene adaptations, we repeat that this is not necessarily true.
Modern hunter-gatherers do not live out the presumed legacy of their (and

our) Plio-Pleistocene ancestors any more than we do. Instead, diversity or similarities in behavior are a result of diversity or similarity in selective pressures and enculturative environments. Our focus here is on social organization as it represents relationships between men and women. It provides a background for a discussion of gender and social inequality in chapter 8.

DIVISION OF LABOR

One of the most important revelations of the "Man the Hunter" conference was that plants formed an important if not essential element of the diets of many hunter-gatherer societies. And since plants are gathered primarily by women, the conference also emphasized the importance of women's work to the hunter-gatherer lifeway. Both critical elements of the *man* the *hunter* model were overthrown. Hunter-gatherer societies were cast as sexually egalitarian societies, ones where men and women were equal. Male hunting fell in importance and women's contribution to subsistence could no longer be ignored (Brown 1970; B. Hiatt 1978; Barry and Schlegel 1982). But is it true that women and men in hunter-gatherer societies contribute equally to diet? Do they both do the same amount of work? Do men always hunt and women always gather?

To answer the first question, Carol Ember (1975) and Betty Meehan (B. Hiatt 1978) gleaned from ethnographies data on the amount of food procured by men versus women (table 7-1). Plotted against ET, their data show that male subsistence contribution is inversely related to effective temperature (figure 7-1; $Y = -3.09x + 107.4$, $r = .605$, $N = 70$, $df = 68$, $p < .01$). The colder the environment, the more food is directly procured by men. Though there are cases where men are almost the sole direct procurers of food, the converse is absent. Given that women have childbearing and breastfeeding responsibilities that men do not have, there is undoubtedly a limit to how little work men can do—perhaps a lower limit of around 25 percent of direct food procurement. In some tropical societies there can be relatively little division of labor. In the dry season in southwestern Madagascar, for example, when animals remain hidden in burrows or tree trunks, Mikea men and women both collect roots (figure 7-2). But as figure 7-2 shows, there are tropical groups (Semang, Muringin, Andamanese, Mbuti, and Tiwi) where men contribute more to subsistence than might be expected, and one cold-environment group, the Yahgan, where men contribute less than anticipated. These are exceptions that may nonetheless prove

Table 7-1. Effective Temperature and Division of Labor

Location	Group	ET	Male food procurement (%)
Siberia	Yukaghir	8.9	90
E. Greenland	Angmagsalik	9	100
S. America	Ona (Selk'nam)	9	75
N. Canada	Copper Inuit	9.1	90
N. Alaska	Nunamiut	9.8	85
S. America	Yahgan	9.9	50
N.W. Coast	N. Tlingit	10	90
Canada	Chipewyan	10.3	100
E. Siberia	Gilyak	10.4	70
Alaska	Kaska	10.4	65
S. Alaska	Chugach Eskimo	10.5	85
N.W. Coast	Bella Coola	10.5	80
Alaska	Eyak	10.5	80
Alaska	Ingalik	10.8	80
Canada	Pikangikum (Ojibwa)	11	90
Canada	Sekani	11.1	95
N.W. Coast	Tsimshian	11.1	70
W. Canada	Chilcotin	11.2	65
N.W. Coast	Quileute	11.3	70
Canada	Beaver	11.3	68
Aleutians	Aleut	11.6	90
E. Canada	Montagnais	11.6	70
Canada	Saulteaux	11.7	70
Japan	Ainu	12	50
Plateau	Flathead	12.1	60
N.W. Coast	Klallam	12.3	75
California	Washo	12.3	55
Plateau	Gros Ventre	12.4	80
N.W. Coast	Squamish	12.6	90
N.W. Coast	Nootka (Nuuchahnulth)	12.6	65
N.W. Coast	Cowichan	12.6	60
E. Canada	Micmac	12.7	85
Plateau	Coeur d'Alene	12.7	70
Plateau	Kutenai	12.7	70
Plateau	Sanpoil	12.7	58
S. America	Tehuelche	12.8	85
California	Tubatulabal	12.9	58
Plains	Crow	13	80
Great Basin	Tosawihi (White Knife)	13	50
Plains	Arapaho	13.2	80
Plateau	Umatilla	13.3	70
California	Achumawi	13.3	60
California	Yurok	13.3	58
Plateau	Tenino	13.3	50
California	Chimariko	13.5	80
California	Maidu	13.5	58
Great Basin	Kaibab (S. Paiute)	14	48
Plains	Comanche	14.4	63
S. America	Botocudo (Kaingang)	14.4	50
California	Wintu	14.6	78
California	Diegueno (Tipai-Ipai)	14.6	50

Table 7-1. Effective Temperature and Division of Labor (*continued*)

Location	Group	ET	Male food procurement (%)
California	S. Yokuts	14.7	73
California	E. Pomo	14.7	63
California	Wappo	14.7	63
Great Basin	Panamint	15	40
Great Basin	Shivwits (S. Paiute)	15.1	48
Australia	Aranda	15.9	30
Australia	Dieri	15.9	30
Southwest	N.E. Yavapai	16	55
S. America	Aweikoma	16.5	70
Africa	Hadza	17.7	20
Australia	Walpiri (Walbiri)	18.4	30
Africa	Ju/'hoansi (Dobe)	18.8	40
Africa	G/wi	19.3	30
Australia	Wikmunkan	19.6	35
Australia	Tiwi	22.6	38
Australia	Murngin	23.5	53
Malaysia	Semang	23.7	80
Africa	Mbuti	23.7	41
Andaman Is.	Andamanese	24.4	50

Sources: Ember 1975 and B. Hiatt 1978.

the rule. The tropical cases appear to be ones in which men either hunt in order to trade meat for horticultural produce, or ones in which men participate in marine fishing. Conversely, the comparatively low input by men into direct food procurement among the Yahgan may reflect the importance of shellfish gathering by women.[1]

The scale used here, however, is based partly on the degree of group dependence on hunting, gathering, and fishing, and tends to equate hunting with male production and gathering with female production. Hunn notes that for high-latitude groups this tends to overcount men's contribution (1981; see chapter 3). Thus, it is no surprise that men appear to procure more food in colder climates than do women. Rhoda Halperin also points out that Ember's measure underemphasizes the level of female labor in areas such as the Arctic where diet is predominantly meat (1980). As we mentioned in the previous chapter, while men directly procure most of the food in the Arctic, women are the men's support network—they mend clothes, repair various kinds of equipment, and prepare food for storage:

When seal hunting has been good, women are extremely busy and may feel somewhat pressed, because seal skins spoil if the blubber is not removed from them

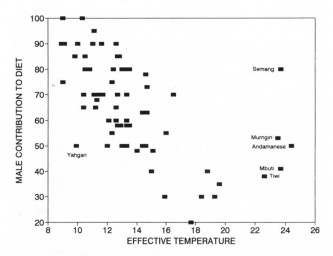

Figure 7-1. Relationship between effective temperature and men's contribution to subsistence (100 = men directly procure all food).

within a day or two. They may also work long hours sometimes if a man is in need, of a new pair of boots or a new fur parka. In this sense, the rhythm of their work is dependent on that of the men. But the men are also dependent on the pace of the women's work. A man cannot hunt until his parka is finished, nor can he move his family to spring camp until his wife has finished making the tent. (Jean Briggs, in Halperin 1980:394)

Halperin argues that the degree of male or female involvement in direct resource procurement varies seasonally among most hunter-gatherers, and that where members of one sex are not directly involved in food procurement, they are involved in activities forming the support network of food procurement (1980). Thus, she argues that "among band-level hunter-gatherers the male-female division of labor remains unspecialized. Female and male contributions to production complement one another, albeit in different ways according to season and overall ecological adjustment." There is no doubt, however, that the degree of male involvement in *direct* food procurement is higher in the Arctic than in the tropics. Halperin's point is important, but as our discussion of female infanticide in chapter 6 pointed out, we should be careful not to presuppose that the complementarity of male-female activities leads to equality between the sexes.

Ethnographic data indicate that hunting (that is, the hunting of large game) is always a highly valued activity (as noted in chapters 3 and 5, this

Figure 7-2. Rabemainty, a Mikea man, digging for roots. Among the Mikea, both men and women gather roots in the dry season. Most hunting, done almost exclusively by men, occurs in the wet season. Photograph by the author, July 1993.

could be for the food value of fatty meat, for the fact that meat is often shared, or both), and the development of hunting skills is a primary way by which men can acquire prestige. As we noted in chapter 3, the lack of meat is sufficient reason for many hunter-gatherers to complain of starvation even when there is plenty of plant food. If men acquire higher status by virtue of the fact that they hunt, why, then, do women not hunt more than they apparently do?

Figure 7-3. Out hunting with bow and arrow near the Malibu River in the Cagayan Province in the northern Philippines in 1982, an Agta woman signals to a female companion that she has spotted game—wild pigs feeding on fruit fallen from a tree. Photograph courtesy of P. Bion Griffin.

In fact, women in hunter-gatherer societies *do* hunt regularly; in particular seasons their targets are usually small game—rabbits and rodents, for example. More often than not, women hunt small game opportunistically, setting out to gather plant food and changing plans if they encounter small game. It is the hunting of large game that is usually men's work. Years ago, it was assumed that women simply did not have the physical strength or endurance to hunt large game. However, hunting requires patience and skill more than strength; and plant collecting, especially digging for tubers, is no less physically demanding than hunting.

Moreover, there are cases of female hunters, even in the Arctic (Romanoff 1983; Landes 1938:137; Watanabe 1968:74), and of women who participate in communal game drives (Turnbull 1965; Bailey and Aunger 1989b).

The best-documented case of women hunters is that of the Philippine Agta (figure 7-3; Estioko-Griffin and Griffin 1981, 1985). The Agta, in fact, appear to be a striking exception among ethnographically known foragers.

About 85 percent of Agta women hunt, although these women hunt less frequently than men (Goodman et al. 1985:1203). There are no significant differences between Agta women hunters and nonhunters in terms of their body size, age, age at menarche, age at first pregnancy, height, weight, or total number of living children. Nor is there much difference in the quarry of male and female hunters: both men and women separately hunt wild pigs and deer, while mixed groups may hunt monkeys. Agta women tend to hunt in groups and use dogs. They also tend to hunt within about ten kilometers of camp, so that they can return at the end of the day. They can walk to a potential hunting area within twenty or thirty minutes of camp. Women hunt while menstruating and while breastfeeding a child.[2] If a child is still breastfeeding, the mother may take the child along in a shoulder sling; older weaned children are left behind in the care of a female relative. Agta women are good hunters, coming home with a kill 31 percent of the time, whereas men average a 17 percent success rate; mixed groups of male and female hunters are even more successful, coming home with kills 41 percent of the time.

Agta women can hunt because they can leave their children with others, and Goodman and her co-workers conclude that "a harsher environment [i.e., one that does not favor brief hunting excursions] or a more retentive or individualistic mode of child care and rearing might have discouraged women's hunting" (1985:1208). As others have argued, there is a basic conflict between childcare and the hunting of large game. The Agta may be the proverbial exception that proves the rule.

Cross-cultural studies, in fact, conclude that childbirth and the nursing of infants are the main constraints on the sexual division of labor (Burton, Brudner, and White 1977:250). Ache women who are still breastfeeding are less efficient foragers than nonbreastfeeding women and spend less time foraging as they allocate more time to their children (Hurtado et al. 1985). Since an infant's primary food is breast milk, and since, as we saw in chapter 6, children may breastfeed until they are several years old, women of childbearing age are frequently accompanied by children. Hunting is not more physically demanding than gathering for adults, but it is so for children. Additionally, since the prey controls the hunt, the hunter cannot interrupt pursuit to tend to a child's needs. Gathering is an interruptible activity, whereas hunting is much less so. Gathering plant foods allows a person to return to camp when necessary, but hunting may require an overnight stay so as to continue tracking the animal in the morning.[3] Stated simply, gathering is more compatible with breastfeeding and childcare than is big-game hunting (Brown 1970).

If this is true we would expect women's participation in hunting to be affected by their childcare practices. Where women cannot be separated from their young children (see chapter 6), women may be unable to hunt very much. Older women without their own children to look after may be able to hunt more than younger women. This appears to the case among the Agta where the most serious hunting is done by women who have reached the end of their childbearing years or who have children old enough to look after themselves in camp. Though women with nursing infants or a number of young children will occasionally hunt if the opportunity arises, it is older women who set out intentionally to hunt (P. Bion Griffin, personal communication, 1990).

On the other hand, if childcare prevents a woman from hunting when young, she may not be able to acquire the experience to be an effective hunter later in life (and the same physical factors that cause men to stop hunting in their old age will also prevent women from doing so). Where this is true, older women may either work for their daughters by foraging for them, as happens among the Hadza, or by watching after their children, as is the case among the Ju/'hoansi (Hawkes et al. 1989).[4] In chapter 6 we saw that Mbuti women probably decide whether or not to participate in hunts based on the return from hunting versus the returns from wage labor. From these cases we see that a woman's decision to hunt has to do with the variables of foraging returns (of gathering versus hunting) and childcare practices, and not with innate abilities or proclivities selected for early in hominid evolution. Given the reproductive differences between men and women, women may get greater fitness benefits from investing in children, and specializing in gathering, whereas men (for reasons discussed in chapter 5) may get greater benefits from the prestige that comes from the hunting and sharing of large game. This difference could, however, become socially defined (affected by the process described in the preceding paragraph), laden with symbolic meanings about gender, and passed on through enculturation.

We cannot close a discussion of the division of labor without pointing out how it could affect gender status. Where men hunt large game because of women's necessary childcare responsibilities, and given that large game is always shared whereas plant foods most often are not (for reasons discussed in chapter 5), then men will in almost all cases be in a better position than women to give food away and thus to acquire the prestige associated with gift-giving. Basic status inequalities between men and women in hunter-gatherer societies (see chapter 8) could be rooted in the division of labor (Collier and Rosaldo 1981:282), but based not on the volume of food collected or complementarity of tasks, but on whether one gender's resources are shared more than the other's outside the family.[5] Thus complicated by issues of sharing and prestige, the division of labor could influence aspects of social organization, such as postmarital residence, descent, and marriage.

POSTMARITAL RESIDENCE, DESCENT, AND MARRIAGE

As we noted in chapter 1, Steward argued that band societies, most commonly represented by hunter-gatherer societies, predominantly display patrilineal descent and patrilocal postmarital residence. Following Murdock's general exposition of social structure (1949), Service argued that the key feature was patrilocal residence, with patrilineal descent following from it. Both Service and Steward agreed that patrilocal residence derived from the presumably natural dominance of men, and also from "the importance of the solidarity of the males in hunting, sharing game, and particularly in offense-defense" (Service 1962:67).[6] Service went on to argue that the prevalence of patrilocal residence in foraging societies in so many different environments indicated that the local habitat had no bearing on postmarital residence and social organization. Service attributed deviations from the patrilocal model (e.g., composite bands, with bilocal or neolocal residence) to population decline brought about by European-introduced disease.

The "Man the Hunter" conference changed much of this. Participants noted that many ethnographic cases did not fit the patrilineal/patrilocal model, yet the social organizations of these societies did not appear to be the result of radical demographic change. June Helm, for example, showed that composite bands of Canadian Athapaskans were not made up of unrelated families (1965). A new model developed after the conference that emphasized bilateral descent and bilocal residence (actually, Murdock suggested that bilocality should be prevalent among hunter-gatherers in unstable bands long before "Man the Hunter"; 1949:204). Hunter-gatherer social organization was seen to be much more fluid and variable than the patrilocal/patrilineal model allowed. By permitting group sizes to adjust to local changes in resource abundance and demographic imbalances (in group sex ratios, for example), and by allowing group fission as the way to settle disputes, bilateral

Table 7-2. Postmarital Descent and Residence

Descent	Residence				
	Patrilocal	**Matrilocal**	**Bilocal**	**Avunculocal**	**Contradictory**
Patrilineal	24	0	0	0	2
Matrilineal	3	9	0	6	4
Bilateral	69	19	18	0	30
Contradictory	3	0	0	0	6
Total	99	28	18	6	42

Sources: Most data from Driver 1961; Driver and Coffin 1975; Murdock 1967.
Note: Data are from 193 hunter-gatherer groups; viri/patrilocality are combined, as are uxori/matrilocality and neo/bilocality; bilateral descent may include some cases of double descent; the contradictory category contains groups with contradictory assignations.
    This table is not a random sample, but a summary of all cases that I have checked. It is biased toward North American groups. All three of the cross-cultural surveys are affected by a latitudinal bias for we have few temperate cases outside of specific culture areas such as the Plains and California. Thus there is the potential for bias toward particular latitudes and, especially, culture areas in these samples (Galton's problem) which can bias interpretations of the table.

descent was considered to be more adaptive (in the cultural ecologists' sense) than unilocal descent. The fluid, bilateral, bilocal hunter-gatherer model of band society soon replaced the patrilineal/patrilocal model.

Ten years later, however, Ember tested the assumption that most known hunter-gatherers have bilocal residence (1978). Her survey of 179 cases showed *patrilocal* residence to be the most common form of postmarital residence (62 percent; omitting equestrians, 64 percent; omitting equestrians and intensive fishing groups, 56 percent). A survey by Kay Martin and Barbara Voorhies of 90 hunter-gatherer societies reached a similar conclusion (58 percent patrilocal; 1975:185), as did my own survey of 193 cases (in 148, or 65 percent, of those cases where there were no contradictory accounts; see table 7-2). In terms of descent, Martin and Voorhies found that 62 percent of their sample was made up of groups with bilateral descent; 63 percent of my sample have bilateral descent (again excluding cases with contradictory accounts). The most common pattern, then, is bilateral descent with patrilocal residence (50 percent of my sample; see note in table 7-2).

These surveys only point to *modern* patterns in descent and residence. As Ember reminds us, "assuming that different residential patterns are the result of different causal conditions, that which is normal as of recent times may only be a statistical artifact of the recent prevalence of certain of those causal conditions" (1975:199). But even if the effects of colonialism and sampling problems were accounted for, we would still be left only with a statistical generalization that could not be projected into the past. Cross-cultural stud-

Table 7-3. Explanations of postmarital residence rules

Residence pattern	Author	Explanation
Patrilocal	Steward, Service	Permits men to be familiar with area to insure success in hunting; provides strength in offense and defense; result of "natural" dominance of men
Matrilocal	Ember, Perry	Associated with long-distance warfare or hunting coupled with women as primary food and childcare providers
Bilocal	Ember, Service, others	Response to fluctuating environments; evens out skewed sex ratios of small groups; results from colonization and breakdown of previous patrilocal rule

ies are useful beginning points, but we now need to ask, what factors condition residence and descent?

Postmarital residence

Several explanations have been proposed for different forms of postmarital residence among hunter-gatherers (table 7-3). Here we will consider only the three most common patterns: matrilocal, bilocal, and, to begin, patrilocal residence.

Steward and Service argued that hunters should live patrilocally in part because men needed to be familiar with a territory in order to hunt successfully in it. As we noted in chapter 1, both Steward and Service thought hunting was of prime importance to hunter-gatherer societies, and so associated the hunter-gatherer lifeway with patrilocal residence. Conversely, if hunting is not important, then women's familiarity with an area should be important, and residence should be matrilocal. Ember tested this hypothesis by looking for correlations between residence practices and the division of labor in a sample of 50 societies (1975). Assuming that men do most of the hunting and fishing and that women do most of the gathering, societies dependent on hunting or fishing should have patrilocal residence, whereas societies dependent on gathering should have matrilocal residence. Ember found a significant tendency toward matrilocality among societies heavily dependent on gathering, and a significant tendency toward patrilocality among societies heavily dependent on fishing. In direct contrast to the patrilineal/patrilocal model, however, no correlation existed between heavy dependence on hunting and patrilocality (Ember 1975; Ember and Ember 1971). Some North American boreal forest groups, for example, have matrilocal residence and yet are heavily dependent on large game such as caribou and moose. In contrast to the Service and Steward formulations, it may not be true that male relatives must remain together in order for them to be successful hunters. Among the patrilocal Efe Pygmies, Bailey and Aunger found that neither hunting efficiency nor hunting success were statistically correlated with the degree of relatedness of the hunters nor the proportion of relatives on a hunt (1989b). On the other hand, working among the nearby Aka Pygmies, Hewlett found that a male with brothers is more likely than a male with no brothers to live in a reliable economic unit (1988).

Ember suggested that in areas where game is not predictable, there is no advantage to men remaining where they grew up, an explanation that has some merit (1975:212). Hunter-gatherers utilize varying mixes of two basic food-getting strategies. In one, the forager learns an area extremely well, exploiting the geography of that area in order to procure food resources. An example is the Gwich'in (Kutchin), who live in Alaska's interior forests. The Gwich'in know the geography of their land extremely well—where springs, game trails, recent burns, and other good hunting places are, as well as sheltered places, firewood, and raw materials. One of their most important foraging tools is a mental map of resource geography.

In the other strategy, the forager learns the various characteristics of the desired food resources, for example, where food is likely to be at certain times of the year or under different weather conditions (R. Nelson 1986:275–76; N. Peterson 1975). The Inuit of Alaska's northern coast provide an example of this strategy. When living on the frozen surface of the sea during the winter, the Inuit face a landscape that changes from day to day as the ice shifts. Here, the Inuit learn animal behavior intimately and use it to predict where seals or fish will be found given the day's configuration of ice, water, and weather.

Hunter-gatherers use a mixture of both strategies, but one may be emphasized depending on the nature of the resources that are used. The fewer resources used, the more likely that one or the other strategy will dominate. There could also be seasonal and long-term shifts in the importance of these strategies. For example, a person could attempt to learn the resource geography of as large an area as possible to be able to call on that knowledge in times of need, while in the short term relying more upon knowledge of animal behavior.

Differences in the short- and long-term predictability of large game could account for some of the variability in postmarital residence among societies heavily dependent on hunting. The more hunter-gatherers depend on hunting, the larger both their yearly foraging ranges and long-term ranges must be (see chapter 4). And the more unpredictable their resource base, the more important it is for them to learn about as large an area as possible. Both these factors could encourage *matrilocal* postmarital residence as a way to learn the area of the wife's country, since the hunter already knows the area in which he grew up. In this case postmarital residence could reflect hunters educating themselves about a region to decrease long-term variance in returns and reduce risk.

Ember also considered the effects of warfare on postmarital residence, an explanation that offers another perspective on matrilocality in societies dependent on hunting. In her sample, matrilocality is associated with external warfare, long-distance fighting between different social groups. Ember argued that external warfare is associated with matrilocality only if warfare places more emphasis on women as the primary procurers of food (Ember and Ember 1971).

However, the degree of direct food procurement may be less important than the extent to which men's contribution to childcare (which includes procuring food) is guaranteed. Warfare could, understandably, reduce a woman's confidence in a man's contribution to child rearing. But such warfare is not common among foragers. Using Ember's observations, Richard Perry argues that matrilocal residence among subarctic Athapaskans (e.g., Dogrib, Han, Sarsi, Sekani) is a function of the need for long-distance hunting, which has the same effect as long-distance warfare: it removes men from the residence, puts them in dangerous situations, and reduces the reliability of their contribution to childcare (1989). This could lead related women to bond together to form support networks among themselves. Given the important effect of the expectation of paternal care on infant survivorship (chapter 6), subsistence strategies that remove men from their families for long periods of time and place them at risk could result in matrilocal postmarital residence as part of a woman's reproductive strategy.

Ember also tested several hypotheses of bilocal residence. One hypothesis suggests that bilocality is a response to fluctuating environments. Where environments are uncertain, the argument goes, camp membership needs to be fluid to allow populations to disperse themselves rapidly in response to changes in the resource base. Bilocality allows families to move back and forth between the locations of the couple's parents. Ember tested this by examining the relationship between bilocal (as opposed to unilocal) residence and the degree of environmental fluctuation as measured by the coefficient of variation in annual rainfall. She found that bilocal groups occur most frequently in environments of variable rainfall; unilocal groups are associated with climatically stable environments.

However, another hypothesis suggests that bilocality allows small groups to even out discrepancies in group sex ratio. As discussed in chapter 6, small groups can undergo dramatic fluctuations in sex ratio. Small groups may allow for more variability in residence in order to permit movement of couples to even out sexual imbalances that could affect food procurement. Ember found a significant correlation between group size and residence, with bilocal residence occurring among hunter-gatherers of small local group size. However, Ember also found that group size and precipitation variability are correlated (this makes sense; precipitation variability is generally high where annual precipitation is low, and low precipitation is associated with low amounts of food). Thus, Ember could not separate environmental from demographic factors in her study.

Ember also tested Service's hypothesis that bilocal residence is the result of the fragmenting effects of contact between hunter-gatherers and European populations. Ember's analysis also supported this contention: bilocal groups are significantly associated with evidence of recent depopulation. Evidence of depopulation was *not* statistically associated with precipitation variability or group size. However, the same process may be at work in all three cases. In areas of high precipitation variability, or where groups are small, or in regions that have undergone depopulation, hunter-gatherers may need to maximize the number of social groups and families to which they have social access to reduce long-term variance in their food supply. As we saw in chapter 5, they can do this through a variety of means, and bilocal residence could be one since it helps a person solidify relations with his or her affinal relatives.

Part of the difficulty in understanding postmarital residence arises from confusing social rules with behavior. In my survey of ethnographic data, instead of rejecting cases for which there were contradictory accounts, I included these under a "contradictory" category. Some contradictions undoubtedly stem from ethnographers' errors, and some from the fact that where one ethnographer records rules of behavior, another records behavior. Some differences also arise from the fact that ethnographers did their fieldwork at different times, when residence and descent patterns may have been different. Both Leacock (1955, 1982) and Dunning (1959) noted a shift from matrilocality to patrilocality in postcontact times among many Canadian Algonquian groups. Dunning also showed that residence would be recorded differently depending on whether data were collected in the summer or winter. As table 7-2 indicates, only 5 percent of the sample had contradictory descent assignations, but 22 percent had contradictory residence rules.

I suspect the discrepancies in residence rules are more apparent than real.

Rules, of course, do exist. They are what people say should be done, but they are by no means what people always do (or even what they say they themselves should do in a specific situation). To understand residence "the empirical patterns of post-nuptial co-residence, stable or shifting, demand as much attention as do formal rules of kin alliance and residence assignment" (Helm 1968:125).

Nicholas Peterson's description of the subtle relations between the ideology and actuality of residence in Australia provides an example (1978). Among many Australian Aborigines, young men desire to live patrilocally in the estate of their father, from whom they inherit various ceremonial and stewardship duties (see chapter 5). This is the ideal situation. However, men tend to be much older than their wives (Chisholm and Burbank 1991; Peterson and Long 1986:154); consequently, a man's parents are often deceased by the time he marries. The wife's parents, on the other hand, are alive, in need of the couple's assistance, and capable of providing the couple with various sorts of aid (such as childcare, social access to different tracts of land, and knowledge). Some couples might be encouraged to reside matrilocally for a while. As the husband ages, he will eventually return to his estate with his family and fulfill the residence rule of patrilocality. Note that at any given point in time, however, local groups will be made up of elderly men living patrilocally, and a few young men residing matrilocally. Neither the ideology nor actuality of residence describes the Aborigines' (or any other culture's) system in its entirety.

The Ju/'hoansi present a similar pattern, although for a different reason. Like many hunter-gatherers in the bilocal residence pigeonhole, a newly married Ju/'hoansi couple lives initially with the bride's parents. This is usually not because the groom's parents are deceased, as with the Australian Aborigines. Instead, the Ju/'hoansi say that this is because the bride is too young to leave her parents, and, additionally, that it allows the bride's parents to see whether the new son-in-law is a good hunter and husband. To these reasons, Wilmsen adds that since children acquire their birthplace as their primary *n!ore* (see chapter 5), but also acquire rights in the *n!ore* of their parents, remaining with the bride's family until a child is born links together land-based kin networks (1989b). The bride's family continues to have responsibilities to their children born at their *n!ore,* as well as to grandchildren born there.

In the 1960s and 1970s, anthropologists were concerned with the rules of band membership among hunter-gatherer societies. They discovered that the patrilocal band was not always the fundamental unit of membership. For some, such as the Chipewyan, it is the hunting unit; the Chipewyan band is a temporary, noncorporate grouping that is physically present only for adventitious occasions (Sharp 1977:378). More to the point, whatever the fundamental corporate group above the family was, anthropologists found that it was not constituted in a simple or straightforward fashion. There were rules that dictated group membership and postmarital residence, but they were layered, and often violated without informants considering the violations to be wrong.

I think the reason is that residence patterns reflect the result of nomadic peoples aligning themselves in different ways with one another. Postmarital residence patterns are not simply rules, but are the outcome of men and women aligning themselves more or less with their or their spouse's kin under different conditions. They are the result of a complex decision-making process that relates to group formation. Residential groups reflect the collective result of individuals' decisions to join (or allow others to join) a foraging group. These decisions should be rooted in the foraging-rate-maximization process described in chapter 6 (see discussion of Smith's member and joiner rules), but are written in a kinship idiom. Henry Sharp, for example, attributes fluctuation in the size and composition of Chipewyan hunting units to "an organized search for maximum individual benefit within a highly structured set of possibilities" (1977:385). In Canadian Athapaskan groups such as the Chipewyan, men are inclined to reside patrilocally because they know the other members of their hunting unit and its traditional terrain well; they are also more likely to gain positions of prestige in their natal hunting unit. On the other hand, there are reasons why a man may wish to reside matrilocally. Because of the nature of kin relations in these societies, younger brothers work for their fathers and older brothers, and are obliged to obey them. Relations between brothers-in-law, however, are more circumspect and shy. A man residing matrilocally can have greater control over his labor and achieve higher returns for his effort. A Dogrib man explained this to June Helm:

With your dad, you kill yourself to do all the work. Going with your older brother is just like going with your dad. He won't work hard. He expects you [as the younger brother] to do most of the work. So you don't take your own brother very often [as a work partner]. You take your brother-in-law most of the time. Brothers-in-law do the work just the same [that is, they share the labor equally]. (Helm 1972:73; see also Sharp 1977:383)

A younger brother may therefore find it more advantageous to reside matrilocally, even though his desire may be to reside patrilocally.[7] Though men may have the same goals, kin and age-structured relations can result in their choosing different postmarital residences.

Men and women, on the other hand, may have different objectives in negotiating group membership (e.g., maximize hunting returns versus invest in childcare). Among the Chipewyan, women prefer to remain with their natal hunting unit (Sharp 1977:383), perhaps because of the support they could expect in child rearing from their sisters or mothers. Such a desire could be especially significant in instances where men are away on long-distance dangerous hunting trips or long-distance raiding, decreasing their reliability as providers. Where neither the husband's or wife's family are more capable of providing assistance in the long term, a couple may reside bilocally so as to keep all options open (this could happen in depopulated areas or environments with temporally and spatially variable resources).

Residence patterns, then, may result from men and women making decisions about the costs and benefits of joining or allowing others to join particular groups. These decisions will be affected by men's and women's activities; as these change over time, the costs and benefits of different residence choices may also change. But it is important to remember that part of the environment here is kin relations, which are highly structured and are not simply built upon people's choices of resources to pursue or of places to live. They channel people's choices. For example, if relations between brothers-in-law were less shy among the Chipewyan, a younger brother might prefer patrilocal residence, even with his father's and older brothers' demands on his time. But, as resource configurations and/or people's choices change (as occurred when the fur trade moved into central Canada), the costs and benefits of different residence patterns change and so do the relations between sets of kin (Sharp 1977). Thus, there should be a constant interplay between kin relations and resource configurations, with changing resources altering the costs and benefits of activities, leading to change, but with existing kin relations channeling that change in particular directions and, in the process, changing kin relations themselves (see Ives 1990 for a discussion drawing upon Canadian Athapaskan societies).

Descent

Many anthropologists assume that descent and postmarital residence are closely connected (Martin and Voorhies 1975:184; Murdock 1949). As table 7-2 shows, patrilineal descent is associated with patrilocal residence; however, whereas matrilineal descent is primarily associated with matrilocal residence, there are also some patrilocal matrilineal societies. Bilateral descent is

largely associated with patrilocal residence, but there are a number of matrilocal and bilocal cases as well. Thus, descent is correlated with residence, but
it is far from perfectly correlated, and thus deserves separate discussion here.

Following Service, Martin and Voorhies suggest that bilateral descent is
more prevalent today than unilineal descent because of the effects of European intrusion, including adoption of the European kinship model. This
may be true in many instances. However, there are at least a few cases where
contact precipitates a shift from bilateral to unilineal descent. The G//ana
of the central Kalahari, for example, shifted from bilateral toward patrilineal
inheritance (Cashdan 1984), and Peter Gardner notes a similar shift among
the Paliyans of India (1988). Moreover, some groups such as the Batek of
Malaysia still maintain a bilateral kinship pattern despite the fact that they
are encapsulated by societies of different descent patterns (Endicott 1981;
Endicott and Endicott 1986). As we pointed out in our discussion of postmarital residence, the argument that contact results in bilateral descent only
specifies one set of proximal conditions rather than the actual cause. The
received wisdom of "Man the Hunter," in fact, was that bilateral kinship was
an adaptation to uncertain environments, and that, like bilocal residence, it
increased the number of relatives one had and their geographic distribution
to reduce the risk of living with spatially and temporally variable resources.

Not everyone accepts this position. John Martin and Donald Stewart point
out that unilineal groups also permit group movement as a response to environmental fluctuation (1982). They argue that patrilineal descent is a function of small-group demography coupled with polygyny. Assuming that
polygyny is permitted, Martin and Stewart argue that the sons of polygynous
males will also become polygynous both because of enculturation and the
fact that they will be able to acquire more wives by having more sisters to
exchange for wives. By creating a shortage of wives in a group, some males
are forced to seek wives elsewhere. If the regional population exists as a
number of small groups, then random variation will alter group sex ratios,
occasionally leaving a shortage of male hunters in some bands. Under these
conditions some groups will seek to recruit young males as hunters, and thus
offer them wives on the condition that they live matrilocally. Martin and
Stewart argue that polygynous men will remain in the territory of their fathers and form patrilineal/patrilocal descent groups consisting of polygynous
men, their brothers, patrilateral parallel cousins, and sons. Thus, they argue,
patrilineal bands form among strongly polygynous hunter-gatherers living in
small groups, with a stable or growing population that has a preference for
viri/patrilocal residence (Martin and Stewart 1982:91).[8]

However, these arguments presuppose concepts of descent and kinship that we often use too simplistically. Consider, for example, the Ju/'hoansi, frequently cited as an example of bilateral descent. The Ju/'hoansi's bilateral descent system is quite flexible. One's name and age can be used by another (older) individual to categorize a nonrelative into the status of relative (as described in chapter 5), and affines can become recognized, through kin-term alteration, as consanguineals (Lee 1979). Wilmsen argues that Ju/'hoansi kinship, marriage, and postmarital residence are all intricately linked to existing social networks that are made up of positions of responsibility and prerogative with regard to the use of land (1989a,b). In what sense is one bilateral group, such as the Ju/'hoansi, like other peoples in the bilateral-kinship category?

A more detailed example comes from Australia, where many groups are often classified as patrilineal in cross-cultural surveys. Do these groups have the same social organization? Does labeling them patrilineal sufficiently capture their descent system and its function?

Among the Pitjandjara, persons, especially men, are united into groups who share an estate where sites of spiritual significance are located and rituals are held (Hamilton 1982a). It is identification with this land, or rather with specific locations in it, that is most crucial, rather than identification with a descent group.[9] For the Pitjandjara, a boy usually, but not always, shares his father's totemic cult (this may be the mother's cult as well, since the preferred marriage is one in which husband and wife have the same totemic affiliation). Though men prefer that their children be born in their country, near the water source associated with their totemic figure, this is not always possible given the exigencies of life in the Western Desert. We mentioned in chapter 5 that in Aboriginal thought, geographic locations can be linked together into a Dreamtime track. If a Pitjandjara boy is born away from his father's totemic country, but near a locality on a track that traverses his father's country, then he will have rights in his father's totemic complex. But if he is born away from his father's country and off the Dreamtime track that includes the father's country, then he takes the cult totem of the country where he was born. His participation in the cult totem of his father is then restricted (but not entirely cut off; as we noted in chapter 5, association can be based on many criteria).

Thus Annette Hamilton asks: in what sense are the Pitjandjara patrilineal, for "rights do not accrue primarily by being born to a particular father, but by being born at a particular place" (1982a:101).[10] Additionally, the Pitjandjara's taboo on using the names of deceased persons, and their tendency to forget the long-dead, operates against the formation of patrilineal descent

$=$ Marriage pairs

⟶   Section membership of woman's
     offspring (male and female)

Figure 7-4. The Mardudjara section system. Redrawn by Dan Delaney. Figure re-drawn from *The Mardudjara Aborigines* by Robert Tonkinson, copyright © 1978 by Holt, Rinehart and Winston, Inc., reproduced by permission of the publisher.

groups. Hamilton contrasts this situation with that of the peoples of Arnhem Land, where the dead are remembered through elaborate mortuary ceremonies, and where members of a patrilineal descent group act corporately. To categorize both these societies as patrilineal tells us less than we already know about their social organization in particular and about the principles of hunter-gatherer social-group formation in general.

The Mardudjara (or Mardu) of Australia's Western Desert provide another example, one that introduces us to the concept of *section systems* (Tonkinson 1978, 1991). In addition to kinship categories, most Aboriginal societies are divided into two, four, six, or eight additional social groupings. Where there are two, these are moieties; where there are four they are called sections, and where there are more than four they are called subsections. Moieties may not be named categories, but sections and subsections always are; unlike kinship, which is defined egocentrically, sections and subsections are socio-centric divisions (Berndt and Berndt 1964; Tonkinson 1978, 1991). Though kinship rules dictate most day-to-day behavior between people, there are also patterned relationships between (sub)sections.

The Mardudjara have a four-section system; people are either Garimara, Banaga, Burungu, or Milangga. Membership in one of the four sections is ascribed at birth and cannot be changed. Referring to figure 7-4, we can describe how the Mardudjara's section system works:

taking, for example, a Garimara female as Ego, or starting point, she will marry a man of Banaga section whom she calls by the term for "spouse." She cannot marry just *any* Banaga man because his section contains her real and classificatory mother's fathers, son's sons, and certain cross-cousins who are classed as "brothers," all of whom are nonmarriageable relatives. . . . The sons and daughters of this Garimara woman will be in the Milaṅgga section and will eventually marry Buṟuṅgu spouses. Her daughter's children will belong to Garimara, her own section, but her son's children will be born into Banaga section, eventually to take their spouses from among the Garimara. (Tonkinson 1978:55–56)

Thus sections are exogamous and therefore play a role in marriage, although they are not marriage classes (Meggitt 1968; Tonkinson 1978:54; Yengoyan 1968), since marriage partners are specified through the kinship system. Additionally, since a child's section depends upon but is not the same as that of his or her mother, section systems do not parallel descent systems. Instead, (sub)sections provide an additional grouping to which individuals belong, and they cut across other groupings based on kinship or estate ownership.

Implicit in section systems are three possibilities for dual groupings. Garimara and Milaṅgga sections could be combined on the one hand (since women of the former bear daughters who belong to the latter, and vice versa), and similarly Banaga and Buṟuṅgu on the other hand, to form matrimoieties. Likewise, members of the Banaga and Milaṅgga sections, and members of the Garimara and Buṟuṅgu sections, can be combined into patrimoieties (these are identified egocentrically, not as socially named divisions among the Mardudjara). Finally, Banaga-Garimara and Buṟuṅgu-Milaṅgga are combined among the Mardudjara into what are called merged alternate generation pairs. By drawing a simple kin diagram of the sectional relationships between marriage and descent as outlined above (or see Tonkinson 1978:figure 3-2), we could see that ego's generation (siblings and cousins) are members of one of the intermarrying pairs of sections. Everyone in the $+1$ (parental) or -1 (offspring/niece/nephew) generation belongs to the other intermarrying pair, while everyone in the $+2$ (grandparental) or -2 (grandchildren) generation belongs to the same pair as ego's generation.

Patrimoieties and merged alternate generations are found among the Mardudjara; matrimoieties are not, but do occur among other Aboriginal societies (although not in the Western Desert). Mardudjara social divisions, especially merged alternate generations, play a role in some ritual obligations and gift-giving. Looking at the kinship relationships of ego it is possible to see that certain relatives always fall into certain sections (see Tonkinson 1978:57). This means two things. First, by lumping together sets of kin terms, sections provide people with a guide for the kind of behavior that is to be expected between people. That is to say, if one knows a person's gender, age, and section, one has a good idea as to how act toward him or her—

even in the case of a stranger—by reducing the possible kin connections (although interaction does not normally occur until the specific kin connection is established). Among the Mardudjara, in fact, section terms are often used to refer to people in place of personal names, which are never used casually (Tonkinson 1978:55). Second, these merged alternate generations contain a majority of kin with whom ego has much less restrained interaction. Ego can joke with those on his or her "side," but he or she must act with respect and deference to those on the "other side." Finally, yet another division consists of ego's generational grouping on one side and some close consanguineal kin—brothers, sisters, and some cross-cousins—on the other. This division figures in male initiation and mortuary rites.

In discussing the similar Walbiri section system, Meggitt sums up the point of our discussion: "Kinship studies alone are simply not enough, not even for comprehending the kinship systems themselves" (1987:132). To understand descent and residence one question we must ask is, what is it that descent and residence rules or tendencies record? Kinship is a way of organizing people by placing them into categories that are accompanied by certain rights and responsibilities. Western society thinks of kinship as a way to categorize biological facts, and so anthropology begins with biological relationships as the basis of different kinds of kinship. But this need not be the case for other cultures. Viewing kinship as a way to categorize blood relationships may lead us astray, because what kinship is actually doing in any given society may be quite different from what we think it does. That is, anthropologists not only impose the categories of patrilineal, matrilineal, and bilateral descent on people, we impose the very concept of kinship on them (Schneider 1984).

We could use our categories of descent and residence as an initial avenue into understanding the organization of interpersonal relationships in a society. The correlations between particular forms of descent and residence suggest that descent, too, is related to decisions about group formation. We suggested that these decisions can be rooted in considerations of foraging costs and benefits and parental investment, and are affected by existing relations between kin and, we could add, existing ideas about how different kinds of kin are created.

Sharp notes, for example, that hunting units try to become as large as possible, for large hunting units are politically powerful (1977). There is a trade-off, however, since the larger a hunting unit is, the more rapidly it depletes resources in its hunting territory and the longer members have to travel to reach trapping lines (1977:385; Sharp states that travel time is the

Table 7-4. Marriage Arrangements among Hunter-Gatherers

Marriage arrangement	Number	Percentage
Bridewealth	23	20.4
Dowry	2	1.8
Gift exchange (between parents of bride and groom)	20	17.6
Absence of any significant exchanges	38	33.6
Brideservice	18	15.9
Token bridewealth	7	6.2
Exchange of sisters or female relative	5	4.5
Total	113	100.0

Source: Murdock 1967.

critical variable in a hunter's decision to remain in a hunting unit). This means that there are limitations on the size of hunting units. These units, as named groups, also rarely last more than three generations due to a number of factors, but Sharp gives priority to the lack of concern with genealogies (partly generated by a taboo on the mention of deceased individuals by name), and to the limited control that elder brothers have over their younger brothers (since the latter can leave). If the resource configuration (or younger brothers' options) were to change such that larger units were possible, would we see a change toward corporate groups with a unilineal bias (and perhaps more consistent postmarital residence patterns) as individuals try to negotiate entry into a group by claiming descent from a deceased individual? Or would prohibitions on speaking of the dead select for a different form of kinship and group formation? Speculations on this topic are endless, but this brief example suggests that there is room for research on descent, and residence, from an evolutionary perspective.

Marriage

Our discussion of Australian Aboriginal section systems leads us to a more general discussion of marriage among hunter-gatherers. From Murdock's ethnographic atlas, we can obtain some idea of the variability in marriage arrangements among hunter-gatherers (Murdock 1967; table 7-4). As the table indicates, marriages without significant gift exchanges make up the largest category, although this accounts only for one-third of the 113 cases. Marriages involving significant bridewealth are the second most common category, but still make up only 20 percent of the sample. Gift exchange

Table 7-5. Cousin Marriage among Hunter-Gatherers

Form	Number	Percentage
Duolateral cross-cousin (MBD or FZS, with parallel cousins forbidden)	15	14.0
Duolateral with maternal cousins only	1	1.0
Matrilateral cross-cousins	5	4.6
Nonlateral (first and second cousins forbidden)	51	47.6
Nonlateral (but information available for first cousins only)	14	13.0
Patrilateral cross-cousin	2	2.0
Quadrilateral (marriage with any first cousin)	7	6.5
Nonlateral (all first and some second cousins forbidden)	3	2.8
Nonlateral (first cousins forbidden but permitted with some second cousins who are not lineage members)	8	7.4
Trilateral (marriage with first cousins except lineage members)	1	1.0
Total	107	99.9

between parents of the prospective couple and brideservice are the third and fourth most common.

Service argued that among patrilocal bands the most common form of marriage is cross-cousin marriage, marriage to a parent's (or other lineal's) opposite-sex sibling's offspring. In the *Man the Hunter* survey, 59 percent of 81 hunter-gatherer societies permitted cross-cousin marriage: 33 percent matrilateral and 26 percent patrilateral (Lee and DeVore 1968:338). Assuming patrilocality, as Service did, cross-cousin marriage forces band exogamy— and supposedly alliances between bands—because all potential mates, a father's sister's or a mother's brother's offspring live in or are associated with the bands of their fathers; these will probably be different than ego's band. And, assuming that warfare was endemic to hunter-gatherers, Service saw these alliances primarily as peacemaking gestures and ways to acquire allies (Service 1962:75). But even as Service himself pointed out, it is always possible to find someone who is a cross-cousin of some kind in another patrilocal band (assuming that a parent is from that band). To say that hunter-gatherers have cross-cousin marriage, therefore, overlooks diversity in the form of these marriages; varieties of cross-cousin marriage among hunter-gatherers are summarized in table 7-5. The largest category is that of nonlateral marriage in which marriage is forbidden with any first or second cousin, but this category only accounts for half of the sample.

As with descent and residence, it is often difficult to judge what marriage rules actually mean. Service recognized this when he noted that "it is doubtful that this [cross-cousin] form of marriage should be considered truly a rule, however, for it is in large measure a construct of anthropologists rather than something conceptualized by the members of the society" (1962:67). True enough, for there are always cultural rules to get around cultural rules. Though Meggitt found that 92 percent of Walbiri marriages fit the Walbiri's stated norm (1987; see also Tonkinson 1991 on the Mardu), L. Hiatt found that only 17 percent of marriages in the Anbarra community of the Gidjingali of northern Australia fit the Gidjingali's norm (1968). In cases where there was no proper marriage partner for a woman (and Hiatt shows that demographic factors make this likely in small communities), her mother and/or her mother's brother would select a husband for her (she need only be a potential husband's classificatory mother's mother's brother's daughter's daughter; or, he should be her actual or classificatory cross-cousin—i.e., there was room for manipulation of social categories). Similarly, among the Pitjandjara, a marriage that is considered less than ideal may be made ideal by recategorizing a person's genealogical status to make the marriage come out right (Yengoyan 1979:404). Analysis of how rules are violated and how they are corrected for a particular case will give a better understanding of social organization than a study of either the rules or behavior alone.

Among the G/wi, for example, the stated rule is that a person should marry his or her cross-cousin. However, Silberbauer found that of seventy-three marriages, only 11 percent were between biological cross-cousins (1981a:149–50). Cross-cousinship among the G/wi, however, is used only as a model to express the ideal prerequisites of marriage: the potential spouses should be joking partners (as biological cross-cousins are among the G/wi), their parents should be on friendly terms, and the parents of the bride or groom should know that the parents of their child's potential spouse are reliable, trustworthy, and of even temperament. Siblings would know this information about one another, but so would close friends. Unrelated G/wi who grow up together and know one another well may call one another by sibling terms—brother and sister—thus their children would address one another as (and for all intents and purposes be) cousins. The marriage rule itself is a shorthand way of communicating the ideal marital relationship. It shows that the relationships between the parents are as important, if not more important, than the actual feelings between the future spouses. (This is also demonstrated by the many societies, especially some Australian Aborigines and Inuit, in which children, especially daughters, are promised as marriage partners before they are born.)

Today, a common explanation of marriage practices builds on observations made some time ago by Lévi-Strauss: marriages construct alliances between different kinship groups of people (and, in fact, Lévi-Strauss argued, constructed those kin groupings [1949]). Service emphasized alliance for the purposes of offense and defense in warfare. This is undoubtedly a possible proximate cause of exogamous marriage rules, but given the lack of warfare among many foragers, it is perhaps more important that affines could provide one another with physical access to resources in times of need via social access to their respecitve group. It is not odd that marriage systems among many hunter-gatherers operate in such a way that husband and wife often come from different areas (e.g., Lee 1979). Among the Pitjandjara, for example, it was preferred that a man's wife have the same totemic affiliations as he did, but that she come from an area away from the area he considers his country, although not too far away (Hamilton 1982a).

Yengoyan argued that the Australian Aboriginal section system served as a way to force people to find marriage partners from distant areas, providing links to resources in times of need (1968). Accordingly, Yengoyan argued that as tribal areas became larger and population density decreased (as a product of decreasing food abundance) section systems should become more elaborate. Four-section systems, he suggested, should be found in areas of higher population density, smaller tribal areas, and high food density, whereas eight-section systems should be found in areas of lower population density, larger tribal area, and lesser food density. However, McKnight shows that data from Australia do not support this prediction; rather, section systems are found among the rich coastal groups, and moieties among some groups of the central desert (1981). The section system also does not necessarily force people to find partners from distant areas since it does not discriminate on geographic grounds (Robert Tonkinson, personal communication, 1992; see also Berndt and Berndt 1964:59).

Marriages do establish social ties and provide close affines who can be called on in times of resource failure. However, specific marriage practices cannot be explained solely by reference to the need for alliances and resource safeguards. People do not intentionally devise marriage systems so they can construct alliances uniquely adapted to particular resource patterns. Understanding marriage, like understanding kinship, means understanding how interpersonal relations and group affiliation are constructed, negotiated, and manipulated over time. Men and women can have different goals to marriage, and thus ascribe different costs and benefits to marriage choices. This establishes the potential for competition between men and women, and among men, as well as the potential for marriage to play a key role in the evolution of social inequality.

GENDER, MARRIAGE, AND SOCIAL INEQUALITY

Jane Collier provides valuable insight into the relationships among gender, marriage, and social inequality through an intriguing analysis of three "ideal-typic" systems of marriage in classless societies: brideservice, equal bridewealth, and unequal bridewealth (1988; Collier and Rosaldo 1981). These are typified by three Plains hunter-gatherer societies, the Comanche, Cheyenne, and Kiowa, respectively. Collier argues that the different potentials for marital instability in these three types of societies—instability that is related to the groom working for the bride's family or for his own elders—organizes marriage in classless societies.

Collier begins by examining the functionalist perspective on inequality, in which it is argued that the individuals who perform the most critical service for society garner the most prestige. On the nineteenth-century North American Plains, for example, a man's avenue to rank and prestige was through warfare and raiding for horses. In so doing, a man acquired horses to hunt and to protect people from enemies. There can be no doubt that these were critical tasks. But Collier points out that it was *only men who already had high rank who had the time to go raiding and participate in activities that would bestow prestige on them.* Apparently, inequality in power preceded the formation of prestige value systems. Raiding and horse-stealing were prestigious not simply because of the need for protection and horses, but because prestigious men did them. How then, did men become prestigious? High-ranking men on the Plains apparently received their status because they had wives, sons-in-law, and brothers-in-law to work for them, to garner more resources for them, and to provide them with the free time for raiding and other activities. Collier's analysis builds upon this observation to link social inequality with the nature of relations between affines. The three different marriage systems described by Collier, however, result in different kinds and intensities of inequality.

In brideservice societies men work for their bride's parents for some length of time after marrying. In these societies, according to Collier, men normally seek their own wives and acquire them through their own actions. The wife's family can neither give nor take back a wife (although the wife can leave—and may even have her parents' assistance in this—the parents do not have the right to control the daughter's behavior). In Comanche society, men sought horses on their own to acquire a wife. (In other hunter-gatherer societies, a man may hunt for his bride's family for a year or more, but eventually move with his wife to his parents' location, or set up a new residence.) The groom is not assisted by his elders in acquiring a wife. If a wife should take lovers, her husband has no recourse except either to provide her with greater attention, take action against the lovers himself, or ignore them.

In equal-bridewealth societies, men acquire a wife or wives through the giving of more or less standardized gifts, gifts that are frequently held or acquired by the groom's seniors, his father, uncles, or older brothers (which they may have acquired from giving the groom's sisters as brides). In bride-wealth societies, the groom's seniors often arrange the marriage with the bride's seniors. Thus, the groom is beholden to his seniors and a kind of gerontocratic society can form (such as is frequently seen in Australia) in which young men must do the bidding of older men in exchange for marriage arrangements. However, the more labor extracted from men, the greater the marital instability because the groom must devote time and energy to his elders and, consequently, not to his wife. She may then seek attention from lovers or return to her family, setting up a dispute between the groom (or his seniors) and the bride's family. This potential for marital instability gives power to the bride's family and requires that the groom seek assistance from his seniors should his wife leave, further indebting himself to them.

In unequal-bridewealth societies, gifts are not standardized, can vary from marriage to marriage, and may be requested throughout the marriage. Wife-givers can extort labor from the husband (and his family) by constantly threatening to take back a wife. This marriage system is associated with social ranking, although it is hard to say how the process begins. Given a differential in prestige, a high-ranking male can refuse to give a daughter in marriage until a large bridewealth is secured or until he locates for his daughter a husband who will be unable to refuse to continue to give bridewealth. Giving a wife to this man, the bride's father can continually demand gifts and labor from the husband "on the grounds that they are not exercising their right to take their kinswomen back" (Collier 1988:233). A high-ranking male can keep his wives easily since her brothers will not wish to break their affinal tie with a high-ranking male (who may provide them with the opportunity to partake in prestigious activities). Low-ranking males, on the other hand, may keep their wives only as long as they comply with the wishes of her male relatives. Since a low-ranking male will spend time work-ing for his wife's relatives, he may provide her with little support in the household, making her unhappy. Does the wife have much to say in this? Not likely, if she wishes to have supportive male relatives in the future. Just as ranking males can extort labor from lower-ranking sons-in-law, men extort cooperation from their sisters (or daughters) by forcing them to remain with a husband who is providing her brothers (or father) with labor. As women lose their autonomy through marriage, so do their husbands also lose theirs. As others have observed, social inequality goes hand in hand with gender inequality (Strathern 1987; Collier and Rosaldo 1981; Bern 1979; see chapter 8).

Collier does not discuss polygyny, but we should note it here because of its bearing on marriage, gender, and inequality. Polygyny is uncommon among ethnographically known hunter-gatherers and, even in societies where it ex-ists, relatively few men are polygynous. In some cases, an older wife will request that her husband marry another woman so that she has assistance with domestic duties and childcare (see Rose 1968). In bridewealth systems, a man may take additional wives because they can contribute to household production. Among the Tolowa in California, wives were used to increase household stores of food. Among many Plains tribes, women processed hides for the fur trade which allowed men to acquire horses, guns, and other goods that helped them move up in rank. Polygyny may be a way for men to increase their wealth and compete with other men, but it may come at a fitness cost to women. James Chisholm and Victoria Burbank found that in an Australian Aboriginal community in Arnhem Land, women in monoga-mous marriages (including serial monogamy) raised more offspring to age five than women in polygynous marriages (1991). (Of the latter, women in sororal polygynous marriages raised a greater percentage of their offspring to age five than women in nonsororal polygynous unions.) This would seem to suggest that, other factors being equal, and looking at the problem only in the simplest terms of reproductive fitness, women should prefer monogamy. Where men control all resources, however, Monique Borgerhoff Mulder suggests that women may choose men on the basis of how many resources they can offer an incoming wife, regardless of whether the man is already married or not (1992). It is not clear, however, if this is always women's choice at work, or the choice of her male kin who may seek a spouse for their daughter/sister who can offer them access to the resources controlled by a potential husband. The cost of not choosing the right spouse could, as Collier's analysis suggests, result in the loss of consanguineal support, and, perhaps as a result, an even lower fitness (see Borgerhoff Mulder 1992 for a fuller discussion of the conditions favoring polygyny).

The ideologies of Collier's three marriage systems differ from one another and play a role in social inequality. "In brideservice societies, people credit men (and women) with forging their own destinies. In equal bridewealth societies, people perceive themselves as being dependent on the beneficent help of seniors and supernatural beings. In unequal bridewealth societies, people consider hereditary rank the most important determinant of a person's fate" (Collier 1988:232). Consequently, it is in unequal-bridewealth societies that people are prepared to accept differential rank and access to power as well as the symbols or activities granting prestige. This creates an ideology that establishes rank as the primary organizing factor of social relations and that conceals and permits exploitation (Collier 1988:242). Specifically, since Collier's analysis points out that it is wife-givers rather than wife-takers who acquire power in the marital relationship in bridewealth societies, the relationship between affines in such societies is not equal, and we may therefore conclude that there is more to marriage in hunter-gatherer societies than the establishment of alliances between two kin groups. Both groups, and all individuals involved, may not benefit equally from the marriage.

CONCLUSIONS

This chapter has examined the division of labor, postmarital residence, descent, and marriage among hunter-gatherers. These topics are all interrelated as the division of labor under different environmental conditions affects the costs and benefits of associating with one corporate group versus another; since men and women do different things, they could easily have different membership preferences. Membership in one or another group is negotiated through kinship and the structured relations it entails between individuals, residence, and marriage.

Although there is no intrinsic reason why women should not hunt as much as men do, gathering is an interruptible activity and is more compatible with taking care of a child than hunting. We might expect women's status to be high where they bring in the most food, but this does not appear to be the case. Instead, by bringing in meat from large game that, as explained in chapter 5, is shared, men have the potential to acquire the prestige that accompanies sharing, and the potential to compete. Women are rarely in this position, and this may establish a basic inequality between men and women in perceived status and may advantage one over the other in decisions about the couple's group membership.

Discussions of postmarital residence and descent point not only to the amount of variability present among foragers, but also to the fact that the terms we use—rules of residence and forms of descent—do not even describe the full range of variation. Rules of residence are related to a number of variables, but all revolve around individuals finding ways to join one group or another. For men, the primary factors may be foraging and warfare (internal versus long-distance), whereas for women it may be assistance in child rearing. We suggested that since residence is part of a process of negotiating group membership, it could be analyzed in terms of a modified version of E. Smith's model discussed in chapter 6.

Research into descent systems now focuses on figuring out what categories are used and how people go about placing themselves and others into those categories. Societies that are classed as having one form of descent may be substantially different from other similarly classed societies in how people are assigned to different kin or other categories. As with postmarital residence, descent and rules of kin relations could also be seen as both resulting from and controlling the kinds of corporate groups that exist, the potential they have for change, and the directions they take in changing. As reflections of and as part of the negotiation of corporate groups that are structured in part by foraging considerations, kinship should also be amenable to an evolutionary analysis.

Finally, we considered variability in marriage relations, finding that again, anthropologists' rules of marriage often mask the process of association. We concluded with Collier's analysis of marriage in three types of systems. From this we saw that marriage is part of the process of group affiliation and too much of this process is masked by looking at marriage only as a way to build alliances to provide networks in times of local subsistence stress. In bridewealth societies, wife-givers enter into a marriage for different reasons than wife-takers: wife-givers get labor, while wife-takers gain prestige. These different agendas result in inequality among men, and between men and women. They also limit some men's and women's autonomy. While Collier's analysis probes the nature of the three ideal-typic systems, it is not intended to account for the conditions under which these systems might arise. We turn to this question in chapter 8.

EGALITARIAN AND NONEGALITARIAN HUNTER-GATHERERS | 8 |

> When a young man kills much meat, he comes to think of himself as a chief or a big man, and he thinks of the rest of us as his servants or inferiors. We can't accept this. We refuse one who boasts, for someday his pride will make him kill somebody. So we always speak of his meat as worthless. In this way we cool his heart and make him gentle.
>
> Ju/'hoansi man (Lee 1979:246)

> You know that every time when the tribes come to our village, we always have four or five more to give blankets away than they have. Therefore, take care, young chiefs! else you will lose your high and lofty name; for our grandfathers were never beaten in war of blood nor in war of wealth, and therefore all the tribes are below us Kwakiutl in rank.
>
> Kwakiutl man (Codere 1950:120)

Ask a class of undergraduates to picture a group of hunter-gatherers, and it is most likely that the Ju/'hoansi will come to mind: small, peaceful, nomadic bands, men and women with few possession and who are equal in wealth, opportunity, and status. Yet, given the prominence of the potlatch in introductory courses, these students are also probably aware of cases that easily overturn this image: large, sedentary, warring, possession-laden Northwest Coast societies, where men boasted of their exploits and power. Anthropologists have used the terms *simple* and *complex* to distinguish these two types of foraging societies (see table 8-1; Price and Brown 1985b). Simple hunter-gatherers include band or family-level groups such as the Australian Pintupi, while complex hunter-gatherers include tribal groups such as the Northwest Coast's Kwakiutl. Complex hunter-gatherers are nonegalitarian societies, whose elites possess slaves, fight wars, and overtly seek prestige. Although complex hunter-gatherers have long been considered to be exceptions to the presumed rule, products of atypical resource-rich environments, archaeologists continue to discover evidence of prehistoric nonegalitarian hunting and gathering societies in many environments.[1] This has created a new interest

Table 8-1. Simple versus Complex Hunter-Gatherers

	Simple	Complex
Environment	Unpredictable or variable	Highly predictable or less variable
Diet	Terrestrial game	Marine or plant foods
Settlement size	Small	Large
Residential mobility	Medium to high	Low to none
Demography	Low population density relative to food resources	High population density relative to food resources
Food storage	Little to no dependence	Medium to high dependence
Social organization	No corporate groups	Corporate descent groups (lineages)
Political organization	Egalitarian	Hierarchical; classes based on wealth or descent
Occupational specialization	Only for older persons	Common
Territoriality	Social-boundary defense	Perimeter defense
Warfare	Rare	Common
Slavery	Absent	Frequent
Ethic of competition	Not tolerated	Encouraged
Resource ownership	Diffuse	Tightly controlled
Exchange	Generalized reciprocity	Wealth objects, competitive feasts

Source: Based in part on Keeley 1988.

(especially among archaeologists), in these societies (Price and Brown 1985a).

The terms *simple* and *complex* are unfortunate. Though no anthropologist thinks that the Bushmen, or Pintupi, or Shoshone are less highly evolved or easier to understand than complex hunter-gatherers, the terms do lead us to think that societies classed as simple are passive ones, and that egalitarianism is simply the lack of hierarchy (for a critique see Flanagan 1989). The word *complex* suggests that there is more going on in societies referred to with such a term. The term focuses attention on specialization of tasks and functions, an important characteristic of these societies, but it directs attention away from social inequality—also an obviously important characteristic but one whose origin is more enigmatic. While recognizing that the simple/complex dichotomy points to some important ways in which foragers differ, we will eschew it in favor of an approach that focuses more on the origin and evolution of social inequality.

This chapter considers differences between egalitarian and nonegalitarian social systems. As we shall see, sedentism, geographic circumscription, storage, population density, resource abundance and resistance to overexploitation, and enculturative processes all appear to be important variables in

Figure 8-1. A family group of Penan in 1986 set up camp, fitting the image of egalitarian foragers. The woman in the foreground, Lisim, with her son Barney (named after a helicopter pilot) on her back is making a roof for the shelter from palm (*Licuala* sp.) fronds. This group lives in a central settlement for five to seven months of the year where they grow rice and cassava. While on a trek in the forest, they stopped here for one night after the men had killed a wild pig. Photograph courtesy of Peter Brosius.

conditioning sociopolitical differences among hunter-gatherers. Therefore, this chapter calls on previous discussions of foraging, mobility, land tenure, exchange, demography, and marriage.

EGALITARIANISM

Let us first consider egalitarianism. James Woodburn describes egalitarian or "immediate-return" societies as those in which there is a short time between the acquisition and the consumption of food, individuals have equal access to resources and methods of resource extraction, and people use mobility as a method of dispute resolution (figure 8-1):

[Egalitarian] societies are nomadic and positively value movement. They do not accumulate property but consume it, give it away, gamble it away or throw it away. Most of them have knowledge of techniques for storing food but use them only occasionally to prevent food from going rotten rather than to save it for some future occasion. They tend to use portable, utilitarian, easily acquired, replaceable artefacts—made with real skill but without hours of labour—and avoid those which are fixed in one place, heavy, elaborately decorated, require prolonged manufacture, regular maintenance, joint work by several people or any combination of these. The system is one in which people travel light, unencumbered, as they see it, by possessions and by commitments. (Woodburn 1980:99)

The term *egalitarian* does not mean that all members have the same amount of goods, food, prestige, or authority. Egalitarian societies are not those in which everyone is equal, or in which everyone has equal amounts of material goods, but those in which everyone has equal access to food, to the technology needed to acquire resources, and to the paths leading to prestige (Woodburn 1979, 1980, 1982). The critical element of egalitarianism, then, is *individual autonomy* (Gardner 1991).

Many hunter-gatherer peoples emphasize autonomy in their everyday lives. The need for autonomy is asserted explicitly, and self-descriptions of many hunter-gatherer societies consist of strong appeals to self-governance (e.g., Myers 1986). Egalitarian societies are those in which each person "is headman over himself" (Lee 1979:348), where each person can achieve prestige, but where prestige should not be used to gain power over another band member. But egalitarianism is *not* simply the absence of hierarchy. Hunter-gatherers are sometimes described as being fiercely egalitarian not because they are willing to take up arms to protect their way of life (though some might be) but because the maintenance of an egalitarian society requires effort. Egalitarian relations do not come easily; they are not the natural result of the absence of stratification.

In fact, there is always a tendency for some individuals to attempt to lord it over others. In response, egalitarian hunter-gatherers have developed a variety of ways to level individuals—to "cool their hearts" as the Ju/'hoansi say. Humor is used to belittle the successful hunter; wives use sexual humor to keep a husband in line; and gambling, accusations of stinginess, or demand sharing maintain a constant circulation of goods and prevent hoarding.[2] Cashdan points out that an egalitarian ethos exists among foragers who need to share as a response to a fluctuating and unpredictable environment (1980). As we noted in chapter 5, sharing may be partly, even largely, a response to variability in foraging returns. Sharing insures future reciprocity. But in so doing, sharing creates tension as it establishes debts and proclaims differences in ability. The self-effacing behavior of foragers such as the Ju/'hoansi makes sharing easier. A hunter who acknowledges his worthlessness while dropping a fat antelope by the hearth relieves the tension created by sharing. The result is not a group of disgruntled would-be misers and dictators, but individuals who are assertively egalitarian, who live a life in which the open hoarding of goods or the imposition of one's will upon another is at odds with cultural norms.

Nonetheless, appeals to autonomy and equality by informants often contradict ethnographic reality in which some members have higher status and greater access to resources than others. We have already seen that people are well aware of, give greater prestige, and probably lose some of their autonomy to men who are good hunters. Differences in autonomy are perhaps especially pronounced between men and women. As we noted in chapter 7, social inequality is embedded in and inseparable from gender inequality. Before we consider nonegalitarian sociopolitical organization, therefore, we need to consider gender equality.

MALE-FEMALE EGALITARIANISM

Prior to "Man the Hunter," women in foraging societies were often seen as chattel and slaves, dominated by male authority in the realms of subsistence, marriage, religion, and sex. After "Man the Hunter," however, equality between men and women was emphasized, and anthropologists portrayed hunter-gatherers as useful role models for a Western society striving for gender equality (Martin and Voorhies 1975). The argument was that in hunter-gatherer society, women, through the daily gathering of plant food, provide as much (if not more) food as men do and therefore have a status equal to that of men (Endicott 1981; Barnard 1980). Even in those societies where women are not directly involved in food procurement (e.g., the extreme Arctic), anthropologists argued that their labor is still integral to the processing of resources (Halperin 1980) and that this maintains their high status (see chapter 7). Claims of gender equality in the two decades following the "Man the Hunter" conference, however, were more asserted than demonstrated through analysis. At least one cross-cultural survey, for example, shows no clear association between women's status and women's economic contribution (Hayden et al. 1986); instead, women's status in hunter-gatherer societies is highly variable. Peggy Sanday sheds light on the relationship between the division of labor and status differences through a cross-cultural study of foragers and nonforagers (1981). She found that where men and women spend a great deal of time separated from one another, that men come to think of women as being subservient to them. Sanday argues that this may make it easier for men to justify, to themselves, the control of their wives, sisters, and/or daughters. But actual domination of women by men appears to occur where men not only spend time away from their spouses, but also where the environment is perceived as hostile. For foragers this appears to be the case where men hunt large game and are away from camp and their spouses for long periods of time. It is in these cases, Sanday points out, that there is a greater male perception of menstrual blood and intercourse as dangerous. Thus, the nature of foraging activities, not the amount of food acquired, may be the significant variable (though the two may be correlated).

As we described in chapter 7, Collier found nonegalitarian relationships between men and women as well as among men in societies that some would quite readily class as egalitarian (1988). Even in that classic egalitarian society, the Ju/'hoansi, women appear to have autonomy and control only when they demand it. Nisa, a Ju/'hoansi woman, had little say in the choice of her first husband and finally had her way only after demanding it repeatedly (Shostak 1981). Ju/'hoansi men do about two-thirds of the talking at public meetings and act as group spokespersons more frequently than women (Lee 1982). In domestic conflicts, Ju/'hoansi women are far more commonly the victims than are men; the same holds true for Australian Aboriginal women (homicide in both these cases, however, is largely a male activity directed at other males). Other studies suggest that foraging women eat less meat than men (see chapter 5; Speth 1990; Spielmann 1989). Walker and Hewlett found that Aka women have significantly more caries than Aka men, suggesting that women eat far more carbohydrate, and less meat, than men (1990).[3] And, in a number of societies, women are forbidden to eat fat during pregnancy and lactation, just when they could use the extra calories, fat-soluble vitamins, and fatty acids (Spielmann 1989).

Female status in hunter-gatherer societies defies easy stereotyping, and interpreting the significance of reported inequalities in ethnographies is difficult. Since equality is a subjective category, interpretation of the degree of sexual equality present in a society is subject to interpreter bias. Male ethnographers, Leacock claims, misinterpreted relations between the sexes by applying the standards of their own culture to hunter-gatherers (1978, 1980). The early literature on foragers, especially that based on observations by explorers and untrained observers, is replete with instances of such misinterpretation. In addition, colonial governments actively sought to alter existing egalitarian relations by imposing European sexual ideology on native peoples. French Jesuits, for example, actively imposed a European, patriarchal ideology on the Montagnais-Naskapi in the seventeenth century (Leacock 1978). Diane Bell suggests that as Europeans imposed their own standards of conduct on Australian Aboriginal society, tension between men and women increased as men turned their frustration and anger on women while women at the same time sought to conform to European (Christian) marital concepts that emphasized love and permanence (1980). Sanday also found that colonialism increases male dominance in indigenous societies (1981). However, she sees this as a function of changes in resource availability and men's versus women's tasks (e.g., warfare and rebellion) rather than a straightforward imposition of European customs.

Additionally, the concept of status itself is ambiguous and difficult to measure cross-culturally. If men and women do different things, does that mean they are unequal? Do we use Western standards of equality, or the sentiments of informants? If the latter, do informants see the reality or the ideology of their society? In response to these questions, Elsie Begler suggests that we avoid the concept of status in favor of authority (1978). Authority is a more straightforward concept than status since it entails identifying who controls the activities of whom, and thus measures autonomy. However, extracting information on authority from the ethnographic record is still difficult, as demonstrated by the Australian Aboriginal case.

Woodburn argues that inequality existed within Aboriginal society because older men arranged marriages between young, uninitiated men and girls or unborn females (1980). This sets up inequality between older and younger men, but, more to the point, means that women are always under the direction of their husbands, brothers, fathers, father's brothers, or mother's brothers. Woodburn, Cowlishaw (1981), and Begler (1978) see this as the precontact situation in Australia. Begler uses several case studies to argue that this situation leads to men having authority over women. Men assist men in retrieving a missing wife, for example, but women are unable to rally support to protect themselves from violent husbands. Violence by men toward women is condoned, Begler argues, because men have culturally defined authority over women. John Bern sees this inequality between men and women as situated within Aboriginal religion (1979). It is true that Aboriginal religion values male rituals more highly than female rituals, and gives greater importance to men's increase ceremonies, but others argue that this religious superiority does not translate into *daily* oppression of women in secular life (see Tonkinson 1988; Hamilton 1980; Merlan 1988).

In evaluating Woodburn's argument, Tonkinson finds that although kinship sets up asymmetrical power relations between categories of kin (men and women), these eventually balance out and no person is in an unequal position relative to others (1988). Isobel White (1978), Catherine Berndt (1978, 1981), and Diane Bell (1980) go further, arguing that women were far more equal to men, especially in the domestic realm, in precontact Australia than just after contact (when ethnographic data were collected). White argued that men and women were partners, though women were always junior partners (1978). Men thought that they themselves played a more important role in religious life—it was their increase ceremonies that insured the growth of plants for women to collect—but White argued that this emphasis on religious life was a function of male jealousy of women's productive and reproductive abilities. Women, on the other hand, accepted secondary status in religious affairs because of the psychological satisfaction they received from the creation of life. (Collier and Rosaldo, however, found no evidence of a concept of women as "Source of All Life" in hunter-gatherer societies [1981].) White also argued that women were seen as junior partners because the age difference at first marriage could often be quite extreme. A woman's first husband could be fifteen to twenty years her senior; this age differential decreased as a woman aged and remarried men closer and closer to her own age. From several case studies, Bell suggested that women controlled many of their second and third marriages; a woman's mother also played a role in the selection of her first husband (1980). It is also possible to find instances where women were physically aggressive toward men, even beating those over whom kinship relations gave them authority; men were also obliged to come to the aid of women to whom they had particular kinship obligations (e.g., Tindale 1974:124–25).

What emerges from this debate is not that previous interpretations are in error (although mistakes have undoubtedly been made), but that there is a fundamental paradox in Aboriginal society between, on the one hand, a strongly egalitarian ethos coupled with high levels of female autonomy in daily life and, on the other, structural inequalities that favor males, especially in domestic quarrels and ritual matters (Tonkinson 1988, 1991). The Yaraldi provide a further example (Berndt and Berndt 1993). In everyday life, Yaraldi women had considerable control over their activities and decisions, and contributed significant amounts of food to the family hearth. There was equality between men and women in religious affairs, and there were no secret-sacred male ritual activities (as are found in many other Aboriginal societies). Both men and women underwent formal initiation ceremonies. The Yaraldi's *kuruwolin* or "sweetheart expedition" gave girls a more active role in selecting a marriage partner. Girls sought their mother's permission to marry, and their fathers did not give them away.

On the other hand, Yaraldi women lacked control over some situations, and were subjected to a double standard. Women acquired their status from their husband, but not vice versa. Girls who sought sexual liaisons with boys who were undergoing initiation were punished, but boys who sought out girls in the process of being initiated went unreprimanded. Men could have more than one wife and carry on affairs, but women were punished for promiscuity. Men initiated together had sexual access to each others' wives, but women were not given the same privilege.

Thus we should replace the question of whether men have higher status than women, and the search for generalizations about gender equality among hunter-gatherers, with more open-ended questions about who has authority, who has power, and under what conditions is it exercised? In so doing, we must inevitably consider links between institutional structures such as economy and marriage practices and their influence on relationships between men and women (Merlan 1988).

Brian Hayden and his colleagues have attempted to analyze such links (Hayden et al. 1986). Arguing that the effects of contact and interpretive problems would be swamped in a large data set, they conducted a cross-cultural survey of female status with thirty-three hunter-gatherer ethnographies. Hayden and his associates collected data on female status in domestic, ritual, intergroup and intragroup politics, as well as data on warfare, degree of dependence on hunting, and environmental characteristics. They found that female status is lowest in all areas of life when the level of resource stress is highest. (Resource stress was measured subjectively, and reflected both periodicity and severity of food shortages.) To explain this association, Hayden argued that in societies undergoing resource stress, population-resource balances are controlled by restraining population size. "By placing women of child-bearing age in positions where they can be easily overworked, they can be pressured by the community to control reproductive activities and infant survival" (Hayden et al. 1986:460). Thus, by seeing women as inferior to men and even potentially dangerous and polluting, males ideologically justify their control of female reproduction and production for the good of the group.

But if controlling the birth rate benefits the group as a whole (a neofunctionalist explanation) then why would women have to be controlled? The assumption appears to be that women are unable to constrain their reproductive abilities and are unwilling to harness their productive abilities, requiring men to control both for them. This seems unlikely, especially in light of the assumption that restricting population growth benefits everyone. It is also not clear from Hayden's argument why women's status would necessarily decrease under conditions of frequent and severe food shortages. It seems just as reasonable that if women's work becomes more critical as environmental variability increases, then their status should be high. In New Guinea, an island with dramatic differences in men's and women's power and autonomy, it is not at all clear if the male concept of women as polluting has any effect on regulating population density (Gelber 1986).

Nonetheless, there may be a relationship between the reliability of the food supply and male-female status differences, for Sanday also found a significantly higher number of sexual-pollution beliefs associated with societies that have unreliable food supplies. An alternative interpretation to the population-regulation argument, however, is that in situations of high year-to-year resource variability, men control women's productive activity in a way that is in the men's but not necessarily in the women's best interest. Collier has already shown how marriage practices may operate to create and maintain nonegalitarian relations between men and women just as they create and maintain nonegalitarian relations between men (chapter 7). As we now turn to the nature of nonegalitarian hunter-gatherer society, we must bear in mind that inequality among men is inextricably tied to inequality between men and women.

NONEGALITARIAN HUNTER-GATHERERS

There are only a few ethnographic examples that fit the anthropological definition of nonegalitarian hunter-gatherers; these include those who lived along North America's Northwest Coast (figure 8-2), some peoples of California (Bean 1978), the Ainu of Japan (Watanabe 1968), and the Calusa of Florida (Widmer 1988). Ethnographically, nonegalitarian hunter-gatherer societies are characterized by high population densities, sedentism or substantially restricted residential mobility, occupational specialization, perimeter defense and resource ownership, focal exploitation of a particular resource (commonly fish), large resident group sizes, inherited status, ritual feasting complexes, standardized valuables, prestige goods or currencies, and

Figure 8-2. Interior of Nootka (Nuuchahnulth) house, Vancouver Island. Note stored, dried fish hanging from ceiling, the cedar boxes for ceremonial paraphernalia on shelves, the decorated whale dorsal fin on the bench to the left. To the right, low plank walls separate family units in the house. The women in the center are roasting fish and heating water with stones from the fire. Pen and ink drawing by John Webber, April 1778, photographed by Hillel Burger. Photograph courtesy of Peabody Museum, Harvard University, no. N26744.

food storage (Keeley 1988; Testart 1982; Watanabe 1983). In contrast to immediate-return societies, Woodburn refers to nonegalitarian societies as "delayed-return" societies and thus places emphasis on resource storage—a delay between the procurement and the consumption of food (1980, 1982).

Nonegalitarian hunter-gatherers also tend to have high rates of violence and condone violence as legitimate. Warfare and raiding for food, land, and slaves were probably fairly common in places such as the Northwest Coast as well as in the interior back from the coast, even before European contact escalated this fighting (Ferguson 1983). This is not to say that egalitarian hunter-gatherers do not experience violence. They certainly do; but there are differences in the kinds of violence found in egalitarian and nonegalitarian societies (Knauft 1987). Among egalitarian hunter-gatherers, interpersonal violence tends to occur between individuals within a social group rather than between groups. Violence is infrequent, although it is often lethal when it does occur, arising unpredictably from the denial of anger that can come with the politics of nonconfrontation that typify egalitarian societies. It also frequently appears to be related to sexual jealousy and marital infidelity (perhaps especially in bridewealth societies). In egalitarian societies, people level an ambitious and potentially violent man through teasing and ridicule. Among nonegalitarian peoples, however, violence may be culturally sanctioned. The frequency of violence in nonegalitarian societies appears to be related to the degree of status differences between men, and in these societies violence often raises a man's status (Knauft 1987).

On the strength of archaeological data it is reasonable to assume that nonegalitarian society developmentally succeeds egalitarian society. If this is true, then, evolutionarily speaking, what happens to a band of "fiercely egalitarian" hunter-gatherers that makes them relinquish some of their autonomy? Why, Mark Cohen rightfully asks (1985), do demand-sharing, belittling, and berating cease to be effective leveling mechanisms? What transforms a group whose members have had their "hearts cooled" to one wherein leaders openly boast of their accomplishments and rank?

A number of variables have been cited as important to the process whereby egalitarian communities develop into nonegalitarian ones. Through a careful analysis of thirty-three foraging societies, Keeley suggested that sedentism (defined as a stay of longer than five months in one village), moderate to high food storage, and, above all, high population density are the most relevant (1988). Keeley converted absolute population densities into measures of population density relative to (terrestrial) environmental productivity. This variable is most highly correlated with measures of nonegalitarian sociopolitical organization. As the relative population density increases, so do measures of nonegalitarian sociopolitical organization. Keeley concluded that "population pressure fits very well the expectations for a necessary and sufficient condition for and the efficient cause of complexity among hunter-gatherers" (1988:404). Foragers who are sedentary, store food, and have a nonegalitarian sociopolitical organization live under population densities that are high relative to their food base.[4]

This observation by itself would strike few anthropologists as odd because these variables have long been linked together into an argument relating them to status differentiation. Some analysts emphasize resource abundance, others point to population pressure or intensification. The resource-abundance argument runs like this: in some favored areas of the world there was such an abundance of resources that people could be sedentary, raise more offspring to reproductive age (increase fertility and/or decrease mortality), collect more resources than needed with the increased labor force, store them in permanent locations, and subsequently participate in economic and prestige competition, what Gould calls "aggrandizing behavior" (1982), resulting in nonegalitarian sociopolitical organizations. Here, sedentism is seen to lift the constraints of a nomadic lifestyle, and thus release human nature. Hayden explains that this process is inevitable because it permits those men (it is always men) with inherently (i.e., genetically determined) domineering personalities to accumulate the goods and food necessary for prestige and economic competition (Hayden 1981a:527). This establishes a patronage system, for through competitive feasting these males are able to acquire prestige and goods for other members of the group.[5]

The population-pressure argument assumes that hierarchies will emerge when circumstances permit because they are necessary to resolve disputes, maintain efficient information flow about the changing availability of resources, and/or redistribute resources under conditions of stress (Ames 1985, but see Ames 1994). In this argument, hierarchy arises from stress on the subsistence base created by high population density, temporally and spatially incongruent resources, and reduced residential mobility. Johnson argues that as the number of "organizational units" increases (individuals, or family units), there is an exponential increase in the number of disputes (Kent 1989) and a similar decrease in the efficiency of decision-making; this is termed scalar stress (Johnson 1982), and there are three possible responses to it:

(1) Groups can fission.

(2) Where this is not possible, "sequential hierarchies" might appear in which normally independent groups, for example, nuclear families, merge into larger units (based on kinship or some other criteria), thus decreasing the number of organizational units and reducing scalar stress. Ritual obligations and activities may play a role in helping to hold these groups together, but they are likely to be very short-lived organizations.

(3) If these groups do last long enough, "vertical hierarchies" appear in which groups have leaders and groups of groups have overarching leaders whose primary role is the processing of information. As noted in chapter 6, Johnson identified six as the number of organizational units that require a special leader. Ken Ames argues that the organizational complexity of a logistically organized, storing economy results in scalar stress and information-flow problems that are resolved by vertical hierarchies (1985).

For others, hierarchy is not the product of population/resource imbalances or subsistence stress, but is the natural result of the intensification of production and resource storage. In this case, it is argued that a food surplus carries with it the inherent potential for manipulation (Woodburn 1982:431; Testart 1982; 1988). Surplus is generated where the intensification of production does not harm the long-term productivity of the environment (thus Hayden suggests that r-selected species will be the most likely initial targets for intensification [1990]). From a Marxist perspective, though environment and demography may play a role in kicking the system into operation, the opportunities for intensification and the subsequent production of surplus for competitive feasts feed into existing inequalities by promoting prestige competition. For some, intensification accelerates an inevitable process of socioeconomic change toward inequality (Lourandos 1985:412, 1988; see Bender 1985).

Each of these three explanations has some difficulty with it. The resource-abundance argument looks only at the benefits of prestige competition, not at its costs; consequently, it does not ask how people weigh the one against the other. People do not acquire prestige, they are given it by others (Riches 1984). Those who give prestige do so at a cost. How do they decide that it is better to elevate some members of the group than to implement another option (e.g., leaving the group)? The population-pressure argument assumes that there is a group-level benefit to hierarchies, but skirts entirely the issue of inequality. Also, it is not clear to me that high-status individuals in places such as the Northwest Coast were responsible for processing information. Given that people could apparently move from household to household, they must have done so based on information about the productive or defensive capabilities of other households in other villages. This information would have come through some channel other than one's current leader. Finally, those explanations that point to intensification and storage as leading to competition and inequality do not explain why competition exists where resources are abundant, or why intensification exists where it does and not in other equally productive areas, or why community members should not continue to implement mechanisms against self-aggrandizing individuals, especially those who seek to intensify production by using the labor of others (see the case of the Hadza below). As we saw in chapter 3, storage is primarily used by foragers to prepare for a period of seasonal food shortage; as Ingold points out, there is nothing inherent in this kind of food storage that mandates inequality (1983).

Part of the problem in thinking about the emergence of inequality is that culture areas containing nonegalitarian hunter-gatherers are often assumed to be regions of abundant resources. I think there are two reasons for this.

First, we often take the limited material culture of nomadic hunter-gatherers as a sign of impoverishment and hard living, whereas the elaborate material culture of sedentary hunter-gatherers is taken to be a sign of affluence (see chapter 1), of resource and by extension food abundance. But this is a Western interpretation of material goods. It is not necessarily the case that a lack of material goods signifies impoverishment (Woodburn 1988:66) or that an abundance of material goods signifies an abundance of easily processed food. It takes time to carve mortuary poles, and paint houses, and weave ceremonial hats and cloaks for feasts, time that could be devoted to some other activity. Is elaborate material culture a sign of affluence or a sign that the cost of the particular social relationships signified by this material culture has increased?

Second, the term abundance can be used carelessly, with little thought given to the costs of processing and storing food (see discussion in chapter 3 of return rates). The Northwest Coast, for example, is frequently cited as a region of food abundance. However, abundance here is of a very particular kind. Millions of salmon travel up some rivers each year, in a number of runs over a period of months, but each run may only last two to three weeks, and the fish can only be taken in large quantities at particular locations along a stream where spearing platforms or fish weirs can be built, or at riffles or falls. Additionally, the number of salmon in a run fluctuates as a function of fish population cycles, but also in relation to changes in river level, temperature, and sediment load (Romanoff 1985; Kew, in Hayden 1992). Thus, the resource is characterized by both temporal and spatial bottlenecks as well as annual fluctuations (see review in Ames 1994). If the fish are to be stored, they must be processed as they come out of the river, which decreases the number that can be taken (and some species do not preserve as well as others). If an insufficient number of fish are taken, the springtime will certainly not be a time of food abundance—and it often was not on the Northwest Coast. Not all Northwest Coast peoples had access to salmon streams; those that did not sought to acquire food from others (see below). Thus, there was not only an added cost to getting food on the Northwest Coast, but an added cost to keeping it as well (see our discussion of tolerated theft in chapter 5). In sum, while it is not wrong to say that food was abundant on the Northwest Coast, that simple phrase must be amended with the recognition that this "abundance" was available only at certain times, in certain places, at a certain cost, and with a certain probability of failure (Suttles 1968).[6]

Nonetheless, resource-abundance, population-pressure, and intensification arguments identify some of the relevant variables that must be considered in understanding the evolution of nonegalitarian sociopolitical organization: the cost/benefit of resource acquisition and group membership, the effects of sedentism, and population growth. To this we should add the nature of men's and women's foraging and other duties, and the enculturative process. The following is only a brief outline of a model describing the origins of two different kinds of inequality among foragers (figure 8-3), one that was anticipated some time ago by Carneiro's circumscription theory of state formation (1970).

The evolution of inequality

Brian Hayden has recently argued that the essential problem to comprehending the evolution of inequality is understanding why it exists under conditions of resource abundance (1994). He argues that "competition will occur if there exists a way to transform abundant resources into highly desired, scarcer goods or services" that is, where the "ability to produce and use excess resources could confer important advantages to individuals and groups" (1994:226–27). This would occur, Hayden argues, where resources are abundant and relatively invulnerable to excessive human exploitation (and also, where the technology for bulk harvesting is available).

In Hayden's model, neither storage nor population pressure on the resources are necessary for competition to result, although population growth and food storage may result as a consequence. Inequality between groups results from the activities of key individuals, "accumulators" who manipulate competitive feasts and who skim off some resources for themselves, their households, and entourages. Others patronize an accumulator by contributing to his feasts because they stand to acquire some of the prestigious goods that the accumulator will eventually receive in return, when he is the guest rather than host of a feast. The course, then, to inequality is charted by an accumulator's ability to organize the labor for the harvesting of excess amounts of a resource.

Hayden makes a valuable contribution here, but there are two points lying beneath his argument that need to be brought to the surface. Given resource abundance or resilience to exploitation, the key to inequality in Hayden's argument lies in the condition that excess amounts of a resource be useful; that is, they are not just excess, but can be used to increase offspring, family security, or confer some other selective advantage (see chapter 5). Hayden

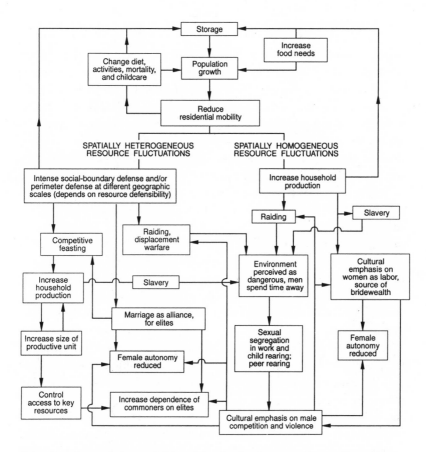

Figure 8-3. A speculative model describing the development of inequality under conditions of spatially heterogeneous and spatially homogeneous resource fluctuations. Drawn by Dan Delaney.

implies that the scarce resources acquired with excess food resources are trade goods, or the labor to construct commemorative monuments or to hold feasts. It is not clear what makes people want these goods, that is, what their selective advantage is. It is probably not an inherent lust for trinkets (see, for example, the case of the predatory Hadza below).

Second, the conditions that promote intensification of resource use are also the conditions that could promote population growth. As we described in chapter 6, population growth rates are expected to be high where there are no dramatic seasonal lows in resource availability (either because of the availability of food year-round, or because of food storage) or where resources, regardless of their return rates, are dense and rebound quickly from human harvesting (Winterhalder and Goland 1993). Nonegalitarian hunter-gatherers live under high population densities. Is this high population density cause or consequence of the way in which the resource base is utilized? The answer to this question awaits more archaeological research in those areas of the world where nonegalitarian foragers lived. On the Northwest Coast, for example, the timing of population growth, resource intensification, and the appearance of nonegalitarian society is still not clear (Ames 1994). As noted in chapter 5, however, high population density relative to the food base is probably a precursor to competitive behaviors such as territoriality and strong social-boundary defense.

Still, Hayden may be correct in pointing to the selective advantage of excess resource extraction, and the significant place of the control of labor in the evolution of inequality. These play a role in the model outlined below, but several analyses have also identified population density, food storage, and the temporal and spatial distribution of resources as key variables (Ames 1994).

I take a reduction in residential mobility, eventually resulting in sedentism, to be the significant "kick" that sets dramatic sociopolitical changes in motion. As described in chapter 4, sedentism results from an interplay between the distribution of food across a landscape and population density. The process will happen more or less quickly depending on the patchiness of the environment, and on the cost of residential mobility compared to foraging. Where resources are localized and travel difficult, residential mobility will decrease most rapidly. Increasing population density exacerbates the conditions that reduce residential mobility by increasing competition for land and hence the cost of movement.

As we described in chapter 6, an increase in the rate of population growth may be strongly linked to a reduction in residential mobility. Reductions in residential mobility increase the use of stored foods and the use of lower-ranked resources with high processing costs. An increased use of foods with high processing costs increases women's work and reduces on-demand breastfeeding which increases fecundity. A reduction in women's aerobic foraging and camp movement may have the same effect. At the same time, the use of stored foods may increase long-term energy balance and increase fecundity. On the other side of the coin, sedentism and storage may both reduce child mortality, and the increased need for labor and peer rearing in sedentary communities may decrease the cost of children and the frequency of birth-spacing infanticide. As we argued in chapter 6, population growth rates, storage, and decreasing residential mobility are linked in a self-reinforcing cycle. This could occur where resources are evenly or patchily distributed, although I suspect that the process will occur most rapidly under the latter condition.

A reduction in mobility and an increase in food storage have additional effects (and one that is exacerbated by the increasing population density they bring about). For a storage economy to operate, a high-return-rate resource must be consistently available in bulk at the appropriate time of year. But no locality is perfectly stable: there are always droughts, insect plagues, spring floods, early frosts, or vicious winters. One response to resource fluctuations is to move to another area. But if storing hunter-gatherers become sedentary through population packing, then mobility is a higher-cost response to local resource failures because other people may have to be displaced, requiring violence (or because those who move to join another group may be considered of lower rank and will have to join at lowered returns—see below). The stored resources are of little use since they are not stored for a rainy day but because they are needed for an anticipated period of scarcity. Therefore, once population reaches the point where all habitable patches are occupied, hunter-gatherers are circumscribed and warfare, or perimeter defense, becomes a viable possibility—the potential benefit (keeping what you have) becoming worth the potential cost (loss of time devoted to foraging or other activities).

This takes on special importance if we look at storing economies on a regional scale. In chapter 5 we saw that a hoarding strategy is predicted to take the place of a sharing strategy unless there is variance in the return rates of foragers and unless retaliation against hoarders is possible. If a group of foragers are situated on a productive resource that fluctuates little from year to year compared to other resource locations in the region, then there is no advantage to sharing with others—their assistance will not be needed. These fortunate foragers have every reason to try and keep as much of their food as possible—and those in less fortunate circumstances now have every reason to try and get it. Looked at in a regional context, but not simply as the practice of accumulation itself, storage carries with it the seeds of conflict. Where resources are highly defensible (concentrated in particular locales such as choice fishing areas along a river), we could expect to see warfare early in the developmental sequence of nonegalitarian societies (early, that is, in an archaeological time scale).

Storage creates a second problem if the resource to be gathered in bulk is only available in such a way that it can be gathered in large quantities for a short period of time. This appears to be the case with many stored foods (e.g., anadromous fish or migratory herd animals). The problem here is that gathering the resource in bulk may require a large number of laborers. Fish weirs, for example, can require the coordinated effort of many workers as can the rapid spearing or netting and processing of fish. The hunting of sea mammals, especially whales, requires the effort of a dozen hunters; the hunting of a herd of bison also may require the efforts of many people. Making a storage economy work, then, may require that someone coordinate and/or control the efforts of some number of foragers. Hayden, for example, argues that the limiting factor on the Northwest Coast "was not the salmon, but the labor required to procure and above all process, dry, and store the salmon" (1994:234).

Lastly, we need to reconsider the value of additional increments of food beyond that which is necessary in a storing economy. Foragers store food for an upcoming lean season but it is not always possible for them to predict how lean that season will be. An especially vicious winter, for example, can make hunting difficult, or increase the rate at which stored food is eaten, either of which could deplete food supplies before spring. It is to the foragers' advantage, therefore, to gather more than is needed; additionally increments beyond the necessary amount can be diverted into competitive feasts, as Hayden suggests, but additional increments of food also increase the probability that foragers will survive a lean season, no matter what circumstances arise. Where storage is necessary, additional increments of food beyond that which is thought to be minimally necessary will confer a selective advantage upon a population.

Our point here is that sedentary hunter-gatherers with their "abundant" resources have not had the constraints of a nomadic lifestyle lifted from them, but have traded one set of constraints for another. If sedentary hunter-gatherers accumulate wealth in the form of food or culturally defined prestige goods through trade, feasting, or warfare, it is not simply because their resource base is abundant enough to allow for such accumulation, but because the long-term consequences of sedentism require it (Bishop 1987:81).

To understand this, consider, as we noted in chapter 5, that nomadic hunter-gatherers acquire physical access to another region primarily by acquiring social access to the group living there (or to those who hold the right to grant permission to use resources there). This social access is more or less defended depending on the costs and benefits of allowing another group in: the incoming group will take some resources, but the host group knows the visitors will reciprocate in the future. The extent to which a host group can allow another group entry depends on whether they think they will need the visiting group's resources in the future, on the possibility of violence if they deny access, and on the amount of resources they can afford to share. More than nomadic groups, sedentary groups who store food may seek to maintain rights to other's resources while trying to limit the rights of others to their own. Well-placed groups with abundant and reliable resources may seek ways to assuage those who are less well-placed to reduce the potential for warfare. Alternatively, less-well-placed groups will seek the least costly ways of acquiring the food of well-placed groups; here, the cost of tendering prestige, and accepting lower returns by doing so may be worth the benefit of receiving needed resources.

If sedentism and storage occur where resources are highly localized (either physically, through their distribution, or effectively through population packing) and population density is high, it would not be advantageous to open one's social door to everyone who knocked. Under these conditions groups could benefit by maintaining access to another group's resources, but could be harmed by letting another group into their own pantry. This sets up a paradox that may result in social access to other groups taking on a different form as residential mobility decreases. Among nomadic huntergatherers, individuals maintain relations with others through trade, sharing, kinship, marriage, and so on (see chapter 5), forming individual and interlocking social networks. Although ethnographic data require further analysis, it is my impression that in the sedentary case, one or a few people maintain links with other groups, whereas other group members are linked only indirectly through these few individuals. Roughly speaking, the transition from egalitarian to nonegalitarian social forms may be paralleled by a transition from egocentric to sociocentric networks.

Thus far we have offered a scenario in which characteristics of resource distribution might encourage sedentism, population growth, territoriality, more tightly controlled social boundaries, and, paradoxically, a need to increase the labor base to exploit a storable resource. How might this situation relate to inequality in an evolutionary framework? We will look at this in terms of the simple case used in chapter 6: that of an individual deciding whether to join a group or to forage alone.

In chapter 6 we pointed out that evolutionary theory predicts that additional members can be expected to try to join a group of size N as long as the return rate from foraging in a group of size $N + 1$ is higher than the return rate from foraging alone. Likewise, those who are already members of a group are willing to include others as long as the per capita return rate does not decrease; when it begins to do so, members will try to exclude others. The question now is what happens when there is no foraging space for an individual (because none is physically available or because other groups are already foraging in all available areas) who wishes to join a group that is already at its optimum size? In this case, competition will result between group members and the newcomer. If a newcomer has no other options, then the cost of group membership can be very high and will still be worthwhile. Group members likewise have to choose between admitting another member (lowering per capita returns; we assume that the mean per capita return will still be higher than foraging alone) and the cost of not admitting the petitioner, which could include physical retaliation by him or her. Evolutionary theory predicts that individuals would not remain in a group of a given size if they acquire more utility by foraging alone or by joining a different-sized group.

James Boone borrows a model from S. Vehrencamp to predict what might occur under these circumstances (Boone 1992). This model assumes that there is a single dominant leader in a group perhaps through the resolution of scalar stress as described by G. Johnson (1982),[7] that the leader's only option is to redistribute benefits within the group to his/her benefit (i.e., the leader can skim), and that the only option of other group members is either to accept the unequal distribution or leave the group. Boone shows that the average per capita utility curve and the utility curve of the group leader are similar to that of figure 6-3, but that the utility curve of the leader predicts a slightly *larger* group size than that of the average per capita utility. In other words, the optimal group size for a leader is slightly larger than for nonleaders assuming that key resources are economically defensible by a group's leader. It is to a group leader's advantage to keep members in the group, even when it is not necessarily to the other members' maximum benefit. (Note that in the Kwakiutl speech that heads this chapter the orator is proud to have "four or five" more people to give blankets away. Also recall the discussion of Chipewyan hunting-unit size in the previous chapter; a leader of a hunting unit will try to make the unit as large as possible even if it eventually leads to increased travel time and declining returns for the existing members.) By joining such a group, a forager gives up some of his/her autonomy, for example, the choice of where and with whom to forage, and how much of a resource they can acquire—and nonegalitarian society has formed. As Boone argues, and Keeley's analysis made clear, inequality is a density-dependent phenomenon. It also occurs only where access to resources can be controlled by a limited number of people. We noted above that storage carries with it the seeds of warfare and raiding. Warfare sets up an additional dilemma in terms of group membership. If an insufficient number of people participate in raiding or, especially, defense, the entire group will suffer. Thus, there is a strong impetus for members of the group who have already decided to fight to encourage others to join. On the other hand, warfare can exact a severe toll, at the very least, in lost opportunities, but also injury, or death. As group size increases, a smaller percentage of people are needed for warfare, and more people can avoid the cost of defense or raiding and free ride on the efforts of others. This could lead to more individuals wanting to join the group since they could escape the cost of warfare and reap the benefits of a resource that current members have decided is worth defending. However, as new members join a group they lower per capita returns for everyone; current members may then have to repel additional joiners. The end result can be an escalating arms race between those who have and those who do not (Boone 1992:317).

The precise nature of relationships between members of a group depends on the shape of the utility functions of key resources. Different utility curves can produce different relations between members of a group (see Boone 1992:321). Figure 8-4 shows one likely relationship between utility and increasing amounts of a resource. This curve could help describe relations between different members of a group by pointing to the cost and benefit of a unit of a resource relative to how much of that resource an individual already has. For those with small amounts (less than A on the x-axis), utility increases proportionately with increasing units of the resource. For those with more (between A and B on the x-axis), utility increases more rapidly with increasing amounts of a resource, and these individuals can be expected to fight harder for those additional increments (perhaps taking from those with less, for whom additional increments are not worth as much). For those individuals who possess a great deal of a resource (more than B on the x-axis), each additional unit is worth relatively little in terms of utility, and they can be expected to give this up more readily, perhaps through competitive feasting. The social benefits of giving resources away may be worth more than the resource itself (see our discussion of trade and tolerated theft in chapter 5).[8]

This curve predicts that individuals in the middle section of the curve would fight the hardest for resources, and those at the bottom would fight the least. Those in the middle of the curve will hoard (demand sharing will have no effect on them), and have the potential for upward movement.

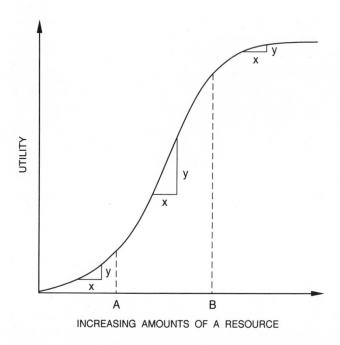

Figure 8-4. One potential utility function describing the relationship between the utility of resources and amounts of that resource. A given unit (*x*) of a resource has different utilities (*y*) for individuals who begin with different amounts of the resource. Redrawn from Boone 1992 by Dan Delaney. Used with permission from E. Smith and B. Winterhalder, eds., *Evolutionary Ecology and Human Behavior* (Hawthorne, N.Y.: Aldine de Gruyter), copyright © 1992.

Those at the top of the curve could appear to be magnanimous (and would have to do so to maintain a larger group size than that which provides the maximum benefit for group members), but are in danger of being toppled by those immediately below them. Leaders could, however, avoid this by enlisting the support of those at the bottom of the curve through distributing resources to them. Those at the very bottom have little potential for social movement, since in contests over resources they will normally lose to those above them (assuming that the benefit of a resource to an individual also measures the effort he or she can put into contests over the resource). One way they can survive is by serving leaders and accepting their largesse. The alternative is to move to another group. If leaders cannot control resources, or if resources are not abundant enough (relative to the current group size) to keep disgruntled members, and if another group is available to join, group members may leave. Recall from chapter 5 the case of Chipewyan hunting units, where leaders could not completely control access to resources, where a forager always had the option of foraging alone or joining another group, and where increasing group size decreased each individual's foraging return rate. Here, the hunting group dissolved after reaching a critical size.

So far, we have considered only the relationships between leaders and other group members. To understand relations between groups, and following the lead set by Cashdan and Winterhalder (see chapter 5), we need to consider how the spatial parameters of resource fluctuations could affect social relations. We will look only at two hypothetical situations, spatially heterogeneous versus spatially homogeneous resource fluctuations (refer to figure 8-3).

Spatially heterogeneous resource variability.   The construction of social relationships based on trade of craft items or stored food is a feasible approach to reducing risk only if the subsistence bases of those participating in the network are not all tied to the same source. Constructing social relationships as a form of insurance becomes viable only if the individuals involved will not be affected by the same resource fluctuation. As mentioned in chapter 5, the degree to which social backup strategies are useful is a function of the spatial heterogeneity of resource fluctuations—the degree to which a resource fluctuation in one region is manifested in an adjacent region. Where resource fluctuations are spatially heterogeneous (probably a characteristic of patchy resource distributions), social relationships are useful as risk-reducing insurance strategies, and we could expect to see the trade of goods or food as a symbolic indicator of social-boundary maintenance and negotiation.

But as population increases, the cost of letting in visitors also increases,[9] and social-boundary defense becomes more costly. It is likely that the number of people absorbed by a host group (through marriage or some other social tie) decreases under these circumstances. Referring again to figure 8-4, leaders could use resources—resources which are themselves worth relatively little to the leader—to establish ties with other groups (e.g., through feasting). Other group members could ride on the coattails of leaders, receiving some of the goods from their connection to other groups, and could therefore be willing to serve their leaders' interests in prestige competition.

Those individuals who gain social access to another group become the funnel through which some or all members of one group have access to the resources of the other. In a sense, these individuals become middlemen who control critical intersections in the social web (Rodman and Counts 1983).

These individuals always walk a fine line, since they must manage an image of generosity and selflessness while maintaining authority and power. That is, on the one hand, they must appear to their own group's members to be able to gain access to the resources of another group, but they must also appear to that other group as in control of their own constituents and able to guarantee access to their own group's resources. The leaders must act generously to their constituents, while encouraging them to assist in elaborate feasts that demonstrate the leader's power to others. This may be why, in nonegalitarian societies, leaders tend to boast of their generosity, an act that would be unthinkable among a people such as the Ju/'hoansi (see Ingold 1983).

Leaders who are middlemen view the maintenance of their power, prestige, and material wealth as essential to their personal well-being. This insures that, once established, social hierarchies will take on a life of their own as ever greater effort must be directed toward prestige activities such as feasting (Hayden 1990). As noted above, leaders may do this in order to acquire culturally valued prestige, but the result is that they keep lower-ranking individuals in their group and control their labor.

Once one or several members of a group recognize and accept that maintaining an actual position of authority, while fostering an image of egalitarianism, is essential to their well-being, they pursue objectives that are different from those of most group members. Consequently, decisions cannot be made on the consensual basis that characterizes egalitarian hunter-gatherer societies. Consensus-based politics "can only operate as a mode of decision-making where there is general agreement about 'the rules of the game'" (Silberbauer 1982:32). As soon as one individual becomes the window of access to another group, he or she develops objectives different from and hidden from the rest of the group; the leader aims to remain the only point of social access to another group and must therefore control the social and productive activities of fellow group members. This, by definition, is inequality, since limitations on individual autonomy are anathema to an egalitarian order (Leacock 1978; Gardner 1991).

The middleman strategy is viable only in a context in which each group tries to restrict social access, and where the members of at least one outside group need or want access to the resources of another.[10] Surplus is necessary to prestige competition, but surplus alone is not the cause of exploitation and sociopolitical inequality. As Josephides points out, the issue is not whether certain individuals produce or consume more than others, but how much they control (1985:219; see also Arnold 1993; Hayden 1994). Among nonegalitarian hunter-gatherers, what middlemen control is access to the resources of some other group of people. Since prestige is always given, not taken, the question is at what point is the giving of prestige, which may encompass working for another individual or giving goods and food for feasts, perceived to be worth what one might get in return? Woodburn notes an interesting case among the Hadza, where certain individuals sought to acquire control over other Hadza by virtue of

what they were able to acquire through their contacts with outsiders which gave them access to valuable goods and associated them with intimidating Europeans. . . . In every instance . . . in which a particular Hadza has been said to be any sort of figure of authority . . . he was someone with contacts with outsiders who was attempting to use these contacts to acquire power over other Hadza. (Woodburn 1979:262, emphasis in original)

But these individuals were not accorded prestige. Instead, they were treated by other Hadza as nothing more than "rather predatory entrepreneurs" (1979:263). Egalitarian hunter-gatherers are famous for their various mechanisms to level individuals who try to acquire prestige. Why, then, aren't aspiring middlemen in formative nonegalitarian societies leveled as well?

Individuals such as the predatory Hadza could be granted prestige where the benefit of granting prestige to an individual outweighs the cost of doing so. This may describe the process that occurred when Russian and other traders first contacted peoples of North America's Northwest Coast. Archaeological data show that at the time of contact peoples of the Northwest Coast had lived in large, sedentary villages, participated in long-distance trade, fought one another, and probably taken slaves for some time. There was a well-developed elite hierarchy in some places. The nature of the meeting of Northwest Coast and European society would have been different had aboriginal society on the coast been more egalitarian. Such a society is easier to penetrate from outside since members of an egalitarian society are pressured to not control one another (Brunton 1989).

Initially, warfare on the coast increased after contact with Europeans as villages fought to control access to European trade goods (Ferguson 1983, 1984). These goods included many things that could have been used in competitive feasts, but also many weapons that could be used in fighting, and tools that improved foraging efficiency. Through armed conflict, some groups dominated the market; coastal groups were especially able to control the trading activities with interior groups such as the Tutchone and Carrier. Those Tutchone and Carrier who were considered rich (by other

Tutchone and Carrier) were those who controlled access not only to the best fishing spots, but also access to the best coastal trading partners (Legros 1985; Bishop 1987). Given the Northwest Coast's sociopolitical environment at the time of contact, the cost of acquiring Western goods (which may have meant being subservient to a village that successfully channeled trading activities through itself) was probably lower than the benefit. Anyone who wanted access to European goods had to go through, give prestige to, and lose autonomy to those who controlled the trade market.[11]

A similar kind of social access between groups is probably achieved through marriages between lineages or kin groups. As we noted above in discussing Collier's analysis, marriage may be one obvious strategy for constructing alliances, but in the kind of marriages we are discussing here, the stakes are too high for divorce, or for the partners (male or female) to disagree. Wife-givers acquire prestige as they capitalize on the labor of wife-takers. Wife-takers, on the other hand, acquire prestige as the marriage provides potential access through the social boundary of another group. If a woman wishes to have any support from her male relatives, she will accept her husband (and if her male relatives wish the marriage to last they will try to select a man to her liking). Women, therefore, become candidates for nuptial politics, the manipulation of power and prestige associated with an intergroup social relationship constructed by marriage. The status and authority of prestigious women may be high in these circumstances, but their autonomy and power could be equally low. This helps to explain the formation of inequality that Collier took as a given in her analysis. (We return to this below, since it does not account for men's initial decision to manipulate women.)

Spatially homogeneous resource variability.   Where resource fluctuations are spatially homogeneous, social relationships as risk-reducing measures are less useful—the cost of admitting visitors is high relative to the benefit, because in times of need the host is always doing as poorly as the visitor. As we noted in chapter 5, one way to insure against subsistence risk in such a situation is for each family to restrict its sharing radius and build up personal stores of food. In these cases, individual resource ownership may appear (perimeter defense on the level of individuals or families), as may various ways to increase household productivity. As above, leaders may find ways to keep people in their household, or otherwise under their control, and accept a lower rate of return than the leader. Also, as above, this could happen where the leader can control access to resources, especially stored food, and where potential joiners have no alternatives, that is, where population density is high relative to the food base.

I suspect that in these societies, women will become valuable for their labor and for their bridewealth, rather than for their potential as players in marriage-based social alliances. Under such circumstances, polygyny may become more common as households try to increase their productivity.[12] Others have already pointed out that women's status decreases as household storage increases (e.g., Sacks 1974). To the extent that an ideology of gender domination is developed, women's lives will be controlled by men, and women's status will decrease.

An example: the Northwest Coast

Some of these propositions can be elucidated by examining cultural variability along the Northwest Coast of North America, where foragers lived in large, sedentary villages, owned slaves, participated in warfare for booty, slaves, food stores, and land, and where in some societies individuals, kinship units, and sometimes even villages were ranked.[13] (Eugene Ruyle even suggested that this amounted to incipient if not fully developed social stratification in some places [1973].) There was also a lively trade in a variety of foodstuffs and material goods such as flint, copper, eulachon oil, canoes, furs, moose and caribou hides, tobacco, baskets, hats, and mats, as well as slaves (see review in Mitchell and Donald 1988).

As a gross characterization, we could say that resource fluctuations shift from being spatially homogeneous to more heterogeneous from the southern to the northern coast (that is, from northern California up to and including the Alaskan panhandle). From south to north on the coast there is an increase in the use of fish, especially salmon (Schalk 1981). Since these are taken from rivers, this means that, from south to north, the bulk of food resources are increasingly localized (Richardson 1982), and there is a greater probability that one village's resource base is not linked to that of another (that is, resource fluctuations become more spatially heterogeneous).[14] Thus, as we move from south to north, we should see an increase in the size of the social group (sequential hierarchies) that owns resource areas, a transition from a more frequent exploitation of women as producers to women as alliance builders, an increase in hierarchy, and an increase in social alliances that are more firmly constructed and more tightly controlled.

As resources become more localized from south to north along the coast they also became more defensible. Access to a good fishing locale was critical for central and northern Northwest Coast societies. At the same time, habitable space is also more limited on the central and northern coasts than on the southern coast. For western Vancouver Island, Drucker states that:

Between the sounds there are areas of low headlands fringed in many places by long, straight beaches on which the surf pounds endlessly. It is said that anciently there were a few groups of people who lived all the year on these "outside" coasts. They suffered many hardships during winter storms when the surf was too heavy for them to launch their canoes. Eventually they made alliances with people of the sounds and abandoned the outer coasts except for spring and summer camp sites. (1951:7)

In addition, the steep terrain of the mountains bordering the central and northern coast as well as the dense temperate rain forest vegetation makes travel difficult, and, as discussed in chapter 4, would have discouraged residential mobility. Everywhere along the coast some of the critical resources— acorns to the south, salmon to the north—were labor intensive, especially for storage preparation (Basgall 1987; Donald 1985). Where fishing weirs and platforms were constructed, or where large boats had to be manned to acquire whales or sea mammals, labor had to be acquired and controlled. As mobility became less of an option in responding to resource shortfalls, the growing population along the coast became increasingly circumscribed, decreasing the cost of warfare relative to its alternatives (which might have included starvation). Labor was therefore also needed for defense of villages and raids against others, in addition to food harvesting and processing.

The model of inequality outlined above is supported by ethnographic data from the Northwest Coast. For groups on the southern coast, such as the patrilocal Tolowa and Yurok of northwestern California, marriage involved bridewealth payments (e.g., red-headed woodpecker scalps, dentalium, obsidian bifaces) and was more important here than elsewhere in California. Marriages were arranged by a wealthy intermediary and were accompanied by little ritual; the most important element appears to have been the schedule of bridewealth payments. Taking a general California pattern to an extreme, wealthy individuals in northwestern California societies such as the Yurok married their children into other wealthy families, and a women's value was judged in terms of her bridewealth (Bean 1978:677).

Marriage was primarily a way to increase household production. To choose a wife, DuBois writes that Tolowa men looked at a woman's hands to see whether they were scratched and worn—evidence of a hardworking disposition (1932). Polygyny was allowed if a man could afford the bride-wealth payments, and it permitted him to increase household production further. The bridewealth payments themselves, acquired by men through the betrothal of their daughters, trade, or direct acquisition, were also a way to increase household production, since they could be traded for food in times of need (Gould 1978:132; this was especially important for men with no wealthy relatives). There were still other ways to increase production. One was half-marriage, in which a poor man paid part of the bridewealth and then gradually paid the rest. In the meantime, his wife remained with her family. The bride's parents therefore could retain her labor for a while, some-times a long while, as well as obtain the bridewealth of any daughters she produced while still living with them. Debt slavery allowed men to work off a debt produced by homicide or some other transgression. Household production was also increased through the taking of slaves.

Though wealthy individuals could hold sway over small villages, there were no permanent tribal or intervillage leaders, and "property and rights pertain[ed] to the realm of the individual" (Kroeber, in Suttles 1968:64). Inland resources such as oak trees and salmon-fishing riffles were owned by individuals or families (Gould 1978, 1982; Pilling 1978:table 2). Resources were accumulated by and for each family (Gould 1982:75).

The Tolowa and Yurok did not engage in organized warfare, as groups to the north did. They were not free of violence, however, for revenge kill-ings did occur between villages. These were settled by intermediaries with payments of wealth objects (Gould 1978).

Further north, in the Wakashan and Salishan linguistic regions, residential groups were more sedentary, spending more time in their winter villages than people to the south. Unlike the Tolowa and Yurok, all individuals and family lines were ranked. Chiefs presided over villages and their households owned the majority of property or the best resource patches; lower-ranking people who used their resource areas had to give some of the food to the chief, who might use it in a feast. Whales that washed up on the beach belonged not to the finder, but to the chief with rights to that particular stretch of beach.

There is also an increase in the importance of the inheritance of wealth and status and more tightly defined ownership units (Drucker 1939, 1951). Among the Kwakiutl the ownership unit was a patrilineally biased bilaterally extended household called a *numaym*. Kwakiutl villages were made up of one to seven *numayms,* consisting (prior to extensive population reduction in the mid-nineteenth century) of some seventy-five to a hundred people.

The *numaym* could lay claim to particular house and resource sites, as well as titles, crests, and potlatching positions (seating places at a competitive feast). Among the Kwakiutl and Nuuchahnulth, the *numaym* owned berry fields and hunting grounds although there was some individual ownership of resources as well (Boas 1966:35–36; Drucker 1939, 1951:247, 251–52).

Wars among the Nuuchahnulth were fought primarily for economic reasons. In precontact times, if a group wanted "the territories and fishing stations of its neighbors, and if they could share in the rights no other way [they] would send out war parties for the express purpose of exterminating the intended victims and seizing their property" (Drucker 1951:333). The Clayoquot, a Nuuchahnulth tribe, drove their neighbors away, taking over their territory; other Nuuchahnulth recalled stories of fighting those who lived on inner channels and salmon streams to control fishing areas (Drucker 1951:37; Ferguson 1984:291). The southernmost Kwakiutl eventually drove some Coast Salish from their villages, taking over their lands; the Kwakiutl fought for control of salmon streams, as did the Salish (Ferguson 1984:297–98). Some argue that the Kwakiutl fought for reasons of revenge, grief, shame, or prestige (e.g., Codere 1950), but Ferguson shows that most precontact and early postcontact warfare was motivated by economic reasons, conflicts over hunting or fishing grounds, or, in times of famine, raids to acquire food stores (1984).

Marriage ceremonies of high-ranking individuals here were more elaborate than in northern California. Among the Kwakiutl, *numayms* were exogamous, and though there appears to have been equal amounts of village endogamy and exogamy (Rosman and Rubel 1971), those of the highest social rank were expected to marry a woman of comparable rank in another village (Ruyle 1973:611–12). Among the Coast Salish, rank was associated with intervillage connections, normally established through marriage (Elmendorf 1971; Suttles 1960). Intervillage marriage ceremonies were sources of tension and apprehension, and were accompanied by elaborate rituals including tests by fire and ritual battles between the two families— demonstrations of each family's power and influence (Boas 1966:57–68). Among the Nuuchahnulth, grooms had to prove their worth by climbing greased ropes, running a gauntlet of torches, or breaching a line of strong men—and this after waiting outside the bride's house for up to four days repeatedly offering the bridewealth payment. The bridewealth payment was important, but it was not the focus of attention as it was in northwestern California. According to Boas, the primary consideration in marriage was "the transfer of names and privileges" from father-in-law to son-in-law

(1966:55). Alliances were constructed between close clusters of tribes, and most warfare or violence was directed outward, toward tribes belonging to other clusters (although close neighbors were still subject to occasional violence; Codere 1990). Ferguson notes that Nuuchahnulth men took wives from less militarily powerful tribes, perhaps to establish alliances for warfare, but also to control trade with Europeans (1984:288). Through marriage and trade, the Nuuchahnulth expanded their territory to improve their salmon resources, reducing variance in the harvest by forced pooling of the returns from different streams. As evolutionary theory would predict, local Nuuchahnulth groups that joined larger federations of villages had poorer salmon streams than those in the federation's territory (Donald and Mitchell 1993).

Kwakiutl villages were ranked, with their ranks correlated with the size of their river's salmon run and, to a lesser extent, with the annual variance in the run (for those villages that had access to sizable runs [Donald and Mitchell 1975, 1994]; some 10 percent of Wakashan villages, for example, did not have access to any streams or only to streams with minor runs [Mitchell and Donald 1988]). As we would expect, villages of smaller salmon runs granted prestige to a village situated on a river with a consistently large run, since the benefit of an alliance with them would probably outweigh its cost (which was undoubtedly less than the cost of raiding or displacement). Villages situated on streams with large, secure runs could afford to hoard resources, partly because the localized fishing places on streams and food stores were defensible locations, and partly because, with low variance in runs, they received no variance-reducing benefit from sharing. They did not need good will; rather, they had to alleviate the cost of demand sharing, which in this case could take the form of raiding by people desperate for a prosperous village's resources. Streamless tribes seem to have frequently been the aggressors in efforts to displace a more fortunate tribe; upriver tribes, whose salmon supply was reduced by those living downstream, directed aggression at them (Ferguson 1984:310, 312). The competitive feasting of potlatching may have offered a way to give some people social access while compensating the host villagers for sharing their resources and relieving them of the cost of defending themselves or retaliating for attacks.

Still further north, among the Tlingit, Tsimshian, and Haida is found the "highest development of formal village organization with permanent discrete social units" (Suttles 1968:64), and the largest village size (Schalk 1981:table 2). There is a "south-to-north gradient of increasing tightness of structure and size of social unit" (Suttles 1968:64; Richardson 1982:97) on the coast, evidenced on the northern coast by the presence of moieties, with three-generation matrilineal households as the primary resource-controlling groups headed by a "keeper of the house" who held all property in trust (Donald 1985). Some Tsimshian chiefs may have held resource-collecting areas individually, in addition to those they controlled for the household. Chiefs among the Tlingit and Tsimshian were men who did not work, and a chief's status could be endangered if he undertook menial tasks (Oberg 1973:87; de Laguna 1983). Adams, writing of the Gitksan, indicates that chiefs strove to increase their household size, suggesting that the optimal household size for them was slightly larger than for those encouraged to join it—as predicted above (1973; see also Hayden 1992 on the Lillooet).

Slavery may have played an important role here. Slavery existed all along the Northwest Coast, and slaves were a major objective of raiding. Although it is difficult to judge the reliability of estimates of the number of slaves, the proportion may have been up to 25 percent in some communities, but 7–15 percent was probably more common. Mitchell and Donald show, at least for the northernmost Northwest Coast, that slaves contributed in important ways to household production (1985; Mitchell 1984). Since the optimal size of a group is predicted to be larger for chiefs than for group members, a chief might have had to coerce individuals occasionally to join, with slavery being the ultimate form of coercion. On the other hand, slaves could also be traded for wealth objects if production fell short of needs (or killed if stores were inadequate to support them); Mitchell provides a list of what slaves were worth among various northern coastal societies (1984; e.g., 1 slave = 15 elk skins among the Tlingit, 100–200 blankets among the Haida). However, slavery may even have been more common in the southern reaches of the coast where the need to increase household production was perhaps felt more keenly (Donald 1985).

On the northern coast, wars were directed to the acquisition of land and food, as well slaves, especially before control of the European fur trade became a key objective. The Tlingit and Tsimshian fought over the Skeena and Nass river estuaries, and the Haida sought to displace the Tlingit on part of the Prince of Wales Archipelago (Ferguson 1984:274). The Tsimshian expanded their territory through war, and both they and the Haida raided neighbors for food supplies. Bella Coola downstream villages were stockaded, and the Kwakiutl and Tsimshian regularly raided them for slaves. Warfare is always expensive, and it appears that as soon as European traders arrived on the scene, warfare for territory ceased, and conflict shifted to fights over access to trade routes and to the traders—the new middlemen.[15]

Societies on the northern coast displayed a more hierarchical sociopolitical structure than those elsewhere on the coast, a structure that was overtly reinforced and maintained through the potlatch. Although it was originally a variety of feasting rituals, it became greatly elaborated after contact (especially among the Kwakiutl) perhaps as a function of disease-induced population decline and an increase in material wealth from the traders. Previous ecological explanations of the potlatch focused on their role as redistribution (Piddocke 1965). However, critics have demonstrated that this was not the function of the potlatch, and, though it did result in the movement of goods, its material role in this regard was limited (Drucker and Heizer 1967; Adams 1973; Kan 1986; Coupland 1985). Instead, the potlatch was a symbolic way of establishing a man's power and prestige. He did this by holding a large feast at which he would give away or sometimes destroy large amounts of food and goods, occasionally including slaves and prestige goods such as coppers (hammered, sometimes embossed, plates of native copper), to a rival from another village. In so doing, the guests recognize the titles, status, and prerogatives of the host. The goods given away at such a feast were acquired from members of his own village, through smaller debt-producing feasts, suggesting that everyone in the village held a stake in a high-ranking man's potlatch and was willing to pay the cost of his receiving prestige.

This form of gift-giving on the coast often was met by remorse on the part of the recipient since the gifts entailed a debt which, until repaid by a larger gift, reduced the recipient's prestige. Among the Kwakiutl, potlatches were held at many different levels. The largest potlatches, those called "doing a great thing" were held between villages. These could be held for many reasons, including the giving of gifts by a man to his new father-in-law, gifts that would eventually be given back to "repurchase" the bride (Codere 1950). (Note the ritualized mechanism for terminating a marriage by the bride's family as anticipated by Collier's analysis of unequal-bridewealth marriages.) Everywhere, potlatching allowed a group to evaluate a ranking individual's authority relative to that of another village or kin group. They might then alter their allegiance, by moving if necessary (Adams 1973). The potlatch existed only on the central and northern coast, where we would expect to see more tightly controlled social boundaries between larger social units (which could muster the labor for a great display of wealth) than on the south coast. Though it created a series of escalating debts, we should note that we have no evidence that the debts established by giving gifts in a potlatch could be repaid by helping the creditor during a time of resource stress (Hayden and Gargett 1990).[16] Ferguson notes, however, that the Bella Bella Heiltsuk, a Northern Kwakiutl tribe, annihilated a Rivers Inlet Kwakiutl tribe who failed to repay a potlatch debt (1984:30). An evolutionary model would suggest that high-ranking individuals stood to enhance their fitness by participating in prestige competition, acquiring greater utility from the social relationships and prestige they gained than from the resources they gave away to get prestige, whereas commoners stood to gain more by assisting than by not assisting high-ranking individuals. One of the ways that commoners may have gained is by the reduced possibility of warfare between themselves and their guests. Adams shows that some Gitksan moved to join other households after potlatches when they felt that their leader was not as powerful as others (1973:99–106; population decrease may have played a role in this as well). Thus, Northwest chiefs probably had to walk a fine line to maintain their support while at the same time managing to build and eventually exploit a labor base.

Enculturation and inequality

Finally, how is it that social relations, and in particular gender relations, change such that women are viewed as secondary to men, as a means to increase household production, or as a means to manipulate social relations with other villages? How do egalitarian relations between men and women change to nonegalitarian ones? These questions cannot be answered without considering the effects of mobility, the division of labor, storage, and marriage, and their effects on ideology within an evolutionary framework. A shift toward nonegalitarian relationships entails dramatic changes in cultural values; from an emphasis on generosity and humility to an emphasis on hoarding and boastfulness; from values that do not sanction violence to those that do. How do such changes in value systems occur?

Though this question goes far beyond the subject of this book, we can make a few observations here based on the potential effects that the circumstances of sedentism and population growth might have on enculturation (see chapter 4). We know that nonegalitarian hunter-gatherers tend to be sedentary and to live under high population densities. We noted in chapter 4 that a shift toward sedentism may precipitate changes in the structure of foraging activities, which in turn can alter child-rearing methods from parent-reared to peer-reared. This in turn can cause a change in the modal personality from one generation to the next. Some of this shift entails changes in how people perceive one another, especially perceptions of individual autonomy and gender relations. Peer-reared children tend to display greater gender differentiation and tend to manipulate the world through social relations rather than through technology. Sanday's cross-cultural study pointed to an association of large-game hunting, a perception that the environment is hostile, and segregation of the sexes in work and child rearing with a predisposition for competition to be culturally endorsed and for women to be seen (by men) as potentially dangerous (1981). As we have seen, sedentism may establish structural conditions that encourage men's absence from a village (long-distance hunting, fishing, trade, or warfare). Eventually, as population grows, some men devote time to prestige-seeking (or giving) activities, and thus remove themselves further from their wives and children. Warfare would also take men away as well as make the environment more hostile.

Therefore, by changing the nature of the enculturative process, the advent of sedentism may, after several generations, alter a population's modal personality toward one that sees social manipulation—the control of another's labor—and competition as the primary way of achieving goals. Sanday's study suggests that this may be true especially for men, and it could set the stage for the increased manipulation of women by men.

We could also expect some variability in the enculturative process within a community that could promote continued manipulation and inequality. Children of high-ranking families will of course learn a different set of particular values and expectations. But the structure of enculturation could also influence child development. It is conceivable that high-ranking men must invest time in prestige-seeking activities, and may have additional wives or slaves to care for children. They may spend less time with their children than others in a village, children who consequently may be more heavily impacted by the more general enculturative process we have associated with sedentism. Sons of high-ranking men would continue to see competition and social manipulation as the keys to success. Low-ranking men, being limited in their resource-acquiring potential, may devote more time to direct childcare, and therefore raise children who are less inclined to competition than the children, especially the sons, of high-ranking individuals. This may leave children of low-ranking families open to exploitation by the competitive attitudes and greater initial resources of children of high-ranking men. If true, this would help account for Collier's observation that in unequal-bridewealth societies people see their fortunes in life as being controlled primarily by birth.

CONCLUSIONS

The study of hunter-gatherer societies offers the opportunity to study a range of human sociopolitical organizations: from egalitarian to nonegalitarian, from societies where men and women are relatively equal, to those where they clearly are not. We are still far from an understanding of what conditions engender egalitarianism or hierarchy, but it is certain that though egalitarianism is not a natural condition of humanity, neither is hierarchy. An evolutionary perspective sees inequality as arising from innate attributes of humans trying to maximize fitness, rather than innate attributes of dominance, and argues that inequality appears under circumstances of competition and circumscription, not only where intensification is possible.

We began with a discussion of egalitarianism, pointing to individual autonomy and a group's ability to operate on a consensual basis as its important characteristics. Individuals who attempt to rule others in egalitarian societies are quickly put in their place through ridicule or ostracism. Yet we saw that even in some of these societies there are inequalities, especially between men and women. Noting that colonial powers had some effect on the gender relations in foraging societies, and noting the difficulties in deriving status from ethnographic data, it still seems that in some societies called egalitarian, women's authority is limited compared to men. The amount of food that a woman contributes directly to the family hearth does not appear to correlate with the level of her autonomy, status, or authority. Instead, inequality seems to be affected by marriage and the relationships it creates between men as wife-takers and wife-givers, and the nature of men's versus women's activities, perhaps especially as they affect the amount of time men spend with their families. Since marriages form alliances between families, and since alliances become more or less important depending on the intensity, frequency, and spatial extent of resource fluctuations, it is logical that the nature of marriage, and consequently the nature of male-female relations, can fruitfully be examined within an evolutionary framework that focuses on the reduction of risk and the formation of social groups in different kinds of environments.

We discussed the nature of nonegalitarian societies, pointing to the association of sedentism, high population density, and storage with social hierarchies. From our discussion it should be clear that there is some variability within the category of nonegalitarian hunter-gatherers that is related in large measure to different resource configurations. This variability must be recognized and analyzed if we are to understand the evolutionary pathways of inequality.[17]

We then presented a perspective on the development of nonegalitarian societies that focused not on the functionalist benefits of hierarchy, but on how hierarchy and inequality result from individual efforts to maximize fitness. Critical here is the nature of group membership. As more individuals join a group that has achieved its optimum group size, the per capita return rate decreases for all members, so there will always be tension between members and potential joiners. If access to resources can be controlled, the cost of joining the group may be that the joiner allows some of the results of his/ her labor to be skimmed by a dominant member, lowering his/her returns below that obtained if returns were simply averaged over the entire group. Simulations suggest the important fact that in this situation the optimal group size is larger for the leader than for the other group members. We suggested that the geographic scale of resource fluctuations and the defensibility of resources could exert a strong influence over the form of nonegalitarian relationships by encouraging middlemen in some cases and increased household production in others. Both of these factors are at work in nonegalitarian societies, although one or the other may be more prevalent depending on the particular resource configuration, or may operate at different social levels. We noted that in either case, women's status could decrease as a function of men's use of marriage as a way to establish social alliances and reduce risk, or as a way to use female labor to increase household production.

Though initially rooted in resource structure and population density, prestige seeking and the resulting hierarchies could result from and be part of a runaway process (Boyd and Richerson 1985), as other individuals (perhaps those in the middle of the utility curve—figure 8-4) mimic the activities of prestigious individuals and shift cultural values to create a greater prevalence of those that emphasize overt prestige seeking. Structured by men's and women's labor, the enculturative process plays a key role in the development of the values that promote competition and values that permit exploitation and inequality. Thus, a change from a mobile to a sedentary existence can put a complex chain of events into motion involving behavioral, psychological, and cultural variables. The scenario is speculative, but it is based on the recognition that social-level phenomena are produced by a complex interplay of regional resource configurations, enculturative processes, and individual decision making. It produces a far more complex, and, from the standpoint of evolutionary theory, more satisfying picture of cultural evolutionary change than functionalist explanations. It is nonetheless incomplete, and understanding the evolutionary development of hierarchy and inequality is one of the greatest challenges facing students of hunter-gatherer societies.

HUNTER-GATHERERS AND PREHISTORY | 9

I want to talk only about proper things, old time.
Annie Ned, Athapaskan (Cruikshank 1990:323)

One of the final questions posed at the "Man the Hunter" conference was "Are the hunter-gatherers a cultural type?" (Lee and DeVore 1968:335). A generation later, we continue to ask ourselves that question.[1] It reflects an ongoing critique of our conceptual tools: what reason is there to expect any category imposed on the continuous diversity of humanity to have neat and tidy boundaries? Most recently, Harvey Feit has concluded that "a universal concept of socially distinctive hunter-gatherer societies may not be a credible anthropological category" (1994:422). Ernest Burch expressed the same sentiments (1994:452). Why did it take anthropology so long to arrive at this conclusion, one that should have seemed obvious decades ago? I suspect that there is a deeply rooted reason for the continued anthropological use of concepts of "the" hunter-gatherer lifeway, one that betrays potentially significant misconceptions of human evolutionary history.

Like our intellectual forebears, we still seem to be overwhelmed by "the fact that hunter-gatherers *appear* to be the most ancient of so-called primitive societies—[by] the *impression* that they preserve the most archaic way of life known to humanity, that characteristic of the whole of the Palaeolithic" (Testart 1988:1; emphasis added). This impression leads many sociocultural anthropologists, even those very familiar with the diversity of hunter-gatherer societies, to seek a glimpse of the past in the present. Leacock and Lee give as one reason for the study of band societies the desire to know "What was human social life like when people lived directly from the fruits of the earth?" (1982b:1). Alain Testart claims that Australian Aboriginal kinship and sharing rules ensure accurate reproduction of society from generation to generation and therefore hypothesizes that "structures and social forms analogous to those observed in Australia were probably present in Palaeolithic societies." He recommends that

if we seek to know about the past, a field of study that has never seemed dishonourable to any discipline other than social anthropology, the point of departure should be hunter-gatherers in favourable regions, hunter-gatherers who might not have been such and probably remain such only by reason of restrictive social forms that for them are quite possibly a distant and glorious heritage. (Testart 1988:12–13)

David Riches considers the possibility that his study of northern hunter-gatherer societies offers "indications as to the basis of certain fundamental institutions in an original human society" (1982:208). Tanaka is more explicit, finding it a "miracle" that the ≠Kade are "still living in the same fashion as human societies of almost 10,000 years ago" (1980:xii). Allen Johnson and Timothy Earle use the Ju/'hoansi and Great Basin Shoshone as analogues for hominid life of the Lower and Middle Paleolithic (1987:55). (Similar views are adhered to much more tenaciously by the public, with less sophisticated reasoning and much less knowledge of ethnography.)

None of these authors would argue that living hunter-gatherers are relic populations untouched by the passage of time. Instead, they would argue that the living conditions of modern hunter-gatherers (small nomadic groups living exclusively by foraging) replicate conditions of the past and that the lifeway of modern foragers is largely structured by these conditions. If the nature of modern foraging lifeways is a product of living conditions, and if those conditions replicate those of the past, then modern foragers should more or less resemble prehistoric ones. Thus, despite pleadings to the contrary, some anthropologists persist in viewing living foragers as our Paleolithic ancestors, although they would admit that the window through which we view them is foggy and cracked. This approach to living foragers is far more sophisticated than that of the nineteenth-century evolutionists, but the end result is not very different.

Archaeology is a difficult route to knowledge of the past—especially to knowledge of past hunter-gatherers, who leave few remains behind—so it is perhaps forgivable that these social anthropologists bypass archaeology altogether and turn instead to the familiar fallacy of analogy. In so doing, they seek to reconstruct an original human society by finding conservative societies that have preserved their prehistoric social organizations, or by subtracting the effects of colonialism from hunter-gatherers encapsulated by the expanding world system, and by attempting to distill the diversity among ethnographically known hunter-gatherers into its essential characteristics.

Why would anthropologists do this? I suspect the primary reason is the idea that the great diversity of human social life stems from one original social form, the hunter-gatherer stage, the developmental period in which, as many textbooks point out, humans have spent 99 percent of their existence. Human societies are usually seen as evolving from what is variously termed an "unspecialized" or "generalized" hunter-gatherer society (one that used to look like the Aranda, today looks like the Bushmen, and tomorrow may probably look like the Ache). This is a time-honored tradition in anthropology (see Kuper 1988).[2] But it is time to move on.

We do not know when and where human society or culture as we know it originated (partly because we don't know how to identify it at its earliest occurrences). Those who allude to the importance of modern foragers in reconstructing an original primitive society do not specify when or where it is to be found. Humans have existed as a separate evolutionary line for some five million years.[3] Paleontologists currently debate whether biologically modern humans arose in Africa, and then spread throughout the globe, replacing or mixing with existing hominid populations, or whether there were several centers of development linked by gene flow. But we do know that biologically modern humans do not appear until sometime in the last 120,000 years—long after earlier hominids had established themselves in Europe, Africa, and Asia.

We also do not know if the appearance of biologically modern humans also signals the appearance of *behaviorally* modern humans. Given that foragers have diverse adaptations to their environments it is difficult to pinpoint one archaeological signature—elaborate burials, for example, or art or complex tools—as the fingerprint of behaviorally modern humans. This issue aside, however, behaviorally modern humans probably also appeared sometime in the last 120,000 years, and certainly by 40,000 years ago. By this date, and regardless of whether humans arose in Africa or somewhere else, humans were living in much of Africa, Europe, Asia, and Australia.[4] Thus behaviorally modern humans had lived and evolved for at least 40,000 and perhaps 120,000 years in a variety of habitats under a variety of ecological and demographic conditions—from the tundra of Pleistocene Europe to the forests of southeast Asia and the shores of Australia. When in this vast expanse of time and space is the original human society to be found?

Perhaps we should look to an earlier time, a time before the appearance of biologically and behaviorally modern humans, a time before our ancestors trekked out of Africa. Using archaeological and paleontological data, Robert Foley demonstrates substantial differences between pre-*Homo sapiens* hominids and modern humans in biological and behavioral attributes (1988). Among early hominids, child growth and maturation were more rapid, home ranges were smaller, and meat was perhaps acquired primarily through scavenging rather than hunting. There is no good evidence for home bases or, thus, for sharing, and one million or more years of remarkable uniformity in hand-axe and pebble-tool technology across three continents (Europe, Asia, Africa) speaks to substantially different mental capacities and behavioral attributes of pre-*sapiens* hominids. Replacement of one species by another (such as the replacement of Neandertals by modern humans some 40,000 years ago in Europe) also points to considerable adaptive differences that permitted competitive replacement. Foley concludes that "early hominids were neither human nor hunter-gatherers" and that "modern hunter-gatherers do not necessarily represent the basal hominid way of life, as was suggested in the 'Man the Hunter' conference" (1988:215, 220). There is little doubt that the Australopithecines and early members of the genus *Homo* were not cultural in the sense that we understand the term. What they were is still much in question, but it is clear that the extension of analogies from living foragers to our most ancient ancestors is certainly inappropriate, and even simple extensions of theoretical premises based on modern foraging may be inaccurate.

Beyond this, Foley explores evolutionary changes that occurred after the appearance of modern humans. Upper Paleolithic humans, for example, were larger and more sexually dimorphic than later, post-Pleistocene humans. Relating this biological difference to male reproductive strategies and the division of labor, he concludes that "What we think of as modern hunting-gathering is a largely post-Pleistocene phenomenon. Rather than being an adaptation ancestral to food production, it is a parallel development" (1988:219). It appears that analogies from living foragers cannot be extended back any time at all. Each chapter of this book has demonstrated variation among ethnographically known hunter-gatherers, variation that can be related, in large part, to environment and demography. If humans lived in various environments, then we can expect them to have lived in various kinds of hunter-gatherer societies.

We must conclude that there is no original human society, no basal human adaptation: studying modern hunter-gatherers in order to subtract the effects of contact with the world system (were that possible) and to uncover universal behaviors with the goal of reconstructing the original hunter-gatherer lifeway is simply not possible—because that lifeway never existed. We should accept it as highly possible, even likely, that modern diversity stems from original diversity in the foraging adaptations of behaviorally modern humans. Recalling the analogy of the founder effect in biological evolution, these different adaptations might have laid the foundations for regional histories of the world, providing a framework within which people developed specific cultural solutions to the challenges of increasing population, contact with other peoples, and environmental changes. As Adam Kuper states:

Even if some very ancient social order could be reconstituted, one could not generalize it. If it is useful to apply evolutionary theory to social history, then it must direct attention to variation in adaptation to all sorts of local circumstances, and so to diversification. Surviving hunter-gatherers certainly do not conform to a single organizational type. Since ecological variations constrain social organization, especially where technology is simple, there must have been considerable differences in social structure between the earliest human societies. (1988:7)

If constructing an image of the original human society motivated attempts to reduce variability in analyses of living foragers, we must go on to ask why anthropologists (and many nonanthropologists as well) wished to do this? Like the Enlightenment social philosophers before them, anthropologists have continued to seek human nature, to discover the traits that lay the foundation for all humankind. This is a worthy enterprise; indeed, it lies at the heart of anthropology and has stimulated much of our research. But despite our rejection of nineteenth-century cultural evolutionism, we have apparently found it hard to abandon the sense that evolution is additive, that the passage of time and changes in social organization have built upon a core of human nature. And so, many anthropologists have been "led to live and work among the hunters because of a feeling that the human condition was likely to be more clearly drawn here than among other kinds of societies" (Lee and DeVore 1968:ix). No social scientist today would say that members of industrial society are more evolved than modern foragers. But we can still hear echoes in the ideas that the material trappings of industrial society and the lust for those material trappings have removed us from our true human nature. So the ghosts of Spencer, Hobbes, and Rousseau persist: hunter-gatherers have been thought to display human nature unfettered by the addi-

338   THE FORAGING SPECTRUM

tions of evolution. By implication, they have witnessed no evolution, no history. Clearly, we can now agree that this is wrong.

Whether there is such a thing as human nature is not a question I am prepared to debate here. Instead, I wish only to point out that there is no reason to suppose that human nature will be drawn more clearly in modern foraging societies than among modern industrial societies. There is additionally no reason to suppose that as we go backward in time to an alleged original human society (even if it did exist) that human nature would become more apparent. Belief in an original human nature is what leads some anthropologists today to explain allegedly common behaviors—everything from warfare to divorce rates—as a product of our genetic heritage, fixed in the distant past by a common selective environment inhabited by early hominids. But humans have lived in many different selective environments; just as there is no one original human society, there is no one original selective environment.

Foragers, past and present, live under specific environmental and social conditions and within particular historical trajectories, as do all peoples. The variability present among living and ancient foragers demonstrates that, as a group, foragers are no more representative of human nature than any other kind of people. They can be used to support any image of human society; generous or greedy, violent or peaceful, monogamous or polygamous, attentive or aloof to children, and so on. This does not mean that the study of foragers has nothing to say about human nature; it is to say, however, that we cannot discover what is common among humans without understanding what is variable. To do otherwise is to simply assume, as the early evolutionists did, what we are trying to discover.

Archaeologists are perhaps even more susceptible than social anthropologists to the urge to create a hunter-gatherer stereotype (and I include myself among the guilty). Given the usually impoverished nature of the archaeological remains of hunter-gatherer societies, especially those of the Pleistocene, archaeologists understandably are tempted to look elsewhere for ways to reconstruct the past. We commonly justify a reconstruction of a prehistoric hunter-gatherer society not by demonstrating the existence of a trait through analysis of archaeological data, but by reference to ethnographic analogy or by appealing to how common it is ethnographically.[5] Like many anthropologists before us, we assume that the widespread occurrence of a trait is a sign of its antiquity. Instead of claiming that widespread traits are the most ancient ones, as Service, Speck, and other early twentieth-century anthropologists did, we argue that some traits are widespread because they are "adaptive" to hunter-gatherer society and therefore to be expected in all cases, present and past. The result is the same. We have already pointed out that our notions of adaptation have frequently been incorrect, and that the prevalence of a trait today could be a product of the prevalence of specific causal conditions among the world's current hunter-gatherer peoples, a product of contact, or life in environments with low return rates or highly variable resources. This theoretical issue aside, we rarely even demonstrate exactly how common a trait is. Appeals to the frequency of a trait, in fact, usually mean that it is found among the Ju/'hoansi, or some other group that closely approximates what the archaeologist *already supposes* the prehistoric case to have been like. The prehistoric past thus begins to look the same everywhere, that is, like the current generalization of ethnographically known hunter-gatherers. We have built up remarkably detailed pictures of early human society complete with family bands of twenty-five people who share food, trace kin relations bilaterally, reside bilocally, eat a generalized diet with women gathering plant food and men hunting, build alliances through monogamous marriage, and regulate their population to avoid environmental degradation. But this detailed picture comes not from archaeological evidence as much as from ethnographic analogy. Such misuse of modern hunter-gatherer research provides spurious support for the idea of a single primitive human society, a uniform hunter-gatherer sociocultural stage. If prehistoric hunter-gatherers all look the same in anthropological literature, it is because we supposed them to be that way from the outset.

Does this mean, then, that archaeologists should reject the creative use of ethnographic data? Of course not. But the translation of information from ethnography to archaeology cannot be direct. Nearly twenty years ago, Martin Wobst warned archaeologists of how ethnographic data, with its wealth of details unrecoverable through archaeology, could "tyrannize" archaeologists by lulling us into envisioning the past before we excavate it (1978). Ethnographic data can, if we let it, limit our ability to recognize unknown prehistoric forms of organization associated with hunting and gathering. Modern hunter-gatherers differ from prehistoric ones not only because they interact with multinational corporations and colonial governments, but because they may and probably have changed for a variety of other reasons (e.g., environmental change or internal social dynamics). The question is not whether change has occurred, but how much and what kind. Even if a pristine, isolated, uncontacted group of hunter-gatherers were found (and there are none), it could not be used as an analogy to reconstruct prehistory. Even if we could take a time machine to Europe or East Africa of 15,000 B.C.—when hunters did indeed live in a world of hunters—the resulting ethnography could not necessarily be projected backward to Europe of 25,000 B.C., or forward to North America of 8,000 B.C. To search for *the* set of conditions under which hunter-gatherers live is irrelevant. The many prehistoric hunter-gatherer societies of the past lived under many different conditions—just as those of the present do.

What, then, is the relationship between the behavioral data of ethnography and archaeological research? To answer this question we must first consider the phenomena archaeology can study. For the most part, archaeology is concerned with explaining cultural behavior as it is manifested over long spans of time. No other discipline has as much time and space at its disposal. Archaeology covers the time from before we were human until the present, from Greenland to Tierra del Fuego. This is archaeology's strength. Its weakness, however, is that the archaeological record is too coarse-grained, for the most part, to record individual events. We often record the past in 1,000- to 10,000-year slices; at best, we see what happened in 25- to 100-year bits. This is a time scale completely different from ethnography, where a 10-year project constitutes a long-term study. Ethnographies record the behavior of individuals, a capacity that is beyond the techniques of archaeology today (and in the foreseeable future). As Michael Jochim puts it, "ethnographies give us brief, individual snapshots, whereas the archaeological record represents fragments of the entire family album" (1991:315). A fundamental difference in time scales precludes the easy transfer of models from ethnography to archaeology.

However, though archaeology may not be able to see the material effects or cultural musings of a lone forager, to understand large-scale changes in foraging strategies—changes from dependence on meat to dependence on plants, or from hunting and gathering to farming—we must understand how that lone forager made decisions. Coarse as it may be, the archaeological record was nevertheless produced by the behavior of individuals. Human cultural evolution is the outcome of millions of decisions involving, among other things, food, mates, kin, non-kin, land, prestige, reputations, spirits, and the cosmos. The results of the decision-making process created diversity in the past and continue to create diversity in the world today. Ethnographic research provides archaeology with an understanding of the daily, on-the-ground, decision-making behavior that is the ultimate source of the archaeological record (leaving aside the effects of natural processes). Our task is to ask, what role do ecological, social, biological, and cultural variables play in decisions? How do hunter-gatherers—indeed, people—decide whether calories, protein, or something else, is the criterion with which to rank foods? How do they decide to share with someone, to let someone into their territory, to move, or to raise a newborn? How do they decide whether to participate in a feast that will garner prestige for someone else?

I am, of course, sympathetic to the use of ethnographic data in reconstructing the past. I am sympathetic to it because if people hunt and gather, and if interaction with the environment exerts any kind of influence over their lifeways, then how living people make decisions should bear some resemblance to how people in the past made decisions as well. This does not mean that living peoples are identical to those of the past, but it does assume that living foragers operate under the same general evolutionary principles as did prehistoric hunter-gatherers, albeit under some new conditions and constraints and different historical circumstances and cultural particulars.

There is no doubt that all living and recent hunter-gatherer societies today are structured in part, perhaps in large part, by interaction with non-hunter-gatherer societies. It would be foolish to apply a model drawn from these societies in a wholesale fashion to prehistory. But it would be equally foolish for archaeologists to ignore the characteristics of these societies because they are contact-induced. Living in the midst of agrarian and industrial societies, sometimes for hundreds of years, modern hunter-gatherers make culturally informed decisions about where to move, when to move, whether to work for wages or not, whether to store food or not, whether to give something away, or hoard it, to arrange a marriage or not, to eat this, that, or something else, to buy food or forage for it, to stay near a village or move away from it, to have children or not. Whenever they make these decisions, they provide archaeology with food for thought. Ethnology should help archaeologists construct more accurate models of the past, models whose success or failure will not depend on ambiguous or inappropriate assumptions, and which therefore will be more accurate tests of hypotheses about prehistory. To borrow Lévi-Strauss's phrase, ethnological data are, for archaeologists, "good to think." We cannot extrapolate from images, descriptions, or statistical generalizations about modern hunter-gatherers to the past. We can, however, use theoretical arguments, tested against ethnological data, to derive expectations for prehistoric hunter-gatherer behavior, given what we reconstruct as their environment and what we think are the evolutionary principles guiding human behavior.

Archaeological models invariably must contain some assumptions about hunter-gatherer behavior, such as whether or not they share, how they forage, and so on. Investigating the sources of variability in how these decisions are made among modern hunter-gatherers allows us to test more accurate models given the anticipated constraints and conditions of the archaeological case (for example, a knowledge of changes in resource distribution based on paleoecological reconstructions). This means specifying the sources of sociocultural variability, rather than searching for generalizations about societies based on gross subsistence or social categories. The ethnographic record is fertile ground in which to develop hypotheses that can then be tested with archaeological data or to test ideas about behavior that cannot be recorded archaeologically, providing justification for their inclusion as assumptions of archaeological models. Inclusion of a behavioral trait must be based on more than its prevalence among ethnographically known hunter-gatherers. For example, a group size of twenty-five is fairly common ethnographically, but it is Winterhalder's demonstration—that a group of twenty-five balances a concern with local resource overexploitation with a concern for minimizing the probability that no one brings home any food—that permits us to use twenty-five as a minimal group size in archaeological models (*if* we can assume food sharing). Winterhalder's argument still needs to be tested against ethnological data, but it is the sort of study that could be of significant benefit to archaeology.

This is different from ethnographic analogy, or, at least, it is a more powerful and secure use of analogy. The variability present in ethnographic data provides us with the information needed to see how human cultural behavior changes in relation to other variables, both internal and external to societies. Understanding how subsistence decisions are made under different conditions allows us to construct a range of competing models to explain prehistoric subsistence change, such as the transition to agricultural economies. We could anticipate different kinds of hunter-gatherer societies depending on, for example, population density, storage, resource characteristics, and the temporal and spatial parameters of resource fluctuations.

Although the archaeology of hunter-gatherers is beyond the scope of this book, understanding the sources of the variability present in ethnographic data will allow us to develop more accurate methods of reconstructing the past. Archaeologists continually try to develop methods, often referred to as middle-range theory, that relate material remains to the behavior that produced them. In this way, we seek signatures of particular kinds of behavior. For example, archaeologists try to use spatial distributions of debris or hearths to reconstruct group size or the length of time a site was occupied. Likewise, the treatment of faunal remains by living peoples can be used to develop methods to sort out hunting, scavenging, and the activities of non-human predators, and to recognize the signs of meat sharing, butchering, and storage. However, since we know that hunter-gatherer behavior can be highly variable, we can also expect hunter-gatherer societies to produce a great variety of archaeological remains, meaning that there are no simple material signatures of behavior. The archaeological remains from hunting can be highly variable depending on whether the population sees meat as primarily a source of calories or protein, on whether they store food or not, or on how meat is shared (this is in addition to the variability that is related to differences in the animal itself, e.g., mobility, size, or fat content).

Lewis Binford has repeatedly argued that methods of interpreting archaeological remains cannot be divorced from an understanding of the variability in hunter-gatherer behavior. He has shown, for example, that the criteria for recognizing residential sites archaeologically—the amounts and kinds of debris left behind as well as the type of housing used—depend on whether a group of hunter-gatherers is more mobile residentially or logistically (Binford 1980, 1990). As described in chapter 4, the organization of group and individual movement is predicated on ecological and demographic variables. Thus, the construction of methods to make inferences from archaeological remains is inextricably linked to an understanding of the variability in behavior. One cannot reconstruct the past without simultaneously trying to explain that past.

We need then, to look at hunter-gatherer prehistory in terms other than broad typological categories such as generalized versus specialized, simple versus complex, storing versus nonstoring, or immediate versus delayed return. Our approach must allow us to continually expand our knowledge of the diversity of human behavior, for ethnographic data undoubtedly record but a limited range of all the ways hunter-gatherers make their lives. We need to approach archaeology not with the goal of assigning a site or time period to a particular typological pigeonhole, but with the intention of reconstructing different cultural elements—diet, mobility, demography, land tenure, social organization—as best we can, then assemble them, like piecing together a jigsaw puzzle with no picture on the box.

If this sounds difficult, it is; but it frees us from the error of uncritical analogy, from the error of seeing all hunter-gatherers through the lens of some imaginary original human society. It leaves us free to discover unanticipated organizational forms associated with prehistoric hunting and gathering, forms that may be related to ecological conditions that no longer exist, or to interaction with kinds of societies that no longer exist, or, for premodern humans, to cognitive capabilities that humanity left behind or expanded on long ago. In approaching the study of modern and prehistoric hunter-gatherers from an explicitly evolutionary theoretical framework, we will continually add to our knowledge and understanding of the development and diversity of humanity. And that, after all, is the reason we do anthropology.

NOTES

CHAPTER 1. HUNTER-GATHERERS AND ANTHROPOLOGY

1. The term *!Kung* has been used extensively in publications on hunter-gatherers since 1965. There has always been some debate over whether this term is the correct one to use, and Richard Lee, the primary ethnographer of the !Kung, has recently elected to use the term *Ju/'hoansi,* which seems to be the term that the people, referred to as !Kung for many years, prefer. Therefore, the term *Ju/'hoansi* (and Lee's choice of spelling) will be used in this book.

2. See Barnard 1983; Arcand 1988; Burch 1994; Hamilton 1982b; Myers 1988b.

3. For a discussion of the role of cosmology and religion in aboriginal land-claims cases, see Wilmsen (1989b,c) and Layton (1986), in subsistence ecology and ideology see Mosko (1987) and Bird-David (1990, 1992a,b), and in individuals' negotiation of cultural precepts in light of changing ecological and social circumstances, see Ridington (1987), Tanner (1979), Sharp (1981), and Myers (1988a:274–75).

4. Bettinger argues that this led to the importance of environmental explanations of hunter-gatherer society (1991).

5. Henry Maine and Lewis Henry Morgan were practicing lawyers. Their interest in primitive society was perhaps stimulated by European colonialism and American expansion (Kuper 1988). Colonial governments had to decide what rights

indigenous peoples of Africa, India, and the New World had to the land and raw materials that colonial powers wanted. Since these people were viewed as being evolutionarily "behind" Europeans, those in legal professions were forced to think about the nature of "early" forms of property ownership. It is not surprising that notions of property figure prominently in early evolutionary schemes.

6. This was not evolution in the Darwinian sense as it did not incorporate natural selection operating upon cultural variability to produce differential transmission of cultural values, norms, etc. over time.

7. A variety of other theoretical assumptions permitted the alignment of cultures into a sequence, e.g., Spencer's homogeneous-heterogeneous principle (heterogeneous societies were more advanced than homogeneous ones; this of course required defining what a society was—larger ones will be more diverse) or Tylor's assumption that language was conservative, especially kin terminologies.

8. Although only three of the nine hunter-gatherer societies Steward considered could be labeled patrilineal bands (1955).

9. In general, indigenous peoples call themselves by terms that reflect *their* divisions of social reality. These often do not meet the social divisions that *anthropologists* find handy. The terms *Eskimo* and *Inuit* are today politically loaded ones, and can be confusing. I follow E. Smith's (1991) usage: *Eskimo* refers to those who speak an Eskimo language such as Yupik and who live in western and southern Alaska or parts of Siberia. *Inuit* (singular, *Inuk*) is a self-referential term used by speakers of Inupiaq or Inuttitut who live in the high Arctic, from northwestern Alaska through Greenland.

10. One could say Radcliffe-Brown willfully ignored variability, for example, when he ignored the presence of non-Aranda-type marriage customs among the Aranda (Rose 1988:195).

11. Patrilocal postmarital residence was emphasized at the conference, but the message of several influential papers (e.g., Damas 1968; Helm 1968) was the importance of bilocal residence (usually following a period of brideservice during which residence was matrilocal or uxorilocal).

12. Nearly every introductory textbook written since 1968 regards hunter-gatherers as living near-perfect lives (a belief that has spilled over into the popular press; supermarket tabloids, for example, still occasionally hail the virtues of "caveman" diets).

13. In this regard archaeology drew upon work from ecology and economics, especially Esther Boserup's population-pressure theory of the origins of agriculture (1965). But I suspect it was the new model of the foraging lifeway that made Boserup's theory so attractive to archaeology since it fit so well with the characterization of foragers as affluent.

14. It is easy to see that Lee's definition of work was unintentionally derived from Western notions of work: it is what people do away from home. It is also easy to see that how one defines work can dramatically alter overall estimates of la-

bor input. Allen Johnson, for example, found that depending on which definition he used, the Machiguenga worked anywhere from 2.5 to 8 hours a day (1975). It is best to break the nebulous category of *work* down into specific activities (see, e.g., R. Bailey 1991:43).

15. It is also clear that subarctic and Arctic peoples have a hard life, dangerous at times, and always with a heavy workload (J. Smith 1978; Rasmussen 1931:134–39).

16. On undernourishment see Howell 1986; Stini 1981. On seasonal fluctuations, see Wilmsen 1978, 1986; Hausman and Wilmsen 1985; Hurtado and Hill 1990; Speth 1990; Spielmann 1989; see chapter 6.

17. See Ember 1978; Ferguson 1984; Knauft 1987; Mitchell and Donald 1985; Swadesh 1948; Warner 1931.

18. Eugene Hunn notes that the ethnographic atlas (Murdock 1967) undercounts the contribution of plant food, demonstrating this point by comparing Plateau subsistence reconstructed from ethnographic data to the atlas's codes (1981). Nonetheless, plants are still not a significant part of diet for many people who live at high latitudes.

19. The "correct" term for the hunter-gatherer Khoisan peoples of southern Africa changes constantly as terms take on new meanings in the politically charged atmosphere of this region. At one time, *Bushmen* and *San* were used freely, but were dropped in favor of *Basarwa* (Basarwa is a made-up term, coming from *Mosarwa* but, by changing the prefix *Mo* to *Ba* linguistically avoids connotations of inferiority). However, this term too has been dropped recently in favor of the previous one, Bushmen (Robert Hitchcock, personal communication, 1993). Though it will no doubt change again, I will use it here.

20. See Abruzzi 1980; Bahuchet and Guillaume 1982; Bailey et al. 1989; Bailey and Peacock 1988; Griffin 1984; Hart and Hart 1986; Headland and Reid 1989; Hoffman 1984; J. Peterson 1978.

21. Richard Grinker has recently produced the first thorough ethnography of the relationships between a tropical foraging group, the Efe, and their horticultural neighbors, the Lese (1994).

22. Though it is true that no tropical forest hunter-gatherers live without trading with other societies, and though some of these groups may have been doing so for centuries, it is not axiomatic that it is impossible to live by foraging in the tropical forest without non-hunter-gatherer neighbors (see, e.g., papers in Headland and Bailey 1991).

23. This raises the intriguing question of whether hunter-gatherers existed in the interstices or along the edges of prehistoric state polities, as, for example, in northern Mexico (W. Taylor 1972), and if people who live largely as hunter-gatherers will be with us for some time to come as groups that opt out of the dominant social order and occupy empty niches (see Feit 1982; Asch 1982; Bird-David 1988).

24. The term was made popular by Richard Fox (1969). See Seligmann and Selig-

mann 1911; Headland and Reid 1989; Schrire 1980, 1984a; Gordon 1984; Denbow 1984; Parkington 1984; Wilmsen 1983, 1989a,b,c.

25. Some of the most insightful and important literature on the inequalities forming between the descendants of foraging populations and colonial powers, and within indigenous populations, comes from Australia (see, e.g., Altman 1989).

26. Wilmsen may have overstated his case; see responses by Harpending 1991; Kent 1992; Lee 1992; Lee and Guenther 1991, 1993; Silberbauer 1991; Solway and Lee 1990.

27. Marx argued that capitalism contained an inherent contradiction. The value of a product was correlated with the amount of labor that went into it. As labor was reduced to increase efficiency in order to compete, products declined in value as did the overall profit in the system. Marx deduced that capitalist organizations would respond by subsuming others, thus becoming larger in size but fewer in number. They would also respond, Marx argued, by shifting production to cheaper labor markets and extend their influences to distant areas, incorporating many noncapitalist societies, including foraging societies, into a world economic system. (However, hunter-gatherers did not have to wait for the appearance of capitalism to be incorporated into distant economic systems.)

28. See also R. Bailey 1991:2; C. Ember 1978; M. Martin 1974; E. Smith 1991:4–5; Winterhalder and Smith 1981:4.

29. E.g., Altman 1987; R. Bailey 1991; Meehan 1982; O'Connell and Hawkes 1981, 1984; E. Smith 1991.

CHAPTER 2. ENVIRONMENT, EVOLUTION, AND ANTHROPOLOGICAL THEORY

1. Shortly after Wissler's study was published, Davidson, who had read Wissler's work closely, published a similar study of Australian Aboriginal culture areas (1928).

2. As a result, the culture-area concept could only have encouraged the view that cultures were static or, at least, were static once they were adjusted to their environment. This is not to say, however, that the culture-area concept has no use in anthropology. Peterson makes interesting use of the concept for Australian Aboriginal society, but only because he recognized the need for an ecological framework for analyzing the interaction between a society and its environment, while allowing for the role of historical and cultural factors (1988).

3. For subsistence studies on the Ituri Forest, see Abruzzi 1980; Bicchieri 1969a,b; Harako 1976, 1981; Ichikawa 1983; Tanno 1976; and Terashima 1980, 1983. For the Kalahari see Lee 1969, 1979; Lee and DeVore 1976; Marshall 1976; Tanaka 1980; and Silberbauer 1981a,b. For Australia see Gould 1968; for the Arctic see Balikci 1970.

4. Cultural ecology's emphasis on homeostasis encouraged "diachronic blindness"

(Winterhalder 1984:307). Historical studies, or the study of human responses to hazards (e.g., droughts) could correct this (Vayda and McKay 1975), although such studies are difficult because they require time frames longer than the life of the average ethnographer and require the use of archaeological or ethnohistoric data (e.g., Hitchcock 1987a,b; Hitchcock and Ebert 1984; Schrire 1984a; Amsden 1977; Winterhalder 1977). However, it is not clear that even with long-term data, cultural ecology could go beyond long-term anecdotal description.

5. We must bear in mind that the Ache study, referred to frequently in this book, focuses on what the Ache do while on hunting treks; we know relatively little about what goes on in the mission settlement—where they spend over 75 percent of their time.

6. Hypergynous marriages, marriages between men of a high-status group and women of a low-status group, are fairly common among living hunter-gatherers, who are usually perceived as being of lower status by neighboring nonforagers. Ten percent of Ju/'hoansi women are married to Bantu cattleherders, for example, and, in the Philippines, up to 25 percent of Batak and 18 percent of Casiguran Agta women are in hypergynous marriages (Bailey 1988).

CHAPTER 3. FORAGING AND SUBSISTENCE

1. Latitude, however, is a poor proxy measure of environmental characteristics. Louisville, Kentucky, and Tonopah, Nevada, are at the same latitude, but one is in a humid deciduous forest, the other in a dry sagebrush desert.

2. For case studies, see Hames and Vickers 1983; Hawkes, Hill, and O'Connell 1982; O'Connell and Hawkes 1984; E. Smith 1983, 1991; Smith and Winterhalder 1992b; Winterhalder 1986a, 1986b, 1987; Winterhalder and Smith 1981.

3. The cost of butchering game can, however, alter a resource's energetic gain dramatically depending on the circumstances under which the game is butchered and how much of the meat can be retrieved, which can be a product of how many people are available for carrying the meat and whether scavengers might steal the kill (see, e.g., Metcalfe and Barlow 1992).

4. Also, Keene took the proportion of calories contributed by protein to be about 8 percent (1979:table 16.4), but in Inuit diets protein generally provides 15–45 percent of calories.

5. For example, in the boreal forest (Winterhalder 1981), the Amazon (Hames and Vickers 1982), Malaysia (Kuchikura 1987, 1988), the central Australian desert (O'Connell and Hawkes 1981, 1984), and the Arctic (E. Smith 1991).

6. It is true, as a number of authors have pointed out, that the marginal-value theorem implies that hunter-gatherers should not overexploit their resource base, or hunt a species to extinction (see chapter 4); it is not necessary to appeal, as some have done, to an inherent conservation ethic among hunter-gatherers.

However, overexploitation could occur where the net-resource-harvest function is of the limited linear kind (see figure 3–6b).

7. See Blurton Jones and Konner 1976; Draper 1975; Heffley 1981; Marshall 1976; Meehan 1982; Silberbauer 1981a:271; Tanner 1979; see also Mithen 1990.

8. This is an especially important question for archaeologists to consider because, though they deal with data that come from time periods of varying length, these periods are always much longer than those of ethnographic studies. They also are conglomerates of male and female behavior which are hard to disaggregate.

9. E.g., Cashdan 1990; de Garine and Harrison 1988; Huss-Ashmore, Curry, and Hitchcock 1988; Minc and Smith 1989.

10. In any case, a resource does not have to be actively included in the diet in order for it to be a backup resource. When their maize crops failed, many Puebloan peoples of the American Southwest, for example, relied on wild plant foods that were not normally included in their diets. Information on backup strategies and starvation foods can also be encoded into a society's mythology, folklore, and ritual (e.g., Minc 1986); the resources need not be continually used to serve as backup foods.

11. E.g., Belovsky 1987; Foley 1985; Keene 1979, 1981; Sih and Milton 1985; E. Smith 1979.

12. Sponsel finds that 39 percent of tropical animals weigh less than 5 kilograms, 54 percent are solitary, 73 percent are nocturnal, and 44 percent arboreal (1986). These facts do not add up to an impressive faunal resource base or one that is easy to exploit. This, by the way, may account for the use of extremely large arrows as shock weapons and poison in the tropical forest, since tropical hunters must shoot game at distances much farther than the thirty to forty feet that bow hunters seem to prefer. It may also have much to do with the quick acceptance of shotguns by tropical forest peoples.

13. Archaeology could similarly benefit from this approach to foraging. Take the case of fish in Tasmania. About 3,500 years ago, the aboriginal inhabitants of Tasmania apparently stopped eating fish (Jones 1978). European colonists found that the Tasmanians considered fish inedible. Were fish tabooed, or just low-ranked relative to other foods? Given the particular resources of Tasmania, optimal-foraging models could predict the conditions under which fish should drop out of the diet for energetic reasons. If these conditions did not hold in the past, then one could argue that fish were removed from the diet for cultural reasons, although the specific reason for their prohibition may always remain unknown.

CHAPTER 4. FORAGING AND MOBILITY

1. Ingold (1987) and Cribb (1991) discuss conceptual differences between the mobility of hunter-gatherers and the mobility of pastoralists.
2. Elsewhere in this book we will use the term *forager* to refer to a generic hunter-gatherer, and not in Binford's sense (1980).
3. Bettinger and Baumhoff propose an alternative to the forager-collector continuum with their *traveler-processor* continuum (1982; see also Bettinger 1991). *Travelers* have high mobility (presumably both residential and logistical) and take only high return rate food resources, especially large game. *Processors* have lower mobility and use a diversity of resources, especially plant foods. The difference in subsistence generates differences in demography, with high rates of female infanticide lowering the growth rate among travelers. Travelers may characterize colonizing populations, whereas processors could encompass Binford's foragers and collectors. Bettinger claims that his model has the advantage of specifying precise relationships between population and resources, and settlement and subsistence (1991:102).
4. I admit to some uncertainty over the Baffinland data, which come from Hantzsch (1977). In Baffinland in 1911 to collect botanical specimens, Hantzsch made the group move more frequently than perhaps they wanted. After Hantzsch's death, the group returned to the coastal port from which they had started in half the time. Whether they were now moving at a regular pace or more quickly to report Hantzsch's death is not clear. Even if the former, it would not raise the estimate to the level of other low-*ET* groups.
5. This observation has pronounced effects for the formation of regional archaeological records of hunter-gatherers (see Binford 1983).
6. McClellan 1975:100; Irimoto 1981:127; Lee 1968:31; Tindale 1972:245; Vickers 1989; Tanaka 1980:66; Cane 1987:395; Endicott and Endicott 1986:150; Kuchikura 1987; Hitchcock and Ebert 1984.
7. Hunter-gatherers only occasionally work this long at collecting *and* processing food (refer to table 1-1), and then only a few days a week. Winterhalder's simulation, discussed in chapter 1, also suggests that this kind of daily work effort would not be adaptive. At this point, however, it does not matter, since shortening the work day would change the absolute returns relative to needs, but not the relationship between the two—and it is the latter that concerns us here. Additionally, the model does not imply that foragers work every day.
8. We assume that the calories collected cover the energy needs of the forager plus his or her dependents; the energy costs of foraging are over and above the basal needs. Adding the energetic costs of foraging into the equation allows the analysis of different foraging and camp-move costs. We also assume that adults collect all food for children; though children do some of their own foraging in some societies, they do very little in others (Blurton Jones, Hawkes, and O'Connell 1989). The factors determining when children forage are too com-

plex to enter into the simple model used here (see chapter 6). It should be apparent from the text, however, that the less food adults have to bring back for children (and the less they are burdened by children while foraging) the further they can forage from camp. This will probably affect women's more than men's foraging.

9. Catchment analysis in archaeology commonly uses a standard foraging radius of 5 or 10 kilometers, based usually on data from the Ju/'hoansi. It should be clear from this model, however, that the length of the effective foraging distance is not a constant.

10. Metcalfe and Barlow have constructed a model predicting how resources will be field-processed depending on characteristics of the resource and the distance back to camp (1992). Ranking different parts of a resource (e.g., the different parts of an animal) in terms of their utility (caloric value), they show that the further foragers are from camp the greater the number of low-utility parts of a resource they will leave behind. Their model has important implications for the interpretation of archaeological data in terms of logistical and residential mobility by predicting what parts of a resource will be left behind at field-processing sites versus brought back to camp.

11. Ritual needs can also increase the time it takes to break camp down. The Cree, for example, make sure that they clean up camp and properly dispose of any faunal remains so as not to insult the spirits of animals. This is necessary to insure that game will return to the area (Tanner 1979:74).

12. For example, if housing must be substantial (e.g., in Arctic climates), then mobility decreases. On the other hand, if mobility must be high, then housing must be less substantial and easily transportable. The decision depends on the materials available for housing and/or for transport, thus the technology of housing and mobility influence one another. The availability of horses may have made Plains Indian life possible, for example, as it reduced mobility costs to an acceptable level, and made possible the transport of the materials needed for housing on the Plains.

13. For examples, see Woodburn 1968; Lee 1976; Griffin 1989; Vickers 1989; Kent and Vierich 1989.

14. The correct term is *sedentarism*. However, the term *sedentism* has a lengthy history of use in anthropology and I elect to continue it.

15. Ingold suggests that these behavioral dimensions have conceptual ones as well, in terms of how related to a particular place hunter-gatherers see themselves (1986).

16. Some osteological studies of prehistoric human skeleton remains suggest that individual hunter-gatherers, especially men, were *more* mobile prehistorically than males in prehistoric sedentary agricultural societies. Thus, it still remains to be seen if the ethnographic pattern is a short-term phenomenon of sedentism itself (and not reflected in the current small sample of archaeological data) or colonial encapsulation.

17. That some foragers learn these areas extremely well is attested to by the maps some Arctic foragers draw from memory encompassing hundreds of square kilometers (see, e.g., Boas 1888:236–40).

18. For mobility as helping to maintain insurance networks, see Yengoyan 1976; Wiessner 1977, 1982. As maintaining trading partners, see Lee 1976:96; Yellen 1977:64; Woodburn 1968:106; Park 1938:629. As instructing children, see Gould 1969b:87.

19. The values employed here can be used to construct a depletion curve of the type amenable to the MVT. It is difficult to decide what the overall environmental return rate should be since it must take travel time into account–but in an area of homogeneous resource distribution, travel time is a function of the size of the foraged area. Nonetheless, using a range of values, the MVT still predicts movement before a year's occupation—in fact, it always predicts movement at a considerably shorter occupation time than the foraging-radius model.

20. On the other hand, one group's decision to become sedentary could leave some land open, permitting others to continue to forage in the interstices between sedentary villages. The extent to which this is possible depends on how patch resources are distributed.

    Archaeologists have also sometimes seen sedentism as an evolutionary threshold from which foragers could not retreat. In chapter 6 we will discuss how sedentism may increase population growth rates and hence encourage a commitment to sedentism. However, from the perspective outlined here it should be apparent that large changes in resource configurations and/or population density could result in a reversal of a settlement trend back to a more residentially mobile lifeway (e.g., see Ames 1991).

21. On the other hand, the sedentary coastal Tlingit used dance to parody interior boreal forest peoples who, in their opinion, wandered about in a pathetic search for food (McClellan 1975:96). And the recently settled G//ana of the Kalahari likewise "speak disparagingly of residents of the Central Reserve who have no fixed home base as 'moving around like animals'" (Cashdan 1984:323).

22. Governments attempting to settle formerly nomadic peoples would do well to realize the role of mobility as an expression of cultural norms and uniqueness, and its importance to a people's psychological as well as physical well-being.

23. See discussion in Lee and DeVore 1968:337–38; Barry, Child, and Bacon 1959; for hunter-gatherer studies see Burbank 1988; Condon 1987; Draper 1975, 1976; Hames 1988; Hewlett 1991a,b, 1992b; Winn, Morelli, and Tronick 1990. Some of these are concerned with childhood in societies undergoing rapid acculturation.

24. For sowing of wild seeds, see Steward 1938; for irrigation, see also Lawton et al. 1976; for burning, see Jones 1969; Lewis 1989, 1991; Lewis and Ferguson 1988; Mills 1986. The sowing of seeds and the irrigation of natural stands of seed plants are clearly aimed at intentionally increasing the productivity of

land. Foragers also sometimes burn land to encourage new growth for the plants themselves or for the wildlife they may attract, but they also burn land for the primary purpose of simply clearing the landscape to make travel easier.

25. This is an important issue because many indigenous peoples around the world, especially former hunter-gatherer peoples, are well aware that some anthropologists, following the affluent-forager model, label them as natural conservationists, and argue that resource-conservation laws should not apply to them, setting up tension and debate between these indigenous peoples and conservation organizations. However, if we find that resource conservation among foragers results from foraging efficiency rather than intentional management, this would *not* mean that foragers or their descendants, living with growing populations that are circumscribed by agricultural or industrial societies, and with access to extensive data (both their own and that collected by land management organizations), do not or could not structure their harvesting so as to manage food resources.

CHAPTER 5. SHARING, EXCHANGE, AND LAND TENURE

1. This does not mean that meat from large game will always be shared, although that is the case in the ethnographic record. Instead, the model predicts that in cases where hunters are always equally successful, meat sharing should be infrequent.

2. It is possible that such dunning leads to ambivalence toward material goods, or even a dislike for possessions. It could also lead to many modern hunter-gatherers saving cash rather than the goods cash can buy (Altman and Peterson 1988), since a person can hide cash, even put it in a bank, and avoid demand sharing by appearing to be cash-poor.

3. Winterhalder also found similar limits on sharing (1986a), as did Hegmon for Hopi horticulturalists (1991).

4. See chapter 2, note 5 for comment on the Ache data. Kaplan and Hill also tested Marvin Harris's conservation hypothesis of sharing. In this hypothesis sharing negates the potential to overexploit resources by discouraging an intensification of effort. By generating a surplus, foragers leave themselves open to accusations of stinginess if they hoard, thus they must share. But if they share and work hard to create a surplus, they will spend much of their time working for others (see Lorna Marshall's discussion of Ju/'hoansi women's foraging in chapter 1). Following a neofunctionalist line of reasoning, Harris argues that sharing indirectly enforces a conservation ethic. This particular test is not especially germane to discussion in this chapter, but it is worth noting that Kaplan and Hill could find no evidence to support it, and found no evidence that the Ache conserved resources.

5. A variant of this hypothesis is that parents should share most with children of

the sex that has the greatest chance of passing genetic material on to future generations.

6. There is also a cultural component here. It is my impression that among many foragers (indeed, many societies) asking for food is often considered inappropriate behavior, but refusing to share food—even when the request is not socially legitimate—is an even worse act. If committed, it could affect others' decisions to share with the refuser in the future. The degree to which this is true will help determine the social costs of sharing; that is, the cost of defending a resource may not always be intrinsic to the resource itself.

7. In discussing the paternity data, Hawkes, a member of the Ache research team, notes that "informants' reports may well be biased" (1990:16). However, even if good hunters do not really father more children it is noteworthy that Ache women name good hunters as possible or likely fathers more frequently than poor hunters. Thus, all involved (the Ache and their anthropologists) may *believe* that good hunters father more children: it may not matter whether the paternity data are biologically accurate.

8. For men, see Dwyer 1983; Ohtsuka 1989; Howell 1986; Hart and Pilling 1960:34. For women, see Biesele and Howell 1981; Howell 1986; Hawkes, O'Connell, and Blurton Jones 1989. There is, however, variability among hunter-gatherer societies in how much work the elderly do. Hawkes and her co-workers note that whereas elderly Hadza women actively forage, providing food for their grandchildren, elderly Ju/'hoansi women do not, possibly because the Kalahari is a much harsher foraging environment than Hadza territory (1989). Elderly Ju/'hoansi women spend much more time than Hadza women in babysitting while the younger mothers forage.

9. It would be interesting to conduct a follow-up study to see how well good Ache and Ju/'hoansi hunters fare as they age.

10. For territories as adaptations to the fur trade, see Leacock 1954, 1980, 1982; but see Knight 1965; see also Scott 1986 for comments on commodity production and privatization. For the Lillooet and other groups in interior British Columbia, see Hayden 1992:545. Harris notes that Speck's later writing tended in the same direction as Leacock's (Harris 1968:359).

11. Radcliffe-Brown's earlier writings on Australian social organization show that he recognized that boundaries between hordes were permeable—people could move between hordes. However, in his later writings, and when writing more generally, hordes were described as closed, with particular individuals using only particular tracts of land (see Peterson and Long 1986:16).

12. Territorial marking may have occurred after Euroamerican settlement restricted land available to Native Californians, but this still suggests the conditions under which marked territories would form. Similar processes could be at work among India's Vedda.

13. This is not unique to Australia, for many Arctic peoples also express feelings

that they belong to a place (Riches 1982:119). Boas, for example, noted that "it is peculiar to the migratory habits of the Eskimo that almost without exception the old man returns to the country of his youth, and consequently by far the greater part of the old people live in their native districts" (1888:58). The Malaysian Batek also express affection for their *pesaka,* or childhood home (Endicott and Endicott 1986:155). And so do the Bushmen as attested to by the quotation at the head of this chapter.

14. Wiessner has not been able to collect data to demonstrate that a !Kung's well-being is related to the number of *hxaro* partners or the spatial distribution of these partners (Wiessner 1982a).

15. The two-year fruiting cycle of the cone in fact permits prediction more than a year in advance. By high resource predictability, Dyson-Hudson and Smith probably mean resources whose timing and location can be known in advance with a high degree of probability, as is true for piñon.

16. It is important to point out that we have very little information on what happens when times are rough—when allowing someone into a territory would have a detrimental effect on the host population. One can only afford to give a gift if it does not jeopardize one's own survival.

17. Not so much for using resources without permission, but for using resources without incurring the obligation to reciprocate sometime in the future. That is, the host group would not be retaliating for the loss of food, but for the loss of a future debt and, hence, security.

18. This is an assumption, of course, since the costs and benefits of social-boundary defense are difficult to measure. No one to my knowledge has done so.

19. It is even more likely that trade relations will focus on specific nutritional concerns (such as protein vs. carbohydrate), since the ability to produce a surplus of food to be traded indicates that calories are not the limiting factor for some populations. Thus, to analyze trade relations among hunter-gatherers or between hunter-gatherers and their neighbors it is necessary to consider nutritional as well as energetic complementarity.

CHAPTER 6. GROUP SIZE AND REPRODUCTION

1. Winterhalder looks only at the effects on group size of variance reduction via pooling of resources. Information processing, reproductive issues, defense, the number of habitable places (e.g., water holes in deserts) or cooperative foraging could also influence group size.

2. Hegmon's analysis of Hopi horticulturalists uncovered a similar pattern (1991); she found that the benefits of sharing did not increase when more than six households shared food (see also McCloskey 1976).

3. An implication of this model is that as population grows, before we see an

increase in average group size we should see an increase in the number of groups—for as groups grow in size, a limit will be reached at which the variance in daily foraging returns is no longer reduced while the rate of local resource depletion continues to increase. Under such circumstances, as noted in the text, group fissioning would probably be the first response.

4. This is not the only curve that applies to group foraging. It could, for example, be the case that per capita return rates only decline where group size is > 1; alternatively, the curve could be bimodal. We present this curve as the most general case.

5. On the other hand, if foraging requires much time, then other nonforaging tasks may have to be embedded into foraging, with a slight reduction in foraging efficiency but an increase in the overall utility of time spent foraging.

6. Archaeologists might also consider how the technology of communal hunts is related to labor requirements and foraging efficiency. Communal hunts require a large number of beaters or drivers. If an insufficient number of people were available technological aids may have been employed to substitute for drivers. Fire, for example, is sometimes used by modern equatorial groups to drive large game (Mills 1986). The Eskimo used stone cairns strategically placed on the horizon and decorated with cloth to simulate hunters. Confused caribou react to the cairns predictably, by running from them, and are thus channeled into ambush sites. Prehistoric bison hunters of the North American Plains used the same tactic. Communal bison hunting on the Plains may not have been possible as a routine subsistence strategy until the horse provided the mobility necessary to cover long distances quickly—making up for the number of drivers that would otherwise be needed to drive a large herd of bison across the open plains.

Alternatively, technological aids like cairns may be a way to limit the number of foragers with whom the collectively acquired food must be shared. By simulating hunters, cairns can effectively bring group size to N and maximize group foraging efficiency; the food, of course, would then be divided among fewer than N people. Therefore, communal hunting technology could be a way to either make up for the lack of additional foragers or a way to keep additional foragers out.

The question of whether foragers will forage communally or individually is also complicated by the fact that a foraging group could alter its technology to accommodate more foragers if demands and potential retributions are strong enough. For example, assume that a group of BaMbuti hunt with bows. When additional BaMbuti decide to hunt individually, the increased number may scare game away, lowering return rates of those already hunting. The hunters' choice in this case is either to keep others from hunting, or to devise a way of hunting that accommodates large numbers of foragers. Given that large numbers of people will be tromping through the forest no matter what, it may be better to find a way to use the additional labor as beaters in a communal effort than to continue to hunt individually with bows. The foraging technology or strategy could itself change as the number or insistence of additional foragers increases.

7. We have already noted that this case is questionable because Birdsell could not measure population density directly. Instead, he measured tribal area, arriving at population density by assuming that tribes averaged about 500 persons in size. We noted the problems in this estimate in the text. Others, however, have shown relationships similar to that documented by Birdsell between more accurate measures of population density and precipitation in other desert environments (Thomas 1981; Martin and Read 1981).

8. Archaeologists will find it interesting that a change in diet breadth in this model results in a transitional period of rapid change between foraging for one versus two resources (this period becomes shorter in the simulation until it is nearly nonexistent as the work day is increased in length).

9. In Belovsky's model, the amount of meat in the diet increases as a population grows, but then decreases as the population moves into the stable-limit-cycle phase, since (1) the dependent-to-adult ratio is lowered as the population enters a period of negative growth, and (2) hunted foods are reduced in abundance once the population enters the stable-limit-cycle phase. The suggestion that initial population growth is associated with greater amounts of meat in the diet is contrary to many archaeological case studies of population growth and diet.

10. For infanticide, see for example Acker and Townsend 1975; Balikci 1967; Birdsell 1968; Carr-Saunders 1922; Chapman 1980; Cowlishaw 1978; Denham 1974; Dickemann 1975; Freeman 1971; Hawkes 1981; Helm 1980; Irwin 1989; Morales 1987; Remie 1985; Riches 1974; Schrire and Steiger 1974a,b, 1981; Van de Velde 1954; Yengoyan 1981.

11. Presumably, the husband and father could be different individuals. Since Tiwi women initially marry very old men, they take a number of younger men as lovers (Goodale 1971:131) and differentiate between the man who allegedly "made" the baby, the biological father, and the woman's husband, the social father.

12. Based on Bugos and McCarthy's kin diagram, among women who had committed infanticide, the rate is 38 percent (not including eight cases where the gender is unknown); 28 percent of all females were killed at birth, whereas 40 percent of all male infants were killed (1984).

13. Data presented by Bugos and McCarthy suggest a secondary sex ratio of 125:100 (1984). Causes of deviations from the expected 1:1 ratio are still largely unknown and could be attributed to a variety of biological factors, such as the side effects of hepatitis B virus (Drew, Blumberg, and Robert-Lamblin 1986; see review by Martin 1994).

14. Helm's discussion also relies on testimonials in the records of early Hudson's Bay traders and explorers (1980). These accounts mention that female infanticide *used to be practiced frequently* by local people, but that the Europeans quickly put a stop to it. It is conceivable that the Europeans convinced themselves that a heinous behavior existed (as Rasmussen did) based on a limited number of cases, then credited themselves for having put a stop to something that never existed (or that existed at a much lower frequency than they thought).

15. Among the polygynous Tiwi, however, young men marry older women. As these men age, they are allowed, by older men, to marry younger and younger women, until they reach an advanced age when they marry the youngest women (Pilling and Hart 1960; Goodale 1971).

16. If female infanticide were performed for this reason, we would predict female infanticide to occur early in the birth sequence, with its frequency decreasing as a function of the number of males already born. To my knowledge, data to test this idea are not available.

17. Infant death can occur through neglect by weaning a child early, by giving it less nutritious food or less attention when sick or injured than that given to other offspring. The result can be a systematically higher rate of infant and toddler mortality of one gender.

18. This suggests a difference in parental attitudes toward females. In the Arctic, female infanticide is accompanied by some very severe attitudes toward women in general. As Irwin points out, it is difficult to sort out the issues of sex-ratio balance, the value of one gender relative to another, and cultural notions of men and women, much less specify the cause of female infanticide (1989). There is a significant need for the analysis of infanticide in terms of a model of cultural transmission.

19. Other factors can intervene for first births. A young woman's decision to kill a firstborn infant is partly related to how much support she can expect to receive. She may be more likely not to keep a newborn since she still has her entire reproductive life ahead of her. Later in life, however, a woman may not wish to restrict her reproductive potential, and, still later, a woman may have acquired what she thinks is the appropriate number of children and feel that she cannot work hard enough to support more. Among those Ayoreo women, for example, who practiced nonpreferential infanticide, the infanticide rate dropped from 65 percent among fifteen- to nineteen- year olds to 22 percent among twenty-five- to thirty-four-year olds, and increased to 31 percent among thirty-five- to thirty-nine-year-olds.

   There are other possible explanations of first-birth infanticide. Working in Australia, Cowlishaw found that infanticide was most often directed at first-born children regardless of gender (1978). She gives a psychological explanation that is based on Australian cultural notions of "women's business" (which includes childbirth), and the need for women to exercise their autonomy, an

important element of Aboriginal culture. They do this by controlling their reproductive powers. We must understand, Cowlishaw argues, that women in
Aboriginal society have little control over their lives, including their marital
partners. They must follow the wishes of their fathers, brothers, and husbands.
Cowlishaw argues that power over their reproductive abilities is the sole power
women have over men. By killing her firstborn, an Aboriginal women denies
"her brother a niece to bestow, or her husband a son to follow him in his ceremonial life" (1978:279; see also Strathern, in Gelber 1986:119). However, not
all Australian ethnographers agree with this characterization of Australian Aboriginal gender relations (see chapter 7).

20. Fertility studies in Africa, however, must take into account the impact of venereal disease, which now appears to be an important variable in central Africa's
"infertility belt."

21. Some studies suggest that increases in fertility are not a function of a reduction
in the birth interval, but an increase in women's childbearing years, a product
of the lowering of the age at first birth (a function of marriage age and/or age
at menarche) and/or an increase in the age of last birth (Roth 1981). Additionally, some variability in birth spacing can be attributed to variability in ovarian
cycle length; the factors controlling this variability are not fully understood
(Campbell and Wood 1988; Ellison, Peacock, and Lager 1989; Ellison 1990,
1994; Wood 1994).

22. Balikci also notes that child homicide may occur among the Netsilingmiut by
a woman's second husband (1967:621).

23. Discussions of fertility revolve almost exclusively around the factors affecting
women. Less attention, and less medical research, is devoted to men. However,
research suggests that the factors considered here that could plausibly affect
men, fluctuations in diet and exercise, appear to have a significant effect on
male fertility (see Campbell and Leslie 1994). This area merits further research.

24. In this case, as a function of government-sponsored infant-bottle-feeding pro-
grams.

25. Harpending and Wandsnider point out that clothing may also inhibit the frequency of breastfeeding (1982).

26. For the Ju/'hoansi, see Wilmsen 1978, 1986; Van der Walt, Wilmsen, and Jen-
kins 1978. For Turkana pastoralists, see Leslie and Fry 1989. For the Ache, see
Hill and Kaplan 1988a,b. For Lese horticulturalists, see Ellison, Peacock, and
Lager 1989. For the Hiwi, see Hurtado and Hill 1989.

   Birth seasonality studies are difficult to assess if they do not demonstrate that
the rate of copulation remains constant throughout the year. Condon and Scaglion (1982), for example, argue that birth seasonality among the Samukundi
Abelam of New Guinea and the post-1970 Copper Eskimo are produced by
the seasonality of labor and settlement patterns that directly affect the rate of
copulation and hence the probability of conception. Brainard and Overfield

(1986) make a similar argument for pre-1955 Western Alaskan Eskimo (who manifest the opposite seasonal pattern of the Copper Eskimo). However, the rate of copulation does not appear to have any bearing on the Ju/'hoansi, Ache, Turkana, or Lese cases.

27. However, these studies have only been conducted with Western populations. Studies duplicating the activity regimes of women in non-Western societies have not been conducted (Ellison 1990, 1994).

28. As hunter-gatherers (and other indigenous populations) are incorporated into the world cash economy, men spend more time away from home working in factories, mines, the military, and so on. Given the arguments presented in this and other chapters, we can expect this to have an effect on population growth as well as child enculturation.

CHAPTER 7. MEN, WOMEN, AND FORAGING

1. We know little about the effect of foraging on sharing or the division of labor where the only game available is small, such as among the Mikea (Stiles 1991). Other than the rare wild boar, the largest game available to the Mikea is hedge-hog-sized. Most ethnographically known foragers have access to at least some large game, game that is the focus of men's work.

2. Dobkin de Rios and Hayden suggested that female odors associated with pregnancy, menstruation, and lactation prevent women from hunting by scaring game away (1985). Their account does not make clear why male odors would not prevent men from hunting. Using a sample of foraging and nonforaging societies, Peggy Sanday found no significant relationship between male dominance and the number of menstrual taboos, one of Dobkin de Rios and Hayden's measure of male dominance (1981). At any rate, pregnancy, menstruation, and lactation do not seem to prevent Agta women from hunting (Kelly 1986).

3. Traditional weapons used to hunt land animals among hunter-gatherers usually do not kill prey on impact. Instead, they either bleed the animal to death, or, if poisons are used, gradually weaken the animal so it can be easily dispatched. This means that game must be tracked, sometimes over long distances, and the hunter must be prepared to go wherever the trail leads him or her, staying out overnight if need be.

4. Hawkes, O'Connell, and Blurton Jones suggest this increases the grand-mother's fitness by contributing to the well-being of her grandchildren (1989).

5. I know of no way to test this idea at present. It is not clear from the literature whether Agta women who hunt have higher status that those who do not. Sanday, however, points out that male dominance tends to be stronger in those societies where men primarily hunt large game—and thus have the resources with which to compete and acquire prestige (1981).

6. As argued in the preceding section, biological differences between men and

women create different costs and benefits of large-game hunting. By placing men in a position to share more outside the family, large-game hunting allows men to acquire the prestige and debts that sharing constructs, and could lead men to have greater control over extrafamilial relations. Combined with the ethnocentric bias of early ethnography, this could lead to the assumption that men are naturally dominant—an important element of the patrilocal-band model.

7. This could create discrepancies in ethnographers' accounts depending on the specific instances and history of the local group studied. For example, though Perry classifies the Beaver as having matrilocal residence (1989), Ridington points out that the recruitment process, through which older members try to enlist as many young people as possible, including their daughters' and sons' spouses, creates a bilaterally extended household (1981). A couple with only daughters might very well convince their daughters' husbands to live with them, making their group appear to have a matrilocal postmarital residence "rule."

8. Martin and Stewart also note that if men marry late in life then fathers will be much older than their sons. Consequently, a son's father could be deceased by the time the son's children reach reproductive age. It would therefore be rare for several generations of lineally related males to live together. They suggest that this could lead to avunculocal postmarital residence or matrilineal authority.

9. Jeremy Keenan points out that where band membership is flexible and fluid, the basis for social relations must be stable (1977). People who belong to a particular band may not live together continually, and the band's existence is not contingent on its members remaining together. Instead, identification with a particular band may be shorthand for identifying some of the sorts of reciprocal obligations one could expect of certain individuals (given their gender, age, and band affiliation).

10. Pitjandjara descent is undergoing change in recent years from a place-based to a father-based system of affiliation.

CHAPTER 8. EGALITARIAN AND NONEGALITARIAN HUNTER-GATHERERS

1. Evidence of prehistoric nonegalitarian foragers is based largely on differential mortuary treatment. Some Early and Middle Woodland societies of the central eastern United States, for example, complexes known as Adena or Hopewell, are best known through their elaborate burial treatment of some of their members. Subsistence data suggest that the majority of their diet was derived from hunted and gathered foods.

2. See, for example, Altman and Peterson 1988; Bird-David 1992b; Lee 1988; Myers 1986, 1988a,b; Peterson 1993; Woodburn 1980.

3. Walker and Hewlett also found that high-status males had fewer caries compared to low-status males, indicating yet another level of inequality in Aka society (1990). However, though some men and women may have eaten less meat than some men, it is not clear whether this had a significant nutritional impact.

4. Widmer does, however, argue that the Calusa did not practice substantial food storage (1988).

5. Like Service's explanation for the patrilocal band, arguments about the evolution of inequality sometimes appeal to the natural predisposition among men to compete and dominate; women never seem to be granted this predisposition. This predisposition is sometimes argued to be rooted in the selective pressures of early (sometimes even prehominid) human evolution. Although it is not a subject that we can discuss in detail here, we should point out that even if it were true that men in all societies are more competitive and domineering than women, it would not demonstrate that this was a function of selective pressures in the Plio-Pleistocene.

6. Thus, Legros's demonstration of socioeconomic inequalities among the Tutchone, who live in a harsh, "nonaffluent" environment, is beside the point (1985). Also, Hayden once argued that complex hunter-gatherers are associated with increased resource reliability— decreased resource fluctuations (1981a). Demonstration of the existence of significant variability in salmon and periods of starvation among the Lillooet Indians of interior British Columbia, however, has made him alter this position (Hayden 1992:538).

7. It bears pointing out, in addition, that I do not think that the evolutionary perspective outlined here is at odds with Marxist perspectives. However, unlike Marxist perspectives, it makes clearer the conditions under which intensification, competition, exploitation, and inequality occur.

8. To put this into simpler terms, think about charitable giving in cash economies. Ten thousand dollars is a small amount of money to a billionaire, and it can be given away in return for the prestige that comes from making donations. However, ten thousand dollars is a relatively large sum for, say, the average college professor; he or she will probably not give it away.

9. The intensity of resource fluctuations independent of population density can also affect this relationship. In addition, the number of parties with whom social relations are viable will in part be a function of the localization of resources; the more localized resources are, the greater the relative number of groups who will want them.

10. One implication of this proposal relevant to archaeology is that nonegalitarian societies form in clusters, not in isolation. Also, within Keeley's ethnographic sample there is no gradual gradient between egalitarian and nonegalitarian societies (1988). Instead, there is a sharp break between these two groups, sug-

gesting (but not demonstrating) that the evolutionary transition between the two social forms may be quick and pervasive.

11. Similarly, European traders sometimes gave boats to those Eskimo men who were most likely to pay off their debt through hunting and trapping, eventually producing a notion of leadership among some Eskimo that "rested not so much on the leader's special productive competence, but more on his abilities in negotiating important facilities from the European trader" (Riches 1982:145).

12. It is not just husbands, but also wives who will try to increase household productivity. Where polygyny does occur, the first wife may encourage her husband to take another wife to ease her burden. The second wife falls under the control of the first as the relationship between a husband and his first wife is now repeated between the first and second wives.

13. See, for example, Ames 1985; Richardson 1982; Schalk 1981; Kelly 1991. For slave owning, see Donald 1983, 1985; Mitchell 1983, 1984, 1985; Mitchell and Donald 1985, 1988. On warfare, see Ferguson 1983, 1984.

14. Reconstructing the prehistoric resource base of the west coast of Britain Peter Rowley-Conwy and Marek Zvelebil also find that salmon runs in different streams are not synchronized and that "as the geographic scale decreases, the coefficient of variability increases, i.e., *the more local the level of consideration, the more marked is the interannual variability*" (1989:43, emphasis added).

15. Maschner finds that evidence for social inequality appears when the population aggregated along the northern coast in large villages that were well-situated for fishing and defensive purposes (1991). The bow and arrow may have come into use at the same time, and may have served in warfare. These cultural changes are correlated with a period of climatic instability that presumably could have increased the intensity and/or frequency of resource fluctuations.

16. Hayden and Gargett note this lack of relevant data, and attempted to test the proposition that big men keep their position because they fulfill the function of providing for peoples' needs in times of stress (1990). They did this by examining the role of high-ranking individuals of the modern Maya cargo system in southern Mexico. They conclude that there is no evidence that high-ranking individuals provided for others; indeed, they note that high-ranking individuals bettered themselves during droughts and times of starvation by exploiting others' desperation.

17. Archaeologists, for example, commonly speak of the presence of exotic goods (e.g., in burials) as signs of social alliances between groups. However, these exotic items can be signs of several different kinds of social relationships—e.g., gift-giving, competitive feasts, bridewealth, raiding—that signal different kinds of evolutionary forces and selective conditions.

CHAPTER 9. HUNTER-GATHERERS AND PREHISTORY

1. E.g., Arcand 1988; Barnard 1983; Hamilton 1982b:236; M. Martin 1974; Myers 1988b; Schrire 1984b; Testart 1988.

2. It is commonly assumed in biology as well that the great diversity of animal life can be traced back to a few simple ancestral forms, or prototypes. Steven Jay Gould exposes this fallacy (1989).

3. If the molecular clock is correct, a speciation event about five million years ago separated hominids from other primates.

4. Perhaps hominids were living in the New World by 40,000 years ago, although evidence for a pre-12,000 B.P. occupation is still tenuous.

5. Prehistory textbooks are replete with examples as their authors strive to present an ethnographic snapshot of what, for example, Magdalenian, Kebaran, or North American Archaic societies were like.

REFERENCES CITED

Abrams, H., Jr.
1987   The Preference for Animal Protein and Fat: A Cross-Cultural Survey. In
        Food and Evolution, edited by M. Harris and E. Ross, pp. 207–23. Phila-
        delphia: Temple University Press.
Abruzzi, W.
1979   Population Pressure and Subsistence Strategies among the Mbuti Pyg-
        mies. *Human Ecology* 7:183–89.
1980   Flux among the Mbuti Pygmies of the Ituri Forest: An Ecological Inter-
        pretation. In *Beyond the Myths of Culture,* edited by E. Ross, pp. 3–31.
        New York: Academic Press.
Acker, C. L., and P. K. Townsend
1975   Demographic Models and Female Infanticide. *Man* 10:469–70.
Adams, J.
1973   *The Gitksan Potlatch: Population Flux, Resource Ownership, and Reciprocity.*
        Toronto: Holt, Rinehart & Winston.
Altman, J. C.
1984   Hunter-Gatherer Subsistence Production in Arnhem Land: The Origi-
        nal Affluence Hypothesis Re-Examined. *Mankind* 14:179–90.
1987   *Hunter-Gatherers Today.* Canberra: Australian Institute of Aboriginal
        Studies.

Altman, J. C., ed.

1989 *Emergent Inequalities in Aboriginal Australia.* Oceania Monograph 38. Sydney: University of Sydney.

Altman, J., and N. Peterson

1988 Rights to Game and Rights to Cash among Contemporary Australian Hunter-Gatherers. In *Hunters and Gatherers,* Vol. 2: *Property, Power, and Ideology,* edited by T. Ingold, D. Riches, and J. Woodburn, pp. 75–94. Oxford: Berg.

Alvard, M. S.

1993 Testing the "Ecologically Noble Savage" Hypothesis: Interspecific Prey Choice by Piro Hunters of Amazonian Peru. *Human Ecology* 21:355–87.

Ames, K.

1985 Hierarchies, Stress, and Logistical Strategies among Hunter-Gatherers in Northwestern North America. In *Prehistoric Hunter-Gatherers: The Emergence of Cultural Complexity,* edited by T. D. Price and J. A. Brown, pp. 155–80. Orlando, Fla.: Academic Press.

1991 Sedentism: A Temporal Shift or a Transitional Change in Hunter-Gatherer Mobility Patterns? In *Between Bands and States,* edited by S. Gregg, Center for Archaeological Investigations Occasional Paper No. 9, pp. 108–34. Carbondale, Ill.: Southern Illinois University Press.

1994 The Northwest Coast: Complex Hunter-Gatherers, Ecology, and Social Evolution. *Annual Review of Anthropology* 23:209–29.

Amsden, C.

1977 A Quantitative Analysis of Nunamiut Eskimo Settlement Dynamics. Unpublished Ph.D. dissertation, Department of Anthropology, University of New Mexico.

Andrews, E.

1994 Territoriality and Land Use among the Akulmiut of Western Alaska. In *Key Issues in Hunter-Gatherer Research,* edited by E. S. Burch, Jr. and L. J. Ellanna, pp. 65–93. Oxford: Berg.

Arcand, B.

1988 Il n'y a jamais eu de Société de Chasseurs-Cueilleurs. *Anthropologie et Sociétés* 12:39–58.

Ardrey, R.

1966 *The Territorial Imperative.* New York: Dell.

Arnold, J.

1993 Labor and the Rise of Complex Hunter-Gatherers. *Journal of Anthropological Archaeology* 12:75–119.

Asch, M.

1982 Dene Self-Determination and the Study of Hunter-Gatherers in the Modern World. In *Politics and History in Band Societies,* edited by R. B. Lee and E. Leacock, pp. 347–72. Cambridge: Cambridge University Press.

Aschmann, H.

1959   *The Central Desert of Baja California.* Ibero-Americana 42. Berkeley: University of California.

Bahuchet, S.

1979   Utilisation de L'Espace Forestier par les Pygmées Aka, Chasseurs-Cueilleurs D'Afrique Centrale. *Social Science Information* 18:99–119.

1988   Food Supply Uncertainty among the Aka Pygmies (Lobaye, Central African Republic). In *Coping with Uncertainty in Food Supply,* edited by I. de Garine and G. Harrison, pp. 118–49. Oxford: Oxford University Press.

Bahuchet, S., and H. Guillaume

1982   Aka-Farmer Relations in the Northwest Congo Basin. In *Politics and History in Band Societies,* edited by E. Leacock and R. B. Lee, pp. 189–211. Cambridge: Cambridge University Press.

Bailey, H.

1960   A Method of Determining Warmth and Temperateness of Climate. *Geografiska Annaler* 43:1–16.

Bailey, R.

1988   The Significance of Hypergyny for Understanding Subsistence Behavior among Contemporary Hunters and Gatherers. In *Diet and Subsistence: Current Archaeological Perspectives,* edited by B. Kennedy and G. Le-Moine, pp. 57–65. Calgary: University of Calgary Press.

1991   *The Behavioral Ecology of Efe Pygmy Men in the Ituri Forest, Zaire.* Anthropological Papers, Museum of Anthropology, University of Michigan No. 86. Ann Arbor: University of Michigan.

Bailey, R., and R. J. Aunger

1989a   Net Hunters vs. Archers: Variation in Women's Subsistence Strategies in the Ituri Forest. *Human Ecology* 17:273–97.

1989b   Significance of the Social Relationships of Efe Pygmy Men in the Ituri Forest, Zaire. *American Journal of Physical Anthropology* 78:495–507.

Bailey, R., and N. Peacock

1988   Efe Pygmies of Northeast Zaire: Subsistence Strategies in the Ituri Forest. In *Coping with Uncertainty in Food Supply,* edited by I. de Garine and G. Harrison, pp. 88–117. Oxford: Oxford University Press.

Bailey, R., G. Head, M. Jenike, B. Owen, R. Rechtman, and E. Zechenter

1989   Hunting and Gathering in Tropical Rain Forest: Is It Possible? *American Anthropologist* 91:59–82.

Balikci, A.

1967   Female Infanticide on the Arctic Coast. *Man* 2:615–25.

1970   *The Netsilik Eskimo.* New York: Natural History Press.

1984   Netsilik. In *Handbook of North American Indians,* Vol. 5: *Arctic,* edited by D. Damas, pp. 415–30. Washington, D.C.: Smithsonian Institution Press.

Barker, G.
1976   The Ritual Estate and Aboriginal Polity. *Mankind* 10:225–39.

Barnard, A.
1980   Sex Roles among the Nharo Bushmen of Botswana. *Africa* 50:115–24.
1983   Contemporary Hunter-Gatherers: Current Theoretical Issues in Ecology and Social Organization. *Annual Review of Anthropology* 12:193–214.
1992   *Hunters and Herders of Southern Africa: A Comparative Ethnography of the Khoisan Peoples*. Cambridge: Cambridge University Press.

Barrett, S.
1910   The Material Culture of the Klamath Lake and Modoc Indians of Northeastern California and Southern Oregon. *University of California Publications in American Archaeology and Ethnology* 5:239–92.

Barry, I. H., and L. M. Paxson
1971   Infancy and Early Childhood: Cross-Cultural Codes 2. *Ethnology* 10:466–508.

Barry, H., and A. Schlegel
1982   Cross-Cultural Codes on Contributions by Women to Subsistence. *Ethnology* 21:165–88.

Barry, H., I. Child, and M. Bacon
1959   The Relation of Child Training to Subsistence Economy. *American Anthropologist* 61:51–63.

Basgall, M.
1987   Resource Intensification among Hunter-Gatherers: Acorn Economies in Prehistoric California. *Research in Economic Anthropology* 9:21–52.

Basu, A.
1969   The Pahira: A Population Genetical Study. *American Journal of Physical Anthropology* 31:399–416.

Baumhoff, M. A.
1958   Ecological Determinants of Population. *University of California Archaeological Survey Reports* 48:32–65.
1963   Ecological Determinants of Aboriginal California Populations. *University of California Publications in American Archaeology and Ethnology* 49:155–236.
1981   The Carrying Capacity of Hunter-Gatherers. In *Affluent Foragers,* edited by S. Koyama and D. H. Thomas, pp. 77–90. Senri Ethnological Studies 9. Osaka, Japan: National Museum of Ethnology.

Beals, R.
1933   Ethnology of the Maidu. *University of California Publications in American Archaeology and Ethnology* 31:335–410.

Bean, L. J.
1978   Social Organization. In *Handbook of North American Indians,* Vol. 8: *California,* edited by R. Heizer, pp. 673–82. Washington, D.C.: Smithsonian Institution Press.

Bean, L. J., and C. Smith
1978   Serrano. In *Handbook of North American Indians*, Vol. 8: *California*, edited
           by R. Heizer, pp. 570–74. Washington, D.C.: Smithsonian Institution
           Press.
Bean, L. J., and D. Theodoratus
1978   Western Pomo and Northeastern Pomo. In *Handbook of North American
           Indians*, Vol. 8: *California*, edited by R. Heizer, pp. 289–305. Washing-
           ton, D.C.: Smithsonian Institution Press.
Beardsley, R., P. Holder, A. Krieger, M. Meggers, J. Rinaldo, and P. Kutsche
1956   Functional and Evolutionary Implications of Community Patterning. In
           Seminars in Archaeology, 1955. Society for American Archaeology Memoir
           11, pp. 129–57. Society for American Archaeology.
Beckett, J.
1965   Kinship, Mobility and Community among Part-Aborigines in Rural
           Australia. In *Kinship and Geographical Mobility*, edited by R. Piddington,
           pp. 2–23. Leiden: E. J. Brill.
Begler, E.
1978   Sex, Status, and Authority in Egalitarian Society. *American Anthropologist*
           80:571–88.
Bell, D.
1980   Desert Politics: Choices in the "Marriage Market." In *Women and Coloni-
           zation: Anthropological Perspectives*, edited by M. Etienne and E. Leacock,
           pp. 239–69. New York: Praeger.
Bellshaw, J.
1978   Population Distribution and the Pattern of Seasonal Movement in
           Northern New South Wales. In *Records of Time Past: Ethnohistorical
           Essays on the Culture and Society of the New England Tribes*, edited by
           I. McBryde, pp. 65–81. Canberra: Australian Institute of Aboriginal
           Studies.
Belovsky, G.
1987   Hunter-Gatherer Foraging: A Linear Programming Approach. *Journal of
           Anthropological Archaeology* 6:29–76.
1988   An Optimal Foraging-Based Model of Hunter-Gatherer Population Dy-
           namics. *Journal of Anthropological Archaeology* 7:329–72.
Bender, B.
1985   Prehistoric Developments in the American Midcontinent and in Brit-
           tany, Northwest France. In *Prehistoric Hunter-Gatherers: The Emergence of
           Cultural Complexity*, edited by T. D. Price and J. A. Brown, pp. 21–57.
           Orlando, Fla.: Academic Press.
Bender, B., and B. Morris
1988   Twenty Years of History, Evolution, and Social Change in Gatherer-
           Hunter Studies. In *Hunters and Gatherers*, Vol. 1: *History, Evolution and*

Social Change, edited by T. Ingold, D. Riches, and J. Woodburn, pp. 4–14. Oxford: Berg.

Bentley, G.

1985   Hunter-Gatherer Energetics and Fertility: A Reassessment of the !Kung San. *Human Ecology* 13:79–109.

Bentley, G., T. Goldberg, and G. Jasienska

1993   The Fertility of Agricultural and Non-Agricultural Traditional Societies. *Population Studies* 47:269–81.

Bentley, G., G. Jasienska, and T. Goldberg

1993   Is the Fertility of Agriculturalists Higher Than That of Nonagriculturalists? *Current Anthropology* 34:778–85.

Berkes, F.

1986   Common Property Resources and Hunting Territories. *Anthropologica* 28:144–62.

Bern, J.

1979   Ideology and Domination: Toward a Reconstruction of Australian Aboriginal Social Formation. *Oceania* 50:118–32.

Berndt, C.

1978   Digging Sticks and Spears, Or, the Two-Sex Model. In *Women's Role in Aboriginal Society,* edited by F. Gale, pp. 64–80. Canberra: Australian Institute of Aboriginal Studies.

1981   Interpretations and "Facts" in Aboriginal Australia. In *Woman the Gatherer,* edited by F. Dahlberg, pp. 153–203. New Haven: Yale University Press.

Berndt, R.

1972   The Walmadjeri and Gugadja. In *Hunters and Gatherers Today,* edited by M. G. Bicchieri, pp. 177–216. New York: Holt, Rinehart and Winston.

Berndt, R., and C. Berndt

1964   *World of the First Australians.* Chicago: University of Chicago Press.

1993   *A World That Was: The Yaraldi.* Melbourne: University of Melbourne Press.

Bernhard, J., and K. Glantz

1992   *Staying Human in the Organization: Our Biological Heritage and the Workplace.* Westport, Conn.: Praeger.

Bettinger, R.

1980   Explanatory/Predictive Models of Hunter-Gatherer Adaptation. In *Advances in Archaeological Method and Theory,* Vol. 3, edited by M. Schiffer, pp. 189–255. New York: Academic Press.

1991   *Hunter-Gatherers: Archaeological and Evolutionary Theory.* New York: Plenum.

Bettinger, R., and M. Baumhoff

1982   The Numic Spread: Great Basin Cultures in Competition. *American Antiquity* 47:485–503.

Bicchieri, M.

1969a   A Cultural Ecological Comparative Study of Three African Foraging
         Societies. In *Contributions to Anthropology: Band Societies,* edited by D.
         Damas, pp. 172–79. National Museum of Canada Bulletin 228. Ottawa:
         National Museum of Canada.

1969b   The Differential Use of Identical Features of Physical Habitat in Con-
         nection with Exploitative, Settlement, and Community Patterns: The
         BaMbuti Case Study. In *Contributions to Anthropology: Ecological Essays,*
         edited by D. Damas, pp. 65–72. National Museum of Canada Bulletin
         230. Ottawa: National Museum of Canada.

Bicchieri, M., ed.

1972   *Hunters and Gatherers Today.* New York: Holt, Rinehart, and Winston.

Biesele, M., and N. Howell

1981   "The Old People Give You Life": Aging among !Kung Hunter-
         Gatherers. In *Other Ways of Growing Old,* edited by P. T. Awass and S.
         Harrell, pp. 77–98. Stanford: Stanford University Press.

Binford, L.

1968   Post-Pleistocene Adaptations. In *New Perspectives in Archaeology,* edited
         by S. R. Binford and L. R. Binford, pp. 313–41. Chicago: Aldine.

1978   *Nunamiut Ethnoarchaeology.* New York: Academic Press.

1980   Willow Smoke and Dogs' Tails: Hunter-Gatherer Settlement Systems
         and Archaeological Site Formation. *American Antiquity* 45:4–20.

1982   The Archaeology of Place. *Journal of Anthropological Archaeology* 1:5–31.

1983   *In Pursuit of the Past.* London: Thames and Hudson.

1990   Mobility, Housing, and Environment: A Comparative Study. *Journal of
         Anthropological Research* 46:119–52.

Binford, L. R., and W. J. Chasko

1976   Nunamiut Demographic History: A Provocative Case. In *Demographic
         Anthropology,* edited by E. B. W. Zubrow, pp. 63–143. Albuquerque:
         University of New Mexico Press.

Bird-David, N.

1988   Hunter-Gatherers and Other People: A Reexamination. In *Hunters
         and Gatherers,* Vol. 1: *History, Evolution, and Social Change,* edited
         by T. Ingold, D. Riches, and J. Woodburn, pp. 17–64. Oxford:
         Berg.

1990   The Giving Environment: Another Perspective on the Economic Sys-
         tem of Gatherer-Hunters. *Current Anthropology* 31:183–96.

1992a   Beyond "The Hunting and Gathering Mode of Subsistence": Culture-
         Sensitive Observations on the Nayaka and Other Modern Hunter-
         Gatherers. *Man* 27:19–44.

1992b   Beyond "The Original Affluent Society": A Culturalist Reformulation.
         Current Anthropology 33:25–48.

Birdsell, J.

1953 Some Environmental and Cultural Factors Influencing the Structuring of Australian Aboriginal Populations. *American Naturalist* 87:171–207.

1958 On Population Structure in Generalized Hunting and Collecting Populations. *Evolution* 12:189–205.

1968 Some Predictions for the Pleistocene Based on Equilibrium Systems for Recent Hunter-Gatherers. In *Man the Hunter,* edited by R. B. Lee and I. DeVore, pp. 229–40. Chicago: Aldine.

1970 Local Group Composition among the Australian Aborigines: A Critique of the Evidence from Fieldwork Conducted Since 1930. *Current Anthropology* 11:115–42.

Birket-Smith, K.

1929 The Caribou Eskimo. *Report of the Fifth Thule Expedition* 5. Copenhagen: Nordisk Forlag.

1953 *The Chugach Eskimo.* Nationalmuseets Skrifter, Etnografisk Raekke 6. Copenhagen.

Bishop, C.

1970 The Emergence of Hunting Territories among the Northern Ojibwa. *Ethnology* 9:1–15.

1983 Limiting Access to Limited Goods: The Origins of Stratification in Interior British Columbia. In *The Development of Political Organization in Native North America,* edited by E. Tooker, pp. 148–61. Washington, D.C.: American Ethnological Society.

1986 Territoriality among Northeastern Algonquians. *Anthropologica* 28:37–63.

1987 Coast-Interior Exchange: The Origins of Stratification in Northwestern North America. *Arctic Anthropology* 24:72–83.

Black, F.

1975 Infectious Diseases in Primitive Societies. *Science* 187:515–18.

Black, L.

1973 The Nivkh (Gilyak) of Sakhalin and the Lower Amur. *Arctic Anthropology* 10:1–106.

Blundell, V.

1980 Hunter-Gatherer Territoriality: Ideology and Behavior in Northwest Australia. *Ethnohistory* 27:103–17.

Blurton Jones, N.

1983 A Selfish Origin for Human Food Sharing: Tolerated Theft. *Ethology and Sociobiology* 4:145–47.

1986 Bushman Birth Spacing: A Test for Optimal Interbirth Intervals. *Ethology and Sociobiology* 7:91–105.

1987 Bushman Birth Spacing: Direct Tests of Some Simple Predictions. *Ethology and Sociobiology* 8:183–203.

1989   The Costs of Children and the Adaptive Scheduling of Births: Towards a Sociobiological Perspective on Demography. In *The Sociobiology of Sexual and Reproductive Strategies,* edited by A. Rasa, C. Vogel, and E. Voland, pp. 265–82. London: Chapman and Hall.

Blurton Jones, N., and M. Konner
1976   !Kung Knowledge of Animal Behavior. In *Kalahari Hunter-Gatherers,* edited by R. B. Lee and I. DeVore, pp. 325–48. Cambridge: Harvard University Press.

Blurton Jones, N., and R. M. Sibly
1978   Testing Adaptiveness of Culturally Determined Behavior: Do Bushmen Women Maximize Their Reproductive Success by Spacing Births Widely and Foraging Seldom? In *Human Behavior and Adaptations,* edited by N. Blurton Jones and V. Reynolds, pp. 135–57. London: Taylor & Francis.

Blurton Jones, N., K. Hawkes, and P. Draper
1994   Differences Between Hadza and !Kung Children's Work: Original Affluence or Practical Reason? In *Key Issues in Hunter-Gatherer Research,* edited by E. S. Burch, Jr. and L. J. Ellanna, pp. 189–215. Oxford: Berg.

Blurton Jones, N., K. Hawkes, and J. O'Connell
1989   Modelling and Measuring Costs of Children in Two Foraging Societies. In *Comparative Socioecology: The Behavioural Ecology of Humans and Other Mammals,* edited by V. Standen and R. Foley, pp. 367–90. Oxford: Blackwell Scientific.

Blurton Jones, N., L. Smith, J. O'Connell, K. Hawkes, and C. Kamuzora
1992   Demography of the Hadza, An Increasing and High Density Population of Savanna Foragers. *American Journal of Physical Anthropology* 89:159–81.

Boas, F.
1888   *The Central Eskimo.* Bureau of American Ethnology Annual Report 6. Washington, D.C.

1907   Second Report on the Eskimo of Baffin Land and Hudson Bay. *Anthropological Papers of the American Museum of Natural History* 15:371–509.

1966   *Kwakiutl Ethnography.* Edited by H. Codere. Chicago: University of Chicago Press.

Bock, K.
1956   *The Acceptance of Histories: Towards a Perspective for Social Science.* University of California Publications in Sociology and Social Institutions 3. Berkeley.

Bongaarts, J., and R. Potter
1983   *Fertility, Biology, and Behavior: An Analysis of the Proximate Determinants of Fertility.* New York: Academic Press.

Boone, J.
1992   Competition, Conflict, and Development of Social Hierarchies. In *Evo-*

lutionary Ecology and Human Behavior, edited by E. Smith and B. Winter-halder, pp. 301–38. Hawthorne, N.Y.: Aldine de Gruyter.

Borgerhoff Mulder, M.

1992   Reproductive Decisions. In *Evolutionary Ecology and Human Behavior,* edited by E. Smith and B. Winterhalder, pp. 339–74. New York: Aldine de Gruyter.

Bose, S.

1964   Economy of the Onge of Little Andaman. *Man in India* 44:298–310.

Boserup, E.

1965   *The Conditions of Agricultural Growth: The Economics of Agarian Change under Population Pressure.* Chicago: Aldine.

Boyd, R., and P. Richerson

1985   *Culture and the Evolutionary Process.* Chicago: University of Chicago Press.

Brainard, J., and T. Overfield

1986   Transformation in the Natural Fertility Regime of Western Alaskan Eskimo. In *Culture and Reproduction: An Anthropological Critique of Demographic Transition Theory,* edited by W. Handwerker, pp. 112–24. Boulder, Colo.: Westview.

Brightman, R.

1987   Conservation and Resource Depletion: The Case of the Boreal Forest Algonquians. In *The Question of the Commons,* edited by B. McCoy and J. Acheson, pp. 121–41. Tucson: University of Arizona Press.

Brody, H.

1987   *Living Arctic: Hunters of the Canadian North.* Seattle: University of Washington Press.

Brown, J.

1970   A Note on the Division of Labor. *American Anthropologist* 72:1073–78.

Brunton, R.

1989   The Cultural Instability of Egalitarian Societies. *Man* 24:673–81.

Bugos, P., and L. McCarthy

1984   Ayoreo Infanticide: A Case Study. In *Infanticide: Comparative and Evolutionary Perspectives,* edited by G. Hausfater and S. Hrdy, pp. 503–20. New York: Aldine.

Burbank, V.

1988   *Aboriginal Adolescence: Maidenhood in an Australian Community.* New Brunswick, N.J.: Rutgers University Press.

Burbank, V., and J. Chisholm

1992   Gender Differences in the Perception of Ideal Family Size in an Australian Aboriginal Community. In *Father-Child Relations: Cultural and Biosocial Contexts,* edited by B. Hewlett, pp. 177–90. New York: Aldine de Gruyter.

Burch, E. S., Jr.

1972   The Caribou/Wild Reindeer as a Human Resource. *American Antiquity* 37:339–68.

1984   Kotzebue Sound Eskimo. In *Handbook of North American Indians,* Vol. 5: *Arctic,* edited by D. Damas, pp. 303–19. Washington, D.C.: Smithsonian Institution Press.

1988   Models of Exchange in North-West Alaska. In *Hunters and Gatherers,* Vol. 2: *Property, Power and Ideology,* edited by T. Ingold, D. Riches, and J. Woodburn, pp. 95–109. Oxford: Berg.

1994   The Future of Hunter-Gatherer Research. In *Key Issues in Hunter-Gatherer Research,* edited by E. S. Burch, Jr. and L. J. Ellanna, pp. 441–55. Oxford: Berg.

Burton, M., L. Brudner, and D. White

1977   A Model of the Sexual Division of Labor. *American Ethnologist* 4:227–51.

Callaway, D., J. Janetski, and O. Stewart

1986   Ute. In *Handbook of North American Indians,* Vol. 11: *Great Basin,* edited by W. D'Azevedo, pp. 336–67. Washington, D.C.: Smithsonian Institution Press.

Campbell, B. C., and P. W. Leslie

1994   Reproductive Ecology of Human Males. *Yearbook of Physical Anthropology,* in press.

Campbell, K., and J. Wood

1988   Fertility in Traditional Societies. In *Natural and Human Fertility: Social and Biological Determinants,* edited by P. Diggory, M. Potts, and S. Teper, pp. 39–69. London: Macmillan.

Cane, S.

1987   Australian Aboriginal Subsistence in the Western Desert. *Human Ecology* 15:391–434.

1990   Desert Demography: A Case Study of Pre-Contact Aboriginal Densities in the Western Desert of Australia. In *Hunter-Gatherer Demography Past and Present,* edited by B. Meehan and N. White, pp. 149–59. Oceania Monograph 19. Sydney: University of Sydney.

Carneiro, R.

1970   A Theory of the Origin of the State. *Science* 169:733–38.

Carr-Saunders, A.

1922   *The Population Problem: A Study in Human Evolution.* Oxford: Clarendon.

Cartmill, M.

1993   *A View to a Death in the Morning: Hunting and Nature through History.* Cambridge: Harvard University Press.

Cashdan, E.

1980   Egalitarianism among Hunters and Gatherers. *American Anthropologist* 82:116–29.

1983   Territoriality among Human Foragers: Ecological Models and an Application to Four Bushman Groups. *Current Anthropology* 24:47–66.

1984   G//ana Territorial Organization. *Human Ecology* 12:443–63.

1985   Coping with Risk: Reciprocity among the Basarwa of Northern Botswana. *Man* 20:454–74.

1987   Trade and Its Origins on the Botletli River, Botswana. *Journal of Anthropological Research* 43:121–38.

1992   Spatial Organization and Habitat Use. In *Evolutionary Ecology and Human Behavior,* edited by E. Smith and B. Winterhalder, pp. 237–66. New York: Aldine de Gruyter.

Cashdan, E., ed.

1990   *Risk and Uncertainty in Tribal and Peasant Economies.* Boulder, Colo.: Westview.

Casteel, R.

1972   Two Static Maximum Population Density Models for Hunter-Gatherers. *World Archaeology* 4:20–40.

1979   Human Population Estimates for Hunting and Gathering Groups Based upon Net Primary Productivity Data: Examples from the Central Desert of Baja California. *Journal of Anthropological Research* 35:85–92.

Cavalli-Sforza, L., ed.

1986   *African Pygmies.* New York: Academic Press.

Cavalli-Sforza, L., and K. Feldman

1981   *Cultural Transmission and Evolution: A Quantitative Approach.* Princeton: Princeton University Press.

Chapman, M.

1980   Infanticide and Fertility among Eskimos: A Computer Simulation. *American Journal of Physical Anthropology* 53:317–27.

Charnov, E. L.

1976   Optimal Foraging, the Marginal Value Theorem. *Theoretical Population Biology* 9:129–36.

Chase, A., and P. Sutton

1987   Australian Aborigines in a Rich Environment. In *Traditional Aboriginal Society,* edited by W. H. Edwards, pp. 68–95. Melbourne: The Macmillan Company of Australia.

Chisholm, J., and V. Burbank

1991   Monogamy and Polygyny in Southeast Arnhem Land: Male Coercion and Female Choice. *Ethnology and Sociobiology* 12:291–313.

Clastres, P.

1972   The Guayaki. In *Hunters and Gatherers Today,* edited by M. G. Bicchieri, pp. 138–74. New York: Holt, Rinehart and Winston.

Codere, H.

1950   *Fighting with Property: A Study of Kwakiutl Potlatching and Warfare, 1792–
1930.* American Ethnological Society Monograph 18. Seattle: University
of Washington Press.

1990   Kwakiutl: Traditional Culture. In *Handbook of North American Indians,*
Vol. 7: *Northwest Coast,* edited by W. Suttles, pp. 359–77. Washington,
D.C.: Smithsonian Institution Press.

Cohen, M. N.

1977   *The Food Crisis in Prehistory: Overpopulation and the Origins of Agriculture.*
New Haven: Yale University Press.

1980   Speculations on the Evolution of Density Measurement and Population
Regulation in Homo Sapiens. In *Biosocial Mechanism of Population Regula-
tion,* edited by M. Cohen, R. Mapass, and H. Klein, pp. 275–303. New
Haven: Yale University Press.

1985   Prehistoric Hunter-Gatherers: The Meaning of Social Complexity. In
Prehistoric Hunter-Gatherers: The Emergence of Cultural Complexity, edited
by T. D. Price and J. A. Brown, pp. 99–119. Orlando, Fla.: Academic
Press.

1989   *Health and the Rise of Civilization.* New Haven: Yale University Press.

Collier, J.

1988   *Marriage and Inequality in Three Classless Societies.* Stanford: Stanford University Press.

Collier, J., and M. Rosaldo

1981   Politics and Gender in Simple Societies. In *Sexual Meanings: The Cultural
Construction of Gender and Sexuality,* edited by S. Ortner and H.
Whitehead, pp. 275–329. Cambridge: Cambridge University Press.

Condon, R.

1987   *Inuit Youth: Growth and Change in the Canadian Arctic.* New Brunswick,
N.J.: Rutgers University Press.

Condon, R., and R. Scaglion

1982   The Ecology of Human Birth Seasonality. *Human Ecology* 10:495–511.

Cook, S.

1976   *The Conflict Between the California Indians and White Civilization.* Berkeley: University of California Press.

Cooper, J.

1939   Is the Algonkian Family Hunting Ground System PreColumbian? *American Anthropologist* 41:66–90.

1946   The Culture of the Northeastern Indian Hunters: A Reconstructive Interpretation. In *Man in Northeastern North America,* Papers of the Robert
Peabody Foundation for Archaeology, edited by F. Johnson, pp. 272–
305. Andover, Mass.: Peabody Museum.

Cooper, Z.
1990   The End of "Bibipoiye" (Dog Not) Days in the Andamans. In *Hunter-Gatherer Demography Past and Present*, edited by B. Meehan and N. White, pp. 117–25. Oceania Monograph 19. Sydney: University of Sydney.

Counts, D. A.
1985   Tamparaonga: "The Big Women" of Kaliai (Papua New Guinea). In *In Her Prime: A New View of Middle-Aged Women*, edited by J. Brown and V. Kerns, pp. 49–64. S. Hadley, Mass.: Bergin and Garvey.

Coupland, G.
1985   Restricted Access, Resource Control and the Evolution of Status Inequality among Hunter-Gatherers. In *Status, Structure and Stratification: Current Archaeological Reconstructions*, edited by M. Thompson, M. Garcia, and F. Kense, pp. 217–26. Calgary: Archaeological Association of the University of Calgary.

Couture, M. D., M. F. Ricks, and L. Housley
1986   Foraging Behavior of a Contemporary Northern Great Basin Population. *Journal of California and Great Basin Anthropology* 8:150–60.

Cowlishaw, G.
1978   Infanticide in Aboriginal Australia. *Oceania* 48:262–83.
1981   The Determinants of Fertility among Australian Aborigines. *Mankind* 13:37–55.

Cox, B., ed.
1973   *Cultural Ecology.* Toronto: McLelland and Stewart.

Coxe, W.
[1787]   *Account of the Russian Discoveries Between Asia and America.* New York:
1804   A. M. Kelley.

Cribb, R.
1991   *Nomads in Archaeology.* Cambridge: Cambridge University Press.

Cronk, L.
1991   Human Behavioral Ecology. *Annual Review of Anthropology* 20:25–53.

Crow, J., and P. Obley
1981   Han. In *Handbook of North American Indians*, Vol. 6: *Subarctic*, edited by J. Helm, pp. 506–13. Washington, D.C.: Smithsonian Institution Press.

Cruikshank, J.
1990   *Life Lived Like a Story: Women's Lives in Athapaskan Narrative.* Lincoln: University of Nebraska Press.

Curr, E.
1886–87   *Australian Race.* Melbourne. 4 vols.

Dahlberg, F., ed.
1981   *Woman the Gatherer.* New Haven: Yale University Press.

Daly, M., and M. Wilson
1988   *Homicide.* New York: Aldine.

Damas, D.
1968   The Diversity of Eskimo Societies. In *Man the Hunter,* edited by R. B.
          Lee and I. DeVore, pp. 112–17. Chicago: Aldine.
1969a   Characteristics of Central Eskimo Band Structure. In *Contributions to An-*
          thropology: Band Societies, edited by D. Damas, pp. 116–38. National Mu-
          seum of Canada Bulletin 228. Ottawa: National Museum of Canada.
1969b   Environment, History, and Central Eskimo Society. In *Contributions to*
          Anthropology: Ecological Essays, edited by D. Damas, pp. 40–64. National
          Museum of Canada Bulletin 230. Ottawa: National Museum of Canada.
1972   The Copper Eskimo. In *Hunters and Gatherers Today,* edited by M. G.
          Bicchieri, pp. 3–50. New York: Holt, Rinehart and Winston.
1975a   Central Eskimo Systems of Food Sharing. *Ethnology* 11:220–39.
1975b   Demographic Aspects of Central Eskimo Marriage Practices. *American*
          Ethnologist 2:409–18.
1984   Copper Eskimo. In *Handbook of North American Indians,* Vol. 5: *Arctic,* ed-
          ited by D. Damas, pp. 397–414. Washington, D.C.: Smithsonian Institu-
          tion Press.

Damas, D., ed.
1969c   *Contributions to Anthropology: Band Societies.* National Museum of Canada
          Bulletin 228. Ottawa: National Museum of Canada.
1969d   *Contributions to Anthropology: Ecological Essays.* National Museum of Can-
          ada Bulletin 230. Ottawa: National Museum of Canada.

D'Anglure, B.
1984   Inuit of Quebec. In *Handbook of North American Indians,* Vol. 5: *Arctic,* ed-
          ited by D. Damas, pp. 476–507. Washington, D.C.: Smithsonian Institu-
          tion Press.

Darwin, C.
[1859]   *The Origin of Species.* New York: New American Library.
1958

Davidson, D.
1926   The Basis of Social Organization in Australia. *American Anthropologist*
          61:557–72.
1928   The Family Hunting Territory in Australia. *American Anthropologist*
          30:614–31.

de Garine, I., and G. Harrison, eds.
1988   *Coping with Uncertainty in Food Supply.* Oxford: Oxford University Press.

de Laguna, F.
1983   Aboriginal Tlingit Sociopolitical Organization. In *The Development of Po-*
          litical Organization in Native North America, edited by E. Tooker, pp. 71–
          85. Washington, D.C.: American Ethnological Society.

de Laguna, F., and C. McClellan
1981   Ahtna. In *Handbook of North American Indians,* Vol. 6: *Subarctic,* edited by
        J. Helm, pp. 641–63. Washington, D.C.: Smithsonian Institution Press.
Denbow, J.
1984   Prehistoric Herders and Foragers of the Kalahari: The Evidence for
        1500 Years of Interaction. In *Past and Present in Hunter Gatherer Studies,*
        edited by C. Schrire, pp. 175–94. Orlando, Fla.: Academic Press.
Denham, W. W.
1974a   Infant Transport among the Alyawara Tribe, Central Australia. *Oceania*
        44:253–77.
1974b   Population Structure, Infant Transport, and Infanticide among Pleisto-
        cene and Modern Hunter-Gatherers. *Journal of Anthropological Research*
        30:191–98.
Denniston, G.
1981   Sekani. In *Handbook of North American Indians,* Vol. 6: *Subarctic,* edited by
        J. Helm, pp. 433–41. Washington, D.C.: Smithsonian Institution Press.
Denys, P.
1908   *Description and Natural History of the Coasts of North America.* Toronto:
        The Champlain Society.
Dewar, R.
1984   Environmental Productivity, Population Regulation, and Carrying
        Capacity. *American Anthropologist* 86:601–14.
Dickemann, M.
1975   Demographic Consequences of Infanticide in Man. *Annual Review of
        Anthropology* 6:107–37.
Divale, W., and M. Harris
1976   Population, Warfare, and the Male Supremacist Complex. *American
        Anthropologist* 78:521–38.
Dixon, R.
1905   The Northern Maidu. *Bulletin of the American Museum of Natural History*
        17(3):119–346.
1907   The Shasta. *Bulletin of the American Museum of Natural History*
        17(5):381–498.
Dobkin de Rios, M., and B. Hayden
1985   Odorous Differentiation and Variability in the Sexual Division of Labor
        among Hunter/Gatherers. *Journal of Human Evolution* 14:219–28.
Donald, L.
1983   Was Nuu-chah-nulth-aht (Nootka) Society Based on Slave Labor? In
        The Development of Political Organization in Native North America, edited
        by E. Tooker, pp. 108–19. Washington, D.C.: American Ethnological
        Society.
1984   The Slave Trade on the Northwest Coast of North America. *Research in
        Economic Anthropology* 6:121–58.

1985   On the Possibility of Social Class in Societies Based on Extractive Subsistence. In *Status, Structure and Stratification: Current Archaeological Reconstructions,* edited by M. Thompson, M. T. Garcia, and F. J. Kense, pp. 237–43. Calgary: Archaeological Association of the University of Calgary.

Donald, L., and D. Mitchell

1975   Some Correlates of Local Group Rank among the Southern Kwakiutl. *Ethnology* 14:325–46.

1994   Nature and Culture on the Northwest Coast of North America: The Case of Wakashan Salmon Resources. In *Key Issues in Hunter-Gatherer Research,* edited by E. S. Burch, Jr., and L. Ellanna, pp. 95–117. Oxford: Berg.

Dowling, J.

1968   Individual Ownership and the Sharing of Game in Hunting Societies. *American Anthropologist* 70:502–7.

Downs, J. F.

1966   *The Two Worlds of the Washo.* New York: Holt, Rinehart and Winston.

Draper, P.

1975   !Kung Women: Contrasts in Sexual Egalitarianism in Foraging and Sedentary Contexts. In *Toward an Anthropology of Women,* edited by R. Reiter, pp. 77–109. New York: Monthly Review Press.

1976   Social and Economic Constraints on Child Life among the !Kung. In *Kalahari Hunter-Gatherers,* edited by R. B. Lee and I. DeVore, pp. 200–17. Cambridge: Harvard University Press.

1985   Two Views of Sex Differences in Socialization. In *Male-Female Differences: A Bio-Cultural Perspective,* edited by R. Hall, pp. 5–25. New York: Praeger.

Draper, P., and A. Buchanan

1992   If You Have a Child You Have a Life: Demographic and Cultural Perspectives on Fathering in Old Age in !Kung Society. In *Father-Child Relations: Cultural and Biosocial Contexts,* edited by B. Hewlett, pp. 131–52. New York: Aldine de Gruyter.

Draper, P., and E. Cashdan

1988   Technological Change and Child Behavior among the !Kung. *Ethnology* 27:339–65.

Draper, P., and H. Harpending

1982   Father Absence and Reproductive Strategy: An Evolutionary Perspective. *Journal of Anthropological Research* 38:255–73.

1987   Parent Investment and the Child's Environment. In *Parenting across the Lifespan: Biosocial Dimensions,* edited by J. Lancaster, A. Rossi, J. Altmann, and L. Sherod, pp. 207–35. New York: Aldine de Gruyter.

Drew, J., B. Blumberg, and J. Robert-Lamblin

1986   Hepatitis B Virus and Sex Ratio of Offspring in East Greenland. *Human Biology* 58:115–20.

Driver, H.
1961   *Indians of North America.* Chicago: University of Chicago Press.

Driver, H., and J. Coffin
1975   Classification and Development of North American Indian Cultures: Statistical Analysis of the Driver-Massey Sample. *Transactions of the American Philosophical Society* 65(3):1–120.

Driver, H., and W. Massey
1957   *Comparative Studies of North American Indians.* Transactions of the American Philosophical Society 47 (part 2). Philadelphia: American Philosophical Society.

Drucker, P.
1939   Rank, Wealth, and Kinship in Northwest Coast Society. *American Anthropologist* 41:55–64.

1951   *The Northern and Central Nootkan Tribes.* Bureau of American Ethnology Bulletin 144. Washington, D.C.

1983   Ecology and Political Organization on the Northwest Coast of America. In *The Development of Political Organization in Native North America,* edited by E. Tooker, pp. 86–96. Washington, D.C.: American Ethnological Society.

Drucker, P., and R. Heizer
1967   *To Make My Name Good: A Reexamination of the Southern Kwakiutl Potlatch.* Berkeley: University of California Press.

DuBois, C.
1932   Tolowa Notes. *American Anthropologist* 34:248–62.

Dunbar, R.
1988   Darwinizing Man: A Commentary. In *Human Reproductive Behavior: A Darwinian Approach,* edited by L. Betzig, M. Mulder, and P. Turke, pp. 161–69. Cambridge: Cambridge University Press.

Dunn, F.
1968   Epidemiological Factors: Health and Disease in Hunter-Gatherers. In *Man the Hunter,* edited by R. B. Lee and I. DeVore, pp. 221–27. Chicago: Aldine.

Dunning, R.
1959   Rules of Residence and Ecology among the Northern Ojibwa. *Southwestern Journal of Anthropology* 15:806–16.

Durham, W.
1976   Resource Competition and Human Aggression, Part 1: A Review of Primitive War. *The Quarterly Review of Biology* 51:385–415.

1991   *Coevolution: Genes, Culture, and Human Diversity.* Stanford: Stanford University Press.

Dwyer, P.
1974   The Price of Protein: Five Hundred Hours of Hunting in the New Guinea Highlands. *Oceania* 44:278–93.

| 1983 | Etolo Hunting Performance and Energetics. *Human Ecology* 11:145–74. |

1985a   A Hunt in New Guinea: Some Difficulties for Optimal Foraging Theory. *Man* 20:243–53.

1985b   Choice and Constraint in a Papua New Guinea Food Quest. *Human Ecology* 13:49–70.

Dwyer, P., and M. Minnegal

1985   Andaman Islanders, Pygmies and an Extension of Horn's Model. *Human Ecology* 13:111–20.

Dyson-Hudson, R., and E. A. Smith

1978   Human Territoriality: An Ecological Reassessment. *American Anthropologist* 80:21–41.

Eder, J.

1978   The Caloric Returns to Food Collecting: Disruption and Change among the Batak of the Philippine Tropical Forest. *Human Ecology* 6:55–69.

1984   The Impact of Subsistence Change on Mobility and Settlement Pattern in a Tropical Forest Foraging Economy: Some Implications for Archaeology. *American Anthropologist* 86:837–53.

1987   *On the Road to Tribal Extinction: Depopulation, Deculturation and Adaptive Well-Being among the Batak of the Philippines.* Berkeley: University of California Press.

Ellanna, L.

1990   Demographic Change, Sedentism, and Western Contact: An Inland Dena'ina Athabaskan Case Study. In *Hunter-Gatherer Demography Past and Present,* edited by B. Meehan and N. White, pp. 101–16. Oceania Monograph 19. Sydney: University of Sydney.

Ellen, R.

1982   *Environment, Subsistence and System: The Ecology of Small Scale Social Formations.* Cambridge: Cambridge University Press.

Ellison, P.

1990   Human Ovarian Function and Reproductive Ecology: New Hypotheses. *American Anthropologist* 92:933–52.

1994   Human Reproductive Ecology. *Annual Review of Anthropology* 23:255–75.

Ellison, P., N. Peacock, and C. Lager

1989   Ecology and Ovarian Function among Lese Women of the Ituri Forest, Zaire. *American Journal of Physical Anthropology* 78:519–26.

Elmendorf, W.

1960   *Structure of Twana Culture.* Washington State University, Research Studies, Monographic Supplement No. 2:1–576. Pullman: Washington State University Press.

1971   Coast Salish Status Ranking and Intergroup Ties. *Southwestern Journal of Anthropology* 27:353–80.

Elsasser, A.
1978   Mattole, Nongatl, Sinkyone, Lassik, and Wailaki. In *Handbook of North American Indians*, Vol. 11: *California*, edited by R. Heizer, pp. 190–204. Washington, D.C.: Smithsonian Institution Press.

Ember, C.
1975   Residential Variation among Hunter-Gatherers. *Behavior Science Research* 3:199–227.
1978   Myths about Hunter-Gatherers. *Ethnology* 17:439–48.

Ember, M., and C. Ember
1971   The Conditions Favoring Matrilocal versus Patrilocal Residence. *American Anthropologist* 73:571–94.

Emlen, J.
1966   The Role of Time and Energy in Food Preference. *American Naturalist* 100:611–17.

Emmons, G. T.
1991   *The Tlingit Indians*. Edited and with Additions by F. de Laguna. American Museum of Natural History Anthropological Papers 70. New York: American Museum of Natural History.

Endicott, K.
1981   The Conditions of Egalitarian Male-Female Relationships in Foraging Societies. *Canberra Anthropology* 14:1–10.

Endicott, K., and K. L. Endicott
1986   The Question of Hunter-Gatherer Territoriality: The Case of the Batek in Malaysia. In *The Past and Future of !Kung Ethnography: Critical Reflections and Symbolic Perspectives, Essays in Honour of Lorna Marshall*, edited by M. Biesele, R. Gordon, and R. B. Lee. Hamburg: Helmut Buske Verlag.

Engels, F.
[1884]   *The Origin of the Family, Private Property, and the State*. Trans. by E. Unter-
1954   mann. Moscow: Foreign Languages Publishing House.

Estioko-Griffin, A., and P. Griffin
1981   Woman the Hunter: The Agta. In *Woman the Gatherer*, edited by F. Dahlberg, pp. 121–51. New Haven: Yale University Press.
1985   Women Hunters: The Implications for Pleistocene Prehistory and Contemporary Ethnography. In *Women in Asia and the Pacific. Towards an East-West Dialogue*, edited by M. Goodman, pp. 61–81. Honolulu: University of Hawaii Press.

Ewers, J.
1955   *The Horse in Blackfoot Indian Culture*. Bureau of American Ethnology Bulletin 159. Washington, D.C.

Eyre, E.
1845   *Journals of Expeditions of Discovery into Central Australia and Overland from Adelaide to King George's Sound, in the Years 1840–1*. London: T. and W. Boone.

Feit, H. A.
1973   The Ethno-Ecology of the Waswanipi Cree; or How Hunters Can Handle Their Resources. In *Cultural Ecology,* edited by B. Cox, pp. 115–25. Toronto: McLelland & Stewart.
1982   The Future of Hunters within Nation States: Anthropology and the James Bay Cree. In *Politics and History in Band Societies,* edited by E. Leacock and R. B. Lee, pp. 373–411. Cambridge: Cambridge University Press.
1994   The Enduring Pursuit: Land, Time, and Social Relationships in Anthropological Models of Hunter-Gatherers and in Subarctic Hunters' Images. In *Key Issues in Hunter-Gatherer Research,* edited by E. S. Burch, Jr. and L. J. Ellanna, pp. 421–39. Oxford: Berg.

Ferguson, B.
1983   Warfare and Redistributive Exchange on the Northwest Coast. In *The Development of Political Organization in Native North America,* edited by E. Tooker, pp. 133–47. Washington, D.C.: American Ethnological Society.
1984   A Reexamination of the Causes of Northwest Coast Warfare. In *Warfare, Culture, and Environment,* edited by R. Ferguson, pp. 267–328. New York: Academic Press.

Flanagan, J.
1989   Hierarchy in Simple "Egalitarian" Societies. *Annual Review of Anthropology* 18:245–66.

Flood, J.
1980   *The Moth Hunters: Aboriginal Prehistory of the Australian Alps.* Canberra: Australian Institute of Aboriginal Studies.

Foley, R.
1982   A Reconsideration of the Role of Predation on Large Mammals in Tropical Hunter-Gatherer Adaptation. *Man* 17:393–402.
1985   Optimality Theory in Anthropology. *Man* 20:222–42.
1988   Hominids, Humans, and Hunter-Gatherers: An Evolutionary Perspective. In *Hunters and Gatherers,* Vol. 1: *History, Evolution, and Social Change,* edited by T. Ingold, D. Riches, and J. Woodburn, pp. 207–21. Oxford: Berg.

Fowler, C.
1982   Food-Named Groups among Northern Paiute in North America's Great Basin: An Ecological Interpretation. In *Resource Managers: North American and Australian Hunter-Gatherers,* edited by E. Hunn and N. Williams, pp. 113–30. Boulder, Colo.: Westview Press.

Fowler, C., and N. Walter
1985   Harvesting Pandora Moth Larvae with the Owens Valley Paiute. *Journal of California and Great Basin Anthropology* 7:155–65.

Fowler, D., and C. Fowler
1971   *Anthropology of the Numa: John Wesley Powell's Manuscripts of the Numic*

Peoples of Western North America. Smithsonian Contributions to Anthropology No. 14. Washington, D.C.

Fox, R.
1969   Professional Primitives: Hunters and Gatherers of Nuclear South Asia. *Man in India* 49:139–60.

Freeman, M.
1971   A Social and Ecologic Analysis of Systematic Female Infanticide among the Netsilik Eskimo. *American Anthropologist* 73:1011–18.

Freuchen, P.
1961   *Book of the Eskimos.* Edited by D. Freuchen. New York: Fawcett.

Frisch, R.
1978   Nutrition, Fatness, and Fertility: The Effect of Food Intake on Reproductive Ability. In *Nutrition and Reproduction,* edited by W. W. Mosley, pp. 99–122. New York: Plenum Press.

Furer-Haimendorf, C. von
1943   *The Chenchus.* London: Macmillan.

Gage, T. B.
1979   The Competitive Interactions of Man and Deer in Prehistoric California. *Human Ecology* 7:253–68.

Gardner, P.
1972   The Paliyans. In *Hunters and Gatherers Today,* edited by M. G. Bicchieri, pp. 404–47. New York: Holt, Rinehart and Winston.
1988   Pressures for Tamil Property in Paliyan Social Organization. In *Hunters and Gatherers,* Vol. 1: *History, Evolution, and Social Change,* edited by T. Ingold, D. Riches, and J. Woodburn, pp. 91–106. Oxford: Berg.
1991   Foragers' Pursuit of Individual Autonomy. *Current Anthropology* 32:543–72.
1993   Dimensions of Subsistence Foraging in South India. *Ethnology* 32:109–44.

Garth, T.
1978   Atsugewi. In *Handbook of North American Indians,* Vol. 11: *California,* edited by R. Heizer, pp. 236–43. Washington, D.C.: Smithsonian Institution Press.

Gatschet, A.
1890   *The Klamath Indians of Southwestern Oregon.* Washington, D.C.: U.S. Government Printing Office.

Geertz, C.
1973   *The Interpretation of Cultures.* New York: Basic Books.

Gelber, M. G.
1986   *Gender and Society in the New Guinea Highlands.* Boulder, Colo.: Westview Press.

Gilberg, R.

1984   Polar Eskimo. In *Handbook of North American Indians*, Vol. 5: *Arctic*, edited by D. Damas, pp. 577–94. Washington, D.C.: Smithsonian Institution Press.

Goddard, P.

1917   The Beaver Indians. *Anthropological Papers of the American Museum of Natural History* 10 (part 5):295–397.

Godelier, M.

1977   *Perspectives in Marxist Anthropology.* Cambridge: Cambridge University Press.

Gomes, A.

1982   *Ecological Adaptation and Population Change: Semang Foragers and Temuan Horticulturalists in West Malaysia.* East-West Environment and Policy Institute Research Report No. 12. Honolulu: East-West Center.

1990   Demographic Implications of Villagisation among the Semang of Malaysia. In *Hunter-Gatherer Demography Past and Present,* edited by B. Meehan and N. White, pp. 126–48, Oceania Monograph 19. Sydney: University of Sydney.

Goodale, J.

1971   *Tiwi Wives: A Study of the Women of Melville Island, North Australia.* Seattle: University of Washington Press.

Goodman, M., P. Griffin, A. Estioko-Griffin, and J. Grove

1985   The Compatibility of Hunting and Mothering among the Agta Hunter-Gatherers of the Philippines. *Sex Roles* 12:1199–1209.

Gordon, R.

1984   The !Kung in the Kalahari Exchange: An Ethnohistorical Perspective. In *Past and Present in Hunter Gatherer Studies,* edited by C. Schrire, pp. 195–224. Orlando, Fla.: Academic Press.

1992   *The Bushman Myth: The Making of a Namibian Underclass.* Boulder, Colo.: Westview Press.

Gould, R.

1968   Living Archaeology: The Ngatatjara of Western Australia. *Southwestern Journal of Anthropology* 24:101–22.

1969a   Subsistence Behavior among the Western Desert Aborigines of Australia. *Oceania* 39:253–74.

1969b   *Yiwara: Foragers of the Australian Desert.* New York: Scribners.

1978   Tolowa. In *Handbook of North American Indians*, Vol. 8: *California*, edited by R. Heizer, pp. 128–36. Washington: Smithsonian Institution Press.

1980   *Living Archaeology.* Cambridge: Cambridge University Press.

1982   To Have and Have Not: The Ecology of Sharing among Hunter-Gatherers. In *Resource Managers: North American and Australian Hunter-*

Gatherers, edited by E. Hunn and N. Williams, pp. 69–92. Boulder, Colo.: Westview Press.

1991   Arid-Land Foraging as Seen From Australia: Adaptive Models and Behavioral Realities. *Oceania* 62:12–33.

Gould, R., D. Fowler, and C. Fowler

1972   Diggers and Doggers: Parallel Failures in Economic Acculturation. *Southwestern Journal of Anthropology* 28:265–81.

Gould, S. J.

1989   *Wonderful Life.* New York: W. W. Norton.

Gragson, T.

1993   Human Foraging in Lowland South America: Pattern and Process of Resource Procurement. *Research in Economic Anthropology* 14:107–38.

Grant, P.

1890   The Saulteau Indians Vers 1804. In *Les Bourgeois de la Compagnie Du Nord-ouest: Recits de Voyages, Lettres et Rapports Inedit Relatifs Au Nord-ouest Canadien,* Vol. 2, edited by L. Masson, pp. 306–66. Quebec: A. Cote.

Grey, G.

1841   *Journals of Two Expeditions of Discovery in Northwest and Western Australia During the Years 1837, 38, and 39.* 2 vols. London: T. and W. Boone.

Griffin, P. B.

1984   Forager Resource and Land Use in the Humid Tropics: The Agta of Northeastern Luzon, the Philippines. In *Past and Present in Hunter Gatherer Studies,* edited by C. Schrire, pp. 95–121. Orlando, Fla.: Academic Press.

1989   Hunting, Farming, and Sedentism in a Rain Forest Foraging Society. In *Farmers as Hunters: The Implications of Sedentism,* edited by S. Kent, pp. 60–70. Cambridge: Cambridge University Press.

Grinker, R.

1990   Images of Denigration: Structuring Inequality Between Foragers and Farmers in the Ituri Forest. *American Ethnologist* 17:111–30.

1994   *Houses in the Rainforest: Ethnicity and Inequality among Farmers and Foragers in Central Africa.* Berkeley: University of California Press.

Gusinde, M.

1934   *The Selk'nam: On the Life and Thought of a Hunting People on the Great Islands of Tierra del Fuego.* Trans. by F. Schultze. New Haven: Human Relations Area Files.

Gussow, Z.

1954   Cheyenne and Arapaho: Aboriginal Occupations. In *American Indian Ethnohistory: Plains Indians,* edited by D. Horr, pp. 27–96. New York: Garland Publishing.

Haines, F.
1955   *The Nez Percés.* Norman: University of Oklahoma Press.
Hall, E.
1984   Interior North Alaskan Eskimo. In *Handbook of North American Indians,* Vol. 5: *Arctic,* edited by D. Damas, pp. 338–46. Washington, D.C.: Smithsonian Institution Press.
Hallowell, I.
1949   The Size of Algonkian Hunting Territories: A Function of Ecological Adjustment. *American Anthropologist* 51:35–45.
Halperin, R.
1980   Ecology and Mode of Production: Seasonal Variation and the Division of Labor by Sex among Hunter-Gatherers. *Journal of Anthropological Research* 36:379–99.
Hames, R.
1987   Game Conservation or Efficient Hunting? In *The Question of the Commons,* edited by B. McCoy and J. Acheson, pp. 92–107. Tucson: University of Arizona Press.
1988   The Allocation of Parental Care among the Ye'kwana. In *Human Reproductive Behavior: A Darwinian Approach,* edited by L. Betzig, M. Mulder, and P. Turke, pp. 237–52. Cambridge: Cambridge University Press.
Hames, R., and W. Vickers
1982   Optimal Diet Breadth Theory as a Model to Explain Variability in Amazonian Hunting. *American Ethnologist* 9:358–78.
Hames, R., and W. Vickers, eds.
1983   *Adaptive Responses of Native Amazonians.* New York: Academic Press.
Hamilton, A.
1980   Dual Social Systems: Technology, Labour and Women's Secret Rites in the Eastern Western Desert of Australia. *Oceania* 51:4–19.
1981   *Nature and Nurture: Aboriginal Child-Rearing in North Central Arnhem Land.* Canberra: Australian Institute of Aboriginal Studies.
1982a   Descended from Father, Belonging to Country: Rights to Land in the Australian Western Desert. In *Politics and History in Band Societies,* edited by E. Leacock and R. B. Lee, pp. 85–108. Cambridge: Cambridge University Press.
1982b   The Unity of Hunting-Gathering Societies: Reflections on Economic Forms and Resource Management. In *Resource Managers: North American and Australian Hunter-Gatherers,* edited by E. Hunn and N. Williams, pp. 229–47. Boulder, Colo.: Westview.
Handwerker, W.
1983   The First Demographic Transition: An Analysis of Subsistence Choices and Reproductive Consequences. *American Anthropologist* 85:5–27.

Hantzsch, B.

1977   *My Life among the Eskimos: Baffinland Journeys in the Years 1909 to 1911.* Edited and translated by L. Neatby. Saskatoon: University of Saskatchewan Press.

Harako, R.

1976   The Mbuti as Hunters. *Kyoto University African Studies* 10:37–99.

1981   The Cultural Ecology of Hunting Behavior among Mbuti Pygmies in the Ituri Forest, Zaire. In *Omnivorous Primates,* edited by R. Harding and G. Teleki, pp. 499–555. New York: Columbia University Press.

Hard, R., and W. Merrill

1992   Mobile Agriculturalists and the Emergence of Sedentism: Perspectives from Northern Mexico. *American Anthropologist* 94:601–20.

Harpending, H.

1991   Review of Wilmsen 1989. *Anthropos* 86:313–15.

Harpending, H., and L. Wandsnider

1982   Population Structure of Ghanzi and Ngamiland !Kung. *Current Developments in Anthropological Genetics* 2:29–50.

Harris, D. R.

1978   Settling Down: An Evolutionary Model for the Transformation of Mobile Bands into Sedentary Communities. In *The Evolution of Social Systems,* edited by J. Friedrich and M. S. Rowlands, pp. 401–17. London: Duckworth.

Harris, M.

1968   *The Rise of Anthropological Theory.* New York: Thomas Y. Crowell.

1979   *Cultural Materialism.* New York: Random House.

Harrison, T.

1949   Notes on Some Nomadic Punans. *Sarawak Museum Journal* 5:130–46.

Hart, J.

1978   From Subsistence to Market: A Case Study of the Mbuti Net Hunters. *Human Ecology* 6:325–53.

Hart, T., and J. Hart

1986   The Ecological Basis of Hunter-Gatherer Subsistence in African Rain Forests: The Mbuti of Eastern Zaire. *Human Ecology* 14:29–55.

Hart, C., and A. Pilling

1960   *The Tiwi of North Australia.* New York: Holt, Rinehart and Winston.

Hassan, F.

1981   *Demographic Archaeology.* New York: Academic Press.

Hausman, A. J., and E. N. Wilmsen

1985   Economic Change and Secular Trends in the Growth of San Children. *Human Biology* 57:563–71.

Hawkes, K.

1981   A Third Explanation for Female Infanticide. *Human Ecology* 9:79–107.

1990   Why Do Men Hunt? Benefits for Risky Choices. In *Risk and Uncertainty in Tribal and Peasant Economies*, edited by E. Cashdan, pp. 145–66. Boulder, Colo.: Westview.

1991   Showing Off: Tests of an Hypothesis about Men's Foraging Goals. *Ethology and Sociobiology* 12:29–54.

1992   Sharing and Collective Action. In *Evolutionary Ecology and Human Behavior*, edited by E. Smith and B. Winterhalder, pp. 269–300. Hawthorne, N.Y.: Aldine de Gruyter.

1993a   Reply to Kaplan and Hill. *Current Anthropology* 34:706–9.

1993b   Why Hunter-gatherers Work: An Ancient Version of the Problem with Public Goods. *Current Anthropology* 34:341–62.

Hawkes, K., K. Hill, and J. O'Connell

1982   Why Hunters Gather: Optimal Foraging and the Ache of Eastern Paraguay. *American Ethnologist* 9:379–98.

Hawkes, K., H. Kaplan, K. Hill, and A. M. Hurtado

1987   Ache at the Settlement: Contrasts Between Farming and Foraging. *Human Ecology* 15:133–61.

Hawkes, K., and J. O'Connell

1981   Affluent Hunters? Some Comments in Light of the Alyawara Case. *American Anthropologist* 83:622–26.

1985   Optimal Foraging Models and the Case of the !Kung. *American Anthropologist* 87:401–5.

Hawkes, K., J. O'Connell, and N. Blurton Jones

1989   Hardworking Hadza Grandmothers. In *Comparative Socioecology: The Behavioural Ecology of Humans and Other Mammals*, edited by V. Standen and R. Foley, pp. 341–66. Oxford: Blackwell Scientific.

Hawkes, K., J. O'Connell, and N. Blurton Jones

1991   Hunting Income Patterns among the Hadza: Big Game, Common Goods, Foraging Goals and the Evolution of the Human Diet. In *Foraging Strategies and Natural Diet of Monkeys, Apes and Humans*, edited by A. Whiten and E. Widdowson, pp. 243–51. Proceedings of the Royal Society of London 334. Oxford: Clarendon Press.

Hayden, B.

1972   Population Control among Hunter/Gatherers. *World Archaeology* 4:205–21.

1975   The Carrying Capacity Dilemma: An Alternative Approach. *American Antiquity* 40:11–21.

1981a   Research and Development in the Stone Age: Technological Transitions among Hunter-Gatherers. *Current Anthropology* 22:519–28.

1981b   Subsistence and Ecological Adaptations of Modern Hunter-Gatherers. In *Omnivorous Primates: Hunting and Gathering in Human Evolution,* edited by G. Teleki and R. Harding, pp. 344–422. New York: Columbia University Press.

1986   Resources, Rivalry, and Reproduction: The Influences of Basic Resource Characteristics on Reproductive Behavior. In *Culture and Reproduction: An Anthropological Critique of Demographic Transition Theory,* edited by W. Handwerker, pp. 176–95. Boulder, Colo.: Westview.

1990   Nimrods, Piscators, Pluckers, and Planters: The Emergence of Food Production. *Journal of Anthropological Archaeology* 9:31–69.

1994   Competition, Labor, and Complex Hunter-Gatherers. In *Key Issues in Hunter-Gatherer Research,* edited by E. S. Burch, Jr. and L. J. Ellanna, pp. 223–39. Oxford: Berg.

Hayden, B., ed.

1992   *A Complex Culture of the British Columbia Plateau: Traditional Stl'atl'imx Resource Use.* Vancouver: University of British Columbia Press.

Hayden, B., and R. Gargett

1990   Big Man, Big Heart? A Mesoamerican View of the Emergence of Complex Society. *Ancient Mesoamerica* 1:3–20.

Hayden, B., M. Deal, A. Cannon, and J. Casey

1986   Ecological Determinants of Women's Status among Hunter/Gatherers. *Human Evolution* 1:449–74.

Headland, T. N.

1988   Ecosystemic Change in a Philippine Tropical Rainforest and Its Effect on a Negrito Foraging Society. *Tropical Ecology* 29:121–35.

1989   Population Decline in a Philippine Negrito Hunter-Gatherer Society. *American Journal of Human Biology* 1:59–72.

Headland, T. N., ed.

1992   *The Tasaday Controversy: Assessing the Evidence.* Special Publication No. 28. Washington, D.C.: American Anthropological Association.

Headland, T. N., and R. Bailey, eds.

1991   Human Ecology Special Issue: Human Foragers in Tropical Rain Forests. *Human Ecology* 19(2).

Headland, T. N., and L. A. Reid

1989   Hunter-Gatherers and Their Neighbors from Prehistory to the Present. *Current Anthropology* 30:43–66.

Heffley, S.

1981   Northern Athabaskan Settlement Patterns and Resource Distributions: An Application of Horn's Model. In *Hunter-Gatherer Foraging Strategies,* edited by B. Winterhalder and E. A. Smith, pp. 126–47. Chicago: University of Chicago Press.

Hegmon, M.

1991   The Risks of Sharing and Sharing as Risk Reduction: Interhousehold
        Food Sharing in Egalitarian Societies. In *Between Bands and States,* edited
        by S. Gregg, pp. 309–29. Center for Archaeological Investigations Occa-
        sional Paper No. 9. Carbondale, Ill.: Southern Illinois University Press.

Heinz, H.

1972   Territoriality among the Bushmen in General and the !Ko in Particular.
        Anthropos 67:405–16.

Heizer, R.

1950   Kutsavi, A Great Basin Indian Food. *Kroeber Anthropological Society Papers*
        2:35–41.

Helm, J.

1965   Bilaterality in the Socio-territorial Organization of the Arctic Drainage
        Dene. *Ethnology* 4:361–85.

1968   The Nature of Dogrib Socioterritorial Groups. In *Man the Hunter,* ed-
        ited by R. B. Lee and I. DeVore, pp. 118–25. Chicago: Aldine.

1972   The Dogrib Indians. In *Hunters and Gatherers Today,* edited by M. G.
        Bicchieri, pp. 51–89. New York: Holt, Rinehart and Winston.

1980   Female Infanticide, European Diseases, and Population Levels among
        the MacKenzie Dene. *American Ethnologist* 7:259–85.

1981   Dogrib. In *Handbook of North American Indians,* Vol. 6: *Subarctic,* edited
        by J. Helm, pp. 291–309. Washington, D.C.: Smithsonian Institution
        Press.

Henry, J.

1941   *The Jungle People.* New York: Vintage.

Hetzel, B.

1978   The Changing Nutrition of Aborigines in the Ecosystem of Central Aus-
        tralia. In *The Nutrition of Aborigines in Relation to the Ecosystem of Central Aus-
        tralia,* edited by B. Hetzel and H. Frith, pp. 39–47. Melbourne: CSIRO.

Hewlett, B.

1988   Sexual Selection and Paternal Investment among Aka Pygmies. In *Hu-
        man Reproductive Behavior: A Darwinian Perspective,* edited by L. Betzig,
        M. Mulder, and P. Turke, pp. 263–76. New York: Cambridge Univer-
        sity Press.

1991a   Demography and Childcare in Preindustrial Societies. *Journal of Anthropo-
        logical Research* 47:1–37.

1991b   *Intimate Fathers: The Nature and Context of Aka Pygmy Paternal Infant Care.*
        Ann Arbor: University of Michigan Press.

1992a   Husband-Wife Reciprocity and the Father-Infant Relationship among
        Aka Pygmies. In *Father-Child Relations: Cultural and Biosocial Contexts,* ed-
        ited by B. Hewlett, pp. 153–76. New York: Aldine de Gruyter.

Hewlett, B., ed.
1992b   *Father-Child Relations: Cultural and Biosocial Contexts.* New York: Aldine
          de Gruyter.
Hewlett, B., and L. Cavalli-Sforza
1986   Cultural Transmission among the Aka Pygmies. *American Anthropologist*
          88:15–32.
Hewlett, B., J. van de Koppel, and M. van de Koppel
1986   Causes of Death among Aka Pygmies of the Central African Republic.
          In *African Pygmies,* edited by L. Cavalli-Sforza, pp. 45–63. New York:
          Academic Press.
Hiatt (Meehan), B.
1967   The Food Quest and Economy of the Tasmanian Aborigines. *Oceania*
          38:99–133.
1968   The Food Quest and Economy of the Tasmanian Aborigines. *Oceania*
          38:190–219.
1978   Woman the Gatherer. In *Woman's Role in Aboriginal Society,* edited by F.
          Gale, pp. 4–15. Canberra: Australian Institute of Aboriginal Studies.
Hiatt, L.
1962   Local Organization among the Australian Aborigines. *Oceania*
          32:267–86.
1965   *Kinship and Conflict: A Study of an Aboriginal Community in Northern Arn-
          hem Land.* Canberra: Australian National University Press.
1966   The Lost Horde. *Oceania* 37:81–92.
1968   Gidjingali Marriage Arrangements. In *Man the Hunter,* edited by R. B.
          Lee and I. DeVore, pp. 165–75. Chicago: Aldine.
Hill, K.
1988   Macronutrient Modifications of Optimal Foraging Theory: An Ap-
          proach Using Indifference Curves Applied to Some Modern Foragers.
          Human Ecology 16:157–97.
Hill, K., and K. Hawkes
1983   Neotropical Hunting among the Ache of Eastern Paraguay. In *Adaptive
          Responses of Native Amazonians,* edited by R. Hames and W. Vickers, pp.
          139–88. New York: Academic Press.
Hill, K., and H. Kaplan
1988a   Tradeoffs in Male and Female Reproductive Strategies among the Ache:
          Part 1. In *Human Reproductive Behavior: A Darwinian Perspective,* edited by
          L. Betzig, M. Mulder, and P. Turke, pp. 277–89. New York: Cambridge
          University Press.
1988b   Tradeoffs in Male and Female Reproductive Strategies among the Ache:
          Part 2. In *Human Reproductive Behavior: A Darwinian Perspective,* edited by
          L. Betzig, M. Mulder, and P. Turke, pp. 291–305. New York: Cam-
          bridge University Press.

1993   On Why Male Foragers Hunt and Share Food. *Current Anthropology* 34:701–6.

Hill, K., K. Hawkes, M. Hurtado, and H. Kaplan

1984   Seasonal Variance in the Diet of Ache Hunter-Gatherers in Eastern Paraguay. *Human Ecology* 12:101–35.

Hill, K., H. Kaplan, K. Hawkes, and A. Hurtado

1985   Men's Time Allocation to Subsistence Work among the Ache of Eastern Paraguay. *Human Ecology* 13:29–47.

Hill, K., K. Kaplan, K. Hawkes, and M. Hurtado

1987   Foraging Decisions among Aché Hunter-Gatherers: New Data and Implications for Optimal Foraging Models. *Ethology and Sociobiology* 8:1–36.

Hitchcock, R.

1982   Patterns of Sedentism among the Basarwa of Eastern Botswana. In *Politics and History in Band Society,* edited by E. Leacock and R. B. Lee, pp. 223–67. New York: Cambridge University Press.

1987a   Sedentism and Site Structure: Organizational Change in Kalahari Basarwa Residential Locations. In *Method and Theory for Activity Area Research,* edited by S. Kent, pp. 374–423. New York: Columbia University Press.

1987b   Socioeconomic Change among the Basarwa in Botswana: An Ethnohistorical Analysis. *Ethnohistory* 34:219–55.

1989   Harmless Hunters, Fierce Fighters or Persistent Pastoralists: The Policy Implications of Academic Stereotypes. Paper Presented at the 89th Annual Meeting of the American Anthropological Association, Washington, D.C.

Hitchcock, R., and J. Ebert

1984   Foraging and Food Production among Kalahari Hunter/Gatherers. In *From Hunters to Farmers: The Causes and Consequences of Food Production in Africa,* edited by J. Clark and S. Brandt, pp. 328–48. Berkeley: University of California Press.

1989   Modeling Kalahari Hunter-gatherer Subsistence and Settlement Systems. *Anthropos* 84:47–62.

Hobbes, T.

[1651]   *Leviathan.* Edited with an introduction by C. A. MacPherson. Balti-
1968   more: Penguin.

Hoffman, C.

1984   Punan Foragers in the Trading Networks of Southeast Asia. In *Past and Present in Hunter Gatherer Studies,* edited by C. Schrire, pp. 123–49. Orlando, Fla.: Academic Press.

Holmberg, A.

1950   *Nomads of the Long Bow: The Siriono of Eastern Bolivia.* Washington, D.C.: Smithsonian Institution Press.

Honigmann, J.
1949   *Culture and Ethos of Kaska Society.* Yale University Publications in Anthropology 40. New Haven, Conn.: Yale University Press.
Horn, H.
1968   The Adaptive Significance of Colonial Nesting in the Brewers Blackbird (*Euphagus cyanocephalus*). *Ecology* 49:282–94.
Horne, G., and G. Aiston
1924   *Savage Life in Central Australia.* London: Macmillan.
Hosley, E.
1981   Environment and Culture in the Alaskan Plateau. In *Handbook of North American Indians,* Vol. 6: *Subarctic,* edited by J. Helm, pp. 533–45. Washington, D.C.: Smithsonian Institution Press.
Howell, N.
1979   *Demography of the Dobe !Kung.* New York: Academic Press.
1986a   Demographic Anthropology. *Annual Review of Anthropology* 15:219–46.
1986b   Feedbacks and Buffers in Relation to Scarcity and Abundance: Studies of Hunter-Gatherer Populations. In *The State of Population Theory,* edited by D. Coleman and R. Schofield, pp. 156–87. Oxford: Basil Blackwell.
Hughes, C. C.
1984   Saint Lawrence Island Eskimo. In *Handbook of North American Indians,* Vol. 5: *Arctic,* edited by D. Damas, pp. 262–77. Washington, D.C.: Smithsonian Institution Press.
Hunn, E. S.
1981   On the Relative Contribution of Men and Women to Subsistence among Hunter-Gatherers of the Columbia Plateau: A Comparison with Ethnographic Atlas Summaries. *Journal of Ethnobiology* 1:124–34.
1982   Mobility as a Factor Limiting Resource Use in the Columbia Plateau Basin of North America. In *Resource Managers: North American and Australian Hunter-Gatherers,* edited by E. Hunn and N. Williams, pp. 17–43. Boulder, Colo.: Westview.
1994   Place-names, Population Density, and the Magic Number 500. *Current Anthropology* 35:81–5.
Huntingsford, G.
1929   Modern Hunters: Some Accounts of the Kamelilo-Kapchepkendi Dorobo (Okiek) of Kenya Colony. *Journal of the Royal Anthropological Institute of Great Britain and Ireland* 69:333–78.
Hurtado, A., and K. Hill
1987   Early Dry Season Subsistence Ecology of Cuiva (Hiwi) Foragers of Venezuela. *Human Ecology* 15:163–87.
1989   Experimental Studies of Tool Efficiency among Machiguenga Women and Implications for Root-Digging Foragers. *Journal of Anthropological Research* 45:207–17.

1990   Seasonality in a Foraging Society: Variation in Diet, Work Effort, Fertil-
           ity and Sexual Division of Labor among the Hiwi of Venezuela. *Journal
           of Anthropological Research* 46:293–346.

1992   Paternal Effect on Offspring Survivorship among Ache and Hiwi
           Hunter-Gatherers: Implications for Modeling Pair-Bond Stability. In
           Father-Child Relations: Cultural and Biosocial Contexts, edited by B. Hew-
           lett, pp. 31–55. New York: Aldine de Gruyter.

Hurtado, A., K. Hawkes, K. Hill, and H. Kaplan

1985   Female Subsistence Strategies among Aché Hunter-Gatherers of Eastern
           Paraguay. *Human Ecology* 13:1–47.

Huss-Ashmore, R., J. Curry, and R. Hitchcock, eds.

1988   *Coping with Seasonal Constraints.* MASCA Research Papers in Science
           and Archaeology 5. Philadelphia: The University Museum, University
           of Pennsylvania.

Ichikawa, M.

1983   An Examination of the Hunting-Dependent Life of the Mbuti Pygmies,
           Eastern Zaire. *African Study Monographs* 4:55–76.

Ingold, T.

1983   The Significance of Storage in Hunting Societies. *Man* 18:553–71.

1986   *Evolution and Social Life.* Cambridge: Cambridge University Press.

1987   *The Appropriation of Nature: Essays on Human Ecology and Social Relations.*
           Manchester: Manchester University Press.

1988   Notes on the Foraging Mode of Production. In *Hunters and Gatherers,*
           Vol. 1: *History, Evolution and Social Change,* edited by T. Ingold, D.
           Riches, and J. Woodburn, pp. 269–86. Oxford: Berg.

Irimoto, T.

1981   *Chipewyan Ecology: Group Structure and Caribou Hunting System.* Senri Eth-
           nological Studies 8. Osaka, Japan: National Museum of Ethnology.

Irwin, C.

1989   The Sociocultural Biology of Netsilingmiut Female Infanticide. In *The
           Sociobiology of Sexual and Reproductive Strategies,* edited by A. Rasa, C. Vo-
           gel, and E. Voland, pp. 234–64. London: Chapman and Hall.

Isaac, B.

1977   The Siriono of Eastern Bolivia: A Reexamination. *Human Ecology*
           5:137–54.

1990   Economy, Ecology, and Analogy: The !Kung San and the Generalized
           Foraging Model. In *Early Paleoindian Economies of Eastern North America,*
           edited by B. Isaac and K. Tankersley, pp. 323–35. Research in Eco-
           nomic Anthropology Supplement 5. Greenwich, Conn.: JAI Press.

Ives, J.

1990   *A Theory of Northern Athapaskan Prehistory.* Boulder, Colo.: Westview
           Press/University of Calgary Press.

Jenness, D.

1922   *The Life of the Copper Eskimos.* Report of the Canadian Arctic Expedition, 1913–1918, Vol. 12. Ottawa.

Jochim, M. A.

1976   *Hunter Gatherer Subsistence and Settlement: A Predictive Model.* New York: Academic Press.

1981   *Strategies for Survival: Cultural Behavior in an Ecological Context.* New York: Academic Press.

1988   Optimal Foraging and the Division of Labor. *American Anthropologist* 90:130–36.

1991   Archaeology as Long-Term Ethnography. *American Anthropologist* 93:308–21.

Johnson, A.

1975   Time Allocation in a Machiguenga Community. *Ethnology* 14:301–10.

Johnson, A., and T. Earle

1987   *The Evolution of Human Societies: From Foraging Group to Agrarian State.* Stanford: Stanford University Press.

Johnson, G.

1982   Organizational Structure and Scalar Stress. In *Theory and Explanation in Archaeology,* edited by C. Renfrew, M. Rowlands, and B. Segraves, pp. 389–421. New York: Academic Press.

Johnson, J.

1978   Yana. In *Handbook of North American Indians,* Vol. 11: *California,* edited by R. Heizer, pp. 361–69. Washington, D.C.: Smithsonian Institution Press.

Johnson, P.

1978   Patwin. In *Handbook of North American Indians,* Vol. 11: *California,* edited by R. Heizer, pp. 350–60. Washington, D.C.: Smithsonian Institution Press.

Jones, F. L.

1963   *A Demographic Survey of the Aboriginal Population of the Northern Territory, with Special Reference to Bathurst Island Mission.* Occasional Papers in Aboriginal Studies No. 1, Social Anthropology Series No. 1. Canberra: Australian Institute of Aboriginal Studies.

Jones, R.

1969   Fire-Stick Farming. *Australian Natural History* 16:224–28.

1974   Tasmanian Tribes. In *Aboriginal Tribes of Australia,* edited by N. Tindale, pp. 317–54. Berkeley: University of California Press.

1978   Why Did the Tasmanians Stop Eating Fish? In *Explorations in Ethnoarchaeology,* edited by R. Gould, pp. 11–47. Albuquerque: University of New Mexico Press.

1980   Hunters in the Australian Coastal Savanna. In *Human Ecology in Savanna Environments,* edited by D. Harris, pp. 107–46. London: Academic Press.

Jones, K., and D. Madsen
1989   Calculating the Cost of Resource Transportation: A Great Basin Example. *Current Anthropology* 30:529–34.

Jorgensen, J.
1980   *Western Indians.* San Francisco: Freeman.

Josephides, L.
1985   *The Production of Inequality: Gender and Exchange among the Kewa.* London: Tavistock.

Kan, S.
1986   The 19th-Century Tlingit Potlatch: A New Perspective. *American Ethnologist* 13:191–212.

Kaplan, H., and K. Hill
1985a   Food Sharing among Ache Foragers: Tests of Explanatory Hypotheses. *Current Anthropology* 26:223–46.
1985b   Hunting Ability and Reproductive Success among Male Ache Foragers: Preliminary Results. *Current Anthropology* 26:131–33.
1992   The Evolutionary Ecology of Food Acquisition. In *Evolutionary Ecology and Human Behavior,* edited by E. Smith and B. Winterhalder, pp. 167–202. Hawthorne, N.Y.: Aldine de Gruyter.

Keegan, W.
1986   The Optimal Foraging Analysis of Horticultural Production. *American Anthropologist* 88:92–107.

Keeley, L.
1988   Hunter-Gatherer Economic Complexity and "Population Pressure": A Cross-Cultural Analysis. *Journal of Anthropological Archaeology* 7:373–411.

Keen, I.
1988   Twenty-Five Years of Aboriginal Kinship Studies. In *Social Anthropology and Australian Aboriginal Studies: A Contemporary Overview,* edited by R. Berndt and R. Tonkinson, pp. 79–123. Canberra: Aboriginal Studies Press.

Keenan, J.
1977   The Concept of the Mode of Production in Hunter-Gatherer Societies. *African Studies* 36:57–69.

Keene, A.
1979   Economic Optimization Models and the Study of Hunter-Gatherer Subsistence Settlement Systems. In *Transformations: Mathematical Approaches to Culture Change,* edited by C. Renfrew and K. Cooke, pp. 369–404. New York: Academic Press.
1981   *Prehistoric Foraging in a Temperate Forest: A Linear Programming Model.* New York: Academic Press.

Kelly, I.
1932   Ethnography of the Surprise Valley Paiute. *University of California Publications in American Archaeology and Ethnology* 31:67–210.

1964   *Southern Paiute Ethnography.* University of Utah Anthropological Papers No. 69. Salt Lake City.

Kelly, K.

1994   On the Magic Number 500: An Expostulation. *Current Anthropology* 35:435–38.

Kelly, R.

1983   Hunter-Gatherer Mobility Strategies. *Journal of Anthropological Research* 39:277–306.

1986   Hunting and Menstrual Taboos: A Reply to Dobkin de Rios and Hayden. *Human Evolution* 1:475–78.

1990   Marshes and Mobility in the Western Great Basin. In *Wetlands Adaptations in the Great Basin,* edited by J. Janetski and D. B. Madsen, pp. 259–76. Brigham Young University, Museum of Peoples and Cultures Occasional Paper No. 1. Provo: Brigham Young University.

1991   Sedentism, Sociopolitical Inequality, and Resource Fluctuations. In *Between Bands and States,* edited by S. Gregg, pp. 135–58. Center for Archaeological Investigations Occasional Paper No. 9. Carbondale, Ill.: Southern Illinois University Press.

Kent, S.

1989a   And Justice for All: The Development of Political Centralization among Newly Sedentary Foragers. *American Anthropologist* 91:703–11.

1989b   Cross-Cultural Perceptions of Farmers as Hunters and the Value of Meat. In *Farmers as Hunters,* edited by S. Kent, pp. 1–17. Cambridge: Cambridge University Press.

1990   Kalahari Violence in Perspective. *American Anthropologist* 92:1015–17.

1992   The Current Forager Controversy: Real versus Ideal Views of Hunter-Gatherers. *Man* 27:40–65.

1993   Sharing in an Egalitarian Kalahari Community. *Man* 28:479–514.

Kent, S., ed.

1989c   *Farmers as Hunters.* Cambridge: Cambridge University Press.

Kent, S., and R. B. Lee

1992   A Hematological Study of !Kung Kalahari Foragers: An Eighteen Year Comparison. In *Diet, Demography, and Disease: Changing Perspectives on Anemia,* edited by P. Stuart-Macadam and S. Kent, pp. 173–200. New York: Aldine de Gruyter

Kent, S., and H. Vierich

1989   The Myth of Ecological Determinism—Anticipated Mobility and Site Spatial Organization. In *Farmers as Hunters: The Implications of Sedentism,* edited by S. Kent, pp. 96–130. Cambridge: Cambridge University Press.

Knauft, B.

1987   Reconsidering Violence in Simple Human Societies: Homicide among the Gebusi of New Guinea. *Current Anthropology* 28:457–500.

Knight, R.

1965   A Re-examination of Hunting, Trapping, and Territoriality among the Northeastern Algonkian Indians. In *Man, Culture, and Animals: The Role of Animals in Human Ecological Adjustments,* edited by A. Leeds and A. P. Vayda, pp. 27–42. American Association for the Advancement of Science Publication 78. Washington, D.C.: AAAS.

Konner, M., and M. Shostak

1987   Timing and Management of Birth among the !Kung: Biocultural Interaction in Reproductive Adaptation. *Cultural Anthropology* 2:11–28.

Konner, M., and C. Worthman

1980   Nursing Frequency, Gonadal Function, and Birth Spacing among !Kung Hunter-Gatherers. *Science* 207:788–91.

Koyama, S., and D. Thomas, eds.

1981b   *Affluent Foragers.* Senri Ethnological Studies 9. Osaka, Japan: National Museum of Ethnology.

Kozak, V., A. Baxter, A. Williamson, and R. Carneiro

1979   The Heta Indians: Fish in a Dry Pond. *Anthropological Papers of the American Museum of Natural History 55,* pp. 351–434. New York: American Museum of Natural History.

Krech, S.

1978   On the Aboriginal Population of the Kutchin. *Arctic Anthropology* 15:89–104.

1983   The Influence of Disease and the Fur Trade on Arctic Drainage Lowlands Dene, 1800–1850. *Journal of Anthropological Research* 39:123–46.

Kroeber, A.

1925   *Handbook of the Indians of California.* Bureau of American Ethnology Bulletin 78. Washington, D.C.

1935   *Walapai Ethnography.* Memoirs of the American Anthropological Association 42. Washington, D.C.

1939   *Cultural and Natural Areas of Native North America.* University of California Publications in American Archaeology and Ethnology 38. Berkeley.

Kuchikura, Y.

1987   *Subsistence Ecology among Semaq-Beri Hunter-Gatherers of Peninsular Malaysia.* Hokkaido Behavioral Science Report, Series E, No. 1. Sapporo: Department of Behavioral Science, Hokkaido University.

1988   Efficiency and Focus of Blowpipe Hunting among Semaq Beri Hunter-Gatherers of Peninsular Malaysia. *Human Ecology* 16:271–305.

Kuper, A.

1988   *The Invention of Primitive Society: Transformations of an Illusion.* London: Routledge.

Landes, R.

1938   *The Ojibwa Woman.* New York: Norton.

Langdon, S.
1979   Comparative Tlingit and Haida Adaptation to the West Coast of the Prince of Wales Archipelago. *Ethnology* 18:101–19.
LaPena, F.
1978   Wintu. In *Handbook of North American Indians,* Vol. 11: *California,* edited by R. Heizer, pp. 324–40. Washington, D.C.: Smithsonian Institution Press.
Laughlin, W. S.
1980   *Aleuts: Survivors of the Bering Land Bridge.* New York: Holt, Rinehart and Winston.
Lawton, H., P. Wilke, M. Decker, and W. Mason
1976   Agriculture among the Paiute of Owens Valley. *Journal of California Anthropology* 3:13–50.
Layne, L.
1987   Village-Bedouin: Patterns of Change from Mobility to Sedentism in Jordan. In *Method and Theory for Activity Area Research,* edited by S. Kent, pp. 345–73. New York: Columbia University Press.
Layton, R.
1986   Political and Territorial Structures among Hunter-Gatherers. *Man* 21:18–33.
Leacock, E.
1954   The Montagnais Hunting Territory and the Fur Trade. American Anthropological Association Memoir 78. Washington, D.C.
1955   Matrilineality in a Simple Hunting Society (Montagnais-Naskapi). *Southwestern Journal of Anthropology* 11:31–47.
1969   The Montagnais-Naskapi Band. In *Contributions to Anthropology: Band Societies,* edited by D. Damas, pp. 1–17. National Museum of Canada Bulletin 228. Ottawa: National Museum of Canada.
1978   Women's Status in Egalitarian Society: Implications for Social Evolution. *Current Anthropology* 19:247–75.
1980   Montagnais Women and the Jesuit Program for Colonization. In *Women and Colonization: Anthropological Perspectives,* edited by M. Etienne and E. Leacock, pp. 25–42. New York: Praeger.
1982   Relations of Production in Band Society. In *Politics and History in Band Societies,* edited by E. Leacock and R. B. Lee, pp. 159–70. Cambridge: Cambridge University Press.
Leacock, E., and R. B. Lee
1982a   Introduction. In *Politics and History in Band Societies,* edited by E. Leacock and R. B. Lee, pp. 1–19. Cambridge: Cambridge University Press.
Leacock, E., and R. B. Lee, eds.
1982b   *Politics and History in Band Societies.* Cambridge: Cambridge University Press.

LeClerq, C.

1910   *New Relations of Gaspesia.* Edited by W. Ganong. Toronto: The Champlain Society.

Lee, R. B.

1968   What Hunters Do for a Living, Or, How to Make Out on Scarce Resources. In *Man the Hunter,* edited by R. B. Lee and I. DeVore, pp. 30–48. Chicago: Aldine.

1969   !Kung Bushman Subsistence: An Input/Output Analysis. In *Contributions to Anthropology: Ecological Essays,* edited by D. Damas, pp. 73–94. National Museum of Canada Bulletin 230. Ottawa: National Museum of Canada.

1974   Male-Female Residence Arrangements and Political Power in Human Hunter-Gatherers. *Archives of Sexual Behavior* 3:167–73.

1976   !Kung Spatial Organization: An Ecological and Historical Perspective. In *Kalahari Hunter-Gatherers,* edited by R. B. Lee and I. DeVore, pp. 73–97. Cambridge: Harvard University Press.

1979   *The !Kung San: Men, Women and Work in a Foraging Society.* Cambridge: Cambridge University Press.

1980   Lactation, Ovulation, Infanticide, and Women's Work: A Study of Hunter-Gatherer Population. In *Biosocial Mechanisms of Population Regulation,* edited by M. Cohen, R. Malpass, and H. Klein, pp. 321–48. New Haven: Yale University Press.

1982   Politics, Sexual and Non-Sexual, in an Egalitarian Society. In *Politics and History in Band Societies,* edited by E. Leacock and R. B. Lee, pp. 37–59. Cambridge: Cambridge University Press.

1984   *The Dobe !Kung.* New York: Holt, Rinehart and Winston.

1985   Work, Sexuality, and Aging among !Kung Women. In *In Her Prime: A New View of Middle-Aged Women,* edited by J. Brown and V. Kerns, pp. 23–35. S. Hadley, Mass.: Bergin and Garvey.

1988   Reflections on Primitive Communism. In *Hunters and Gatherers,* Vol. 1: *History, Evolution, and Social Change,* edited by T. Ingold, D. Riches, and J. Woodburn, pp. 252–68. Oxford: Berg.

1992   Art, Science, or Politics? The Crisis in Hunter-Gatherer Studies. *American Anthropologist* 94:31–54.

Lee, R. B., and I. DeVore, eds.

1968   *Man the Hunter.* Chicago: Aldine.

1976   *Kalahari Hunter-Gatherers: Regional Studies of the !Kung San and Their Neighbors.* Cambridge: Harvard University Press.

Lee, R. B., and M. Guenther

1991   Oxen or Onions? The Search for Trade (And Truth) in the Kalahari. *Current Anthropology* 32:592–601.

1993   Problems in Kalahari Historical Ethnography and the Tolerance of Error. *History in Africa* 20:185–235.

Legros, D.
1985   Wealth, Poverty, and Slavery among 19th Century Tutchone Athapas-
        kans. *Research in Economic Anthropology* 7:37–64.
Leland, J.
1986   Population. In *Handbook of North American Indians,* Vol. 11: *Great Basin,*
        edited by W. D'Azevedo, pp. 608–19. Washington, D.C.: Smithsonian
        Institution Press.
Leslie, P., and P. Fry
1989   Extreme Seasonality of Births among Nomadic Turkana Pastoralists.
        American Journal of Physical Anthropology 79:103–15.
Lévi-Strauss, C.
1949   *Les Structures élémentaires de la parenté.* Paris: Presses Universitaires de
        France.
Lewis, H.
1989   Ecological and Technological Knowledge of Fire: Aborigines versus
        Park Rangers in North Australia. *American Anthropologist* 91:940–61.
1991   Technological Complexity, Ecological Diversity, and Fire Regimes in
        Northern Australia. In *Profiles in Cultural Evolution,* edited by A. Rambo
        and K. Gillogly, pp. 261–88. Anthropological Papers, Museum of An-
        thropology, University of Michigan, No. 85. Ann Arbor.
Lewis, H., and T. Ferguson
1988   Yards, Corridors, and Mosaics: How to Burn a Boreal Forest. *Human
        Ecology* 16:57–77.
Long, J.
1971   Arid Region Aborigines: The Pintupi. In *Aboriginal Man and Environ-
        ment in Australia,* edited by D. Mulvaney and J. Golson, pp. 262–70.
        Canberra: Australian National University Press.
Lourandos, H.
1985   Intensification and Australian Prehistory. In *Prehistoric Hunter-Gatherers:
        The Emergence of Cultural Complexity,* edited by T. D. Price and J. A.
        Brown, pp. 385–423. Orlando, Fla.: Academic Press.
1988   Palaeopolitics: Resource Intensification in Aboriginal Australia and Pa-
        pua New Guinea. In *Hunters and Gatherers,* Vol. 1: *History, Evolution, and
        Social Change,* edited by T. Ingold, D. Riches, and J. Woodburn, pp.
        148–60. Oxford: Berg.
Lubbock, Sir J.
1865   *Pre-Historic Times, as Illustrated by Ancient Remains and the Manners and
        Customs of Modern Savages.* London: Williams and Norgate.
MacArthur, R., and E. Pianka
1966   On Optimal Use of a Patchy Environment. *The American Naturalist*
        100:603–9.
MacLachlan, B.
1981   Tahltan. In *Handbook of North American Indians,* Vol. 6: *Subarctic,* edited

by J. Helm, pp. 458–68. Washington, D.C.: Smithsonian Institution Press.

MacLeish, K., and J. Launois

1972   Stone Age Men of the Philippines. *National Geographic* 142:219–50.

Madsen, D., and J. Kirkman

1988   Hunting Hoppers. *American Antiquity* 53:593–604.

Mailhot, J.

1986   Territorial Mobility among the Montagnais-Naskapi of Labrador. *Anthropologica* 28:92–107.

Maine, H.

1861   *Ancient Law.* London: J. Murray.

Malaurie, J.

1956   *The Last Kings of Thule: A Year among the Polar Eskimos of Greenland.* London: Allen & Unwin.

Marks, S.

1976   *Large Mammals and a Brave People: Subsistence Hunters in Zambia.* Seattle: University of Washington Press.

Marshall, L.

1976   *The !Kung of Nyae Nyae.* Cambridge: Harvard University Press.

Martin, C., and D. Read

1981   The Relation of Mean Annual Rainfall to Population Density for Some African Hunters and Gatherers. *Anthropology UCLA* 7:151–60.

Martin, J. F.

1973   On the Estimation of Sizes of Local Groups in a Hunting Gathering Environment. *American Anthropologist* 75:1448–68.

1994   Changing Sex Ratios: The History of Havasupai Fertility and Its Implications for Human Sex Ratio Variation. *Current Anthropology* 35:255–80.

Martin, J. F., and D. Stewart

1982   A Demographic Basis for Patrilineal Hordes. *American Anthropologist* 84:79–96.

Martin, M. K.

1974   *The Foraging Adaptation—Uniformity or Diversity?* Addison-Wesley Module in Anthropology No. 56. Reading, Mass.: Addison-Wesley Publishing Company.

Martin, M. K., and B. Voorhies

1975   *Female of the Species.* New York: Columbia University Press.

Maschner, H.

1991   The Emergence of Cultural Complexity on the Northern Northwest Coast. *Antiquity* 65:924–34.

Mason, O. T.

1894   Technogeography, or the Relation of the Earth to the Industries of Mankind. *American Anthropologist* 7(2):137–61.

Mathiassen, T.

1928   *Material Culture of the Iglulik Eskimos*. Report of the Fifth Thule Expedition, pp. 1921–24, Vol. 7(1). Copenhagen: Gyldendalske Boghandel, Nordisk Forlag.

Mauss, M.

[1924]   *The Gift*. Trans. by W. D. Halls. New York: Norton.

1990

Mauss, M., and H. Beuchat

1906   Essai sur les variations saisonnières des sociétés Eskimos. *L'Année Sociologique* 9 (1904–1905):39–132.

McCarthy, F., and M. McArthur

1960   The Food Quest and the Time Factor in Aboriginal Economic Life. In *Records of the American-Australian Scientific Expedition to Arnhem Land*, Vol. 2: *Anthropology and Nutrition*, edited by C. Mountford, pp. 145–94. Parkville, Victoria: Melbourne University Press.

McClellan, C.

1975   *My Old People Say: An Ethnographic Survey of Southern Yukon Territory*. National Museum of Man Publications in Ethnology 6. Ottawa.

McClellan, C., and G. Denniston

1981   Environment and Culture in the Cordillera. In *Handbook of North American Indians*, Vol. 6: *Subarctic*, edited by J. Helm, pp. 372–86. Washington, D.C.: Smithsonian Institution Press.

McCloskey, D.

1976   English Open Fields and Behavior Toward Risk. *Research in Economic History* 1:144–70.

McGee, W.

1898   *The Seri Indians*. Seventeenth Annual Report of the Bureau of American Ethnology, pp. 1–344. Washington, D.C.

McKennan, R.

1959   *The Upper Tanana Indians*. Yale University Publications in Anthropology 55. New Haven.

1981   Tanana. In *Handbook of North American Indians*, Vol. 6: *Subarctic*, edited by J. Helm, pp. 562–76. Washington, D.C.: Smithsonian Institution Press.

McKnight, D.

1981   Distribution of Australian Aboriginal Marriage Classes: Environmental and Demographic Influences. *Man* 16:75–89.

Meehan (Hiatt), B.

1977a   Hunters by the Seashore. *Journal of Human Evolution* 6:363–70.

1977b   Man Does Not Live by Calories Alone: The Role of Shellfish in a Coastal Cuisine. In *Sunda and Sahul*, edited by J. Allen, J. Golson, and R. Jones, pp. 493–531. London: Academic Press.

1982   *Shell Bed to Shell Midden.* Canberra: Australian Institute of Aboriginal
           Studies.

1983   A Matter of Choice? Some Thoughts on Shell Gathering Strategies in
           Northern Australia. In *Animals and Archaeology 2: Shell Middens, Fishes
           and Birds,* edited by C. Grigson and J. Clutton-Brock, British Archaeo-
           logical Reports, International Series 381, pp. 3–17. Oxford.

Meggitt, M.

1962   *The Desert People.* Sydney: Augus and Robertson.

1968   "Marriage Classes" and Demography in Central Australia. In *Man the
           Hunter,* edited by R. B. Lee and I. DeVore, pp. 176–84. Chicago:
           Aldine.

1987   Understanding Australian Aboriginal Society: Kinship Systems or Cul-
           tural Categories? In *Traditional Aboriginal Society,* edited by W. H. Ed-
           wards, pp. 113–37. Melbourne: The Macmillan Company of Australia.

Meigs, P.

1939   *The Kiliwa Indians of Lower California.* Ibero-Americana 15. Berkeley:
           University of California.

Meillassoux, C.

1973   On the Mode of Production of the Hunting Band. In *French Perspectives
           in African Studies,* edited by P. Alexandre, pp. 187–203. London: Oxford
           University Press.

Merlan, F.

1988   Gender in Aboriginal Social Life: A Review. In *Social Anthropology and
           Australian Aboriginal Studies: A Contemporary Overview,* edited by R.
           Berndt and R. Tonkinson, pp. 17–76. Canberra: Aboriginal Studies
           Press.

Metcalfe, D., and K. R. Barlow

1992   A Model for Exploring the Optimal Trade-Off Between Field Pro-
           cessing and Transport. *American Anthropologist* 94:340–56.

Mills, B.

1986   Prescribed Burning and Hunter-Gatherer Subsistence Systems. *Haliksa'i:
           UNM Contributions to Anthropology* 5:2–26.

Milton, K.

1985   Ecological Foundations for Subsistence Strategies among the Mbuti Pyg-
           mies. *Human Ecology* 13:71–78.

Minc, L.

1986   Scarcity and Survival: The Role of Oral Tradition in Mediating Subsis-
           tence Crises. *Journal of Anthropological Archaeology* 5:39–113.

Minc, L., and K. Smith

1989   The Spirit of Survival: Cultural Responses to Resource Variability in
           North Alaska. In *Bad Year Economics,* edited by P. Halstad and J. O'Shea,
           pp. 8–38. Cambridge: Cambridge University Press.

Mitchell, D.

1983   Seasonal Settlements, Village Aggregations, and Political Autonomy on the Central Northwest Coast. In *The Development of Political Organization in Native North America,* edited by E. Tooker, pp. 97–107. Washington, D.C.: American Ethnological Society.

1984   Predatory Warfare, Social Status, and the North Pacific Slave Trade. *Ethnology* 23:39–48.

1985   A Demographic Profile of Northwest Coast Slavery. In *Status, Structure and Stratification: Current Archaeological Reconstructions,* edited by M. Thompson, M. Garcia, and F. Kense, pp. 227–36. Calgary: Archaeological Association of the University of Calgary.

Mitchell, D., and L. Donald

1985   Some Economic Aspects of Tlingit, Haida, and Tsimshian Slavery. *Research in Economic Anthropology* 7:19–35.

1988   Archaeology and the Study of Northwest Coast Economics. *Research in Economic Anthropology* Supplement 3:293–351.

Mithen, S. J.

1989   Modeling Hunter-Gatherer Decision Making: Complementing Optimal Foraging Theory. *Human Ecology* 17:59–83.

1990   *Thoughtful Foragers.* Cambridge: Cambridge University Press.

Moore, O.

1965   Divination—A New Perspective. *American Anthropologist* 59:69–74.

Morales, T.

1987   An Examination of Infanticide Practices among Mobile and "Sedentary" Hunter-gatherers. *Haliksa'i: UNM Contributions to Anthropology* 6:1–19.

Morgan, L.

[1877]   *Ancient Society.* Edited by E. Leacock. New York: Meridian.
1963

Morris, B.

1982   The Family, Group Structuring and Trade among South Indian Hunter-Gatherers. In *Politics and History in Band Societies,* edited by E. Leacock and R. B. Lee, pp. 171–87. Cambridge: Cambridge University Press.

Mosko, M.

1987   The Symbols of "Forest": A Structural Analysis of Mbuti Culture and Social Organization. *American Anthropologist* 89:896–913.

Murdock, G.

1949   *Social Structure.* New York: Macmillan.

1958   Social Organization of the Tenino. *Miscellanea Paul Rivet* 1:299–312.

1967   The Ethnographic Atlas: A Summary. *Ethnology* 6(2).

1980   The Tenino Indians. *Ethnology* 19:129–49.

Murphy, R., and J. Steward
1955   Tappers and Trappers: Parallel Processes in Acculturation. *Economic Development and Cultural Change* 4:335–55.
Myers, F.
1982   Always Ask: Resource Use and Land Ownership among Pintupi Aborigines of the Australian Western Desert. In *Resource Managers: North American and Australian Hunter-Gatherers,* edited by E. Hunn and N. Williams, pp. 173–96. Boulder, Colo.: Westview.
1986   *Pintupi Country, Pintupi Self.* Washington, D.C.: Smithsonian Institution Press.
1988a   Burning the Truck and Holding the Country: Property, Time and the Negotiation of Identity among Pintupi. In *Hunters and Gatherers,* Vol. 2: *Property, Power, and Ideology,* edited by T. Ingold, D. Riches, and J. Woodburn, pp.52–74. Oxford: Berg.
1988b   Critical Trends in the Study of Hunter-Gatherers. *Annual Review of Anthropology* 17:261–82.
Nabokov, P.
1967   *Two Leggings: The Making of a Crow Warrior.* New York: Crowell.
Neel, J., and K. Weiss
1975   The Genetic Structure of a Tribal Population, the Yanomama Indians. XII. Biodemographic Studies. *American Journal of Physical Anthropology* 42:25–51.
Nelson, E.
1899   *The Eskimo About Bering Strait.* Bureau of American Ethnology Annual Report for 1896–1897, Vol. 18, No. 1. Washington, D.C.
Nelson, R.
1986   *Hunters of the Northern Forest.* Second edition. Chicago: University of Chicago Press.
Nerlove, S. B.
1974   Women's Workload and Infant Feeding Practices: A Relationship with Demographic Implications. *Ethnology* 13:207–14.
Noli, D., and G. Avery
1988   Protein Poisoning and Coastal Subsistence. *Journal of Archaeological Science* 15:395–401.
Nurse, G., and T. Jenkins
1977   Health and the Hunter-Gatherer. *Monographs in Human Genetics* 8.
Oberg, K.
1973   *The Social Economy of the Tlingit Indians.* Seattle: University of Washington Press.
O'Connell, J. F., and K. Hawkes
1981   Alyawara Plant Use and Optimal Foraging Theory. In *Hunter-Gatherer*

Foraging Strategies, edited by B. Winterhalder and E. A. Smith, pp. 99–125. Chicago: University of Chicago Press.

1984   Food Choice and Foraging Sites among the Alyawara. *Journal of Anthropological Research* 40:504–35.

O'Connell, J., K. Hawkes, and N. Blurton Jones

1988   Hadza Scavenging: Implications for Plio-Pleistocene Hominid Subsistence. *Current Anthropology* 29:356–63.

O'Connell, J., P. Latz, and P. Barnett

1983   Traditional and Modern Plant Use among the Alyawara of Central Australia. *Economic Botany* 37:80–109.

Ohtsuka, R.

1989   Hunting Activity and Aging among the Gidra Papuans: A Biobehavioral Analysis. *American Journal of Physical Anthropology* 80:31–39.

Orians, G. H., and N. E. Pearson

1979   On the Theory of Central Place Foraging. In *Analysis of Ecological Systems,* edited by R. Mitchell and G. Stairs, pp. 155–78. Columbus, Ohio: Ohio State University Press.

Osgood, C.

1936   The Distribution of the Northern Athapaskan Indians. *Yale University Publications in Anthropology* 7:3–23.

O'Shea, J.

1981   Coping with Scarcity: Exchange and Social Storage. In *Economic Archaeology: Towards an Integration of Ecological and Social Approaches,* edited by A. Sheridan and G. Bailey, pp. 167–86. British Archaeological Reports, International Series 96. Oxford.

Oswalt, W.

1967   *Alaskan Eskimos.* San Francisco: Chandler.

Owen, R.

1965   The Patrilocal Band: A Linguistically and Culturally Hybrid Social Unit. *American Anthropologist* 67:675–90.

Pálsson, G.

1988   Hunters and Gatherers of the Sea. In *Hunters and Gatherers,* Vol. 1: *History, Evolution, and Social Change,* edited by T. Ingold, D. Riches, and J. Woodburn, pp. 189–204. Oxford: Berg.

Panowski, E.

1985   Analyzing Hunter-Gatherers: Population Pressure, Subsistence, Social Structure, Northwest Coast Societies, and Slavery. Unpublished Ph.D. dissertation, Department of Anthropology, University of New Mexico.

Park, W.

1938   The Organization and Habitat of Paviotso Bands. *American Anthropologist* 40:622–26.

Parkington, J.
1984   Soaqua and Bushmen: Hunters and Robbers. In *Past and Present in Hunter Gatherer Studies*, edited by C. Schrire, pp. 151–93. Orlando, Fla.: Academic Press.

Pate, D.
1986   The Effects of Drought on Ngatatjara Plant Use: An Evaluation of Optimal Foraging Theory. *Human Ecology* 14:95–115.

Pennington, R., and H. Harpending
1988   Fitness and Fertility among Kalahari !Kung. *American Journal of Physical Anthropology* 77:303–19.

Perry, R.
1989   Matrilineal Descent in a Hunting Context: The Athapaskan Case. *Ethnology* 28:33–52.

Petersen, R.
1984   East Greenland Before 1950. In *Handbook of North American Indians*, Vol. 5: *Arctic*, edited by D. Damas, pp. 622–39. Washington, D.C.: Smithsonian Institution Press.

Peterson, J.
1978   The Ecology of Social Boundaries: Agta Foragers of the Philippines. *Illinois Studies in Anthropology* 11. Urbana: University of Illinois Press.

Peterson, N.
1973   Camp Site Location amongst Australian Hunter-Gatherers: Archaeological and Ethnographic Evidence for a Key Determinant. *Archaeology and Physical Anthropology in Oceania* 8:173–93.

1975   Hunter-Gatherer Territoriality: The Perspective from Australia. *American Anthropologist* 77:53–68.

1976   The Natural and Cultural Areas of Aboriginal Australia. In *Tribes and Boundaries in Australia*, edited by N. Peterson, pp. 50–71. Canberra: Australian Institute of Aboriginal Studies.

1978   The Importance of Women in Determining the Composition of Residential Groups in Aboriginal Australia. In *Woman's Role in Aboriginal Society*, edited by F. Gale, pp. 16–27. Canberra: Australian Institute of Aboriginal Studies.

1979   Territorial Adaptations among Desert Hunter-Gatherers: The !Kung and Australians Compared. In *Social and Ecological Systems*, edited by P. Burnham and R. Ellen, pp. 111–29. New York: Academic Press.

1988   The Natural and Cultural Areas of Aboriginal Australia: A Preliminary Analysis of Population Groupings with Adaptive Significance. In *Social Anthropology and Australian Aboriginal Studies: A Contemporary Overview*, edited by R. Berndt and R. Tonkinson, pp. 50–71. Canberra: Aboriginal Studies Press.

1993   Demand Sharing: Reciprocity and the Pressure for Generosity among Foragers. *American Anthropologist* 95:860–74.

Peterson, N., and J. Long

1986   *Australian Territorial Organization.* Oceania Monograph 30. Sydney: University of Sydney.

Peterson, N., and T. Matsuyama, eds.

1991   *Cash, Commoditisation and Changing Foragers.* Senri Ethnological Studies 30. Osaka, Japan: National Museum of Ethnology.

Peterson, W.

1981   Recent Adaptive Shifts among Palanan Hunters of the Philippines. *Man* 16:43–61.

Pianka, E.

1978   *Evolutionary Ecology.* New York: Harper and Row.

Piddocke, S.

1965   The Potlatch Systems of the Southern Kwakiutl: A New Perspective. *Southwestern Journal of Anthropology* 21:244–64.

Pilling, A.

1978   Yurok. In *Handbook of North American Indians,* Vol. 8: *California,* edited by R. Heizer, pp. 137–54. Washington, D.C.: Smithsonian Institution Press.

Pookajorn, S.

1985   Ethnoarchaeology with the Phi Tong Luang (Mlabri): Forest Hunters of Northern Thailand. *World Archaeology* 17:206–21.

1988   *Archaeological Research of the Hoabinhian Culture or Technocomplex and Its Comparison with Ethnoarchaeology of the Phi Tong Luang, a Hunter-Gatherer Group of Thailand.* Tübingen: Institüt fur Urgeschichte der Universität Tübingen.

Povinelli, E.

1992   "Where We Gana Go Now": Foraging Practices and Their Meanings among the Belyuen Australian Aborigines. *Human Ecology* 20:169–201.

Price, T. D., and J. A. Brown

1985a   Aspects of Hunter-Gatherer Complexity. In *Prehistoric Hunter-Gatherers: The Emergence of Cultural Complexity,* edited by T. D. Price and J. A. Brown, pp. 3–20. Orlando, Fla.: Academic Press.

Price, T. D., and J. A. Brown, eds.

1985b   *Prehistoric Hunter-Gatherers: The Emergence of Cultural Complexity.* Orlando, Fla.: Academic Press.

Radcliffe-Brown, A.

1922   *The Andaman Islanders.* Cambridge: Cambridge University Press.

1930   Former Numbers and Distribution of the Australian Aborigines. *Official Yearbook of the Commonwealth of Australia* 23:671–96.

1930–31 Social Organization of Australian Tribes. *Oceania* 1:34–63, 206–46, 322–41, 426–56.

1956 On Australian Local Organization. *American Anthropologist* 58:363–67.

Rafferty, J.

1985 The Archaeological Record on Sedentariness: Recognition, Development, and Implications. In *Advances in Archaeological Method and Theory,* Vol. 8, edited by M. Schiffer, pp. 113–56. New York: Academic Press.

Rai, N.

1990 *Living in a Lean-To: Philippine Negrito Foragers in Transition.* Anthropological Papers, Museum of Anthropology, University of Michigan No. 80. Ann Arbor.

Rambo, T.

1985 *Primitive Polluters: Semang Impact on the Malaysian Tropical Rain Forest Ecosystem.* Ann Arbor: University of Michigan Press.

Rappaport, R.

1968 *Pigs for the Ancestors.* New Haven: Yale University Press.

Rasmussen, K.

1929 *Intellectual Culture of the Hudson Bay Eskimo,* I: *Intellectual Culture of the Iglulik Eskimo.* Report of the Fifth Thule Expedition, 1921–1924, 7(1). Copenhagen: Gyldendalske Boghandel.

1931 *The Netsilik Eskimos: Social Life and Spiritual Culture.* Report of the Fifth Thule Expedition, 1921–1924, 8(1,2). Copenhagen: Gyldendalske Boghandel.

1932 *Intellectual Culture of the Copper Eskimos.* Report of the Fifth Thule Expedition, 1921–1924, 9. Copenhagen: Gyldendalske Boghandel.

Ray, D.

1984 Bering Strait Eskimo. In *Handbook of North American Indians,* Vol. 5: *Arctic,* edited by D. Damas, pp. 285–302. Washington, D.C.: Smithsonian Institution Press.

Ray, V.

1932 The Sanpoil and Nespelem. *University of Washington Publications in Anthropology* 5:1–237.

Raymond, A., and E. Sobel

1990 The Use of Tui Chub as Food by Indians of the Western Great Basin. *Journal of California and Great Basin Anthropology* 12:2–18.

Reidhead, V.

1979 Linear Programming Models in Archaeology. *Annual Review of Anthropology* 8:543–78.

1980 Economics of Subsistence Change. In *Modeling of Prehistoric Subsistence Economics,* edited by T. Earle and A. Christensen, pp. 141–86. New York: Academic Press.

Remie, C.
1985   Toward a New Perspective on Netjilik Inuit Female Infanticide. *Etudes/Inuit/Studies* 12:101–27.

Renouf, M.
1991   Sedentary Hunter-Gatherers: A Case for Northern Coasts. In *Between Bands and States,* edited by S. Gregg, pp. 89–107. Center for Archaeological Investigations Occasional Paper No. 9. Carbondale, Ill.: Southern Illinois University Press.

Rhode, D.
1990   Transportation Costs of Great Basin Resources: An Assessment of the Jones-Madsen Model. *Current Anthropology* 31:413–19.

Richardson, A.
1982   The Control of Productive Resources on the Northwest Coast of North America. In *Resource Managers: North American and Australian Hunter-Gatherers,* edited by E. Hunn and N. Williams, pp. 93–112. Boulder, Colo.: Westview.

Riches, D.
1974   The Netsilik Eskimo: A Special Case of Selective Female Infanticide. *Ethnology* 13:351–61.
1982   *Northern Nomadic Hunter-Gatherers.* London: Academic Press.
1984   Hunting, Herding and Potlatching: Towards a Sociological Account of Prestige. *Man* 19:234–51.

Ridington, R.
1981   Beaver. In *Handbook of North American Indians,* Vol. 6: *Subarctic,* edited by J. Helm, pp. 350–60. Washington, D.C.: Smithsonian Institution Press.
1987   Knowledge, Power, and the Individual in Subarctic Hunting Society. *American Anthropologist* 14:98–110.

Rodman, W., and D. Counts
1983   Introduction. In *Middlemen and Brokers in Oceania,* edited by W. Rodman and D. Counts, pp 1–20. Association for Social Anthropology in Oceania Monograph 9. Lanham, Md.: University Press of America.

Rogers, E.
1967a   Subsistence Areas of the Cree-Ojibwa of the Eastern Subarctic: A Preliminary Study. *National Museum of Canada Bulletin* 204:59–90.
1967b   *The Material Culture of the Mistassini.* National Museum of Canada Bulletin 218. Ottawa.
1969a   Band Organization among the Indians of Eastern Subarctic Canada. In *Contributions to Anthropology: Band Societies,* edited by D. Damas, pp. 21–50. National Museum of Canada Bulletin 228. Ottawa: National Museum of Canada.
1969b   Natural Environment—Social Organization—Witchcraft: Cree versus

Ojibway—a Test Case. In *Contributions to Anthropology: Ecological Essays,* edited by D. Damas, pp. 24–39. National Museum of Canada Bulletin 230. Ottawa: National Museum of Canada.

1972   The Mistassini Cree. In *Hunters and Gatherers Today,* edited by M. G. Bicchieri, pp. 90–137. New York: Holt, Rinehart and Winston.

Rogers, E., and E. Leacock

1981   Montagnais-Naskapi. In *Handbook of North American Indians,* Vol. 6: *Subarctic,* edited by J. Helm, pp. 169–89. Washington, D.C.: Smithsonian Institution Press.

Romaniuk, A.

1974   Modernization and Fertility: The Case of the James Bay Indians. *Canadian Review of Sociology and Anthropology* 11:344–59.

Romanoff, S.

1983   Women as Hunters among the Matses of the Peruvian Amazon. *Human Ecology* 11:339–43.

1985   Fraser Lillooet Salmon Fishing. *Northwest Anthropological Research Notes* 19:119–60.

Roper, D.

1991   John Dunbar's Journal of the 1834–5 Chawi Winter Hunt and Its Implications for Pawnee Archaeology. *Plains Anthropologist* 36:193–214.

Roscoe, P.

1990   The Bow and Spreadnet: Ecological Origins of Hunting Technology. *American Anthropologist* 92:691–701.

Rose, F. G. G.

1960   *Classification of Kin, Age Structure, and Marriage amongst the Groote Eylandt Aborigines.* Berlin: Akademie-Verlag.

1968   Australian Marriage, Land-Owning Groups, and Initiation. In *Man the Hunter,* edited by R. B. Lee and I. DeVore, pp. 200–208. Chicago: Aldine.

1988   Boundaries and Kinship Systems in Aboriginal Australia. In *Social Anthropology and Australian Aboriginal Studies: A Contemporary Overview,* edited by R. Berndt and R. Tonkinson, pp. 192–206. Canberra: Aboriginal Studies Press.

Rosman, A., and P. Rubel

1971   *Feasting with Mine Enemy: Rank and Exchange among Northwest Coast Societies.* New York: Columbia University Press.

Roth, E.

1981   Sedentism and Changing Fertility Patterns in a Northern Athapascan Isolate. *Journal of Human Evolution* 10:413–25.

Roth, E., and A. Ray

1985   Demographic Patterns of Sedentary and Nomadic Juang of Orissa. *Human Biology* 57:319–26.

Roth, H.

1890   *The Aborigines of Tasmania*. London: Kegan, Paul, Trench and Trubner.

Rowley-Conwy, P., and M. Zvelebil

1989   Saving It for Later: Storage by Prehistoric Hunter-Gatherers in Europe. In *Bad Year Economics,* edited by P. Halstead and J. O'Shea, pp. 40–56. Cambridge: Cambridge University Press.

Rubel, P., and A. Rosman

1983   The Evolution of Exchange Structures and Ranking: Some Northwest Coast and Athapaskan Examples. *Journal of Anthropological Research* 39:1–25.

Ruyle, E.

1973   Slavery, Surplus and Stratification on the Northwest Coast: The Ethnoenergetics of an Incipient Stratification System. *Current Anthropology* 14:603–31.

Sackett, L.

1979   The Pursuit of Prominence: Hunting in an Australian Aboriginal Community. *Anthropologica* 21:223–46.

Sacks, K.

1974   Engles Revisited: Women, the Organization of Production, and Private Property. In *Women, Culture and Society,* edited by M. Rosaldo and L. Lamphere, pp. 207–22. Stanford: Stanford University Press.

Sahlins, M.

1968   Notes on the Original Affluent Society. In *Man the Hunter,* edited by R. B. Lee and I. DeVore, pp. 85–89. Chicago: Aldine.

1972   *Stone Age Economics*. Chicago: Aldine.

Sanday, P.

1981   *Female Power and Dominance: On the Origins of Sexual Inequality*. Pittsburg: University of Pittsburg Press.

Satterthwait, L.

1987   Socioeconomic Implications of Australian Aboriginal Net Hunting. *Man* 22:613–36.

Savishinsky, J.

1974   *The Trail of the Hare*. New York: Gordon and Breach Science Publishers.

Savishinsky, J., and H. Hara

1981   Hare. In *Handbook of North American Indians,* Vol. 6: *Subarctic,* edited by J. Helm, pp. 314–25. Washington, D.C.: Smithsonian Institution Press.

Schalk, R.

1978   Foragers of the Northwest Coast of North America: The Ecology of Aboriginal Land Use Systems. Unpublished Ph.D. dissertation, Department of Anthropology, University of New Mexico.

1981   Land Use and Organizational Complexity among Foragers of Northwestern North America. In *Affluent Foragers,* edited by S. Koyama and D. Thomas, pp. 53–76. Senri Ethnological Studies 9. Osaka, Japan: National Museum of Ethnology.

Schebesta, P.

1929   *Among the Forest Dwarfs of Malaya.* Trans. by A. Chambers. London: Hutchinson Press.

Schlegel, A., and A. I. Barry

1991   *Adolescence: An Anthropological Inquiry.* New York: Free Press.

Schneider, D.

1984   *A Critique of the Study of Kinship.* Ann Arbor: University of Michigan Press.

Shnirelman, V. A.

1994   Cherchez le Chien: Perspectives on the Economy of the Traditional Fishing-Oriented People of Kamchatka. In *Key Issues in Hunter-Gatherer Research,* edited by E. S. Burch, Jr. and L. J. Ellanna, pp. 169–88. Oxford: Berg.

Schrire, C.

1980   An Inquiry into the Evolutionary Status and Apparent Identity of San Hunter-Gatherers. *Human Ecology* 8:9–32.

1984a   Wild Surmises on Savage Thoughts. In *Past and Present in Hunter Gatherer Studies,* edited by C. Schrire, pp. 1–25. Orlando, Fla.: Academic Press.

Schrire, C., ed.

1984b   *Past and Present in Hunter Gatherer Studies.* Orlando, Fla.: Academic Press.

Schrire, C., and R. Gordon, eds.

1985   *The Future of Former Foragers: Australia and Southern Africa.* Cultural Survival Occasional Paper 18. Cambridge, Mass.

Schrire, C., and W. L. Steiger

1974a   A Matter of Life and Death: An Investigation into the Practice of Infanticide in the Arctic. *Man* 9:161–84.

1974b   Demographic Models and Female Infanticide. *Man* 10:470–72.

1981   Arctic Infanticide Revisited. *Etudes/Inuit/Studies* 5:111–17.

Scott, C.

1986   Hunting Territories, Hunting Bosses and Communal Production among Coastal James Bay Cree. *Anthropologica* 28:163–73.

1988   Property, Practice, and Aboriginal Rights among Quebec Cree Hunters. In *Hunters and Gatherers,* Vol. 2: *Property, Power and Ideology,* edited by T. Ingold, D. Riches, and J. Woodburn, pp. 35–51. Oxford: Berg.

Scott, E. C., and F. E. Johnston

1982   Critical Fat, Menarche, and the Maintenance of Menstrual Cycles: A Critical Review. *Journal of Adolescent Health Care* 2:249–60.

Seligmann, C., and B. Seligmann

1911   *The Veddas.* Cambridge: Cambridge University Press.

Service, E.
1962   *Primitive Social Organization.* New York: Random House.
1966   *The Hunters.* Englewood Cliffs, N.J.: Prentice-Hall.
Sharp, H.
1977   The Chipewyan Hunting Unit. *American Ethnologist* 4:377–93.
1981   The Null Case: The Chipewyan. In *Woman the Gatherer,* edited by F. Dahlberg, pp. 221–44. New Haven: Yale University Press.
Sharpe, D.
1975   Methods of Assessing the Primary Productivity of Regions. In *Primary Productivity of the Biosphere,* edited by H. Lieth and R. Whittaker, pp. 147–66. New York: Spring-Verlag.
Shostak, M.
1981   *Nisa: The Life and Words of a !Kung Woman.* Cambridge: Harvard University Press.
Sih, A., and K. Milton
1985   Optimal Diet Theory: Should the !Kung Eat Mongongos? *American Anthropologist* 87:396–401.
Silberbauer, G.
1972   The G/wi Bushmen. In *Hunters and Gatherers Today,* edited by M. G. Bicchieri, pp. 271–326. New York: Holt, Rinehart and Winston.
1981a   *Hunter and Habitat in the Central Kalahari Desert.* Cambridge: Cambridge University Press.
1981b   Hunter/Gatherers of the Central Kalahari. In *Omnivorous Primates,* edited by R. Harding and G. Teleki, pp. 455–98. New York: Columbia University Press.
1982   Political Process in G/wi Bands. In *Politics and History in Band Societies,* edited by E. Leacock and R. B. Lee, pp. 23–35. Cambridge: Cambridge University Press.
1991   Morbid Reflexivity and Overgeneralization in Mosarwa Studies: Review of E. N. Wilmsen, Land Filled with Flies. *Current Anthropology* 32:96–99.
Simms, S.
1987   *Behavioral Ecology and Hunter-Gatherer Foraging: An Example from the Great Basin.* British Archaeological Reports, International Series 381. Oxford.
Siskind, J.
1973   Tropical Forest Hunters and the Economy of Sex. In *Peoples and Cultures of Native South America,* edited by D. Gross, pp. 226–41. Garden City, N.Y.: Doubleday/Natural History Press.
Slobodkin, R.
1969   Leadership and Participation in a Kutchin Trapping Party. In *Contribu-*

tions to Anthropology: Band Societies, edited by D. Damas, pp. 56–89. National Museum of Canada Bulletin 228. Ottawa: National Museum of Canada.

Slocum, S.

1975   Woman the Gatherer. In *Toward an Anthropology of Women,* edited by R. Reiter, pp. 36–50. New York: Monthly Review Press.

Smith, C.

1978   Tubatulabal. In *Handbook of North American Indians,* Vol. 11: *California,* edited by R. Heizer, pp. 437–45. Washington, D.C.: Smithsonian Institution Press.

Smith, D. G.

1984   Mackenzie Delta Eskimo. In *Handbook of North American Indians,* Vol. 5: *Arctic,* edited by D. Damas, pp. 347–58. Washington, D.C.: Smithsonian Institution Press.

Smith, E. A.

1979   Human Adaptation and Energetic Efficiency. *Human Ecology* 7:53–74.

1981   The Application of Optimal Foraging Theory to the Analysis of Hunter-Gatherer Group Size. In *Hunter-Gatherer Foraging Strategies,* edited by B. Winterhalder and E. A. Smith, pp. 36–65. Chicago: University of Chicago Press.

1983   Anthropological Applications of Optimal Foraging Theory: A Critical Review. *Current Anthropology* 24:625–51.

1985   Inuit Foraging Groups: Some Simple Models Incorporating Conflicts of Interest, Relatedness, and Central-Place Sharing. *Ethology and Sociobiology* 6:27–47.

1987   Optimization Theory in Anthropology: Applications and Critiques. In *The Latest on the Best: Essays on Evolution and Optimality,* edited by J. Dupre, pp. 201–49. Cambridge: Cambridge University Press.

1988   Risk and Uncertainty in the "Original Affluent Society": Evolutionary Ecology of Resource Sharing and Land Tenure. In *Hunters and Gatherers,* Vol. 1: *History, Evolution, and Social Change,* edited by T. Ingold, D. Riches, and J. Woodburn, pp. 222–51. Oxford: Berg.

1991   *Inujjuamiut Foraging Strategies.* Hawthorne, N.Y.: Aldine de Gruyter.

Smith, E. A., and R. Boyd

1990   Risk and Reciprocity: Hunter-Gatherer Socioecology and the Problem of Collective Action. In *Risk and Uncertainty in Tribal and Peasant Economies,* edited by E. Cashdan, pp. 167–92. Boulder, Colo.: Westview.

Smith, E. A., and S. A. Smith

1994   Inuit Sex-Ratio Variation: Population Control, Ethnographic Error, or Parental Manipulation? *Current Anthropology* 35:595–624.

Smith, E. A., and B. Winterhalder
1992a   Natural Selection and Decision Making: Some Fundamental Principles. In *Evolutionary Ecology and Human Behavior,* edited by E. Smith and B. Winterhalder, pp. 25–60. Hawthorne, N.Y.: Aldine de Gruyter.

Smith, E. A., and B. Winterhalder, eds.
1992b   *Evolutionary Ecology and Human Behavior.* Hawthorne, N.Y.: Aldine de Gruyter.

Smith, J. G. E.
1978   Economic Uncertainty in an Affluent Society: Caribou and Caribou Eater Chipewyan Adaptive Strategies. *Arctic Anthropology* 15:68–88.
1981   Chipewyan. In *Handbook of North American Indians,* Vol. 6: *Subarctic,* edited by J. Helm, pp. 271–84. Washington, D.C.: Smithsonian Institution Press.

Snow, J.
1981   Ingalik. In *Handbook of North American Indians,* Vol. 6: *Subarctic,* edited by J. Helm, pp. 602–17. Washington, D.C.: Smithsonian Institution Press.

Sollas, W.
1911   *Ancient Hunters and Their Modern Representatives.* London: Macmillan.

Solway, J.
1985   Middle-Aged Women in Bakgalagadi Society (Botswana). In *In Her Prime: A New View of Middle-Aged Women,* edited by J. Brown and V. Kerns, pp. 36–47. S. Hadley, Mass.: Bergin and Garvey.

Solway, J., and R. B. Lee
1990   Foragers, Genuine or Spurious? Situating the Kalahari San in History. *Current Anthropology* 31:109–46.

Speck, F.
1915   The Family Hunting Band as the Basis of Algonkian Social Organization. *American Anthropologist* 17:289–305.
1921   Beothuk and Micmac. *Indian Notes and Monographs* (series 2) 22:1–187.

Speck, F., and L. Eiseley
1939   The Significance of Hunting Territory Systems of the Algonkian in Social Theory. *American Anthropologist* 41:269–80.

Spencer, B., and F. Gillen
1927   *The Arunta.* London: Macmillan.

Speth, J.
1990   Seasonality, Resource Stress, and Food Sharing in So-Called "Egalitarian" Foraging Societies. *Journal of Anthropological Archaeology* 9:148–88.

Speth, J., and S. Scott
1989   Horticulture and Large Mammal Hunting: The Role of Resource Depletion and the Constraints of Time and Labor. In *Farmers as Hunters: The*

Implications of Sedentism, edited by S. Kent, pp. 71–79. Cambridge: Cambridge University Press.

Speth, J., and K. Spielmann

1983   Energy Source, Protein Metabolism, and Hunter-Gatherer Subsistence Strategies. *Journal of Anthropological Archaeology* 2:1–31.

Spielmann, K.

1986   Interdependence among Egalitarian Societies. *Journal of Anthropological Archaeology* 5:279–312.

1989   A Review: Dietary Restrictions on Hunter-Gatherer Women and the Implications for Fertility and Infant Mortality. *Human Ecology* 17:321–45.

Spielmann, K., ed.

1991   *Farmers, Hunters, and Colonists: Interaction Between the Southwest and the Southern Plains.* Tucson: University of Arizona Press.

Spielmann, K. A., and J. F. Eder

1994   Hunters and Farmers: Then and Now. *Annual Review of Anthropology* 23:303–23.

Spier, L.

1930   Klamath Ethnography. *University of California Publications in American Archaeology and Ethnology* 30:11–338.

1978   Monache. In *Handbook of North American Indians,* Vol. 11: *California,* edited by R. Heizer, pp. 426–36. Washington, D.C.: Smithsonian Institution Press.

Sponsel, L.

1986   Amazon Ecology and Adaptation. *Annual Review of Anthropology* 15:67–97.

Stanner, W. E. H.

1965   Aboriginal Territorial Organization: Estate, Range, Domain and Regime. *Oceania* 36:1–26.

Stark, B.

1981   The Rise of Sedentary Life. In *Supplement to the Handbook of Middle American Indians: Archaeology,* edited by V. Bricker, pp. 345–72. Austin: University of Texas Press.

Stearman, A.

1984   The Yuqui Connection: Another Look at Siriono Deculturation. *American Anthropologist* 86:630–50.

Stefansson, V.

1914   The Stefansson-Anderson Arctic Expedition of the American Museum: Preliminary Ethnological Report. *Anthropological Papers of the American Museum of Natural History* 14:1–395.

Stephens, D. W.

1990   Risk and Incomplete Information in Behavioral Ecology. In *Risk and Uncertainty in Tribal and Peasant Economies,* edited by E. Cashdan, pp. 19–46. Boulder, Colo.: Westview.

Stephens, D. W., and J. Krebs
1986   *Foraging Theory.* Princeton: Princeton University Press.

Steward, J. H.
1933   Ethnography of the Owens Valley Paiute. *University of California Publications in American Archaeology and Ethnology* 33:233–350.
1936   The Economic and Social Basis of Primitive Bands. In *Essays in Anthropology Presented to Alfred Louis Kroeber,* edited by R. H. Lowie, pp. 331–50. Berkeley: University of California Press.
1938   *Basin Plateau Aboriginal Sociopolitical Groups.* Bureau of American Ethnology Bulletin 120. Washington, D.C.
1941   Culture Element Distributions: XVIII. Nevada Shoshone. *University of California Anthropological Records* 4(2):209–359.
1943   Culture Element Distributions: XXIII. Northern and Gosiute Shoshone. *University of California Anthropological Records* 8(3):263–392.
1955   *Theory of Culture Change.* Urbana: University of Illinois Press.
1968   Causal Factors and Processes in the Evolution of Pre-Farming Societies. In *Man the Hunter,* edited by R. B. Lee and I. DeVore, pp. 321–34. Chicago: Aldine.
1969a   Observations on Bands. In *Contributions to Anthropology: Band Societies,* edited by D. Damas, pp. 187–90. National Museum of Canada Bulletin 228. Ottawa: National Museum of Canada.
1969b   Postscript to Bands: On Taxonomy, Processes, and Causes. In *Contributions to Anthropology: Band Societies,* edited by D. Damas, pp. 288–95. National Museum of Canada Bulletin 228. Ottawa: National Museum of Canada.

Steward, J. H., and L. Faron, eds.
1959   *Native Peoples of South America.* New York: McGraw-Hill.

Stewart, O.
1941   Culture Element Distributions, XIV: Northern Paiute. *University of California Anthropological Records* 4(3):361–446.

Stiles, D.
1991   Tubers and Tenrecs: The Mikea of Southwestern Madagascar. *Ethnology* 30:251–63.

Stini, W.
1981   Body Composition and Nutrient Reserves in Evolutionary Perspective. In *Food, Nutrition, and Evolution: Food as an Environmental Factor in the Genesis of Human Variability,* edited by D. Walcher and N. Kretchmer, pp. 107–20. New York: Masson Publishing USA.

Strathern, M.
1987   Introduction. In *Dealing with Inequality: Analyzing Gender Relations in Melanesia and Beyond,* edited by M. Strathern, pp. 1–32. Cambridge: Cambridge University Press.

Stuart, D.

1972   Band Structure and Ecological Variability: The Ona and Yahgan of
        Tierra del Fuego. Unpublished Ph.D. dissertation, Department of An-
        thropology, University of New Mexico.

1980   Kinship and Social Organization in Tierra del Fuego: Evolutionary Con-
        sequences. In *The Versatility of Kinship,* edited by L. Cordell and S. Beck-
        erman, pp. 269–84. New York: Academic Press.

Sugawara, K.

1988   Visiting Relations and Social Interactions Between Residential Groups
        of the Central Kalahari San: Hunter-Gatherer Camp as a Micro-
        Territory. *African Study Monographs* 8:173–211.

Suttles, W.

1960   Affinal Ties, Subsistence, and Prestige among the Coast Salish. *American
        Anthropologist* 62:296–305.

1968   Coping with Abundance: Subsistence on the Northwest Coast. In *Man
        the Hunter,* edited by R. B. Lee and I. DeVore, pp. 56–68. Chicago:
        Aldine.

Sutton, M.

1985   The California Salmon Fly as a Food Source in Northeastern California.
        Journal of California and Great Basin Anthropology 7:176–82.

Swadesh, M.

1948   Motivations in Nootka Warfare. *Southwestern Journal of Anthropology*
        4:76–93.

Tanaka, J.

1980   *The San Hunter-Gatherers of the Kalahari: A Study in Ecological Anthropol-
        ogy.* Tokyo: University of Tokyo Press.

Tanner, A.

1979   *Bringing Home Animals: Religious Ideology and Mode of Production of the
        Mistassini Cree Hunters.* London: Hurst.

Tanner, V.

1944   Outline of the Geography, Life and Customs of Newfoundland-
        Labrador. *Acta Geographica* 8:1–907.

Tanno, T.

1976   The Mbuti Net-Hunters in the Ituri Forest, Eastern Zaire. *Kyoto Univer-
        sity African Studies* 10:101–35.

Taylor, J.

1984   Historical Ethnography of the Labrador Coast. In *Handbook of North
        American Indians,* Vol. 5: *Arctic,* edited by D. Damas, pp. 508–21. Wash-
        ington, D.C.: Smithsonian Institution Press.

Taylor, K.

1966   A Demographic Study of Karluk, Kodiak Island, Alaska 1962–1964. *Arc-
        tic Anthropology* 3:211–40.

Taylor, W.

1964   Tethered Nomadism and Water Territoriality: An Hypothesis. *Acts of the 35th International Congress of Americanists,* pp. 197–203.

1972   The Hunter-Gatherer Nomads of Northern Mexico: A Comparison of the Archival and Archaeological Records. *World Archaeology* 4:167–78.

Terashima, H.

1980   Hunting Life of the Bambote: An Anthropological Study of Hunter-Gatherers in a Wooded Savanna. *Senri Ethnological Studies* 6:223–67.

1983   Mota and Other Hunting Activities of the Mbuti Archers: A Socio-ecological Study of Subsistence Technology. *African Study Monographs* 3:71–85.

Testart, A.

1982   The Significance of Food Storage among Hunter-Gatherers: Residence Patterns, Population Densities, and Social Inequalities. *Current Anthropology* 23:523–37.

1987   Game Sharing Systems and Kinship Systems among Hunter-Gatherers. *Man* 22:287–304.

1988   Some Major Problems in the Social Anthropology of Hunter-Gatherers. *Current Anthropology* 29:1–31.

1989   Aboriginal Social Inequality and Reciprocity. *Oceania* 60:1–16.

Thomas, D. H.

1981   Complexity among Great Basin Shoshoneans: The World's Least Affluent Hunter-Gatherers. In *Affluent Foragers,* edited by S. Koyama and D. Thomas, pp. 19–52. Senri Ethnological Studies 9. Osaka: National Museum of Ethnology.

Thomas, R.

1973   *Human Adaptation to a High Andean Energy Flow System.* Occasional Papers in Anthropology No. 7. State College, Pa.: Pennsylvania State University.

Thomas, R., B. Winterhalder, and S. McRae

1979   An Anthropological Approach to Human Ecology and Adaptive Dynamics. *Yearbook of Physical Anthropology* 22:1–46.

Thompson, H.

1966   A Technique Using Anthropological and Biological Data. *Current Anthropology* 7:417–24.

Thomson, D.

1932   Ceremonial Presentation of Fire in North Queensland. *Man* 32:162–66.

Thornthwaite Associates

1962   Average Climatic Water Balance Data of the Continents, Part I. *Publications in Climatology* 15:15–287.

1963   Average Climatic Water Balance Data of the Continents, Parts II-IV. *Publications in Climatology* 16:5–476.

1964   Average Climatic Water Balance Data of the Continents, Parts VI-VII. *Publications in Climatology* 17:235–610.

Tindale, N.

1972   The Pitjandjara. In *Hunters and Gatherers Today,* edited by M. G. Bicchieri, pp. 217–68. New York: Holt, Rinehart and Winston.

1974   *Aboriginal Tribes of Australia.* Berkeley: University of California Press.

Tobey, M.

1981   Carrier. In *Handbook of North American Indians,* Vol. 6: *Subarctic,* edited by J. Helm, pp. 413–32. Washington, D.C.: Smithsonian Institution Press.

Tonkinson, R.

1974   *The Jigalong Mob: Aboriginal Victors of the Desert Crusade.* Menlo Park, Calif.: Cummings Publishing.

1978   *The Mardudjara Aborigines.* New York: Holt, Rinehart and Winston.

1988   "Ideology and Domination" in Aboriginal Australia: A Western Desert Test Case. In *Hunter-Gatherers,* Vol. 2: *Property, Power, and Ideology,* edited by T. Ingold, D. Riches, and J. Woodburn, pp. 150–64. Oxford: Berg.

1991   *The Mardu Aborigines.* New York: Holt, Rinehart and Winston.

Townsend, J.

1981   Tanaina. In *Handbook of North American Indians,* Vol. 6: *Subarctic,* edited by J. Helm, pp. 623–40. Washington, D.C.: Smithsonian Institution Press.

Turnbull, C.

1961   *The Forest People.* New York: Simon and Schuster.

1965   *Wayward Servants: The Two Worlds of the African Pygmies.* Garden City, N.Y.: Natural History Press.

1968   The Importance of Flux in Two Hunting Societies. In *Man the Hunter,* edited by R. B. Lee and I. DeVore, pp. 132–37. Chicago: Aldine.

1972   Demography of Small-Scale Societies. In *The Structure of Human Populations,* edited by B. Harrison, pp. 283–312. Oxford: Clarendon Press.

Turner, L.

1889   *Ethnology of the Ungava District, Hudson Bay Territory.* Eleventh Annual Report of the Bureau of American Ethnology, pp. 159–350. Washington, D.C.

Tylor, E.

1871   *Primitive Culture: Researches into the Development of Mythology, Philosophy, Religion, Language, Art, and Custom.* London: J. Murray.

UNESCO

1974   *Atlas of World Water Balance.* Paris: The UNESCO Press.

Van Arsdale, P. W.

1978   Population Dynamics among Asmat Hunter-Gatherers of New Guinea: Data, Methods, Comparisons. *Human Ecology* 6:435–67.

Van der Walt, L. A., E. N. Wilmsen, and T. Jenkins
1978   Unusual Sex Hormone Patterns among Desert-Dwelling Hunter-Gatherers. *Journal of Clinical Endocrinology and Metabolism* 46:658–63.

Van de Velde, F.
1954   L'Infanticide chez les Esquimaux. *Eskimo* 34:6–8.

Vanoverbergh, M.
1925   Negritos of Northern Luzon. *Anthropos* 20:148–99, 399–443.

Vayda, A., ed.
1969   *Environment and Cultural Behavior.* Garden City, N.Y.: Natural History Press.

Vayda, A., and B. McCay
1975   New Directions in Ecology and Ecological Anthropology. *Annual Review of Anthropology* 4:293–306.

Vickers, W.
1989   Patterns of Foraging and Gardening in a Semi-Sedentary Amazonian Community. In *Farmers and Hunters: The Implications of Sedentism,* edited by S. Kent, pp. 46–59. Cambridge: Cambridge University Press.

Vincent, A.
1984   Plant Foods in Savanna Environments: A Preliminary Report of Tubers Eaten by the Hadza of Northern Tanzania. *World Archaeology* 17:131–47.

Walker, P., and B. Hewlett
1990   Dental Health, Diet, and Social Status among Central African Foragers and Farmers. *American Anthropologist* 92:383–98.

Wallace, W.
1978   Hupa, Chilula, and Whilkut. In *Handbook of North American Indians,* Vol. 11: *California,* edited by R. Heizer, pp. 164–79. Washington, D.C.: Smithsonian Institution Press.

Wallis, W., and R. Wallis
1955   *The Micmac Indians of Eastern Canada.* Minneapolis: University of Minnesota Press.

Warner, W.
1931   Muringin Warfare. *Oceania* 1:457–91.
1937   *A Black Civilization.* Gloucester, Mass.: Harper & Row.

Watanabe, H.
1968   Subsistence and Ecology of Northern Food Gatherers with Special Reference to the Ainu. In *Man the Hunter,* edited by R. B. Lee and I. DeVore, pp. 69–77. Chicago: Aldine.
1972   The Ainu. In *Hunters and Gatherers Today,* edited by M. Bicchieri, pp. 448–84. New York: Holt, Rinehart and Winston.
1983   Occupational Differentiation and Social Stratification: The Case of Northern Pacific Maritime Food Gatherers. *Current Anthropology* 24:217–19.

Weiss, K., and P. Smouse
1976   The Demographic Stability of Small Human Populations. *Journal of Human Evolution* 5:59–73.

Weyer, E.
1932   *The Eskimos.* New Haven: Yale University Press.

White, I.
1978   Aboriginal Women's Status: A Paradox Resolved. In *Woman's Role in Aboriginal Society,* edited by F. Gale, pp. 36–49. Canberra: Australian Institute of Aboriginal Studies.

White, N.
1985   Sex Differences in Australian Aboriginal Subsistence: Possible Implications for the Biology of Hunter-Gatherers. In *Human Sexual Dimorphism,* edited by J. Ghesquiere, R. D. Martin, and F. Newcombe, pp. 323–61. London: Tagler & Francis.

White, N., B. Meehan, L. Hiatt, and R. Jones
1990   Demography of Contemporary Hunter-Gatherers: Lessons from Arnhem Land. In *Hunter-Gatherer Demography Past and Present,* edited by B. Meehan and N. White, pp. 171–85, Oceania Monograph 39. Sydney: University of Sydney.

Widmer, R.
1988   *The Evolution of the Calusa: A Nonagricultural Chiefdom on the Southwest Florida Coast.* Tuscaloosa: University of Alabama Press.

Wiessner, P.
1977   *Hxaro:* A Regional System of Reciprocity for Reducing Risk among the !Kung San. Unpublished Ph.D. dissertation, Department of Anthropology, University of Michigan.
1982a   Measuring the Impact of Social Ties on Nutritional Status among the !Kung San. *Social Science Information* 20:641–78.
1982b   Risk, Reciprocity and Social Influences on !Kung San Economics. In *Politics and History in Band Societies,* edited by E. Leacock and R. B. Lee, pp. 61–84. Cambridge: Cambridge University Press.

Williams, B.
1968   The Birhor of India and Some Comments on Band Organization. In *Man the Hunter,* edited by R. B. Lee and I. DeVore, pp. 126–31. Chicago: Aldine.
1974   *A Model of Band Society.* Society for American Archaeology Memoir 29. Washington, D.C.

Williams, N. M.
1982   A Boundary Is to Cross: Observations on Yolngu Boundaries and Permission. In *Resource Managers: North American and Australian Hunter-Gatherers,* edited by E. Hunn and N. Williams, pp. 131–54. Boulder, Colo.: Westview.

1986   *The Yolungu and Their Land: A System of Land Tenure and the Fight for Its Recognition.* Stanford: Stanford University Press.

Williams, N. M., and E. S. Hunn, eds.

1982   *Resource Managers: North American and Australian Hunter-Gatherers.* Boulder, Colo.: Westview.

Wilmsen, E. N.

1973   Interaction, Spacing Behavior, and the Organization of Hunting Bands. *Journal of Anthropological Research* 29:1–31.

1978   Seasonal Effects of Dietary Intake on Kalahari San. *Federation of American Societies for Experimental Biology, Proceedings* 37:65–72.

1982   Studies in Diet, Nutrition, and Fertility Performance. *Social Science Information* 21:95–125.

1983   The Ecology of Illusion: Anthropological Foraging in the Kalahari. *Reviews in Anthropology* 10:9–20.

1986   Biological Determinants of Fecundity and Fecundability: An Application of Bongaarts' Model to Forager Fertility. In *Culture and Reproduction: An Anthropological Critique of Demographic Transition Theory,* edited by W. Handwerker, pp. 59–82. Boulder, Colo.: Westview.

1989a   *Land Filled with Flies.* Chicago: University of Chicago Press.

1989b   Those Who Have Each Other: Politics of Aboriginal Land Tenure. In *We Are Here: Politics of Aboriginal Land Tenure,* edited by E. Wilmsen, pp. 43–67. Berkeley: University of California Press.

1992   A Myth and Its Measure. *Current Anthropology* 33:611–14.

Wilmsen, E. N., ed.

1989c   *We Are Here: Politics of Aboriginal Land Tenure.* Berkeley: University of California Press.

Wilmsen, E. N., and J. Denbow

1990   Paradigmatic History of San-Speaking Peoples and Current Attempts at Revision. *Current Anthropology* 31:489–524.

Wilmsen, E. N., and D. Durham

1988   Food as a Function of Seasonal Environment and Social History. In *Coping with Uncertainty in Food Supply,* edited by I. de Garine and G. Harrison, pp. 52–87. Oxford: Oxford University Press.

Wilson, P.

1988   *The Domestication of the Human Species.* New Haven: Yale University Press.

Winn, S., G. A. Morelli, and E. Z. Tronick

1990   The Infant in the Group: A Look at Efe Caretaking Practices. In *The Cultural Context of Infancy,* edited by J. K. Nugent, B. M. Lancaster, and T. B. Brazelton. Norwood, N. J.: Ablex.

Winterhalder, B.

1977   Foraging Strategy Adaptations of the Boreal Forest Cree: An Evaluation of Theory and Models from Evolutionary Ecology. Unpublished Ph.D. dissertation, Department of Anthropology, Cornell University.

1981   Foraging Strategies in the Boreal Forest: An Analysis of Cree Hunting and Gathering. In *Hunter-Gatherer Foraging Strategies,* edited by B. Winterhalder and E. A. Smith, pp. 66–98. Chicago: University of Chicago Press.

1983   Opportunity Cost Foraging Models for Stationary and Mobile Predators. *American Naturalist* 122:73–84.

1984   Reconsidering the Ecosystem Concept. *Reviews in Anthropology* 2:301–13.

1986a   Diet Choice, Risk, and Food Sharing in a Stochastic Environment. *Journal of Anthropological Archaeology* 5:369–92.

1986b   Optimal Foraging: Simulation Studies of Diet Choice in a Stochastic Environment. *Journal of Ethnobiology* 6:205–23.

1987   The Analysis of Hunter-Gatherer Diets: Stalking an Optimal Foraging Model. In *Food and Evolution,* edited by M. Harris and E. Ross, pp. 311–39. Philadelphia: Temple University Press.

1993   Work, Resources and Population in Foraging Societies. *Man* 28:321–40.

Winterhalder, B., and C. Goland

1993   On Population, Foraging Efficiency, and Plant Domestication. *Current Anthropology* 34:710–15.

Winterhalder, B., and E. A. Smith

1992   Evolutionary Ecology and the Social Sciences. In *Evolutionary Ecology and Human Behavior,* edited by E. Smith and B. Winterhalder, pp. 3–24. Hawthorne, N.Y.: Aldine de Gruyter.

Winterhalder, B., and E. A. Smith, eds.

1981   *Hunter-Gatherer Foraging Strategies: Ethnographic and Archaeological Analyses.* Chicago: University of Chicago Press.

Winterhalder, B., W. Baillageon, F. Cappelletto, I. Daniel Jr., and C. Prescott

1988   The Population Ecology of Hunter-Gatherers and Their Prey. *Journal of Anthropological Archaeology* 7:289–328.

Wissler, C.

1926   *The Relation of Nature to Man in Aboriginal America.* New York: Oxford University Press.

Wobst, H. M.

1974   Boundary Conditions for Paleolithic Social Systems: A Simulation Approach. *American Antiquity* 39:147–78.

1978   The Archaeo-Ethnology of Hunter-Gatherers or the Tyranny of the Ethnographic Record in Archaeology. *American Antiquity* 43:303–9.

Wood, J. W.

1990   Fertility in Anthropological Populations. *Annual Review of Anthropology* 19:211–42.

1994   *Dynamics of Human Reproduction: Biology, Biometry, Demography.* Hawthorn, N.Y.: Aldine de Gruyter.

Woodburn, J.

1968   An Introduction to Hadza Ecology. In *Man the Hunter,* edited by R. B. Lee and I. DeVore, pp. 49–55. Chicago: Aldine.

1972   Ecology, Nomadic Movement, and the Composition of the Local Group among Hunters and Gatherers: An East African Example and Its Implications. In *Man, Settlement, and Urbanism,* edited by P. J. Ucko, R. Tringham, and G. Dimbleby, pp. 193–206. New York: Schenkman.

1979   Minimal Politics: The Political Organization of the Hadza of North Tanzania. In *Politics and Leadership: A Comparative Perspective,* edited by W. Shack and P. Cohen, pp. 244–66. Oxford: Clarendon Press.

1980   Hunters and Gatherers Today and Reconstruction of the Past. In *Soviet and Western Anthropology,* edited by A. Gellner, pp. 95–117. London: Duckworth.

1982   Egalitarian Societies. *Man* 17:431–51.

1988   African Hunter-Gatherer Social Organization: Is It Best Understood as a Product of Encapsulation? In *Hunters and Gatherers,* Vol. 1: *History, Evolution, and Social Change,* edited by T. Ingold, D. Riches, and J. Woodburn, pp. 31–64. Oxford: Berg.

Worsley, P.

1961   The Utilization of Natural Food Resources by an Australian Aboriginal Tribe. *Acta Ethnographica* 10:153–90.

Wynne-Edwards, V.

1962   *Animal Dispersion in Relation to Social Behavior.* Edinburgh: Oliver and Boyd.

Yellen, J.

1976   Settlement Pattern of the !Kung: An Archaeological Perspective. In *Kalahari Hunter-Gatherers,* edited by R. B. Lee and I. DeVore, pp. 48–72. Cambridge: Harvard University Press.

1977   *Archaeological Approaches to the Present: Models for Reconstructing the Past.* New York: Academic Press.

Yellen, J., and H. Harpending

1972   Hunter-Gatherer Populations and Archaeological Inference. *World Archaeology* 4:244–53.

Yengoyan, A.

1968   Demographic and Ecological Influences on Aboriginal Australian Marriage Sections. In *Man the Hunter,* edited by R. B. Lee and I. DeVore, pp. 185–99. Chicago: Aldine.

1972   Biological and Demographic Components in Aboriginal Socio-Economic Organization. *Oceania* 43(2):85–95.

1976   Structure, Event and Ecology in Aboriginal Australia. In *Tribes and*

Boundaries in Australia, edited by N. Peterson, pp. 121–32. Canberra: Australian Institute of Aboriginal Studies.

1979 Economy, Society, and Myth in Aboriginal Australia. *Annual Review of Anthropology* 8:393–415.

1981 Infanticide and Birth Order: An Empirical Analysis of Preferential Female Infanticide among Australian Aboriginal Populations. *Anthropology UCLA* 7:255–73.

Yesner, D. R.

1980 Maritime Hunter-Gatherers: Ecology and Prehistory. *Current Anthropology* 21:727–50.

1994 Seasonality and Resource "Stress" among Hunter-Gatherers: Archaeological Signatures. In *Key Issues in Hunter-Gatherer Research,* edited by E. S. Burch, Jr. and L. J. Ellanna, pp. 151–67. Oxford: Berg.

INDEX